THE FAMILY
Handyman.

Home Improvement
2012

THE FAMILY
Handyman

Home Improvement
2012

by The Editors of *The Family Handyman* magazine

THE FAMILY HANDYMAN HOME IMPROVEMENT 2012
(See page 288 for complete staff listing.)
Editor in Chief: Ken Collier
Project Editor: Mary Flanagan
Contributing Designers: Joel Anderson, Bruce Bohnenstingl, Teresa Marrone
Contributing Copy Editors: Donna Bierbach, Peggy Parker
Indexing: Stephanie Reymann

Vice President, Publisher: Lora Gier

The Reader's Digest Association, Inc.
President & Chief Executive Officer: Robert E. Guth

Warning: All do-it-yourself activities involve a degree of risk. Skills, materials, tools, and site conditions vary widely. Although the editors have made every effort to ensure accuracy, the reader remains responsible for the selection and use of tools, materials, and methods. Always obey local codes and laws, follow manufacturer's operating instructions, and observe safety precautions.

ISBN 978-1-60652-256-1   1-60652-256-6

Address any comments about *The Family Handyman Home Improvement 2012* to:
Editor, Home Improvement 2012
2915 Commers Drive, Suite 700
Eagan, MN 55121

To order additional copies of *The Family Handyman Home Improvement 2012,* call 1-800-344-2560.

For more Reader's Digest products and information, visit our Web site at rd.com.
For more about *The Family Handyman* magazine, visit familyhandyman.com.

Printed in the United States of America.
1 3 5 7 9 10 8 6 4 2

INTRODUCTION

"Whenever you are asked if you can do a job, tell 'em, 'Certainly I can!' Then get busy and find out how to do it."
                                          —Theodore Roosevelt

By nature, do-it-yourselfers are resilient, eager learners. We like challenges, the process of overcoming them and the satisfaction of a job well done.

Here at *The Family Handyman* magazine, we've done a lot of learning this year. But instead of just honing our home improvement skills, we've been developing our digital tools as well. We're building our Web site, familyhandyman.com, each and every day, adding new how-to articles, hints and tips, blog and forum posts and contests.

While we've been working diligently to build our online presence, we have not neglected our roots. Our editors still spend much of their time in the field and in the shop creating the best do-it-yourself home improvement content available in print or on the Web. With passion, our editors, consultants and field editors continue to strive for excellence in each article we publish.

In the pages of *The Family Handyman Home Improvement*, you'll learn how to improve the storage space in your bathroom vanity, tile and grout like a pro, trim a window, run electrical power anywhere, repair your kitchen appliances, build a beautiful flat-screen TV bookcase, fix masonry, gutters and soffits and build a retaining wall. And that's just for starters! There are 20 pages of money-saving car maintenance and repair projects and dozens of hint, tips and chuckle-worthy Great Goofs—it can be fun to learn from other people's mistakes!

Whenever you're about to tackle a new home improvement project, you can count on *The Family Handyman* and familyhandyman.com for the best how-to advice and instruction in print or online. All the best of luck on your DIY projects!

                              —The staff of *The Family Handyman* magazine

Contents

EXTERIOR MAINTENANCE & REPAIRS

OUTDOOR STRUCTURES, LANDSCAPING & GARDENING

AUTO & GARAGE

BONUS SECTION

SAFETY FIRST–ALWAYS!

Tackling home improvement projects and repairs can be endlessly rewarding. But as most of us know, with the rewards come risks. DIYers use chain saws, climb ladders and tear into walls that can contain big and hazardous surprises.

The good news is, armed with the right knowledge, tools and procedures, homeowners can minimize risk. As you go about your projects and repairs, stay alert for these hazards:

Aluminum wiring

Aluminum wiring, installed in about 7 million homes between 1065 and 1973, requires special techniques and materials to make safe connections. This wiring is dull gray, not the dull orange characteristic of copper. Hire a licensed electrician certified to work with it. For more information visit inspectny.com/aluminum/aluminum.htm.

Spontaneous combustion

Rags saturated with oil finishes like Danish oil and linseed oil, and oil-based paints and stains can spontaneously combust if left bunched up. Always dry them outdoors, spread out loosely. When the oil has thoroughly dried, you can safely throw them in the trash.

Vision and hearing protection

Safety glasses or goggles should be worn whenever you're working on DIY projects that involve chemicals, dust and anything that could shatter or chip off and hit your eye. Sounds louder than 80 decibels (dB) are considered potentially dangerous. Sound levels from a lawn mower can be 90 dB, and shop tools and chain saws can be 90 to 100 dB.

Lead paint

If your home was built before 1979, it may contain lead paint, which is a serious health hazard, especially for children six and under. Take precautions when you scrape or remove it. Contact your public health department for detailed safety information or call (800) 424-LEAD (5323) to receive an information pamphlet. Or visit epa.gov/lead.

Buried utilities

A few days before you dig in your yard, have your underground water, gas and electrical lines marked. Just call 811 or go to call811.com.

Smoke and carbon monoxide (CO) alarms

Almost two-thirds of home fire deaths from 2003 to 2006 resulted from fires in homes with missing or nonworking smoke alarms. Test your smoke alarms every month, replace batteries as necessary and replace units that are more than 10 years old. As you make your home more energy-efficient and airtight, existing ducts and chimneys can't always successfully vent combustion gases, including potentially deadly carbon monoxide (CO). Install a UL-listed CO detector, and test your CO and smoke alarms at the same time.

Five-gallon buckets and window covering cords

Since 1984, more than 275 children have drowned in 5-gallon buckets. Always store them upside down and store ones containing liquid with the covers securely snapped.

According to Parents for Window Blind Safety, just under 500 children have been seriously injured or killed in the United States in the past few decades after becoming entangled in looped window treatment cords. For more information, visit pfwbs.org or cpsc.gov.

Working up high

If you have to get up on your roof to do a repair or installation, always install roof brackets and wear a roof harness.

Asbestos

Texture sprayed on ceilings before 1978, adhesives and tiles for vinyl and asphalt floors before 1980, and vermiculite insulation (with gray granules) all may contain asbestos. Other building materials, made between 1940 and 1980, could also contain asbestos. If you suspect that materials you're removing or working around contain asbestos, contact your health department or visit epa.gov/asbestos for information.

For additional information about home safety, visit homesafetycouncil.com.
This site offers helpful information about dozens of home safety issues.

1 Interior Projects, Repairs & Remodeling

IN THIS CHAPTER

HomeCare&Repair

TIPS, FIXES & GEAR FOR A TROUBLE-FREE HOME

REPLACE DAMAGED WEATHER STRIPPING

Damaged weather stripping can allow a lot of air to leak around old entry doors. Several surface-mount solutions work well to seal the cracks, but they're unattractive. A better-looking alternative is silicone rubber tubing weather stripping. It costs about 40¢ to $1 per ft. and is available in several colors and diameters. Call Resource Conservation Technology (800-477-7724) for buying information. For a complete list of products and installation instructions, go to conservationtechnology.com/building_weatherseals_caulkable.html.

Before you order the tubing, close the door and inspect the perimeter to see how large the gap is between the door and the frame. Measure and record the size of the gap at three places along both sides and at the top of the door. Use the chart at conservationtechnology.com to choose the right size tubing based on the size of the gap. Order different diameters for each side and the top if the gap sizes are different.

If the gap varies along one edge, order progressively larger sizes and insert the smaller seal about 1/2 in. inside the larger seal where they join. You'll also need a tube of commercial-grade neutral-cure silicone caulk, which you can get from Conservation Technology. With the new silicone tubing in place, your old door will be as airtight as modern doors at a fraction of the cost of replacing the door and frame.

1 **Pry off the old weather strip.** This old door had damaged brass weather strip held on by hundreds of tiny nails. We used a small pry bar to remove the nails and weather strip. For the best-looking job, fill the nail holes and repaint the jamb before installing the silicone tubing.

2 **Use silicone caulk for adhesive.** After cleaning the area with toluene, xylene or MEK, apply a thin bead of silicone caulk to the inside corner of the jamb offset. This is where you'll add the new silicone tubing.

3 **Install the silicone tubing.** Press the tubing into the wet silicone caulk. Leave it a little long and trim off the excess with scissors. Butt the tubing at corners. Keep the tubing clean and dust free before installing it to ensure good adhesion.

COOKIE CUTTER CARPET PATCH

Are you tired of looking at that wine stain your brother-in-law so graciously gifted you last Christmas? Before replacing the carpet in the entire room to the tune of $30 a yard, first try a cookie cutter repair kit for $30. They're available online (search for "cookie cutter carpet tool") and at flooring supply stores. The idea is to cut out the stain from the highly visible area and replace it with a patch from a remnant, a closet or from under the sofa.

An adhesive pad holds the new piece in place. Some adhesive pads require ironing. For a stronger bond, use carpet seam sealer around the perimeter to fuse the backing of the patch to the backing of the surrounding carpet. You can buy seam sealer for about $5 at home centers.

The kit we tried came with thorough instructions, but here are a few things to keep in mind: You'll need to cut out the stained portion first so you can cut out a replacement piece with an identical pattern. Even if your carpet appears to have no pattern, it does. Before installing the new piece, examine the backing on the carpet. It should look like a grid of sorts (you may have to lift it up a bit). The orientation of the grid on the patch should line up with the surrounding carpet.

Try to clear a path for the cutting knives. The fewer carpet fibers you cut, the better. This is harder to do with

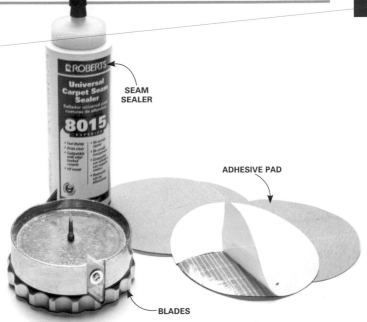

SEAM SEALER

ADHESIVE PAD

BLADES

looped-pile carpeting like Berber. If you're lucky enough to have a remnant, try a practice run on that. As with most seams in carpeting, it might take a while for the patch to blend in, but it will be less noticeable than the eye-grabbing merlot stain.

Cut out the stain. Twist to slice out the damaged area. Do the same in a closet to cut a perfect patch.

ADHESIVE PAD

Stick in the patch. Lay in an adhesive-backed pad to secure the carpet patch. Make sure the nap direction of the patch matches the nap of the surrounding carpet.

HomeCare&Repair

REPLACE A STAIR SPINDLE

It's true: The spindles on your old stair rail weren't installed with the notion that they would someday need to be replaced, but don't be intimidated—they can be, even if the spindles are trapped in holes at the top and bottom.

First, you need to remove the damaged spindle. If the spindle isn't completely broken in half, finish the job with a saw. Then persuade both pieces out of their respective holes.

Next, find the proper size spade or Forstner bit, and overdrill the top hole. Be careful not to punch all the way through the rail. Mark your bit with masking tape if you have to. Overdrilling the hole in the handrail will allow you to push the new spindle up into the railing and then back down into the hole at the base.

You may need to cut down the new spindle to make it fit, but mind which side you trim down. If you cut too much off one side or the other, the shape of the replacement spindle may not line up exactly with the existing spindles. If the old spindle was glued in and the bond is still strong, you may have to cut the damaged spindle out flush and bore two new holes. If you think that the damaged spindle may be held in with a brad nail, don't use your most expensive Forstner bit to bore the new holes.

To find a matching spindle, start local. Try the lumberyard closest to your house. There's a good chance the builder of your home purchased it there. If not, the folks working there may know where it came from. Otherwise you could try an online source. Here are a few: cheapstairparts.com, stairpartsnow.com and stairwarehouse.com. If you can't find a new one, you may need to have one custom made by a local wood turner.

1 Yank out the broken spindle. Wiggle while you pull and make sure you don't break off the end of the spindle in the hole. You may need a big pair of pliers to do the job.

2 Deepen the upper hole. Extra depth lets you insert the top of the spindle far enough to get the bottom end of the spindle into the lower hole.

3 Test the fit. Don't go for the glue until you're sure the new spindle fits. Insert the upper end, then drop the spindle into place.

HANG A NEW DOOR

The kids shouldn't have been playing floor hockey indoors with a real puck because those babies can go right through a hollow-core door. But the damage is done and now somebody (i.e., you!) has to replace the door. You have two choices. Yank the old door and jamb, trim and all, and replace with a prehung door. Or, spend less time and save $70 and up by installing a blank door slab in the existing jamb and leave the trim intact. Hanging a slab is easier than you think. All you need is a hammer and chisel, clamps, a square and a drill and hole saw. Measure the width of the old door. Sizes are all standard, so you'll be able to find a replacement at the home center.

Line up both doors and lightly clamp them together (**Photo 1**). Next, mark the new slab (**Photos 2 and 3**). Mortise the hinge openings using a chisel and utility knife (**Photo 4**). Once you've finished mortising the hinges, set the door upright and bore the lockset holes.

If the old door was trimmed at the bottom and you were happy with the gap at the floor, cut the new door to match. Mount the hinges on the new door and hang the door. If you don't need any further adjustments, remove the door again, then finish it to match the rest of the woodwork and rehang it. Now it's on to the next item on your fix-it list.

1 You already have the perfect template. Carefully align the top and hinge edges of both doors and clamp them together.

2 Transfer the hinge locations. Use a Speed Square and a sharp pencil to transfer the hinge locations to the new slab.

3 Trace the hinge. Unscrew the hinge and tape it in place to trace the rest of the hinge outline. Be sure to match the distance from the edge of the door to the edge of the hinge (the same as it was on the old door).

4 Chisel and slice. Chisel out the opening, leaving the corners for last. Then use a sharp utility blade to score around the corner radius. Pop out the corner slug with the chisel.

FIX A PERSISTENT DRYWALL CRACK

If you have a door or window with a crack on either side traveling up to the ceiling, there's probably a drywall butt joint behind it. Installers aren't supposed to seam drywall at the end of doors, but sometimes they do. Houses settle, and wood expands and contracts, and that area is very susceptible to cracks. A taped joint just isn't strong enough to handle the stress. Patch the crack and it'll nearly always show up again. The only real fix is

CUT DOWN CENTER OF OPENING

CRACK

CUT DOWN CENTER OF STUD

HORIZONTAL CUT 48" FROM CEILING

1 Saw and slice the drywall around the crack. Remove the door trim and cut the drywall horizontally (with a drywall saw or utility knife) to the nearest stud. Then use a utility knife to slice down the center of the vertical stud and also down the center above the door.

TAPERED EDGE BUTTED TO CEILING

2 Cut and screw on the patch. Cut the patch with the tapered side facing the ceiling and screw it into place with a few 1-1/4-in. screws.

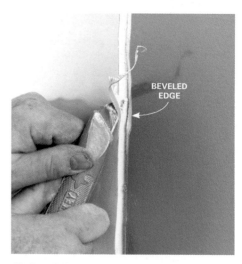

BEVELED EDGE

3 Bevel the edges. Bevel all the cut edges. That will give the joint compound more "bite" and remove any jagged paper edges.

4 Mud, tape, sand, mud. Apply joint compound and tape to the vertical seams and embed the tape. Then tape the bottom horizontal seam and finish at the wall-to-ceiling seam. Follow up with sanding and two additional coats.

to cut out the drywall and put in a solid sheet spanning the crack-prone zone. The entire job costs less than $15 and takes about eight hours (spread over a few days). Sure, you'll have to repaint, but you have to do that anyway, every time you repatch.

Start by cutting out the cracked drywall (**Photo 1**). Then cut all the way through the taped joint at the ceiling. Remove the old pieces of drywall and any exposed screws and nails. Cut a single sheet of drywall to match the new opening. Screw the new sheet into place (**Photo 2**). Then clean up all the cut edges (**Photo 2**). Tape and mud the new seams using paper or mesh tape and lightweight joint compound (**Photo 4**). To avoid repainting and patching against the ceiling, "flat tape" that seam by embedding tape in the mud against the surface (**Photo 4**).

TWO GREAT WAYS TO REMOVE GROUT

The worst part of regrouting is the incredibly tedious, tough hand-scraping to get the old stuff out. Now you have two much better options. If you already own a variable-speed reciprocating saw, try a Milwaukee Carbide-Grit Grout Blade (No. 48-08-0415; $7 from amazon.com). It works really well. Just make sure to use the slowest speed until you get the feel of the process.

If you don't have a recip saw and you're dying to get your hands on a new oscillating tool, this is your chance. The Dremel No. 6300 03 Multi-Max ($100) and the Rockwell RK5101K SoniCrafter kit ($120) are two tools that work with grout removal blades. Both are available at amazon.com.

An oscillating tool (**bottom photo**) is a bit easier to control than the recip saw because it's smaller and has a much shorter blade stroke. Plus, you can rotate the cutting head, so it's a tad more versatile.

With either tool you'll need to be careful not to chip the tile. We've tried both systems and they work equally fast. The oscillating tool does get you a bit tighter into corners. With either method, you'll still have to scrape some areas by hand.

THE RECIP SAW METHOD
Install the carbide-grit grout blade into your recip saw so it points down while the saw handle is pointing up. Apply power and "saw" out the grout.

THE OSCILLATING TOOL METHOD
Chuck up either a 1/16-in.- or 1/8-in.-wide blade (depending on the grout width) and go to town. Rotate the blade and rechuck it to maneuver into tight corners.

HomeCare & Repair

REPLACE A LAMINATE FLOOR PLANK

You can fix minor chips and scratches in a laminate floor with filler products from the home center. But if the damage is severe, you have to replace the plank (you did save a few from the installation, right?). It's a job you can do yourself in about two hours. In addition to a spare plank, you'll need a circular saw, hammer and chisel, router or table saw, drill and wood glue.

Some flooring experts recommend removing the base molding and unsnapping and numbering every plank until you get to the damaged portion. That works if the damaged plank is close to the wall. But trust us, if the damaged section is more than a few rows out from the wall, it's actually faster to just cut it out. If your laminate floor is glued together, the unsnapping routine won't work at all. See "Removing Glued Planks," p. 17.

Start by drawing a cutting line 1-1/2 in. in from all four edges of the plank. Drill a 3/8-in. relief hole at each corner of the cutting line and again 1/4 in. in from each corner of the plank.

Cut out the center section with a circular saw, cutting from hole to hole (**Photo 1**). Next, cut from the center section into each corner, stopping at the drilled hole (**Photo 2**). Finally, cut a relief cut from the center section out toward the seam of each plank. Tap a chisel into each relief cut to break out the uncut portion. Then remove all the cut pieces.

The new plank has a groove at one end and one side, as well as a tongue at the opposite end and side. But you can't install it until you cut off the bottom lip of both grooves and the side tongue. Use a utility knife to remove them (**Photo 3**). Here's a tip for cutting the groove. Stick the blade inside the groove and cut off the bottom from the inside (or use a table saw).

Apply a bead of wood glue to all four edges of the new plank. Insert the glued tongue of the new plank into the groove on the existing flooring and drop the plank into place. Wipe off any excess glue and load books on the plank until it's dry.

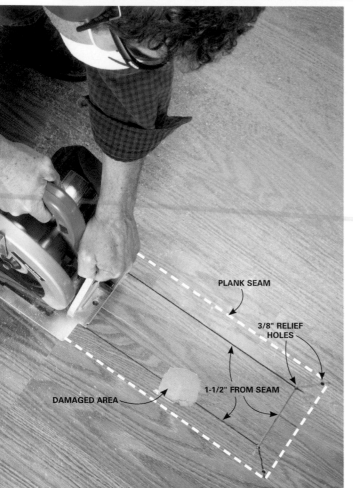

PLANK SEAM
3/8" RELIEF HOLES
DAMAGED AREA
1-1/2" FROM SEAM

1 **Remove the center section.** Set the depth of your circular saw a tad deeper than the floor thickness. Then lift the blade guard and dip the blade into the cutting line.

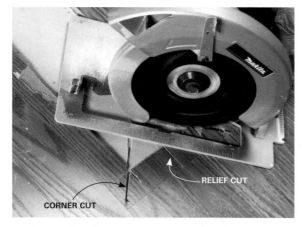

CORNER CUT
RELIEF CUT

2 **Cut to the corners.** Cut from the center section to the drilled hole in each corner—but no farther! Break out the remainder with a chisel.

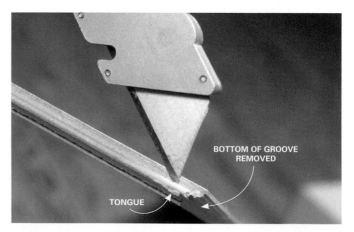

BOTTOM OF GROOVE REMOVED
TONGUE

3 **Remove the bottom lip.** Score the tongue several times with a utility knife. Then snap it off with pliers. Shave off any remaining scraps with your knife.

Removing glued planks

Most of the early laminate floors were fastened with glue. But that doesn't mean you can't do an "in-place" patch on those floors too. Follow all the cutting directions shown for a snap-together floor. Then use pliers to break the glue bond (**Photo 1**). Clean off the old glue (**Photo 2**) and lay in the new plank.

SPACER

1 **Raise the floor to gain leverage.** Slip a dowel or scrap piece of flooring under the seam. Grab the section with pliers and tilt it down until the glued seam cracks apart. Then snap it upward to break any remaining glue.

2 **The old glue has to go.** Use a flat-blade screwdriver or small chisel to chip out the old glue. Get the surfaces as smooth as possible for a flush fit and a good glue bond.

ADD A SHOWER SHELF

On new tile walls, the correct way to install a ceramic corner shelf is to set it directly into the thin-set mortar during tile installation. But you can add a corner shelf (or another soap dish) on existing tile.

Stop by a tile shop and pick up a "flat-back" corner shelf unit (about $20). Then buy soap scum remover, double-face foam tape and a tube of silicone caulk. Clean off all the soap scum or the bond might fail.

Apply a strip of foam tape on each mounting flange, stopping 1 in. short of the ends. Test-fit the shelf before you remove the wax liner paper from the tape. Shim any gaps with additional layers of foam tape. Once the shelf fits squarely into the corner, apply the silicone caulk (**Photo 1**).

Locate a spot in the middle of a row of tiles (no horizontal grout lines running through the caulk). Then remove the liner, square up the shelf and press it against the tile (**Photo 2**). Once the tape grabs, let go, wipe off the excess caulk and then tool the joint with a damp fingertip. If you blow the placement, you'll have to muscle off the shelf, completely clean off the back and reapply fresh tape, so be careful.

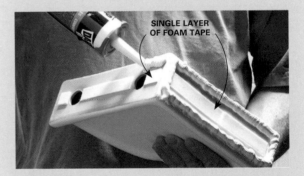

SINGLE LAYER OF FOAM TAPE

1 **Tape, shim and caulk.** Add extra layers of foam tape to compensate for an "out-of-square" corner. Then lay a thick bead of caulk around the entire perimeter.

MOUNT IN CENTER OF TILE

2 **Double-check before you stick.** Make final adjustments before driving it home—you only get one shot at placement. Once the foam tape touches the wall, you're done.

HomeCare&Repair

BEEF UP ENTRY DOOR SECURITY

You can spend hundreds on a fancy "pick-proof" dead bolt for your entry door. But you're kidding yourself if you think that'll stop most burglars. The truth is, most don't know how to pick a lock. They gain entry with one really well-placed kick or body slam that splits the doorjamb (and often the door as well), and they walk right in. You can stop burglars in their tracks by beefing up your door and jamb with reinforcing hardware. The components cost about $120 and take about an hour to install. Here's how to do it.

1 **Reinforce the door.** Slide the reinforcement plate onto the door and insert the dead bolt and dead latch. Secure them with 1-1/2-in.-long stainless steel screws. Then secure the plate to the door with the matching screws from the kit.

2 **Mark the latch and bolt centers.** Extend the dead bolt slightly and close the door. Mark the center of the bolt on the edge of the doorjamb with a pencil. Then mark the center of the latch on the jamb.

LATCH ALIGNMENT HOLE

CENTERLINE MARK

3 **Attach a jamb reinforcement plate.** Extend the pencil marks to the door stop. Then line up the center of the latch alignment hole on the reinforcement plate with the centerline mark. Slide the plate into place. Predrill two holes and run the supplied screws almost all the way into the jamb with your drill. Stop before they're seated or you'll bow the door frame.

Start by measuring the entry door thickness and the spacing between the entry knob and the dead bolt cylinder. Then buy either a single or a double wrap-around door reinforcement plate kit (less than $20 at any home center or hardware store) and four 1-1/2-in.-long stainless steel wood screws. Then get a doorjamb reinforcement kit (StrikeMaster II is one brand; $100 from homedepot.com or amazon.com).

Remove the entry knob and dead bolt cylinder. Then remove the dead bolt and latch and toss the short screws. Install the wrap-around door reinforcement plate and reinstall the latch and dead bolt plates using the longer stainless steel screws (**Photo 1**). Next, mark both the latch

and the dead bolt "centers" on the strike side of the jamb (**Photo 2**). Remove the latch and strike plates and weather stripping from the jamb. But leave any weather stripping that's attached to the door stop. Then align the reinforcement plate, predrill a few mounting holes and add screws (**Photo 3**). Check the reinforcement plate alignment before snugging the screws by hand. Do not overtighten.

If the prescored dead bolt knockout lines up with the marking along the jamb, remove it and finish installing the remaining screws. If it doesn't line up, drill a new dead bolt hole with a 3/4-in. bimetal hole saw. Finally, replace two screws in each hinge with the longer screws provided in the kit.

FIX A SWOLLEN SINK BASE BOTTOM

Let's face it—it's easy to get water on the floor of your sink base cabinet. We'll never understand why cabinetmakers use particleboard for the base, but they do. And once it starts swelling, your only option is to replace it. But you don't have to cut out the entire bottom. Here's an easier way to install a new sink base bottom.

Remove the drain lines (and garbage disposer, if there is one) to get maneuvering room. Then trace a cutting line about 3 in. in from all four edges. Then

cut out the middle section of the swollen sink base with a jigsaw (**Photo 1**). Next, cut a piece of 1/2-in. plywood to the interior size of the sink base. Cut slots for the water supply tubes. Then seal the edges and face of the plywood with urethane varnish. Then install the new plywood floor and fasten it to the old floor (**Photo 2**). Caulk around the edges and pipes to prevent water from seeping under the new floor. Then reattach the P-trap and garbage disposer.

1 **Remove the middle section.** Drill a 3/4-in. hole in each corner of the traced cutout line. Then run your jigsaw along the line. Remove the old, swollen floor.

2 **Drop in the new floor and screw it into place.** Predrill holes around the perimeter using a countersink bit. Then install brass-colored drywall screws.

HomeCare&Repair

PATCH A TEXTURED CEILING

INSIDE OF
FRAMING

TRUSS
FINDER

BETWEEN
FRAMING

DRYWALL
SAW

1 **No power saws for this step.** Probe with a nail to find the framing on either side of the breakout. Mark the cut between the framing, then make those two cuts until you hit the framing. Then cut alongside the framing at the sides.

We're not going to ask how you managed to step through your living room ceiling. But we can tell you that pros fix that mistake quite often, charging about $300 to patch the hole and retexture it. But you can do the job yourself for about $75. You'll have to paint the entire ceiling afterward, and even then the patched area won't match perfectly; even a pro can't achieve that. Perfection calls for scraping off and retexturing the entire ceiling after the patch is complete.

You'll only need a small piece of drywall and a couple of scraps of any 3/4-in.-thick wood or plywood, plus standard taping supplies and materials. And you'll need to rent a texture gun. But first, scrape off a small sample of your texture material and find a match for it at a home center. If it doesn't carry it, try a local drywall supplier.

Start by cutting out the damaged area (**Photo 1**). Avoid cutting the vapor barrier, or reseal it with red moisture barrier tape if you do. Screw backer boards above the unsupported drywall ends of the enlarged hole and install the new patch (**Photo 2**).

Mist water over the surrounding ceiling texture in an area about 24 in. out from the patch to soften it so you can scrape it off to prep for the taping work (**Photo 3**). Then tape, mud and skim-coat the entire patch. Sand it smooth and you're ready to spray.

Rent a professional spray texture gun and practice on scrap drywall or cardboard. Apply a light coat of texture and add more in stages until you get a match. Lightly blend it into the existing texture.

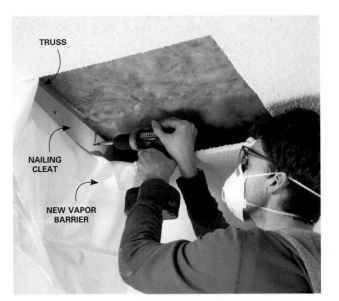

2 **Patch the hole.** Screw 3/4-in.-thick cleats to the sides of the trusses and replace or repair the vapor barrier. Then patch in a fresh piece of drywall.

3 **Reapply texture.** Wet the texture on the edges of your patch and allow it to soak in for several minutes before you scrape. Tape the joints and then reapply texture.

FREE UP A STICKING DEAD BOLT

You use your dead bolt every day without giving a thought to maintenance. But one of these days, it's going to fight back and refuse to open. Don't panic; it's just crying for a few shots of lube. You can get it working again with dry Teflon lube spray. It's a bet-ter choice than graphite because it sprays on wet to soak into the lock mechanism. The solvent evaporates, leaving behind a dry, slippery powder. Start by lubing the lock cylinder (**Photo 1**). If that doesn't free it, you'll need to lube the bolt mechanism (**Photo 2**).

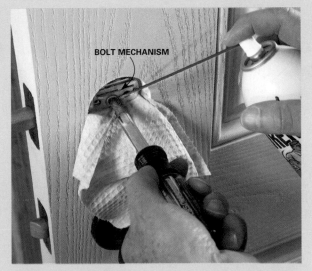

1 **Shoot the keyway.** Leave the lock cylinder on the door and spray inside the keyway. Then insert your key and twist it several times to work in the lube.

2 **Shoot the bolt.** Remove the two screws that hold the lock cylinder and pull it from the door. Then saturate the bolt mechanism with the spray lube and twist it back and forth with a flat-blade screwdriver. Reinstall the lock cylinder and you're good to go.

STAINLESS STEEL
KITCHEN BACKSPLASH

Fast. Easy. Elegant.

by Jeff Gorton

ncredible drama, itty-bitty effort. If there's an easier way to get this much impact, we don't know what it is. Stainless steel tiles are easy to install, last forever and don't require grouting. If there's any downside, it's that they cost about $15 to $20 per sq. ft. You can install the tile directly over any wall surface that's flat and sound, but clean the wall first so the adhesive will stick.

Besides standard carpentry tools, you'll need a rotary tool ($40 to $90) fitted with a metal-cutting disc, and a tile-cutting diamond wet saw. You can rent the wet saw (about $40 a day) or buy a table saw–type wet saw for under $100.

Order the tile

Stainless steel tile is available from several online sources. We ordered ours from Aqua Design at stainlesssteeltile.com. Once you find a tile size and style you like, decide on an installation pattern. You can combine different shapes to form a design or install the tiles in a traditional stacked or subway style like ours. Most stainless steel tiles have a backing that makes them easy to install. Some even have a peel-and-stick back. At Aqua Design, you can choose from cork, hardboard and cement board backing. Cork is good for backsplash installations. Use cement board in wet areas like showers.

Use graph paper or a computer drawing program to plan the pattern and calcu-

Stainless steel, aluminum and copper tiles are available in many styles, in brushed or shiny finishes. The tile at left is embossed; some tiles are even bowed to create a basket-weave look.

late how many pieces of each size of tile you'll need. Order several extra tiles in case you miscut one or miscalculate the amount. We decided on a subway pattern using 12 x 2-1/4-in. tiles. If you have an open end on your wall and you're installing the tile in a subway pattern, make sure to order half tiles to start every other row (Photo 2).

1 **Try out the layout.** Hang the tiles with masking tape to determine the best layout. By shifting the tiles to the left or right, you can avoid cutting small slices of tile to fill in at the ends.

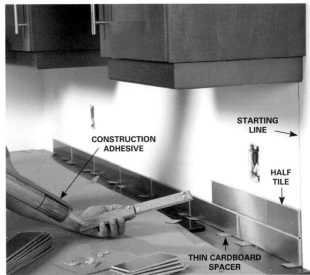

2 **Go light on the glue.** All it takes is a small dab at each corner. If you use too much, the glue will squeeze out between tiles. Place cardboard shims under the first course to provide space for caulk.

Prepare for tiling

Before you get started, find a long straight board or metal straightedge and use it to determine whether the walls in the backsplash area are flat. If the walls have humps or depressions, the tile will be uneven. For a great-looking job, you should fix these problems now, either by filling in the low spots with a layer of joint compound or by filling alongside humps and feathering them out to make them less pronounced.

Next, plan the installation to avoid skinny tile cuts if possible. **Photo 1** shows one method. You can also make a scale drawing and sketch the layout on paper, or make a template of your backsplash with butcher paper or cardboard and lay the tiles over it. The idea is to adjust the layout for the most pleasing look.

It's dangerous to work around live outlets with metal tiles. Before you begin the installation, turn off the power to the kitchen outlets and lights at the main electrical

panel. We removed the outlets and switches in the backsplash area and capped the wires because we planned to replace the ivory-color devices with gray ones. If you plan to keep the same outlets and switches, wrap two layers of wide blue painter's tape around the entire device to cover the face and terminal screws. Then twist the device so that you can push it partially into the box where it will be out of the way. Leave the power turned off while you install the tiles.

Before you reinstall the outlets and switches, add box extensions to bring the face of the electrical box flush to the face of the tile. You'll find plastic box extensions at home centers and hardware stores. Arlington Industries is one manufacturer.

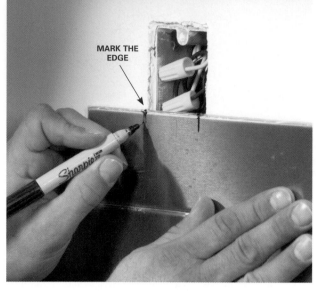

3 **Mark for an outlet cut.** Hold the tile in position to mark both sides of the electrical box. Then remove the tile and measure the distance from the tile below to the bottom of the box and mark this on the tile.

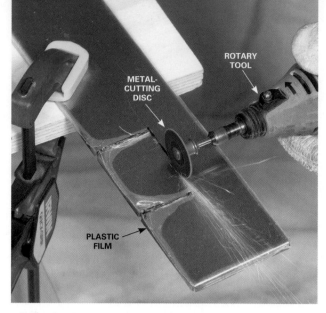

4 **Notch with a rotary tool.** Clamp the tile and cut the notch. Cut notches with a rotary tool. Don't worry about the protective film on the tile; it will loosen along the cut, but it won't melt or burn.

5 **Mark, don't measure.** To avoid mistakes in measuring, hold the tile in place and mark it instead. For accuracy, use a fine-tip permanent marker. Hold a border tile in position and mark where it intersects the next full tile. Draw a level line across the tile at the mark.

6 **Cut cool with a wet saw.** Make straight cuts with the wet saw. A dry diamond or abrasive blade will cut stainless steel, but the heat buildup may damage the tile.

Glue the tiles to the wall

The cork-backed stainless steel tiles we used are held to the wall with construction adhesive (Liquid Nails is one brand; $2 at home centers). You can leave spaces between the tiles and grout them just like ceramic tiles, but they look better set tight together. Grout lines detract from the metallic look. Peel off the protective plastic coating after you're finished installing the tiles.

The best way to cut stainless steel tiles is with a diamond wet saw. Cut the tile face up so that any lip that forms is on the back of the tile. Handle the tile carefully.

The cut metal edges are very sharp. It's difficult to cut notches with a wet saw. A rotary tool fitted with a metal-cutting disc is a good tool for cutting notches and other intricate shapes (Photo 4).

Rest the first row of tile on thin cardboard shims (Photo 2). Cardboard from the back of a legal pad is the right thickness. This leaves a space for caulk under the tiles and allows you a little room to adjust the tile if the countertop isn't perfectly flat. When you're done installing the tile, fill this gap with a very thin bead of clear silicone caulk. ⌂

VANITY
SANITY

*Three sensible solutions
for disorder down under*

by **David Radtke**

Most vanities are poor storage spaces because they're designed for the convenience of plumbers, not for you. While that big, open box is nice for installing pipes, it leaves you with jumbled storage and wasted space.

But you can convert that box into useful space by installing any or all of these three upgrades. You'll expand the real estate under your sink and make it easy to find anything in seconds. Even a beginning DIYer can build all three projects in a weekend, at a total cost of about $75.

1 Swing-out shelf
Get everything within reach! This spacious, double-level shelving unit pivots in and out effortlessly.

2 Mini rollout
No more tipping! This rollout has taller sides for taller products as well as full-extension hardware.

3 Drawer top trays
Get organized! Make these nifty sliding trays for all your vanity drawers.

Swing-out shelf

Here's the answer to all that inaccessible clutter on the floor of your vanity. With one pull, you can bring stored items out of the dark recesses and into easy reach.

Chances are, the measurements shown in Figure A won't be best for your vanity. The surest way to determine the right size for your shelf is to cut a quarter circle from cardboard and test the fit. If your vanity has double doors, you can still build this shelf, but you may need to open both doors to swing it out. Here are some tips for building your swing-out shelf:

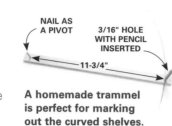

NAIL AS A PIVOT

3/16" HOLE WITH PENCIL INSERTED

11-3/4"

A homemade trammel is perfect for marking out the curved shelves.

- To make the curved shelves, just mark a half circle and then cut it into two equal quarter circles.
- A pneumatic brad nailer makes assembly a cinch. If you don't have a brad nailer, use trim screws. The awkward shape of the shelves makes hand nailing difficult. Whether you use nails or screws, also use glue.
- We finished our shelf with a couple of coats of polyurethane. A can of spray lacquer is also a good option.
- Piano hinges come in various lengths, but you probably won't find exactly what you need for your shelf. That's OK; you can cut it to length with a hacksaw.

Figure A

Part A 1/2" x 11-3/4" x 12"
Part B 1/2" x 13" x 12"
Part C 1/2" x 11-3/4" radius
Part D 1/8" x 1-3/4" x 24"

Materials
1/2" plywood (A–C)
1/8" hardboard (D)
No. 4 screws and No. 6 finish washers
Piano hinge
Cabinet pull

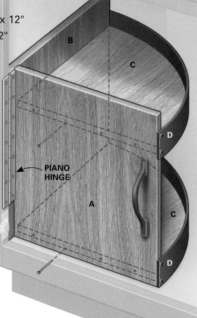

PIANO HINGE

HARDBOARD EDGING

NO. 4 SCREWS AND NO. 6 FINISH WASHERS

1 **Install the edging, then trim it.** Cut the hardboard edging a few inches too long, fasten it with screws and slice off the excess with a fine-tooth saw. Finish washers give the screws a neater look.

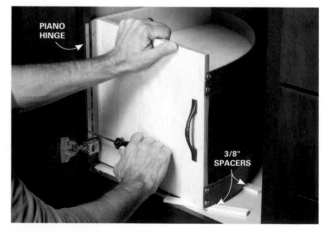

PIANO HINGE

3/8" SPACERS

2 **Hang it on a hinge.** Raise the shelf with spacers and align the shelf back with the inside edge of the face frame. Screw the piano hinge to the shelf back, then to the cabinet. You may have to notch the shelf back to clear the door hinge.

Mini-rollout

This handy little rollout has tall sides, fronts and backs to keep bottles and cleaners in place as you open it. Our dimensions are given in **Figure B**, but you can alter the size to suit your needs. Here are some building tips:

- Assemble the drawer boxes with glue plus trim screws, finish nails or brad nails.
- We used a 14-in. "full-extension" drawer slide. This type of slide is typically mounted on the side of a drawer, but it also works well as a light-duty undermount slide. If your home center doesn't carry full-extension slides in the length you need, go to any online cabinet hardware supplier. You can use a standard undermount slide, but your tray won't extend fully.
- Finish the rollout with two coats of polyurethane or spray lacquer.
- If you add a cabinet pull as we did, be sure to set the base back a bit so the vanity door can close.

Figure B

Part A 1/2" x 3-1/2" x 16"
Part B 1/2" x 3-1/2" x 16"
Part C 1/2" x 3-1/2" x 3"
Part D 1/2" x 3-1/2" x 16"

Materials
1/2" plywood
14" full-extension drawer slide
Cabinet pull

1 Mount the drawer slides. Separate the two parts of the drawer slide. Screw them to the tray and the base, aligned flush at the fronts.

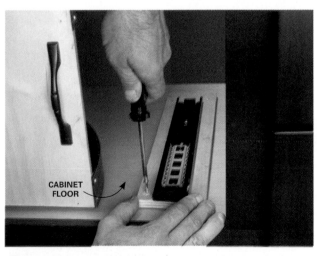

2 Elevate the drawer slide with a separate base. Fasten the tray base to the cabinet floor with No. 6 x 1-in. screws, then slide on the drawer.

3 Drawer top trays

Drawers are often too deep for small bathroom stuff like razors, medicine and cosmetics. That means wasted space. These handy sliding trays reduce that waste and increase drawer real estate by 50 percent.

- To size the tray, measure the drawer: Subtract 1/16 in. from the width of the drawer space and divide the length in half. Cut a piece of 1/8-in. hardboard this size.
- You can make the tray any depth you like. If the opening in the vanity is taller than the height of the drawer, your tray can protrude above the drawer sides.
- Finish the tray with a couple of coats of polyure-thane or spray lacquer.
- Stored items tend to slide around in the trays, so we added shelf liner (available at home centers and discount stores). 🏠

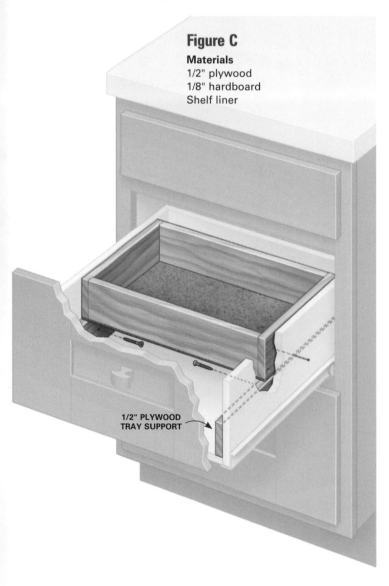

Figure C

Materials
1/2" plywood
1/8" hardboard
Shelf liner

1/2" PLYWOOD
TRAY SUPPORT

TRAY
SUPPORTS

1 Add tray supports. Fasten strips of plywood to the drawer to support the tray. You only need two screws per support.

SHELF
LINER

2 Line the trays. Cut shelf liner to fit the trays. Liner helps stored items stay put when you slide the tray.

PRO SECTION | REAL-WORLD TIPS FOR HANGING DOORS

by Jeff Gorton

You already know the standard approach to hanging a door: Set it in the rough opening, then level, shim and nail it. This traditional approach works fine in a perfect world where walls are always plumb, floors are level and you have plenty of time to fuss with the fit. But in the real world, some nonstandard tricks can help you finish the job faster and better.

SHIMS

HINGE LOCATION MARK

SHIM THE EASY WAY

Mark the location of the hinges on the drywall alongside the opening so you'll know where to place the shims. Place shims at the top and bottom hinge locations using a long level or a straight board and a short level. Then add the center shims.

Shim before the door goes in

The usual method of holding the door frame in place while you shim behind the hinge side is awkward. It's a lot easier to shim the hinge side of the rough opening before you put in the door frame. After that, it's a simple job to set the frame in place, screw or nail it to the shims, and then shim the strike side. Measure the width of the rough opening before you start shimming to see how much shim space is available. Usually the rough opening allows for about 1/2 in. of shimming on each side of the frame. If the rough opening is extra wide, you can use fewer shims by tacking scraps of 1/2-in. plywood at the hinge locations first, and then add shims to plumb the jamb.

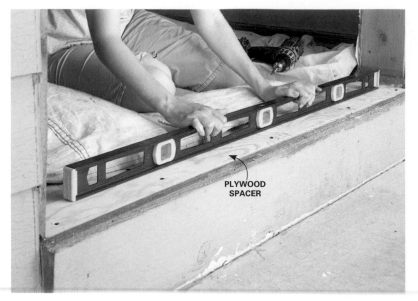

AVOID CLEARANCE PROBLEMS
Screw a strip of plywood to the bottom of the rough opening to raise the door and prevent it from rubbing on the floor inside.

Make sure your exterior door clears the rug

Most of the time, you can simply set your new exterior door frame directly on the subfloor and the door will easily clear carpeting or a throw rug. But if you're replacing an old door with a thick sill, or if the floor will be built up with tile, thick carpet or an extra layer of wood, you could have a problem. And there's no easy solution after the door is installed. You can't simply trim the bottom, because then the door won't seal against the sill. To avoid this problem, add a spacer under the door before you install it. The key is to determine where the top of the tile, carpet or throw rug will be, and then raise the door frame to leave about a 1/2-in. space under the door (**photo left**).

Set interior jambs on spacers

If you set the doorjambs directly on the subfloor, there's a good chance the door will rub against the carpet later. Of course, you can cut off the bottom of the doors, but it's easy to avoid this extra work by planning ahead. Find out the thickness of the finish floor and then calculate where the bottom of the door will be. Plan the installation so there will be about 1/2 to 3/4 in. of space under the door. Usually setting the doorjambs on scraps of 3/8- to 1/2-in.-thick trim will put the door at the correct height.

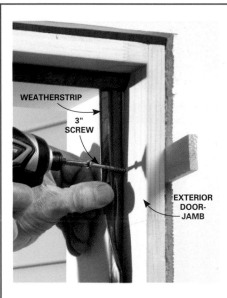

HIDE THE SCREWS
Pull back or remove the weather strip on the latch side of the door frame and drive screws where they'll be hidden.

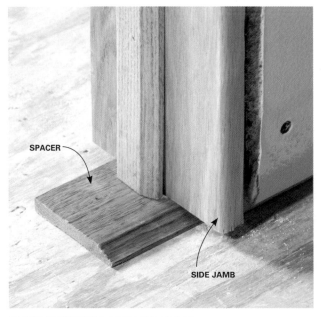

AVOID TRIMMING DOOR BOTTOMS
Raise doorjambs with scraps of trim to make sure the door will clear the carpeting.

Hidden screws make exterior doors stronger

There are many benefits to using screws rather than nails to install exterior doors. They can be adjusted and won't easily pull out or loosen. But you don't want to leave the painter with the task of filling big, ugly screw holes. The trick is to hide the screws under the weather stripping on the latch side. On the hinge side, you can simply replace one screw in each hinge with a matching 3-in.-long screw. Always start by drilling a clearance hole that allows the screw to slide freely in and out of the hole. This ensures the screw will pull the jamb tight to the shims, and allows for adjustment if needed. Don't let the spinning screw rub against the weather strip—it will slice right through. I know this from bitter experience.

Tune up the rough opening

Twisted or out-of-plumb rough openings raise havoc with door installations. If you install the jambs to follow the walls, the door is likely to swing open or shut on its own. On the other hand, if you plumb the jambs against the out-of-plumb rough opening, the trim will be hard to install.

As long as the bottom of the wall isn't held in place by flooring, there's a simple solution. Just move the studs on both sides of the opening back to plumb. Don't think you can do this with your trim hammer, though. You'll need a maul or a sledgehammer.

1 **Check for plumb. Check both sides of the door opening.** If they're more than 1/4 in. out of plumb, adjust them before you install the door.

2 **Nudge the wall.** Protect the wall with a 2x4 scrap while you move the bottom of the wall over with a sledgehammer. When the wall is plumb, toe-screw the bottom plate to the floor to hold it in place.

How one pro installs a door in four easy steps

John Schumacher, owner of Millwork Specialties Ltd. in Minnesota, has been installing doors and millwork for more than 20 years. He's learned to avoid callbacks by doing the job right the first time. Here's his door installation method in a nutshell.

1. PLUMB THE HINGE JAMB

The hinge side of the door has to be plumb or the door will swing open or closed on its own. Start by shimming the hinge side of the rough opening. First make marks to indicate the centers of the hinges. Then use a long level or a long, straight board along with a short level to plumb the shims. Tack a pair of tapered shims at the top hinge. Then install the bottom shims and finally fill in the middle.

2. SCREW THE HINGE-SIDE JAMB TO THE STUD

Remove the door from the frame and set it aside. Remove the hinge leaves from the jamb. Set the door frame in

the opening with the jamb resting on the finished floor or on a spacer. Drive 3-in. screws through the jamb where they'll be hidden by the hinges.

3. ADJUST THE GAP ALONG THE TOP

Slide shims between the floor and the latch-side jamb until the head jamb is level. Now reinstall the door hinges and the door. Adjust the shims under the latch-side jamb until the gap between the top of the door and the top jamb is even.

4. SHIM AND NAIL THE LATCH-SIDE JAMB

Shim behind the latch-side jamb to make an even gap between the door and the jamb. Usually three or four sets of shims, evenly spaced along the jamb, are plenty. Drive two finish nails into each set of shims to hold the jamb in place. Cut off the protruding shims with a fine-tooth saw or a utility knife.

Trim the bottom to level the top

Old houses are notorious for having sloping floors. Even some newer houses settle in unexpected ways. If you don't cut the jamb to compensate for the out-of-level floor, you could have a problem getting an even space between the top of the door and the head jamb. This is critical if you're installing a door over existing flooring where the jambs have to fit tightly to the floor. **Photos 1 and 2** show how to trim the jambs to fit a sloping floor.

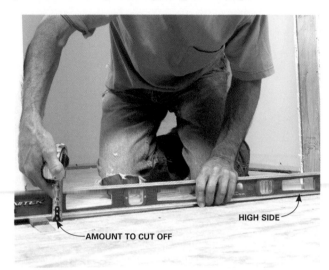

1 **Check with a level.** Level across the opening and shim up one side until the bubble is centered. The distance between the level and the floor tells you how much to cut off the jamb.

2 **Cut the high-side jamb.** Trim the jamb with a fine-tooth saw. A "Japanese"-style pull saw cuts fast and leaves a clean cut.

Hide screws behind the hinges

Screws are better for securing the hinge jamb because nails can work loose. You can easily replace one of the short hinge screws with a long screw, but it can be difficult to find a strong screw that matches the other screws. Here's a trick we learned. Hide the screw behind the hinge. It only takes a minute or two to remove all the hinges and gain access to this area. Then you can drive a self-drilling screw through the jamb with ease. Make sure the jamb is straight and plumb before you reinstall the hinges.

USE SCREWS, NOT NAILS
Screw through the jamb in the hinge mortise. The screws will hold better than nails and will be hidden by the hinges.

Troubleshooting tips
DOOR WON'T LATCH

Out-of-plumb jambs or a warped door can cause this. If the door won't latch because it's hitting the latch-side stop on the top or bottom, the fix is to move the stop. If it only needs a little adjustment, you can just tap it over with a hammer and a block of wood. Otherwise, pry it off carefully, and with the door closed and latched, reinstall it against the door.

DOOR BINDS AND RESISTS CLOSING

If the door isn't rubbing against the jamb, but there's tension when you try to close it, then it's binding on the hinge jamb. Usually this means you haven't shimmed correctly and the jamb isn't at a right angle to the wall. Fix this problem by adjusting the hinge-side shims to twist the jamb back to a right angle with the wall. 🏠

TILE WITHOUT TROUBLE

*Easier installation,
less frustration*

by **Gary Wentz**

In theory, setting tile is easy. You just stick tiles to the wall or floor and fill the gaps with grout. But in the real world, tile jobs are full of frustrations. This collection of tips—collected from pros and DIYers—may not eliminate all your tile troubles, but it will help you avoid the most common headaches.

Mix it smooth

After all the prep and layout work, you're finally ready to set tile and see some results. The last thing you want to do is stop and wait. But giving the thin-set time to absorb water, or "slake," is the key to a smooth, chunk-free mix. A chunky mix will drive you crazy when you try to comb the thin-set onto the wall or floor. After slaking, remix and add a smidgen of water if needed. Play the same waiting game when you mix up the grout later.

FOR A SMOOTH MIX, WAIT
Mix up the thin-set or grout, then let it stand for about 10 minutes. That allows dry chunks time to absorb water before you do the final mixing.

Start with a flat floor

Tiling a wavy floor is a nightmare. You push and pry to get each tile flush with its neighbors and you still end up with "lippage" (edges that protrude above adjoining tiles, usually at corners). So before you tile, check the floor with a 4-ft. straightedge. If you find low spots more than 1/4 in. deep, screed thin-set over them to create a flat surface.

For really bad floors, self-leveling compound (also called "self-leveling underlayment") is a lifesaver. You just mix the powder with water and pour to create a flat, smooth surface. A perfect tile base doesn't come cheap, though—expect to pay about $2 per sq. ft. Some products require metal or plastic lath; some don't.

Self-leveling compound is almost goof-proof, but there are two big pitfalls. First,

PLASTIC LATH

SELF-LEVELING COMPOUND

HEATING CABLE

POUR A PERFECT FLOOR
Self-leveling compound gives you a flat, smooth base for tile. It's also a fast way to embed in-floor heating mats or cables.

it will slowly seep into the tiniest crack or hole, leaving a crater in the surface. So before you put down the lath, grab a caulk gun and fill every little gap—even small nail holes. Second, you have to work fast. Most compounds begin to harden in about 30 minutes. To get the whole floor poured in that time frame, you need at least one helper to mix the compound while you pour. And even with help, you'll have to move quickly.

Remove the baseboard

You can leave base trim in place, lay tile along it and caulk the gap. But that "shortcut" will look second rate and cost you hours of fussy measuring and cutting. With baseboards gone, your cuts don't have to be precise or perfect; the baseboard will hide chipped edges and small mistakes. If you're just dead-set against pulling off baseboards, consider adding base shoe molding along the bottom of the baseboard after you set the tile.

BASEBOARD REMOVED

GIVE YOURSELF SOME WIGGLE ROOM
With baseboards removed, measurements and cuts don't have to be precise. That means faster work and fewer mis-cut tiles on the scrap pile.

Set against guide boards

The usual way to position the first rows of tile is to snap chalk lines. But there are two problems with that method: First, chalk lines are hard to see if you've slopped thin-set over them. Second, the first row of tile can move as you set the next row. Guide boards solve both problems. Position the boards the same way you would position layout lines and screw them to the floor. Be sure to choose perfectly straight boards or cut strips of plywood. Also, wrap the edge of the guide with duct tape so the thin-set won't stick to it.

GUIDE BOARD

BOARDS ARE BETTER THAN LINES
Unlike chalk lines, guide boards don't get lost under thin-set or allow tiles to shift as you set other tiles.

Get a straight start on walls

The obvious way to tile a wall is to start at the bottom and work your way up. And that works fine if the base of the wall (usually the floor or bathtub) is perfectly flat and level. If not, the tile will simply amplify the imperfections; you'll end up with misaligned tiles and grout lines that vary in width.

To get a straight, level start, position a ledger on the wall, leaving a gap below—about 1/2 in. less than a full tile. The ledger shown here is a length of steel angle held in place by wood blocks screwed to the wall. A strip of plywood or a perfectly straight board will do the job too.

SET TILES ON A LEDGER
Fasten a straight ledger to the wall to support the tiles. Remove the ledger later and trim tiles to fill the gap below.

Tackle tough cuts with a grinder

A grinder isn't the best tool for cutting tile. It whips up a nasty dust storm and often leaves jagged or chipped edges. Plus, it's just plain slower than a tile cutter or wet saw. But equipped with a diamond blade, a grinder will cut curves and make enclosed cuts that those other tools can't. Choose a "dry-cut" blade ($25) and do the cutting outdoors.

CUT OUTLET HOLES
Outline the light switch or outlet box on the face of the tile. Cut as much as you can, then finish the cut from the back, where you can overcut the corners slightly.

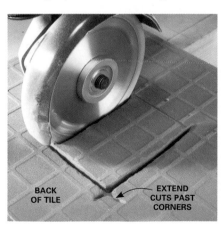

BACK OF TILE

EXTEND CUTS PAST CORNERS

Clean up right away!

When you're done setting the tile, stand back for a minute to admire it. Then get back to work. First, drop your mucky tools in a bucket of cold water. That will slow—but not stop—the hardening of the thin-set. Next, inspect all the joints for thin-set that has squeezed out between tiles and clean it out before it hardens. Also look for thin-set smudges on the face of the tile. If a smudge has hardened and won't wipe off easily, wet it and scrub with a synthetic abrasive pad (the kind you use to scour cookware). Use minimal elbow grease; if you rub really hard, it's possible to dull polished stone or even glazed tile. Now go clean up those tools.

SQUEEZE-OUT

CLEAN OUT THE SQUEEZE-OUT
Plow excess thin-set out of joints with a utility knife, a pencil or a tile spacer. Whatever you use, do it now, not later.

Slow down the drying

Pros like to finish the job fast and will sometimes use fast-setting thin-set. For the rest of us mortals, slower is better, and even the standard products sometimes harden or dry out too fast. Here are two ways to give yourself extra working time: First dampen the backer board or concrete with a sponge before you spread the thin-set. A damp surface won't immediately suck moisture out of the thin-set. Second, mix the thin-set with latex additive rather than water ($25 for 2 gallons). Latex additive dries slower than water and boosts adhesion in both thin-set and grout. It also makes grout more stain-resistant. (A few latex additives are designed to speed the hardening process; check the label.) If thin-set or grout begins to harden before you can use it, just toss it. Don't add water and remix. That's a recipe for weak bonding and trouble later. ⌂

Question&Comment

DIY GRANITE COUNTERTOPS

I'd really like to install granite countertops in my kitchen. Is there any way I can do that myself? What's involved, how much could I save, and where can I get the materials?

Yes, you can install granite countertops yourself. If you have straight countertops with no inside corners, it's actually quite an easy DIY project. However, if your kitchen is like most, you'll have to do some cutting and seaming. But if you have basic woodworking skills, that's not as intimidating as it might sound.

The key is to find a company that provides the granite along with most of the cutting, shaping and machining of the sink and faucet openings. Doityourselfgranite. com is one online source for both the slabs and the fabrication work. Go online and search for "granite countertop suppliers" for many others. Send the company a sketch of your kitchen layout with dimensions. The staff will review it, pencil in where the seams should go and provide the quote. The prices at doityourselfgranite.com range from $18 to $25 per sq. ft. depending on the granite style you choose.

The only tricky part is cutting butt joints wherever there are inside corners, which you'll have to do yourself. That involves making a straight cut just short of the bull nose and then cutting the miter with a special jig that's provided with the rest of the tools.

The cut doesn't have to be perfect; fillers and polishing will take care of small irregularities. Don't get scared off by these cuts. Just be sure to measure twice and cut slowly—the diamond blade does all the hard work for you. Doityourselfgranite.com even includes a misting system that attaches to your saw to keep the blade cool and eliminate dust. After installation, you fill, dye to match and polish all the seams, making them nearly invisible.

Doityourselfgranite.com offers substantial discounts on the tools you'll need if you buy them at the time of your slab order. Even after buying the tools and paying the shipping charges, you'll still save about $1,500 for countertops for the average-size kitchen.

It takes about a month for the slabs to arrive. At that point, you install 3/4-in. plywood over your base cabinets and call in favors from all your friends. You'll need their help to heft those heavy slabs out of the shipping container and into the house. So buy beer—and lots of it.

SEAM FILLER

SEAM GRINDING TOOL

POLISHING COMPOUND

SEAM POLISHING PAD

DIAMOND BLADE

DYE PACKS

YOU'LL NEED SPECIAL SUPPLIES
Order seam filler, dye packs, a diamond blade, a polishing stone and pad, and polishing compound from your granite supplier.

HOW DO I FIX THIS? FLAT-PANEL TV MOUNT

I want to mount my flat panel TV, but one side of the bracket doesn't line up with the studs, even if I adjust the TV all the way to one side. When I try to catch two studs, the TV placement just isn't centered where I want it. Can I use toggle bolts in the drywall?

That's not a good idea; toggle bolts are just not up to the task. Moen (yeah, the faucet company) developed a great wall anchor system for attaching bathroom grab bars. Now it offers a 150-lb.-rated SecureMount version for mounting flat screen TVs. Moen recommends these for fixed or pivoting but not swing-out mounts. We've tried them and they're fabulous. Just drill a 1-1/4-in. hole, insert the sleeve and slide in the anchor piece. Pull it close to the wall with the disposable pull tool. It locks the anchor in place so you won't lose it in the wall while you insert the screw. Buy a set of two for $16 at moen.com/securemountanchors.

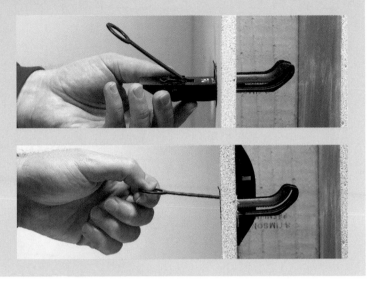

GROUTING POROUS TILE

I've begun grouting a small part of an enormous slate floor that I laid in the basement. The grout is impossible to clean from all the cracks and crevices. Do you have any advice before I tackle the rest?

Yes. You can't just slather grout over any porous or uneven surfaces such as split-slate tiles or limestone or similar stone tile that has crevices, holes or open cracks. The grout will fill in those areas and even if you're able to clean them out, you'll never have enough time to clean everything before the grout sets up.

Here's an effective three-step system. It takes longer than conventional grouting techniques, but you'll get perfectly clean tile with far less hassle.

The only special tool you might not have is a grout bag, which masons use for tuck-pointing. Find one for about $10 with the masonry tools at the home center. Also pick up a

bottle of "grout release" at a tile store. A quart costs less than $15. To start, clean out all the grout lines by vacuuming and scraping out any thin-set projecting above the tile. Then wipe the surface with a damp rag until it's free of dust.

The three photos show how to apply the grout. When you're finished with one batch, let the grout set until you can't leave a thumbprint in it. Then begin tooling the joints with a slightly damp sponge to shape and even them out. Keep wiping away any excess grout until the tile looks clean.

After you see a hazy film form, polish the tile with a dry cloth just as you would with conventional tile.

1 Wipe on grout release. Wipe on the grout release with care. Try to keep it out of the grout joints or the grout won't bond to the tile. Let it dry before grouting.

2 Squeeze in the grout. Twist the bag like you're icing a cake to force the grout into each joint. This takes time, so only mix small batches until you get a feel for how much flooring to bite off at once.

3 Pack the joints. Compress the grout into each joint by dragging the margin trowel over the joint. Then scrape the excess grout away until it's even with the tile.

WEEKEND BATHROOM MAKEOVER

Transform your bathroom without the hassle of a complete remodel.

by **Jeff Gorton**

You don't have to spend thousands of dollars and put up with weeks of construction mess to transform your bathroom. In many cases, you can give your bathroom a fresh, new look by replacing the dated vanity cabinet, sink, faucets and light fixtures. And with a little planning and perseverance, you can get most of the work done in a weekend. In this story, we'll walk you through the steps for this weekend bathroom makeover and show you a few tricks to save you some money and speed up the job.

Here's what we did:

- Installed a new IKEA cabinet in place of the old vanity.
- Replaced an old single-bowl vanity top with a modern double-bowl top and faucets from IKEA.
- Added a big mirror to make the room feel spacious.
- Improved the lighting by adding sconces on the sides of the mirror.
- Added style and punch with decorative glass tile.
- Tied it all together with new birch trim to match the cabinet.

For more details on vanity tear-out and installation, sink hook-up, sconce wiring and tiling, you can go to familyhandyman.com and search for the topic you're interested in.

We were looking for a way to radically change the appearance of this '70s-era bathroom without breaking the bank. And after shopping around, we settled on IKEA cabinets and fixtures. They're modern, moderately priced and easy to install. To spice things up, we splurged a little on the glass tiles. But even at $10 per sq. ft., the tile only added about $270 to the cost. Altogether we spent about $1,300 for this project.

Before you launch into a bath redo like this, make sure the flooring extends under the vanity cabinet. This may take a little detective work. You can usually tell by carefully inspecting the intersection of the floor and cabinet. If there's no flooring under the cabinet, you'll have to either replace the floor or find a new vanity cabinet with the same or larger footprint. If you're lucky, you may find matching flooring to patch in, but this is rare.

Tear out the old stuff

Every bathroom is different, and this phase of the job may be quick and easy or present a few challenges. Start by closing the shutoff valves to the faucet and disconnecting the plumbing under the sink. If the drain parts are the old steel type, don't try to reuse them. You'll save yourself headaches by simply replacing the trap assembly with a modern PVC version. Buy a 1-1/4-in. PVC trap kit at a home center or hardware store. If you have a plastic laminate vanity top, look for screws on the underside and remove them. Cultured marble tops like the one shown here are usually held on by caulk and need to be pried off (**Photo 1**). If tile surrounds your vanity top, you'll have to remove the tile first.

Next remove the screws that hold the cabinet to the wall and remove the cabinet. Complete the tear-out by removing the mirror or medicine cabinet and light fixtures. Turn off the power to the bathroom light at the main electrical panel and double-check the wires with a voltage sniffer to make sure the power is off before you disconnect the light.

1 Tear out the vanity. Disconnect the plumbing and pry off the old top. Then remove the vanity cabinet and old medicine cabinet or mirror.

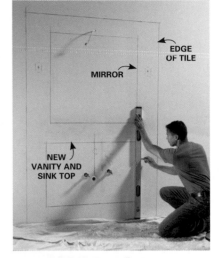

2 Draw outlines on the wall. Outline the new fixtures, mirror and tile on the wall. Then decide where the new lights should go and mark these.

3 Reroute electrical lines. Cut a large hole so it's easy to mount a new junction box and drill holes for the new wiring. Don't worry about patching the wall; the hole will be covered by the mirror.

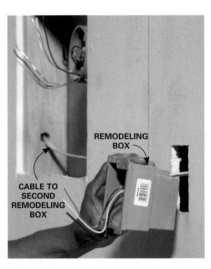

4 Mount the new light boxes. Run a cable from the junction box to the new remodeling boxes. Slide the box into the hole and tighten the screws to clamp it onto the drywall.

Mark the new plan on the wall

Drawing a full-scale plan of the new layout on the wall will save you headaches later (**Photo 2**). You'll need the dimensions of the vanity cabinet, vanity top, tile and light fixtures. It's best if you have these items on-site to make sure there are no surprises. In addition, it's important to dry-fit the drain parts so you'll know exactly where to position the new vanity cabinet. The IKEA cabinet we used included a custom (and very unusual) drain assembly that required us to center the new cabinet on the existing drain. Traditional vanity cabinets are more forgiving.

After you've determined the vanity cabinet location and marked it on the wall, plan the tile layout. Lay a row of tile

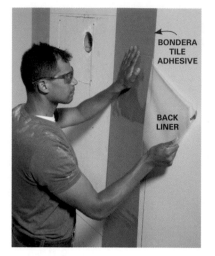

5 **Apply the tile adhesive.** Line up the edge of the Bondera tile adhesive with the tile line. Peel off the back liner as you press the adhesive to the wall.

BONDERA TILE ADHESIVE

BACK LINER

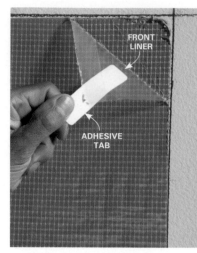

6 **Peel off the front liner.** Use the sticky tabs included with the tile adhesive to peel off the front liner. Once you get it started, it's easy to peel off the rest.

FRONT LINER

ADHESIVE TAB

7 **Install the tile.** Position the tile carefully and press it just hard enough to hold it in place. When you're sure the tile is straight and the joints line up, tamp the tile with a grout float to adhere it.

BONDERA TILE ADHESIVE

GLASS MOSAIC TILE SHEET

8 **Grout the tile.** Press grout into the joints with a grout float. Sweep the float in diagonal strokes until the joints are completely filled. Then scrape off the excess grout with the edge of the float.

requires every electrical box to be accessible. In other words, you can't connect wires in a junction box and then cover it with drywall or glue a mirror over it. But luckily it's OK to put a junction box behind a mirror as long as the mirror isn't permanently attached. This allows you some flexibility when adding light fixtures. If the old wires won't reach to the new box location, you can simply add a junction box as we show here and extend new wires from it to the new fixture locations (**Photo 3 and 4**).

In our case, the wiring was straightforward. There was one cable extending from the switch to the original light fixture. We removed a section of drywall to simplify the installation of the junction box and new wires. Then we chose an electrical box large enough to accommodate the new wires (go to familyhandyman.com and search for "electrical box size" for more information). We nailed the new junction box to the stud and ran the old wires into the box. Then we cut holes for the new remodeling boxes at the fixture locations, drilled holes through the studs and ran new cable from the junction box to each fixture location (**Photo 4**). We used remodeling boxes to simplify exact placement and avoid extra wall patching.

Tile the walls

It's easier to tile before you install the vanity cabinet because you don't have to cut the tile to fit around it. You can save money on tile by omitting it behind the vanity cabinet and mirror. Just extend the tile a few inches beyond the outlines of the mirror and cabinet. Also, you don't have to cut tile to fit tightly to the electrical boxes as long as the light fixture will cover the missing tiles.

Rather than spread thin-set mortar on the wall to adhere the tile, we installed a sticky mat called Bondera (**Photos 5 and 6**). Bondera tile adhesive has a few advantages over thin-set, especially for installation of glass mosaic tile like ours. First, you can grout right away. You don't have to wait for the thin-set to set up. And you don't have to worry about thin-set oozing out from behind the tile and into the grout spaces.

Bondera adhesive isn't perfect, though. First, at about $4 per sq. ft., it's way more expensive than thin-set. Also,

on the floor to determine the exact width and height of the tiled area and mark this on the wall. Now draw lines to indicate the position of the mirror. Finally mark the location of the new light fixture boxes. Hold the light fixtures up on the wall to determine the best height and make marks. Then center them between the mirror and the tile border. After you double-check all your layout marks, you're ready to move on to the wiring.

Add wiring for the new sconces

Again, every bathroom will be different. Maybe you already have sconces, but need to relocate them for the new mirror position. Keep in mind that the National Electrical Code

repositioning the sheets of tile was a little tricky. They won't slide like they do on thin-set. You have to place them gingerly onto the mat and not embed them firmly until you're sure they're properly aligned. You can pull off the sheet of tile and reposition it if you haven't pressed too hard. Follow the instructions included with the Bondera adhesive, or go to bonderatilematset.com for an installation video and more instructions.

If you're leaving tile out like we did, the trick is to make sure the tile meets up accurately as you surround the blank space. Run tile up one side to just above the cabinet space and across the bottom, making sure the side column is perfectly plumb (follow your layout line) and the bottom row is perfectly level. Then extend lines from these two points with a level. Remember, don't press too hard on the tile until you're sure it's all lined up correctly (**Photo 7**). When the tile is lined up perfectly, embed it in the mat by tamping on it with a grout float. As soon as you're done tiling, you can mix up some grout and fill the grout spaces (**Photo 8**).

Mix the grout to toothpaste consistency and let it sit for 15 minutes. Remix it and add a tiny dash of water if it got too thick. Go to familyhandyman.com and type "grout" into the search box for more grouting tips and instructions.

Mount the vanity cabinet and top

IKEA cabinets require assembly but are easy to put together. After assembling the cabinet, mount it on the wall using temporary blocks to hold it up. If you don't have studs at the mounting bracket location, use toggle bolts. Regardless of what type of vanity cabinet you're installing, first locate the studs. Then drive 3-in. washer head screws through the cabinet hanging rail into the studs to hold it in place (**Photo 9**).

Next mount the faucets to the sink top and assemble the drain parts and faucet connections. If you're replacing a single faucet with two faucets, you can connect them both to the existing shutoff valves by adding a "tee" as shown in **Photo 10**. These IKEA faucets included proprietary supply tubes with 1/2-in. pipe thread fittings on the

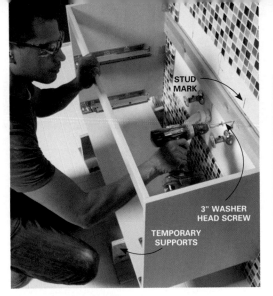

STUD MARK

3" WASHER HEAD SCREW

TEMPORARY SUPPORTS

9 **Hang the cabinet.** Support the cabinet on temporary stands. Then drive screws through the hanging rail into the studs to secure the cabinet.

Get the look

Tile: Premium Glass Mosaics Black and White Blend at Home Depot. $10 per 12 x 12-in. sheet.

Light fixtures: Hampton Bay No. 287451 Wall Sconce at Home Depot. $40.

The following products are available at IKEA stores and online from ikea.com:

Vanity cabinet: Godmorgon two-drawer sink cabinet. $248.

Vanity top: Bredviken sink. $300.

Faucets: Dalskar. $100.

Towel bar: Sävern. Article No. 901.625.97. $20.

Bondera tile adhesive: A new way to set tile

To install the glass mosaics for this project, we replaced the traditional thin-set mortar tile adhesive with a product called Bondera. It's basically a mat that's sticky on both sides, allowing you to stick it to the wall like wallpaper, and then stick tiles to the face. Bondera adhesive is available at Lowe's and online for about $40 for a 12-in.-wide x 10-ft.-long roll. The main advantages over thin-set are that you can grout right away and that you don't have to worry about it oozing into the grout joints. It's not perfect, though. Whereas thin-set can take up some wall irregularities, Bondera adhesive isn't forgiving. If your wall is wavy, your tile will be too. And you can't slide the tile around to reposition it. You can nudge it a little, but for major adjustments you'll have to pull off the tile and try again.

Here's what Dean, our tile guru, has to say:

"I'm impressed! The tile really sticks to this stuff. It would be great for my kitchen backsplash jobs. I'd save a trip back and the customer would be happy to have me out of the kitchen a day sooner."

end. Your faucets may be different. Take the faucet and any included tubes with you to the home center or hardware store so you can assemble them in the store to find the right parts.

After you've mounted the faucets and assembled the drain parts, you're ready to install the sink. Spread a thin bead of silicone caulk on the top edge of the cabinet and carefully lower the sink top onto it. Let the caulk set up for a few hours before you connect the plumbing to make sure the sink doesn't get jostled out of position. Complete the job by marking and cutting the PVC tailpiece (**Photo 11**) and connecting the supply lines. Turn on the water and check for leaks.

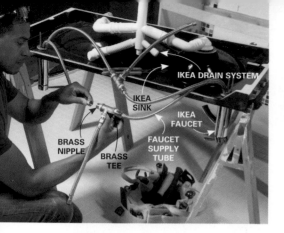

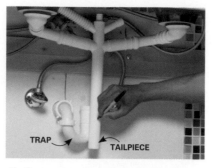

10 Mount the faucets. Follow the faucet instructions to mount the faucets to the sink. Installing the faucets and drain plumbing is easier if you do it before installing the sink on the cabinet.

11 Connect the plumbing. Mark the tailpiece so that it will extend into the trap a few inches when it's cut off. Cut it off with a hacksaw. Remove the trap. Slip it over the tailpiece and reconnect it. Connect the supply tubes to the shutoff valves. Turn on the water and check for leaks.

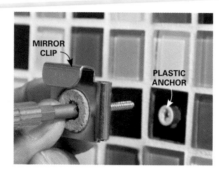

12 Drill mirror clip holes. Keep the glass bit cool by spraying water on it as you drill. Run the drill at slow to medium speed. Let up on the pressure when you're almost through the tile.

13 Install the mirror clips. Tap a plastic hollow-wall anchor into the hole and screw the clip into the anchor. If the hole landed over a stud, you don't need the anchor.

The trick to drilling a hole in glass tile is to go slow and keep the glass bit wet.

1/4" GLASS BIT

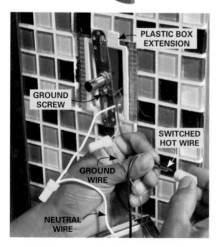

14 Wire the light fixtures. Slip a box extension into the electrical box if the tile is more than 1/4 in. thick. Then mount the fixture strap to the box and connect the wires.

15 Finish up. Hang the mirror, paint the walls and mount the light fixtures. We installed new trim to match the cabinet.

Add the finishing touches

Now you're on the home stretch. In our bathroom, we repainted the walls and replaced the old moldings with strips of flat birch to match the new cabinet. **Photo 12** shows how to drill holes in the glass tile for the mirror mounting clips. The mirror mounts we found at the home center included a pair of spring-loaded clips for the top and fixed clips for the bottom. Measure your mirror and mark the clip positions on the tiles with a permanent marker. The top clips have to be mounted about 3/8 in. low to allow the spring clip to function properly. Then use a 1/4-in. glass bit, available at home centers and hardware stores, to drill the holes (**Photo 12**). The key is to go slowly and keep the bit and tile wet to avoid overheating, which would crack the tile and ruin the bit. Tap a plastic anchor into the holes and attach the clips with pan head screws. Install the mirror by putting the top edge into the clips and lifting it up. Then let it drop down into the lower clips.

Finish by mounting the light fixtures. Make sure the power is turned off. Then strip the ends of the wires about 1/2 in. (read the instructions on the wire connector package for the exact amount). Electrical boxes can be recessed up to 1/4 in. in noncombustible materials like tile, but since our tile was just over 1/4 in. thick, we added a box extension set flush to the tile surface before attaching the fixture strap with the mounting screws (**Photo 14**). Wrap the bare copper ground wire three-quarters of the way around the grounding screw on the fixture strap and tighten the screw. Then extend the remainder of the bare ground wire to the ground wire on the fixture and connect them with a wire connector. Complete the wiring by connecting the white neutral wires together and the switched hot wires together. ⌂

PRO TIPS for
HANGING DRYWALL

by **Mark Petersen**

Hanging drywall is not all that complicated, but there is a right and a wrong way to do it. Here are some tips to save you time and money, and make taping easier.

Cut outside corners flush with the framing

It's tempting to cut the first piece of an outside corner flush with the framing and run the perpendicular piece flush with the first. Don't do it! If you run the first piece just a little too long, the second piece will flare out. If you cut the second piece a bit too long, it will have to be shaved down to accommodate the corner bead. A good-quality metal corner bead will cover a gap and hold up as well as a perfectly flush corner—without the fuss.

CORNER BEAD WILL COVER

Inside corners: Measure exact, then subtract

When you're working in a smaller area like a closet and have to cut a piece that's going to fit between two perpendicular walls, don't try to cut exactly. Precision is a worthy goal, but you're not building a piano. All the inside corners are going to receive mud and tape anyway. If the piece is too big and you try to force it into place (which you will do), besides scraping up the drywall on an adjacent wall, you're more than likely going to damage the piece you're trying to install.

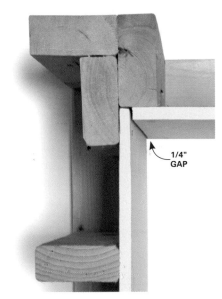

1/4" GAP

Master the basics

Even pros sometimes forget a few of the basics of good drywall installation. Here are some that we think are important to know:

- Think ahead when you deliver the drywall. For example, don't bury the sheets for the ceiling behind the ones for the walls. Stack all the sheets so the finished side is facing out. Place the drywall throughout the job site where it is most handy and won't be in the way. Order 12-ft.-long sheets whenever possible. Order 54-in.-wide sheets for 9-ft. walls. Consider having your drywall delivered; it costs about $1 more per sheet.
- Most manufacturers now offer a stiffer, 1/2-in. drywall that can be used on ceilings in certain situations. Half-inch is considerably easier to hang than 5/8-in., but make sure the drywall you use conforms to the fire code in your area.
- If you use a chalk line to mark your pieces before you cut them, use blue chalk. Red, orange or any other color is likely to bleed through the finish.
- If you write down measurements or mark the stud lines with a pencil, do it very, very lightly. Even

modest pressure on drywall with a pencil will show up on your finished walls.
- In our neck of the woods, screws need to be spaced no more than 12 in. on ceilings and 16 in. on walls. Nails require 8-in. spacing on ceilings and 7-in. on walls. Technically, the fastening schedule code is whatever the manufacturer requires. That information can usually be found online.
- Don't overtighten the screws. If a screw breaks the paper, its holding power has been compromised. And don't undertighten the screws or taping will be an awful job!
- Leave about a 1/2-in. gap between the drywall and the floor. You don't want drywall to wick up moisture from concrete or from an inevitable spill in an upper level room. In addition, a gap at the floor makes it easier for carpet to be tucked under the trim.
- On a long wall, it's not always possible to steer clear of seams located directly over a window or door, but a seam that's in line with the horizontal edge of a window or door should be avoided at all costs. It's sure to crack.

CUT COUNTER-CLOCKWISE

Gaps mean extra work

All tear-outs and gaps that won't be completely covered by a cover plate have to be taped and feathered out—more work. So use your spiral saw carefully (and see the tip below about heavy plastic electrical boxes!). If a gap around an electrical box is just filled with mud and the cover plate is overtightened, the mud will crack and crumble out of the gap. The areas around outlets are particularly vulnerable because of the pressure of plugging in and unplugging electrical cords.

NEEDS TO BE TAPED

SPIRAL SAW BIT BURN-THROUGH

Spiral saws— a hanger's best friend

Spiral saws save time and money if they're used properly. Here are a few tips for getting the most out of this important drywall tool:

- Make sure you're using a sharp bit, and have extra bits handy because they will break.
- Don't insert the bit too far into the spiral saw. About 1/8 in. of the bit's shank should be exposed. This allows the bit to flex and reduces the chance of breaking.
- Make sure the bit is adjusted to the proper depth. If the bit extends too far, you may cut right through an electrical box or nip a wire inside it. If the bit doesn't extend far enough, the tip of the bit may hop right over an electrical box or recessed light and head off in the wrong direction.
- Cut in the proper direction. Go clockwise when cutting freehand. When cutting around an electrical box or recessed light, move the spiral saw in a counterclockwise direction. The spinning motion of the bit should pull toward the object that's being cut around.
- Never overtighten the drywall or drive screws too close to the cutting area. The pressure will crack and tear the drywall as you're finishing the cut.

Don't hang drywall too close to door jambs

Window and door jambs are not always straight. Often, the jamb has to be adjusted when you install the casing. This can't be done if the drywall is cut too close to the jamb. When you're using a spiral saw, guide it with the wood that makes up the rough opening, not the window jamb itself.

LEAVE ENOUGH ROOM TO STRAIGHTEN WINDOW JAMB

USE ROUGH OPENING AS THE GUIDE

THICKER PLASTIC

Use heavy boxes and watch out for the wires

Buy electrical boxes made from hard plastic. A spiral saw can cut right through boxes made from soft plastic (usually blue), sending the saw off on an unfortunate path.

Make sure wires are tucked in far enough so the spiral saw won't cut them. Fishing new wire can be an expensive inconvenience, but cutting a live wire could be worse.

What butt joint?

A butt joint in drywall will result in a raised layer of tape and mud because the edges aren't tapered. A good taper can minimize the ridge over a butt joint, but it's hard to eliminate it altogether. If you're installing drywall by yourself or installing in a space where it's impossible to deliver 12-ft. sheets, butt joints are going to be unavoidable. And if you're dealing with wall sconces or areas where raking light means a truly flat wall is imperative, a butt joint backer may be the answer.

A butt joint backer is basically

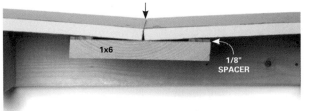

VOID FOR MUD

1x6

1/8" SPACER

a 4-ft.-long, 5- or 6-in.-wide board with 1/16-in. to 1/8-in. spacers added along the edges. You can purchase them at a drywall supply store or make your own. You could use an inexpensive 1x6 pine board and either glue or staple strips of ripped-down wood to the outside edges.

Installing the backer is easy. First, install the sheet of drywall, making sure the end doesn't land on a stud. Next, attach the butt joint backer to the back of that piece. Finally, fasten the second piece of drywall to the backer. When installed properly, the butt joint backer will cause the ends of each piece to suck in, resulting in a recess similar to the recess created by two tapered edges.

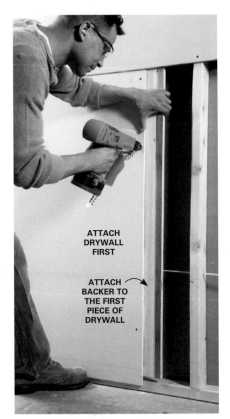

ATTACH DRYWALL FIRST

ATTACH BACKER TO THE FIRST PIECE OF DRYWALL

Hang it, then cut it

You can save time and be guaranteed a perfect fit if you cut out the door opening after you hang the sheet. Once the sheet is up, score the back of the piece, pull the scrap forward and finish it off by cutting the paper on the front side.

CUT SIDES WITH SAW

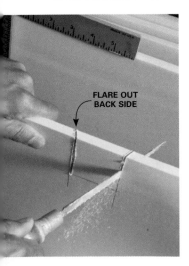

FLARE OUT BACK SIDE

Back-beveling gives you wiggle room

Even in a world of spiral saws and screw guns, two classic tools—handsaws and keyhole saws—are still essential on any drywall job. One advantage of hand-sawing is the ability to create a back bevel. This allows for a little more leeway when you're sliding a piece into place, because if you need to trim, you won't have to remove as much material.

Avoid a large gap at the floor

When you're dealing with a wall that is a few inches over 8 ft., two sheets of 4-ft. drywall will leave you with a large gap at the floor. While most base trim will cover that gap, the tapered edge on the bottom sheet will have to be filled with mud or it will show above the trim line, and that's a lot of extra work (and bending over!). Instead of leaving a gap at the bottom, leave a gap in the center of the wall, and fill it with 3/8-in. drywall. The thinner drywall is a snap to tape over smoothly. ⌂

STRIP OF 3/8" DRYWALL

1/2" GAP AT FLOOR

HandyHints®

TIDIER WALL DRILLING

I hate having to drag out the vacuum to clean up a small pile of drywall or plaster dust after a minor wall repair. A cone-style coffee filter makes a great dust catcher. Tape the seam side to the wall beneath your repair and the filter will automatically hang wide open and catch the dust. Then just toss the filter when you're done.

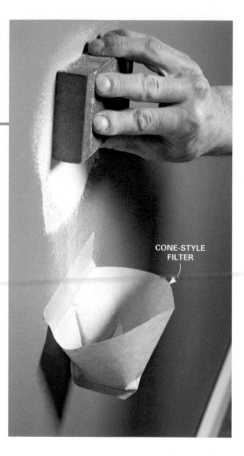

CONE-STYLE FILTER

PAINTED WOOD HANDLES

LOW-COST CHIMNEY DRAFT BLOCKER

If you don't use your fireplace that often, here's a simple, inexpensive way to keep warm air from escaping up your chimney. Cut a piece of plywood the same size as your fireplace opening. Paint the plywood with flat black latex paint and let it dry. Once you press the plywood into the dark fireplace opening, it will magically disappear. You can make simple handles out of small pieces of wood screwed together and painted black.

PRECISION HOLE DRILLING

When you're drilling into ceramic tile to install a towel rack or toilet paper holder, your drill bit has a tendency to "wander" on the slippery tile while starting the hole. Keep your drill bit in place by overlapping a couple of pieces of painter's tape over the spot you want to drill. Then mark the tape for the hole and slowly drill into the tape (I like to drill a pilot hole first) until the bit "bites" into the tile. Works like a charm.

PILOT BIT

A TOUGHER TOWEL RACK

After my kids pulled the towel rack off the bathroom wall a second time, I came up with a better way to mount it. I cut a piece of oak a little longer than the mounting bracket spacing, routed the edges and finished it to match the bathroom trim. Then I screwed it to the wall studs and mounted the towel bar to its new base. No matter how tough my kids are on that towel rack, it holds fast.

LOOSE NAIL SOLUTION

I wanted to hang a picture in my son's room using an existing nail hole. The hole was a little too big, so the nail kept sliding in too far. Rather than making a new nail hole, I put a tiny dab of super glue on the tip of the nail, pushed it into the hole and held it where I wanted it. After 30 seconds, the nail was tight and I hung the picture.

SUPER GLUE

PRECISE TILE MEASURING

When you're tiling a floor and you need to cut odd edge pieces, try this. Lay the field tile first. When you get to the outside edges, get exact measurements by making a paper template. Cut a piece of sturdy paper the exact size of the tile you're using and set it in place. At the wall, crease the paper and fold it over at the correct angle. Then transfer the angle to the actual tile using a wax marker or heavy pencil. You'll get a much more accurate cut and fit.

PAPER TEMPLATE

BETTER TUB CAULKING

Here's an old plumber's trick to try before you caulk the seal between your tub and the tile wall. Step inside the tub. If it flexes or you feel any movement at all, fill the tub with water and stand in it while you caulk (make sure to use silicone). Let the caulk dry before you drain the water. The weight of the water (and you) will settle the tub slightly downward or outward. This will help the caulk seal last longer because it will never be stretched when you use the tub.

WEEKEND
KITCHEN MAKEOVER

Four fresh and easy projects to transform an outdated kitchen into something fabulous—for $600!

by **Elisa Bernick**

Have a boring, outdated kitchen that's calling out for help? Here are four quick, inexpensive projects that will transform your kitchen into something truly special. A brand new countertop coating system turns tired laminate into a stunning and durable faux granite surface. Precut metal inserts add a high-style feature to cabinet doors. Splash-proof wallpaper makes a striking and bulletproof backsplash. And a stainless steel panel adds an exciting and easy-to-clean wall surface behind your range.

None of these projects is difficult, and of the four, only the cabinet inserts require power tools. It's helpful to have a partner for these projects, but even if you're working alone, once you have the materials in hand, you can finish one or all four of these projects in a weekend or two.

So if your tired kitchen is in need of a style infusion, these projects are a simple way to wake things up.

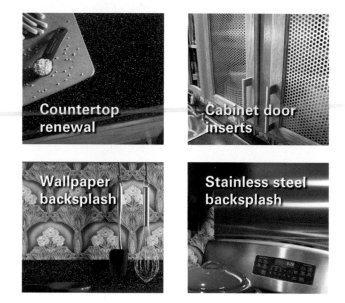

Countertop renewal

Cabinet door inserts

Wallpaper backsplash

Stainless steel backsplash

COUNTERTOP RENEWAL: $250

Rust-Oleum's new Countertop Transformations coating system ($250 for 50 sq. ft. of counter at Lowe's, Menards, Ace Hardware and other retailers) is a simple way to transform worn or damaged laminate countertops into a new countertop surface. The product is available in five colors ranging from light to very dark (our homeowners chose Charcoal).

The big pluses of this system are it's not smelly or difficult, you don't have to remove your countertops (!), the instructions are clear, and the kit comes with everything you need (except basic painting tools), plus it includes a very detailed DVD. This product can be applied to any laminate or hardwood countertop in reasonable condition. Burns and scratches are fine, but fill deep dents and chips before you use it.

After using this product, we can report that it's surprisingly easy to apply. In terms of durability, the manufacturer compares it to laminate. We can't speak to its long-term durability, but when we tried to scratch the newly resurfaced countertop with car keys, it was surprisingly tough—no marks at all. And you can reapply the system to renew the surface later if you want.

Sand and clean

The first step is to completely degloss the laminate surface using the sanding tools included in the kit (**Photo 1**). You can save on sanding time by using an orbital sander with 60- or 80-grit sandpaper on the flat areas (but you'll add cleaning time vacuuming up the dust). Use a light touch so you don't sand through any areas or create uneven surfaces. Vacuum up the dust and wipe all surfaces with a damp cloth until they're completely dust-free. Use painter's tape and plastic to mask off base cabinets, the sink, appliances, the walls above the backsplash and the floor. Cover the sink drains so nothing falls into them.

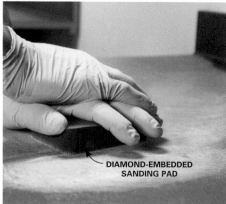

DIAMOND-EMBEDDED SANDING PAD

1 **Rough up the surface.** Degloss the countertop with the diamond-embedded sanding pad in the kit so the base coat will stick to it. You'll know it's deglossed when there are tiny scratches everywhere.

Apply the base coat

This step is time-sensitive, so before you apply the base coat, have the decorative chips in the dispenser and ready to go. Once you've applied the base coat, you'll have a 20-minute window to apply the decorative chips before it dries. If you have a long countertop or several countertop areas, work in pairs (**Photo 2**) and complete one section (including the chip application) before moving on to the next.

Apply the base coat thickly using a brush on the backsplash and a microfiber roller (not included in the kit) on the flat surface and front edge. You really need to lay it on thickly and evenly, and maintain a wet edge on the entire surface for the best result. The kit includes a wetting agent you can spray on to keep the base coat moist and ready for the decorative chips.

Apply the decorative chips

Moving quickly, use the dispenser to broadcast the decorative chips so they completely cover the backsplash, flat area and front edges of the counter. Don't skimp. The kit comes with a ton of chips, so use more than you need to cover every bit of the base coat. We found that it works best to get down on your knees and zing the chips hard by hand against the front edge for the best coverage (**Photo 3**). Inspect for any uncovered base coat, apply more chips and let dry undisturbed for a minimum of 12 hours, but no more than 24.

Sand and smooth

After the base coat is dry, vacuum up the loose chips. Then use the chip scraper to knock down the rough chip edges. Use a light touch so you don't gouge the surface at the corners and edges. Vacuum again.

2 **Apply the base coat.** This coat is the background color and a sticky bed for the chips. One person brushes it on the backsplash; the other rolls on the rest. Work fast; you have 20 minutes to complete this and the next step.

3 **Heap on the chips.** The multicolored chips hide brush marks and give the countertop a textured, speckled appearance. Move quickly to cover every bit of base coat before it dries.

4 **Sand the chips smooth.** Sand hard on the flat surfaces but lightly along the front edge to avoid sanding completely through the chips and base coat. The goal is a smooth, lightly textured surface.

Tip

Make a very light last pass with 120-grit sandpaper for extra smoothness.

Sand the rough chip surfaces smooth to prepare them for the topcoat. The kit includes a sample of how smooth the countertop should be. The challenge is to sand it smooth without sanding through the chips. Use the sanding block and a lighter touch on the backsplash and front edges since these areas are likely to have fewer chips on the surface (**Photo 4**). The sanding process will appear to lighten the chip surface, but the topcoat will darken it again. Vacuum and wipe clean with a damp cloth until all the sanding dust has been removed.

Apply the topcoat

The clear topcoat is a two-part formula that you mix and then apply to the countertop. Once you've mixed the formula, you must use it within four hours.

Just as you did with the base coat, use a paintbrush to apply a thick layer of topcoat to the backsplash and back few inches of the countertop. Use a 6-in. high-density roller (not included) to roll a thick, even layer of the topcoat onto the flat counter area and the front edge (**Photo 5**). Once every surface is covered, go back and roll a final pass of the topcoat in one direction to avoid lap and brush marks. Let dry to the touch (four to six hours) and remove the tape and plastic. The countertop will be ready for light use in 48 hours and completely cured within a week.

5 **Apply the clear topcoat.** Vacuum up every speck of sanding dust. Then brush a thick, even layer of topcoat on the backsplash and roll out the rest. Reroll a final pass in one direction and let it dry undisturbed for 48 hours.

WALLPAPER BACKSPLASH: $50

Wallpaper as a durable kitchen backsplash? You bet. We bought "splash-proof" vinyl wallpaper (in the "Wallis" pattern; $50 per roll) from grahambrown.com, which offers a variety of wallpapers designed for kitchens and baths. Splash-proof wallpaper resists moisture and humidity, and stands up to scrubbing.

1 **Cut out windows with scissors.** Make "relief cuts" with sharp scissors until the paper lies flat against the wall. Then use a razor to make the final cuts by following the contours of the molding.

Tough paper is easy to hang

We're not going to show you everything you need to know to hang wallpaper (for that, visit familyhandyman. com and search for "hanging wallpaper"). Instead, we're going to show you techniques that are unique to hanging vinyl.

The great news is that vinyl wallpaper goes up easier than other wallpapers because it's not as flimsy. Most vinyl wallpapers require a premixed vinyl paste (read the manufacturer's instructions). We used a heavy-duty clay-based paste available at any wallpaper store. Before starting, make sure your wall is primed with a primer/sealer for vinyl wallpapers (also available at wallpaper stores).

Set a plumb line with a level to start your first sheet. On small pieces, you can use a paintbrush to apply the paste to the back of the wallpaper. "Book" each piece for five minutes before hanging it (see our online story for more on this technique). Booking allows the paper to relax and return to its original width before it goes on the wall.

Photos 1 – 3 offer pro tips for making the job go smoothly.

2 **Glue corners tight.** Vinyl won't stick to itself. To keep corner seams secure, overlap the corner by 1/2 in. and brush the overlapped section with vinyl-to-vinyl adhesive before pressing the next piece into place.

1/2" OVERLAP

VINYL-TO-VINYL ADHESIVE

3 **A sharp blade is critical for trimming.** Vinyl wallpaper dulls razor blades quickly, so each blade is good for only one or two cuts. Wallpaper razor knives ($6) give you more control than utility knives.

WALLPAPER RAZOR KNIFE

STAINLESS STEEL BACKSPLASH: $50

A stainless backsplash is a striking complement to stainless appliances. It's also durable, easy to clean and a cinch to install.

The edges will be sharp, so wear gloves and protect the surfaces in your kitchen. On the back side of the panel, use a caulk gun to apply a bead of heavy-duty construction adhesive (Loctite PL 400 is an example) across the entire panel surface. Use a wide putty knife to spread the adhesive evenly (**Photo 1**).

A cleat beneath the panel will support the backsplash as the adhesive cures (**Photo 2**). Position the panel carefully and then press it firmly against the wall. Starting at one end, use a clean, soft rag to smooth the backsplash into place and remove any air bubbles. When you're finished, remove the protective plastic coating.

HEAVY-DUTY CONSTRUCTION ADHESIVE

1 **Apply construction adhesive.** Smooth the construction adhesive across the entire panel with a wide putty knife. Spread it evenly so you don't leave bumps that will show through the thin metal.

PROTECTIVE COATING

SUPPORT CLEAT

2 **Support the panel with a cleat.** Screw a cleat to the wall so the backsplash will be supported while the adhesive cures. Carefully position the backsplash and press it firmly into place.

Buying sheet metal

You can order a stainless steel sheet online (one source is discountsteel.com) or from a local metal shop. You'll need to know the size, gauge and finish. A thickness of 20 or 22 gauge is best for this project. Handle it carefully to prevent denting it. To match your appliances, order a "304-#4" brushed (sometimes called satin or architectural) finish and ask to have the edges smoothed or deburred so the panel doesn't arrive razor sharp. Most shops will do this for free or for a nominal cost. The panel will arrive with a protective plastic coating. Don't remove this until you've installed the panel on the wall.

Steel accessories top it all off

The Johnsons used IKEA's Grundtal stainless steel rails and accessories to add affordable and stylish off-the-counter storage to their new kitchen. The screw-in rails match the existing appliances and are available in three lengths, priced from $7 to $11. The Grundtal line also includes the spice rack shown ($20) and much more. Visit ikea.com.

CABINET DOOR INSERTS: $250

Installing new panels in old cabinet doors can really dress up a kitchen (and new panels are *a lot* cheaper than new cabinets). Insert materials include glass, translucent plastic, copper, metal, fabric, wicker and many others. Adding "feature" inserts to just one or two of your cabinet doors can be striking and very inexpensive. Our homeowners decided to install perforated metal inserts in all of their upper cabinet doors. They initially wanted to use stainless steel to match their appliances, but went with aluminum after discovering that it costs a third of the price and has a similar look (see "Buying Metal Inserts," right, for tips on ordering).

Remove the panels

To cut away the lips that secure the door panel (**Photo 1**), you'll need a "pattern bit"—a straight bit with a bearing that's the same diameter as the cutting diameter. You can buy a pattern bit for about $25, but most are too long to use with a 3/4-in.-thick guide. You may have to shop online to find a shorter bit. One source is routerbits.com. (Search for "3001" to find a bit with a cutting depth of 1/2 in.)

If you're working with just one or two cabinet doors, the only guide you'll need is a straight board. If you have a stack of doors to rout, a more elaborate guide will save you time (**Photo 2**). The stops automatically position the guide without measuring, and you can rout two sides without repositioning.

Examine the back of the door before you rout. If you find any nails, pull them out so they don't chip your router bit. Before you start cutting, set your router depth so the bit just touches the panel. After you cut away the lips,

PANEL

LIP

PATTERN BIT

1 **Locate the lips.** A door panel fits into grooves in the door's frame. To remove a panel, just cut away the lips on the back of the door.

GUIDE

STOP

2 **Rout away the lips.** Run a pattern bit along a guide to remove the lips. Any straight board will work as a guide, but an L-shaped guide with stops speeds up the job.

simply lift out the door panel. The router bit will leave rounded corners at each corner of the door frame; square them off with a chisel or utility knife.

Install the metal inserts

Prefinish 1/4-in. quarter-round molding and use it to secure the inserts (**Photo 3**). When you place the insert into the door frame, make sure the punched side is face up (the punched side will feel slightly raised around the holes). Fasten the quarter round with 5/8-in. nails or brads. If you don't have a brad nailer or pinner, you can use a hammer; just be careful not to dent the metal.

QUARTER-ROUND MOLDING

3 **Install the metal.** Frame the back of the insert with quarter-round molding to hold it in place. If you use a nail gun, aim carefully so you don't shoot through the face of the door.

Buying metal inserts

Some home centers carry sheets of metal (including perforated) and will cut them for you for a small fee. But you'll find a much bigger selection online. Look for metal in the 16- to 20-gauge range. We bought directly from McNichols Co. (mcnichols.com) and did all our ordering over the phone. Its Web site is full of information (and a bit confusing). Look at its "Products" drop-down menu and go from there.

Do your measuring after you remove the cabinet doors to get accurate insert measurements. Order inserts 1/8 in. shorter in both the length and the width so the inserts just fit in the opening. If stainless is out of your price range, consider aluminum or plain steel (called "mill finish"). You can spray-paint your metal any color you want. No matter what finish you order, wash the metal with paint thinner to rinse off the manufacturing oils. If you choose not to paint the steel, spray it with a clear lacquer to prevent it from rusting.

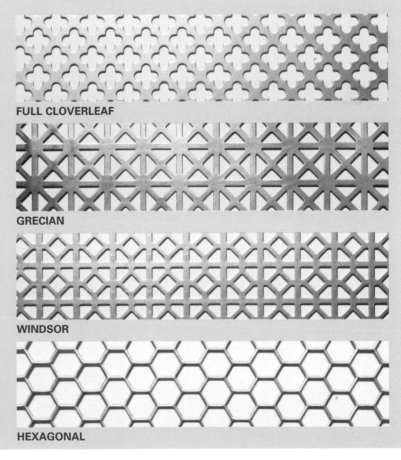

FULL CLOVERLEAF

GRECIAN

WINDSOR

HEXAGONAL

MORE IDEAS ONLINE

Need more inspiration for injecting new energy into your tired kitchen? We've got tons of ideas for you at **FAMILYHANDYMAN.COM**. Here's a sampling of what you'll find online.

A. INSTALL LAMINATE COUNTERTOPS

There are tons of gorgeous new laminates available. Remove your old laminate counters and install new ones, then complete the transformation by installing a new sink and faucet. To learn how, visit familyhandyman.com and search for "install laminate countertops."

B. CREATIVE CABINET FACELIFTS

Remodel your kitchen at a bargain cost with these cabinet upgrades, including new doors and drawer fronts, open shelving, improved storage and painted frames. Visit familyhandyman.com and search for "cabinet facelift."

C. LOWER CABINET ROLLOUTS

Vertical rollouts convert half-empty base cabinets into high-capacity food storage. Visit family-handyman.com and search for "kitchen rollouts."

D. ABOVE-CABINET DISPLAY SHELVES

Create an attractive display shelf in the empty space above your kitchen cabinets. This project requires only basic carpentry skills, and you can build it in a day! Visit familyhandyman.com and search for "above cabinet shelving."

E. TILE BACKSPLASH & NEW RANGE HOOD

Change boring to bold by installing a tile backsplash combined with a new range hood and a custom, over-the-oven shelf for spices and seasonings. Visit familyhandyman.com and search for "tile backsplash."

F. UNDER-CABINET LIGHTING

Add dramatic countertop lighting in a weekend without tearing up your walls to install the wiring. Visit familyhandyman.com and search for "under cabinet lighting."

G. GRANITE TILE COUNTERTOPS

Use granite tile to create the look of a stone slab or solid surface countertop for your kitchen or bathroom—for a fraction of the cost. Visit familyhandyman.com and search for "granite tile countertops." ⌂

PERFECT WINDOW TRIM

You don't even need a tape measure!

by **Travis Larson**

Like most veteran carpenters, I've trimmed hundreds—maybe even thousands—of windows. So trimming out a window is second nature to me. But when I see windows that were trimmed by a rookie or watched rookies trim a window, I realize it's not quite as easy for others.

The truth is, most carpenters don't even use a tape measure. Nope, it's all done by eye, using a sharp pencil, a miter saw and an 18-gauge nailer. I'll show you how to pull off a window trim job that'll look every bit as good as a trim guy's—without hours of frustration. We're working with standard trim, between 3/8 and 1/2 in. thick—the types you'll find at any home center.

STEP 1: Mark the length

JAMB CENTER

SCRIBE FLUSH

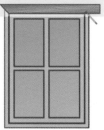

Cut a 45-degree angle on one end of the trim and hold it so the short end of the angle overhangs halfway, or 3/8 in., onto the jamb. Then mark the other end flush with the inside of the jamb. That'll give you a 3/16-in. reveal.

STEP 2: Get the spacing right

3/16"

Hold the trim 3/16 in. away from the jamb at both ends and along the base of the trim. Nail the trim to the jamb with 1-in. brads spaced about every 6 in. Nail the thick part of the trim to the framing with 2-in. brads.

STEP 3: Check the fit, then cut to length

3/16"

Cut a 45-degree miter on one end of the trim board. Adjust the miter as needed for a perfect fit. Then scribe the cut length 3/16 in. past the bottom of the jamb. Nail the trim onto the jamb first and then to the framing, as you did with the top piece.

STEP 4: Glue and pin for a solid miter

GLUE SQUEEZE-OUT

Glue and pin together the miter from both directions with 1-in. brads. Wipe the glue squeeze-out with a damp rag right away.

STEP 5: Trim the other side

Repeat all the same steps on the other side of the window, fitting first the top miter, and then marking and cutting the bottom one. Nail the trim into place.

STEP 6: Fit the first bottom miter

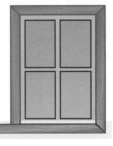

Cut an overly long piece of trim and cut a miter on one end. Overlap the far end to check the fit. Mark and recut the miter as needed for a perfect fit.

STEP 7: Fit the opposite miter

Cut a test miter on the other end and check the fit. Adjust the miter as necessary until you're satisfied with the joint.

STEP 8: Scribe for length

With the saw still set for the previous miter, flip the trim over and scribe the length for the end that has that miter. Transfer the mark to the front side and make the cut.

Dealing with problem drywall

If you have drywall that's "proud" (sticking out past the jamb) or recessed behind the jamb, you have to deal with it before trimming or the trim won't lie flat. Here's what to do:

If the drywall projects past the jamb 1/8 in. or less, and is close to the window jamb, just chamfer the edge with a utility knife. Check to see if you've pared off enough drywall by holding a chunk of trim against the drywall and jamb. If it rocks and won't sit flush against both surfaces, carve out some more.

If the drywall's recessed behind the jamb, don't nail the trim to the framing at first. Only nail it to the jamb and pin the mitered corners together. After the window is trimmed, slide shims behind each nail location to hold out the trim while nailing, then cut off the shims. Caulk the perimeter of the trim to eliminate gaps before painting.

If the drywall projects more than 1/8 in., crush in the drywall with a hammer. Just be sure the crushed area will be covered by trim. In this situation, your miters won't be 45 degrees. You may need to go as low as 44 degrees to get a tight miter.

Avoiding trim-induced headaches

Here are a few tips to help you avoid a few trim hassles:

■ Whenever you can, cut with the thick side of the trim against the miter saw fence. You'll be less likely to tear out the narrow tapered edge that way.

■ Cutting right up to the pencil mark almost always leaves pieces too long, so remove the pencil line with the blade. You'll most likely still have to shave off more.

■ Sneak up on cuts by starting long and dipping the saw blade into the wood while you work your way to the cutoff mark.

■ Trim out the biggest windows first. That way, you can reuse miscuts for the smaller windows and not run out of material.

■ When nailing 3/4-in.-thick trim, use 15-gauge 2-1/2-in. nails for the framing and 18-gauge 2-in. brads for nailing to the jamb.

■ To prevent splitting, avoid nailing closer than 2 in. from the ends.

Tools&Skills

NO-MUSS, NO-FUSS GROUTING

To paraphrase Rodney Dangerfield, grout gets no respect. Grout can ruin an otherwise great tile job. And yet grout and proper grouting technique are often treated as an afterthought, like the final few half-hearted steps of a tired runner stumbling over the finish line. Grout deserves better. Your tile deserves better.

The keys to a professional-quality grout job aren't secrets shrouded in mystery. On these pages, we'll show you some tips and techniques that will help your next grout job go more smoothly and give your tile a professional-grade finished look.

Start with clean joints

Start by vacuuming out all that remodeling dust, debris and any chips of dried thin-set from grout joints (Photo 1).

PROTRUDING THIN-SET MORTAR

1 **Clean the joints.** Vacuum the grout lines, then scrape any protruding thin-set mortar and vacuum again. Don't scrape too hard or you may chip the tile glazing.

Tools&Skills

2 Tape off the tile. For easier cleanup, tape off painted walls to protect them from grout. Also tape off trim or inset tiles that feature imprinted patterns with crevices (Photo 9).

4 Load the grout float. Tip the bucket toward you. Drag some grout "up the slope," then scoop it onto the float.

If there are high spots where thin-set has oozed out and dried, use a sturdy-edged tool to scrape it out and then vacuum again, including the tile surfaces. The last thing you want is to push all that muck back into the joint as you are floating your grout in.

Mix grout by hand

Pour some grout out of the bag into a mixing bucket. Pour water in a little at a time and start mixing by hand using

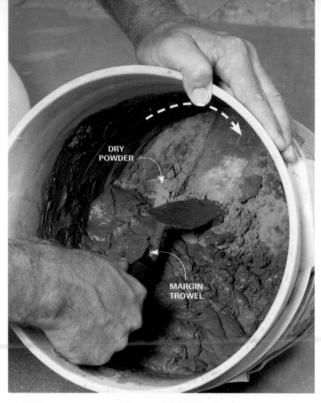

3 Mix the grout until it's powder free. Mix the grout with a margin trowel until all the powder is dissolved. Roll the bucket frequently while mixing. Scrape the bottom to make sure all the grout is mixed.

a margin trowel. Tip the bucket toward you and roll it in a "cement mixer" style as you mix (**Photo 3**). Be sure to scrape any dry, unmixed grout from the bottom of the bucket with your margin trowel. Keep mixing until all the powder has been absorbed and it has the consistency of peanut butter. When you're getting close, dribble in water from a sponge. It only takes a little too much to create soup. And don't mix grout with a drill and mixing paddle. This method churns the grout and introduces air into the mix. That weakens the cured strength and causes a type of discoloration called "shading." Besides, we're trying to mix grout here, not make soufflé.

Let the grout "slake"

When your grout has reached peanut butter status, stop! Go and make a sandwich, take out the trash, whatever. Let the grout slake (rest) for about 10 minutes. This allows the chemicals in the grout to work their magic. Skipping this step may result in weaker, crack-prone joints. After slaking, the grout will feel a bit stiffer, but don't add more water. Remix the grout by hand again to loosen it up.

Load the joints

You're now ready to grout. Tip the bucket toward you (like you did when mixing) and "drag" some grout with your float up the side of the bucket toward you. This pulls a "working batch" closer to you and makes it easier to scrape up a decent amount of grout onto your float. Push the float tight against the side of the bucket and scrape

5 **Spread the grout.** Smear the grout diagonally across the tile to force it deep into the joints and prevent it from being sucked back out as your float slides along.

off a dollop of grout (**Photo 4**). Any excess that falls off will only fall into the bucket and not off the edge and onto the floor.

Always grout the walls first, and after they're finished, the floor. That'll keep you from messing up a finished floor. Apply the grout diagonally across the tile joints to squish the grout into the joints (**Photo 5**). Use whichever side or corner of the float is necessary to fully compress grout into the entire joint. On vertical surfaces, apply grout upward. That way you won't drop so much on the floor.

Clean off excess grout

After you've filled all the joints, make your first "cleanup" passes with the float. Your goal is merely to get as much excess grout as possible off the face of the tile. Hold the float at a sharp angle to the tile and scrape excess grout from the surface. Use a serpentine motion to make it faster and easier (**Photo 6**).

Sponge bath

Once the grout has started to harden (20 to 30 minutes), begin sponging (**Photo 7**). Don't use just any sponge, especially one from the kitchen; choose a "hydrophilic" (water-loving) sponge. They're sold near the tile supplies. Make sure it's damp, not wet, and sweep diagonally across the face of the tile and wipe the grout off the tile surface. On your first few passes, the grout will smear all over the tile and look like a mess—that's OK. Just rinse out your sponge often in a bucket of clean water (never in the sink) and keep wiping until most of the smeared-on grout is gone.

Tools&Skills

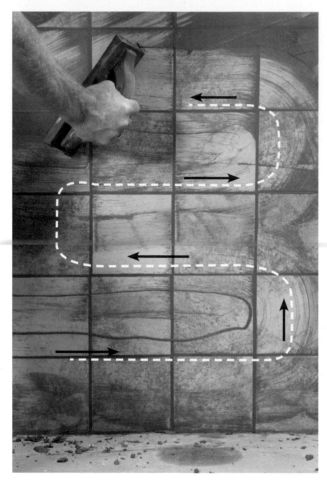

6 **Squeegee off the excess.** Remove the bulk of the grout by wiping in a serpentine motion. This helps evenly distribute the grout and prevents the grout float edge from digging into grout lines.

Tool the grout lines

When the surface has been cleaned, begin "tooling" (smoothing and leveling) the grout lines with the sponge. Hold the sponge in your palm and, gently pressing down with your index finger, run the sponge over any grout joints that look too high or uneven (Photo 8). The goal is consistent, even-depth grout joints. Don't push too hard; let the sponge do the work.

Sanded vs. unsanded grout

Sanded grout is stronger than unsanded grout and resists shrinkage and cracking better. As a rule of thumb, sanded grout should be used in joints larger than 1/8 in. Realistically, as long as you can force the grout into the joint, use sanded grout. But on soft stone tiles like polished limestone or marble, use only unsanded grout or you'll scratch the surface.

7 **Sponge off the surface.** Sweep a damp (not wet!) sponge diagonally across the tile. Rinse your sponge often and repeat until you're left with a thin haze.

8 **Tool the lines.** Depress the sponge with your index finger and smooth out high or uneven grout lines. Don't push too hard. Your goal is grout joints all the same shape and depth.

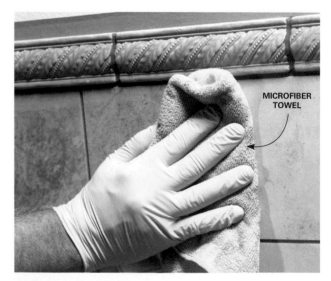

MICROFIBER TOWEL

9 **Buff out the haze.** After the grout film has dried, polish away the haze with a cotton towel or, better yet, a microfiber towel.

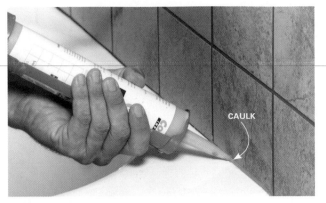

CAULK

10 **Don't grout inside corners.** Use a grouting caulk on inside corners after grouting and cleaning. Don't overfill the void; you'll just make it harder to tool and clean.

Keep some for repairs

It's a good idea to hold on to a small quantity of unused grout for future touch-ups. Grout will easily absorb ambient moisture, so store it in an airtight container such as a resealable plastic bag or a canning jar.

Towel off the haze

After all the joints have been dressed, step away for about a half hour to let the surface dry and form a haze. Then wipe away the haze with a towel. Regular towels work, but microfiber towels are the hot ticket for this task. With more fibers, they remove grout haze much quicker and cleaner than a regular towel.

Caulk all inside corners

Don't grout inside corners. Inside corners that are grouted will always crack over time. Choose a matching color caulk designed to coordinate with the grout you've used. It's sold in matching colors near the grout.

GreatGoofs®

Plaster—it's what's for dinner

My parents were turning the attic space directly over the dining room into an extra bedroom. That space had no flooring, which was one of the first jobs they tackled. One evening, they set out our dinner and went upstairs to work while we ate. Suddenly we heard a scream and a crash and saw Mom's foot come through the ceiling! She'd forgotten all about the lack of flooring and stepped right through the ceiling. She wasn't hurt, but the soup that night was pretty crunchy due to the plaster dust and all.

7 PAINTING BASICS

Simple tips for a flawless finish and faster cleanup

by **Emrah Oruc**

1 Set up a staging area

Step one in any painting job is to establish a spot for your stuff. Think through the whole project, gather up all the tools and supplies you'll need and pile them just outside the room. All the gear will be out of your way but within easy reach. And you won't be tripping over it, constantly moving it or hunting for it during the job.

Plastic drop cloths lead to paint tracks

Plastic sheets are great for protecting woodwork or furniture, but they're a bad choice for floors. They're slippery on carpet and they don't stay put. Even worse, plastic promotes tracking. That's because spills and drips sit on the surface and dry very slowly, giving you plenty of time to step in the paint and track it around. Fabric, on the other hand, lets paint dry fast, from above and below. Canvas drop cloths are best, but a double layer of old bed sheets works well too.

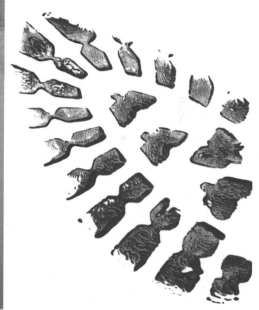

2 Prime every patch

You've filled in the dents and dings, and now it's time to paint, right? Wrong! All those patches, even the tiny ones, must be primed. The unprimed patches will absorb paint and leave noticeable dull spots. This phenomenon is called "flashing," and just like the other type of flashing, it's embarrassing and unprofessional. When you apply primer, don't just brush it on. The tiny ridges of brush marks will show through the paint coat. Instead, "stipple" it on by dabbing your brush against the wall. The bumpy texture will better match the texture of rolled-on paint.

3 Avoid paint freckles

Rolling paint on the ceiling showers you with a fine mist. A baseball cap is essential and safety glasses let you watch your work without squinting. To make skin cleanup easier, rub lotion on your face, arms and hands. At the end of the day, your paint freckles will wash right off.

5 Overnight storage

If that "quick" painting project didn't go as fast as you'd hoped and you need an extra day, seal your brushes in a freezer bag. As long as it's airtight, you can store brushes for up to a week without cleaning. But don't push it; any longer and they'll dry out and stiffen up, making cleanup that much harder.

6 Wipe down the walls

Static electricity makes dust, lint and even pet hair stick to walls. Rolling paint without cleaning the wall will enshrine them Pompeii-style for all to see. Plus, paint adheres better to clean walls. So wipe down the walls with a damp sponge and warm water before painting. Add a smidgen of dishwashing liquid to the water. A couple of drops is just enough to cut through oil and greasy fingerprints without creating suds that you'll have to wipe off later.

7 Keep a scrapbook

 Those labels on paint can lids are like the paint's DNA. They contain all the information needed to duplicate the color and sheen. So the next time you buy paint, ask the clerk to print out a second set of labels and make sure you keep the color chips. Keep them together in a folder so that matching the color later will never be a problem. ⌂

PRO PAINTER'S FAVORITE BENCH

by Travis Larson

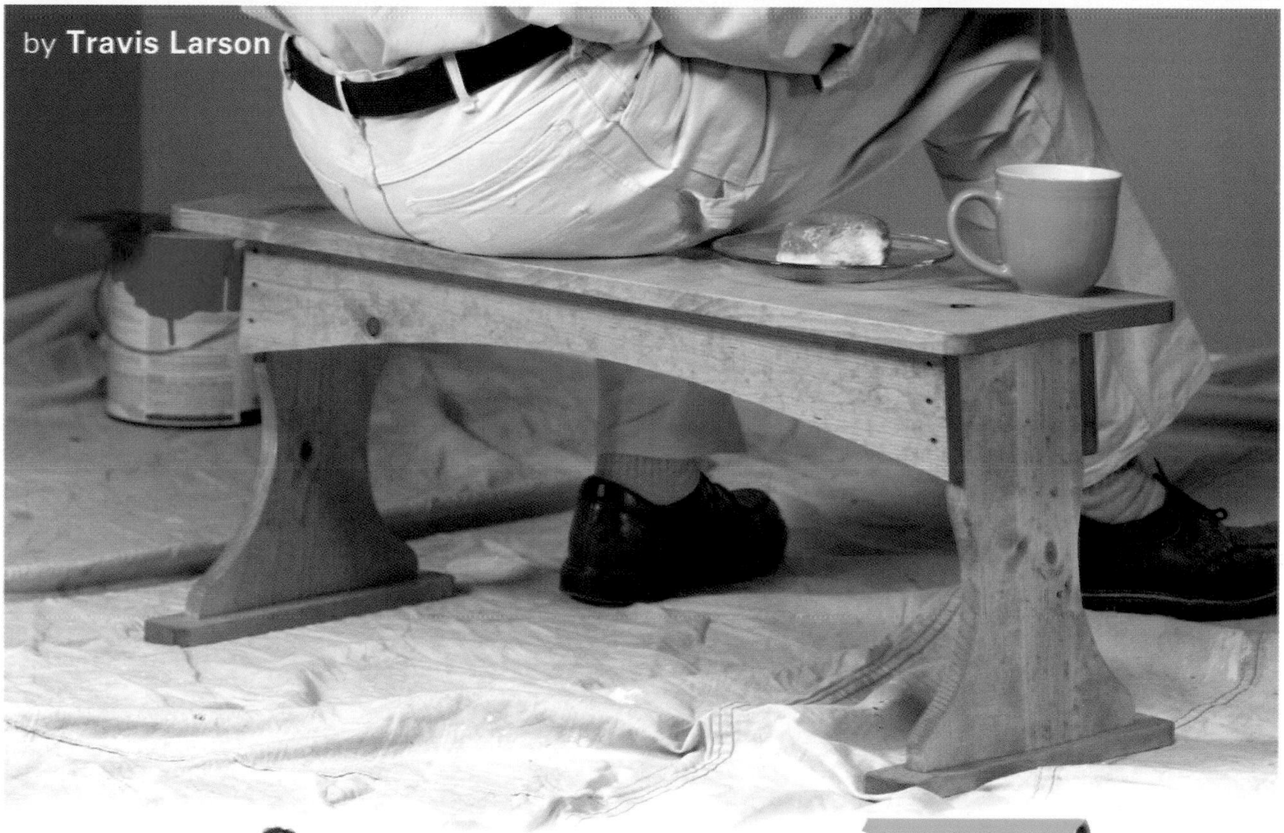

SPECIAL SECTION PAINTING

Bill and
his bench

It's a
mobile
work
table.

I was talking to Bill Nunn, one of our rock-star painting consultants, and my eyes rested on his elegant (and elegantly beat-up) bench. He always has it with him, so I asked him to tell me about it.

Twenty-plus years ago, he set out to design the ultimate painter's bench. It had to be light, so he chose pine. It needed to be the right height to stand on for high brush work and, of course, to sit on for breaks. It had to be easy to move, so he gave it a handle. Then it had to be easy to haul through countless doorways while he worked. That called for curved stretchers so he could comfortably tuck it under his arm.

Bill designed not only the ultimate painter's bench but also a great platform for many other home improvement jobs. And with the right wood or finish, it would be just as fitting as a high-end boot bench or a stool for the man cave. Here's how to build your own.

It's mini
scaffolding.

It's a break
bench.

Two boards and quarter

Buy yourself a 6-ft. 1x12 and an 8-ft. 1x6. Pine will cost you about $15. Choose any wood species you like, but select the flattest 1x12 you can find. While you're at the home center, pick up a small box of 2-in. finish screws and a No. 1 square-head screw bit. Oh, and make sure you still have a quarter in your pocket when you get home (more on that later).

Make all final cuts on a table saw

Figure B shows you how to lay out the parts. Cut all the parts to rough length (1/2 in. overlong) first. You can use a circular saw for that. Then rip the parts to final width by crosscutting on the table saw with the miter gauge, including the 5-degree bevels at both ends of the legs (Photo 1). (You could make all the cuts with a circular saw, but you'll get much better results with a table saw.)

Scribe and cut the curves

Notice in Figure B that there's a 1/4-in.-wide slat. That's for scribing the curves on one leg and one stretcher. When you rip the slat, choose wood that doesn't have any knots or it'll snap when you're bending it. Either get a helper to help you make the scribes or use clamps and nails (Photo 2). It's simple: Just mark your starting and stopping points, bend the slat and make your scribes. Clamp both boards together and make the cuts with a jigsaw (Photo 3). Then clamp both boards together again and smooth out the curves with a belt sander (Photo 4).

Pocket change

Here's the part about the quarter. Use it to mark all the outside corners for rounding (Photo 5). Also trace around the quarter to mark the ends of the handholds. Then use a 1-gallon paint can to draw the front and back of the hand-

1 Cut accurate angles with your table saw. Use your table saw's miter gauge when you cut all the parts to final length. Screw a 1x2 to your miter gauge so you can clamp on a stop block for identical cuts. Cut parallel 5-degree bevels on the top and bottom of the legs.

2 Mark perfect curves. Mark the starting and stopping points of the stretcher curves, then scribe them using the 1/4-in.-thick scribing slat. Use the same trick to mark the curve on the legs.

3 Gang-cut the curves. Clamp together the stretchers and legs and cut the curves with a jigsaw. This trick will give you identical matching parts and keep you from having to mark curves more than once.

4 Gang-sand the curves. Belt-sand the curved parts to eliminate saw marks and smooth out the curves. A belt sander works best, but an orbital sander will do the job too.

Figure A
Painter's bench

Overall dimensions: 36" x 15" x 12"

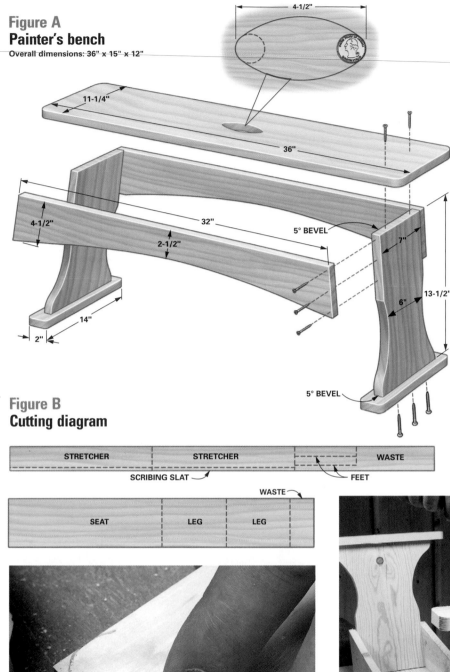

4-1/2"

11-1/4"

36"

32"

4-1/2"

2-1/2"

5° BEVEL

7"

14"

2"

6"

13-1/2"

5° BEVEL

Figure B
Cutting diagram

STRETCHER	STRETCHER		WASTE

SCRIBING SLAT

FEET

WASTE

SEAT	LEG	LEG	

hold. Soften all the edges with 100-grit sandpaper, and if you wish, sand all the parts for finish before assembly.

Assemble the bench

Make all your connections with 2-in. finish screws for a rock-solid bench. A bonus is that the small heads are inconspicuous. Predrill 1/8-in. pilot holes, especially if you're building with hardwood. Screw the stretchers to the legs first and then center and fasten the bench seat to both the legs and the stretchers. Lastly, flip the bench upside down and screw the feet to the bottom of the legs (**Photo 6**). Finish your masterpiece any way you wish. Or go au naturel—the bench, not you! ⌂

5 Round off sharp corners. Use a quarter to outline the outside corners, then cut and sand all of them.

FINISH SCREW

6 Assemble the bench. First attach the stretchers to the legs. Then screw the bench seat to the legs and stretchers, and finally, center and screw the feet to the legs.

TFH BEST IN DIY

PAINTING GEAR

Paint better, faster and easier with our picks for the best in DIY painting gear

by **Jeff Gorton**

Here at *The Family Handyman*, we spend a lot of time painting—on the projects you see in the magazine, at job sites, in our own homes. And nobody spends more time (or money) looking for better ways to paint: Whenever we see a new painting gadget, we buy it and try it, and we're always pestering painting pros for their recommendations. And this year we asked our Field Editors to pitch in from across North America. We added up all that effort and experience and came up with this collection of painting gear.

Easy-clean Chinex brush

The editors here love Chinex bristle paintbrushes. But it's not just us. Our set builder doesn't use anything else. And the pros we talked with agree that paintbrushes made with Chinex bristles are nearly perfect. They work equally well for oil-base and water-base paints. But the best feature of Chinex bristles is how easy they are to clean. Many of the new formulations of water-base paint dry quickly and stick tenaciously to other types of synthetic bristles, leaving you with a tough cleanup job. Chinex bristles solve this problem. Paint rinses out easily, giving you a brush that's "like-new" clean. Corona, Wooster and Purdy make brushes with Chinex bristles. Expect to spend $15 to $20 for a 2-1/2-in. Chinex bristle brush.

The Family Handyman EDITORS' CHOICE

Cut your brush-cleaning time in half. A quick rinse is usually all you need to get these brushes clean.

Sturdy aluminum bench

Everyone who tries this sturdy aluminum bench wants one. We use it as a temporary paint mixing and pouring platform, stand on it to cut in along the ceiling, and sit on it during coffee breaks. It's lightweight and folds up flat for easy storage. It's a good value, too. You can pick one up at home centers for about $45. If you prefer a classic wooden version, see "Pro Painter's Favorite Bench" on p. 67.

A better edge-painting tool

If you don't paint every day, "cutting-in" a room can be frustrating. It's no wonder there have been so many attempts over the years to make a tool that simplifies the task. The Accubrush edge-painting tool is one of the best we've tried. It makes cutting-in quick and easy. With just a little practice, you can paint perfectly straight lines along ceilings and moldings. You'll still have to finish some areas with a brush, though, since the tool can't paint right up to adjacent edges. Go to painthelpers.com to see a video of how it works and to purchase the tool. Prices range from $40 to $125 depending on the kit you choose.

SMALL BRUSH

Connect a pole to the ceiling-edging tool and you can paint along the ceiling without even getting on a ladder.

Handy Paint Pail

We tried all kinds of paint containers and came to a unanimous conclusion: Nothing beats the Handy Paint Pail because it has a comfortable, stretchy rubber handle that makes the pail easy to hold with one hand. Better yet, a magnetic brush holder lets you suspend the brush in paint when it's not in use so the bristles don't dry out. And disposable liners are available so you can avoid the messy job of cleaning the paint pail once you're done. You'll find the Handy Paint Pail ($10) at home centers, hardware stores and paint stores.

Hot paint stripper

Stripping paint is tough work no matter how you do it. But we like this tool because it eliminates nasty chemicals and dangerous dust. Old-timers may remember using torches to loosen paint for scraping. The Speedheater uses infrared heat to do the same thing, but at a lower, safer temperature. You don't have to worry about burning down your house or breathing dangerous fumes caused by vaporized lead in the paint. It does get hot, so make sure to follow the instructions and safety precautions carefully. A Speedheater kit ($472—ouch!) that includes a case and scrapers is available online at speedheaterstore.com.

Remove old paint with heat instead of chemicals. Soften the paint with the infrared stripping tool. Then remove it with a sharp scraper while it's still warm.

Pro masking tool

The 3M Hand-Masker is popular with painting contractors because it provides a fast, affordable and convenient way to cover trim or walls with masking tape, paper and plastic to keep the paint off. But these masking machines aren't just for pros. If you do a lot of painting and are looking for a quick way to protect woodwork, doors, windows and cabinets from paint spatters, check these out. The least expensive version (shown here) costs about $20. It comes with a 6-in. blade that can be extended to 12 in. These Hand-Maskers hold a roll of masking tape and a roll of paper and apply the tape to the edge of the paper as you pull it out. You use the blade to cut the paper and tape to the desired length. You can even buy a roll of super-thin plastic sheeting and use that instead of paper to cover walls or other large areas. You'll find 3M Hand-Maskers at paint stores, home centers and on online.

MASKING PAPER

Mask off baseboards quickly with a hand-masking tool. It applies the tape to the paper and cuts it to the right length with a twist of your wrist.

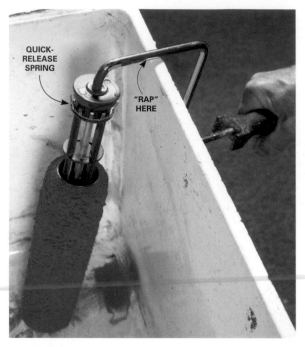

QUICK-RELEASE SPRING

"RAP" HERE

Rap the frame against the edge of the laundry tub or the lip of a 5-gallon bucket. The roller will pop off.

Easy-off roller frame

There are a lot of roller frames on the market, but we like this one the best. Like other premium roller frames, it's sturdy, so it doesn't bend when you apply pressure. And it has better bearing surfaces than cheap frames for easy, squeak-free rolling. But the feature that really sets this roller frame apart is the quick-release springs that hold the roller cover firmly in place while you're rolling and yet release easily when you want to remove the roller for cleaning. You simply rap the metal frame against the edge of a bucket or laundry tub and the roller cover pops off—no more struggling to get a slippery, paint covered roller cover off the frame. Sherlock frames also have a hexagon recess and holes in the bottom of the handle to accept a matching Sherlock extension pole (see "Quick-Connect Paint Pole" on p. 73). You'll find Sherlock frames (about $8) at home centers and paint stores.

Versatile brush comb

A brush comb is an essential tool for keeping your paintbrushes in top-notch shape. This Warner version adds a few features that make it our top pick. In addition to two brush combs, it has a semicircular cutout you can use to squeegee excess paint from your roller prior to cleaning, and a nub on the end to clean paint can rims. Check your local paint stores and home centers or search online for Warner No. 279 Brush and Roller Cleaner ($3).

ROLLER-CLEANING CUTOUT

Keep your brushes in top-notch shape by combing the bristles before you wrap them for storage.

Speedy roller cleaner

The Rejuv-a-Roller is so easy to use that we don't mind cleaning roller covers. Instead of buying cheap roller covers and throwing them away, we can buy top-quality covers and reuse them. Here's how it works: Slip the roller cover into the tube and plug the end. Then connect the hose to a faucet and turn on the water. When the water runs clear from the bottom holes, the roller is clean. If you own a roller spinner, you can speed up drying and fluff the roller nap by giving it a quick spin. But it's not necessary. For more product and ordering information go to timelessinnovations.com or search online for Rejuv-a-Roller (about $25).

ROLLER COVER

PLUG

Cleaning roller covers couldn't be easier. Just slip them into the tube and turn on the water.

SPECIAL "GRIP TIP"

Quick-connect paint pole

When it's time to paint, this is the extension pole we fight over. The quick-connect feature allows you to easily connect and disconnect the roller frame without having to screw and unscrew the pole. In addition, the pole is hexagon-shaped to prevent it from spinning, and is super easy to extend. Just push the button to release. Then pull in or push out the top section until the spring-loaded pin drops into a hole in the pole to lock it in place. The Sherlock GT Convertible shown here (the 2-ft. to 4-ft. size; $28) includes a screw-in adapter that stores in the handle and allows you to convert any roller frame into a quick-connect version. Find Sherlock poles at paint stores, some home centers and online.

Clip on the roller frame, adjust the length and go. In seconds, you're rolling walls or ceilings with a pole that's the perfect length.

Field Editor Favorites

We asked our Field Editors to send in their choices for the best DIY painting gear. Their picks ranged from battery-powered sprayers to favorite putty knives. But there were a couple favorites that stood out from the crowd.

Brush and roller spinner

Our Field Editors don't like cleaning up painting gear, so it's no surprise that this brush and roller spinner is one of their choices for best painting gear. You'll find roller spinners ($15 to $25) at any good paint store.

A few quick handle pumps is all it takes. But be sure to keep the roller in a bucket or deep sink to avoid a mess.

Most comfortable brush

Our Field Editors loved this little brush from Wooster because it's so darned comfortable to hold. But they also liked being able to get into tight spots where the long handle of a conventional brush would be in the way. You'll find Wooster ShortCut brushes ($5.50) at paint stores and home centers. Purdy's XL-Cub ($10) is a similar small-handled brush.

Getting into tight spots is easy with this compact paint brush.

Paint spout

How can you go wrong spending less than a dollar for a tool that simplifies paint pouring and reduces the mess? This handy spout snaps onto the rim of a gallon or quart can and directs the paint where you want it. Plus it prevents paint from running down the side of the can and creating a mess on the floor or drop cloth. You'll find these at home centers and paint stores, or search online for "snap on paint can spout."

HandyHints®

STICKY SIDE OUT

FUZZ-FREE PAINT ROLLERS

I've been painting for 30 years, and there's one thing I do before every paint job when using a new roller sleeve. I wrap some duct tape (sticky side out) around my hand and rub all sides of the roller sleeve across the tape. This is an easy way to get rid of all the loose fuzz on the roller cover that would otherwise end up on the wall.

MORE COMFORTABLE PAINTING

Whenever I paint ceilings, crown molding or the upper part of walls, I strap a travel pillow around my neck. It looks a little funny, but it sure beats waking up with a sore neck the next day!

TRAVEL PILLOW

PAIN-FREE WALL PREP

One of my least favorite paint prep tasks is washing down the walls and ceiling. This step is especially important in kitchens and bathrooms where grease and soap residue can build up. I use a sponge mop to clean the ceiling and high on the walls. It not only saves my back, but it beats going up and down the ladder with a dripping sponge and helps me move around the room a lot faster. This works great for cleaning up sanding dust from drywall taping too.

2 Electrical & High-Tech

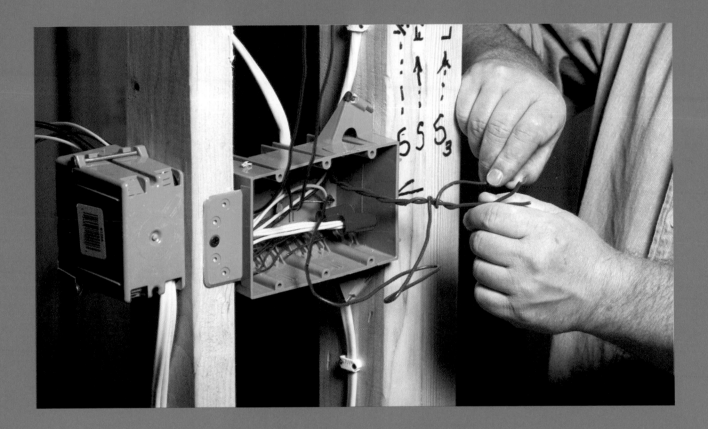

IN THIS CHAPTER

FIX AN OVERSIZE ELECTRICAL BOX CUTOUT

We've all done it—cut the electrical box opening too large. Sure, you can cover it with a "jumbo" electrical plate, but that can look pretty stupid, especially if there are other boxes nearby. Instead of squishing joint compound into the gap (it'll always crack), try this fix.

First prepare the gap and fill it with compound (**Photo 1**). Then apply joint tape and additional mud coats (**Photo 2**).

1 Fill with setting-type compound. Bevel the back of the drywall with a utility knife. Then fill in the gap with fast-setting joint compound.

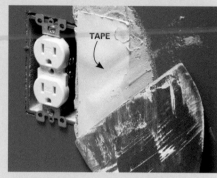

TAPE

2 Mud and tape. Spread the fast-setting compound into the gap and surrounding area and embed the tape right up to the edge of the electrical box. Let it set up and apply the final two coats of lightweight compound. Sand with a medium-grit sanding sponge.

WIFI RANGE EXTENDER

Having trouble picking up your WiFi signal in the shop or garage? Here's an easy solution. This Hawking range extender (HWREN1; $65 to $90 online or at electronic retailers) rebroadcasts your home's wireless signal to areas where you're having trouble picking up a signal. Ideally you'd place the range extender halfway between your wireless access point (WAP) and the trouble spot. The unit comes with a CD to guide your setup. Check to make sure it's compatible with your computer before you buy it.

HOW TO ADD CAPACITY TO AN ELECTRICAL BOX

I want to replace my light switch with one of those multi-button fan/light switches, but it won't fit in the box unless I jam it in. Is that safe?

No. Even though the current "box fill" may meet code, it's not safe to jam the new device in. You have two options: Add a plastic surface-mount extender box (like Leviton No. 6197-W; $8 from amazon.com; **Photo 1**), or remove the old 12.5-cu.-in. box and replace it with a flush-mount 20-cu.-in. box that's 7/8 in. deeper (like Carlon No. B120R Old Work Electrical Box, $2; **Photo 2**).

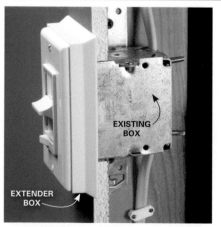

EXISTING BOX

EXTENDER BOX

1 The easy but less elegant way. Remove the old switch (power off) and screw the extender box on top of the old box. Then install the new switch and cover plate on the extension box.

REPLACEMENT BOX

2 The harder but more attractive option. Disconnect the old switch and label all the wires (power off). Saw out the old box, remove the wires and set in a deep remodeling box. Reconnect the wires and install the new switch.

DIM YOUR "DIMMABLE" CFL BULBS

Many dimmable CFL bulbs don't work well with a standard incandescent dimmer. If that's your situation, don't blame the bulb. Standard dimmers were never designed to run CFL bulbs and can cause "drop-out" (the bulb turns off before you finish dimming) and "flicker" (the bulb turns off when a high-voltage appliance goes on). Or the bulb won't light up on "dim" settings, forcing you to push the dimmer to full bright and then bring it down again.

Replacing a conventional dimmer with a CFL-compatible electronic dimmer switch will solve the problems. Lutron DVWCL-153PH Diva ($26) or Leviton No. 6673-10W ($24) are two models available at home centers and amazon.com. They're pricier than standard dimmers, and they only work with certain brands of CFLs (check the manufacturer's Web site for compatible bulbs). Just swap out your existing dimmer for one of these new models and dim the light fantastic.

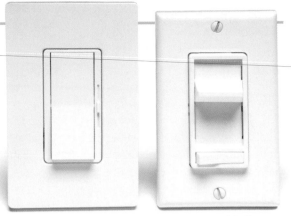

ELECTRICAL & HIGH-TECH

Smart dimmers play nice with "dimmable" bulbs
Upgrade your dimmer to an electronic CFL-compatible model that really works. It provides full-range dimming, starts at any brightness level and eliminates flickering.

INSTALL A WALL-HUGGER RECEPTACLE

That new espresso machine looks great in your kitchen, and it even hides the receptacle. But it would look even better if the cord didn't make it stick out from the wall 3 in. Solve that problem by replacing the existing electrical box with a recessed "remodeling box" (such as Arlington No. DVFR1W-1; $11 from amazon.com). It will take about an hour.

Flip the breaker to the receptacle and check it with a voltage sniffer to make sure it's dead. Then remove

the old box (go to familyhandyman.com and search for "electrical box").

Once the old box is out of the way, you'll have to enlarge the hole (**Photo 1**). Be sure to enlarge the opening on the side away from the stud. Then pull the old wires into the new box (**Photo 2**). Work the box into the wall while you pull the wires through. Then tighten the clamps and install the receptacle and cover (**Photo 3**).

1 **Cut a larger hole.** Align the new box with the stud side of the existing opening and level it. Then trace the larger profile onto the wall. Cut the larger opening with a drywall saw.

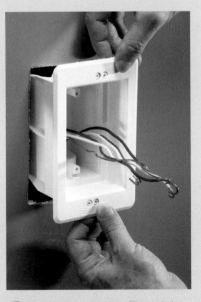

2 **Insert the new box.** Thread the old wires into the top or bottom clamp and pull on them until the cable jacket comes through. Slide the box into the opening and tighten the retaining tabs.

3 **Tighten and trim.** Then connect the receptacle. Secure the receptacle and install the receptacle cover plate and trim bezel.

HomeCare&Repair

REPLACE A WELL PUMP PRESSURE SWITCH

Your well pump gets its marching orders from the switch mounted on the pressure tank. When the switch acts up (and they all do eventually), you'll see all kinds of strange behavior (pump won't turn on, turns on erratically or won't shut off). Replacing the pressure switch is cheap and takes only about an hour.

Diagnose a cranky switch by rapping on it with a screwdriver handle. If the pump runs (you'll hear it click) or quits, you've nailed the problem. But even if it doesn't respond, it's still worth replacing the switch. Replace it with a new one (about $24 at rural home centers and amazon.com).

Switches come in three pressure ranges: 20 to 40, 30 to 50 and 40 to 60 psi. Always replace your switch with one of the same rating (usually printed inside the plastic cover of your old switch). Also buy a new pressure gauge (less than $10) and a 1/4-in. x 6-in. galvanized nipple (about $1.50).

Flip the breaker to the pump switch and check it with a voltage sniffer to make sure it's off. Then disconnect the wiring (**Photo 1**).

Close the valve from the pressure tank to the house. Then drain the pressure tank. Next, remove the old switch (**Photo 2**) and gauge (**Photo 3**).

Wrap the pipe threads with Teflon tape and reassemble. Install the wiring, close the faucet and repower the pump.

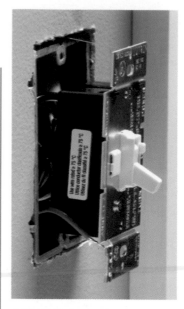

REPLACING A DIMMER? CHECK THE RATING

If you're installing a dimmer switch, keep in mind that each switch is rated to handle a maximum wattage. If you're trying to dim six 100-watt lightbulbs, use a switch rated for at least 600 watts. Newer models are fairly generous with their allowances (usually about 600 watts), but that won't cut it if you're trying to dim seven 100-watt bulbs.

1 **Shut off the power, then disassemble.** Label each wire with tape. Then unscrew the conduit locking ring and pull the wires and conduit out of the switch.

2 **Swap the switch.** Unscrew the old switch and nipple. Replace with new parts.

1/4" NIPPLE

Check the rating Make sure the wattage rating on your new dimmer is at least as high as the old one.

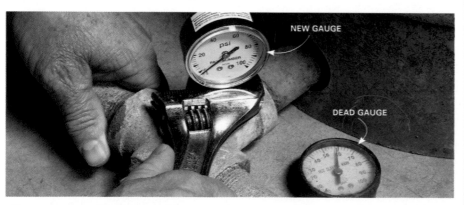

NEW GAUGE

DEAD GAUGE

3 **Replace the pressure gauge.** Slap your adjustable wrench around the flats on the gauge and unscrew it. Then screw in a new one and tighten it down.

RUN POWER ANYWHERE

The easiest way to bring electricity to a shed, garden or lamppost

by **Jeff Gorton**

Dragging extension cords across the yard to power the weed whip, fumbling around in a dark shed... most of us take these hassles for granted. But it doesn't have to be that way. With a day's work, you can run electrical lines to any part of your yard. This article will show you how to bring power to a shed, but the process is almost identical if you want to simply mount an outlet on a post planted in the soil. A licensed electrician would charge at least several hundred dollars plus materials to run lines from your house to a shed 50 ft. away (not including any work inside your house). You can do the job yourself for a materials cost of about $140.

We'll show you how to run wires through rigid metal conduit (RMC). This method offers the best protection of the wiring and requires the least amount of digging. It also lets you install a GFCI outlet at the end of the line rather than at the house, which means you'll never have to run

back to the house to reset a tripped GFCI. For information on completing the wiring inside the outbuilding or connecting to power in your house, go to familyhandyman. com and search for "wiring."

If you want to provide a dedicated circuit to the shed, hire an electrician to make the final connection in your main electrical panel. Otherwise you can connect to an existing circuit if the circuit has enough capacity and the box you're connecting to has enough volume for the additional wires.

To run the wires inside rigid conduit, you'll need a hacksaw, a pipe bender capable of bending 1/2-in. rigid conduit with an outside diameter of 3/4 in. ($30), and a fish tape long enough to reach through the buried pipe ($15 to $60). You'll also need a pair of pipe wrenches to screw the sections of pipe together, a drill and 1-in. bit capable of penetrating your siding, and wire cutting and stripping tools. The total cost of this project is typically about $2.20 for every foot of buried conduit, plus about $25 for LB fittings and miscellaneous hardware.

A few weeks before you start the project, contact your local building department to obtain an electrical permit if one is required. Then a few days before you dig, call 811 to have your underground utility lines marked. Learn more at call811.com.

Plan the route

There are several factors to consider in planning the route from the house to the shed. Obviously the shorter the trench, the less digging you'll have to do, but you also have to determine where you're going to connect to power inside the house and how easy it will be to get there. In some cases, a little more digging could save you from having to tear into a basement ceiling. Start by locating a power source, whether it's your main panel, a ceiling box, outlet or other electrical box. Then figure out the best spot for the new conduit to enter the house. Since the National Electrical Code (NEC) limits the number of bends you can make in the pipe to a total of 360 degrees, you have to plan the route carefully. The two 90-degree bends from the ground into the house and shed consume 180 degrees, leaving you 180 degrees more for any additional bends.

With the route planned, you can measure for the amount of wire and conduit you need and head to the hardware store or home center. Add 10 ft. to the length of wire and pipe to make sure you'll have enough.

It's smart to drill the hole into the house before you start digging just in case you run into an obstacle and

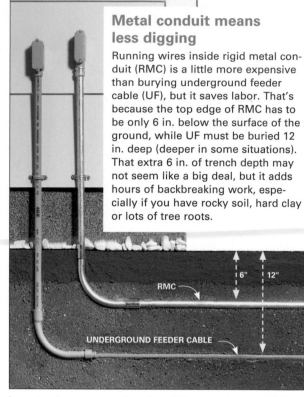

Figure A: Cable depth

Metal conduit means less digging

Running wires inside rigid metal conduit (RMC) is a little more expensive than burying underground feeder cable (UF), but it saves labor. That's because the top edge of RMC has to be only 6 in. below the surface of the ground, while UF must be buried 12 in. deep (deeper in some situations). That extra 6 in. of trench depth may not seem like a big deal, but it adds hours of backbreaking work, especially if you have rocky soil, hard clay or lots of tree roots.

RMC
6" 12"
UNDERGROUND FEEDER CABLE

have to choose a new location. When you're sure of the exit point, dig a trench from the house to the shed. If you're going across a lawn, remove a slice of sod the width of a spade from the surface and set it aside to reuse after you bury the pipe. Then use a mattock or narrow spade to dig the trench (**Photo 1**). Pile the dirt on plastic tarps so you don't have to rake it out of the grass later.

8"-DEEP TRENCH
SOD FOR PATCHING

1 **Dig the trench.** Use a mattock to dig the trench. The narrow head means less dirt to remove and less to put back. Slice out strips of sod with a spade so you can neatly patch the lawn later.

LB
8"-DEEP TRENCH

2 **Plan the bend.** Measure from the bottom of the trench to the bottom of the LB fitting. Mark that measurement on the conduit.

THREADED END
CONDUIT BENDER
TORPEDO LEVEL

3 **Bend the conduit.** Pull back on the conduit bender until the end stands straight up. A magnetic level lets you know when you've got a perfect 90-degree bend.

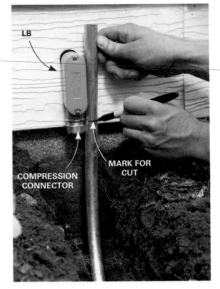

4 **Join the conduit.** Assemble the conduit run aboveground to make tightening the connections easier. Support the conduit with 2x4s until you've connected all but the last section.

5 **Plan the last piece.** Measure for the last section of conduit. Adjust the measurement for the distance the LB protrudes from the wall. Then mark the pipe and bend it.

6 **Mark and connect.** Hold the bent conduit in place to mark it for cutting. Since there are no threads on the end of the pipe, screw a compression fitting into the LB and connect the conduit to it.

Mount the LBs and metal boxes

The rigid conduit will come out of the ground and into a fitting called an "LB." The LB has a removable cover that simplifies the task of pulling wire by eliminating a sharp right-angle turn. The trickiest part of this project is mounting the LBs and connecting them to metal boxes inside the house and shed. In general, you'll have to choose a box location and then calculate the length of electrical metallic tubing (EMT) needed to reach from the back of the LB to the box. If you're going into a basement or crawl space, the length of the conduit usually isn't critical. Start by drilling a small hole with a long bit to make sure you're in the right spot. Then drill a 1-in. hole for the LB and conduit. Screw a 1/2-in. conduit connector into the back of the LB and then attach a piece of 1/2-in. EMT that's long enough to reach an easily accessible box in the basement or crawl space. After you've mounted the LB to the siding, go inside and add a conduit connector and a metal electrical box to the other end of the EMT. This box is where you'll make the connections from your house wiring to the new shed wiring.

On the inside of the shed, you'll screw a 4 x 4-in. square metal box to the side of the stud. Then connect the LB to the box using the parts shown in **Figure B**.

Run the metal conduit

The 10-ft. lengths of RMC are threaded on both ends and include a coupling on one end. You'll start by bending the first pipe and threading an LB onto the end. Then thread the pipes together one at a time until you reach the other

end, where you'll cut and bend the last piece of conduit to fit and connect it to the LB with a compression connector. **Photos 1 – 6** show the process.

Temporarily attach the LB to the shed and measure between it and the bottom of the trench (**Photo 2**). Add 3/4 in. for the threads that'll go into the LB and subtract the bending allowance listed on your bender (usually 6 in.) from this measurement for the bend. Mark this length on a piece of conduit, measuring from the end with bare threads. Then find a level spot to bend the conduit. Align the mark on the conduit with the arrow on the bender. Push with your foot and pull back on the pipe handle to

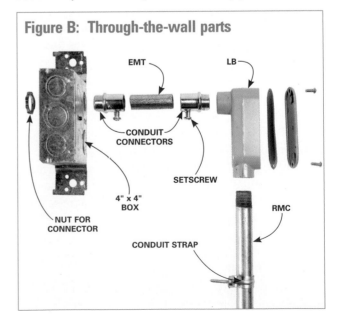

Figure B: Through-the-wall parts

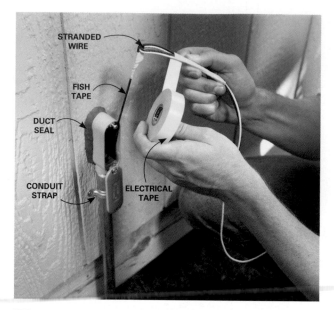

7 **Tie the wire to the fish tape.** Feed the fish tape through the conduit. Loop the wires through the fish tape and wrap them with electrical tape. Also wrap the hook on the fish tape so it can't snag. Use stranded wire, not solid wire.

8 **Pull the wires.** Pull the wires through the conduit. This is a two-person job—you need a helper at the other end to feed the wires into the conduit.

bend the pipe (**Photo 3**). Use a level or the bubble built into some benders to tell when you reach 90 degrees. Take the bent conduit back to the trench and screw the LB onto the end. **Photo 4** shows how to connect lengths of conduit until you reach the house.

Bend the last piece of conduit up and cut it off to fit into the compression connector (**Photos 5 and 6**). Start by measuring from the last piece of conduit to the house wall (**Photo 5**). If the LB is held away from the wall by siding, subtract this distance from the measurement. Then add 3/4 in. for the threading and subtract for the bend. Mark the last piece of conduit, starting from the bare threads. Once again, place the bender arrow on the mark and bend the conduit. Face the threaded end of the conduit when you make this bend, not the end with the coupling. Mark the conduit (**Photo 6**) and cut it with a hacksaw. Remove burrs from the inside of the pipe by smoothing with a file or by inserting the bare metal handles of pliers into the pipe and twisting. Complete the conduit run by threading on the last piece of conduit. You'll have to lift the previous piece of conduit to create clearance as you spin the bent pipe around. Finally, slip the end of the conduit into the compression connector and tighten the compression nut with a wrench. Wrap a conduit strap around the conduit and screw it to the house to secure the conduit. Also press a rope of "duct seal" around the top of the LB to keep water out.

Pull the wires

Remove the covers from the LBs and push a fish tape through the conduit. Then pull the wire through the

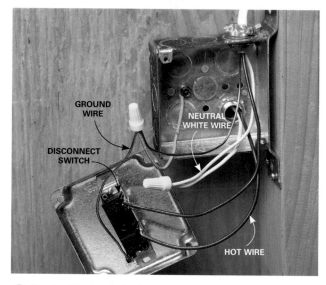

9 **Start with a switch.** Connect the wires inside the shed to a switch. Then run them to a GFCI receptacle.

conduit (**Photos 7 and 8**). You'll need two wires, one white and one black, for one circuit, or more if you intend to wire a three-way switch from the house or add more than one circuit. Use THWN-2 14-gauge stranded wire if you get power from a 15-amp circuit or THWN-2 12-gauge stranded wire for a 20-amp circuit. Leave enough extra wire on each end to reach the inside metal box plus 12 in.

The NEC requires a means, such as a single-pole switch, to disconnect the power where it enters the shed. **Photo 9** shows how to connect the switch, ground wire and neutral wires. Run wires from the switch to a GFCI receptacle, and from there to the rest of the outlets or lights in your shed. ⌂

HandyHints®

CLEVER CHANNEL CHANGING

To change the channels on our finicky television, the remote control has to be directly in its line of sight. This meant I had to get up out of my favorite chair and walk over to line up the remote with the TV. Then I came up with this solution: I put a mirror at a 45-degree angle between the chair and the TV. I made sure I could see the TV in the mirror (it took me a few tries to find the right angle). Now all I do is aim the remote at the mirror and the reflected signal changes the channel without my getting up out of my chair. This works with DVD players, converter boxes and any other electronics requiring a remote control.

Tip Try this first without the mirror. Sometimes bouncing the signal off the wall works too.

BREAD BAG TAG

I.D. CABLES WITH BREAD TAGS

The little plastic tags used to close bread bags are handy for identifying the cables on your computer components. Just write the name of the device on the tag and slip it around the cable. No more wondering which cable belongs to which device.

LAMP PULL CHAIN

GLOW-IN-THE-DARK LAMP SWITCH

The pull chain on the fluorescent lamp fixture in my basement is around the corner from the doorway, and it's hard to see it even with the hall light on. To make it easier to find in the dim light, I drilled a hole in the middle of a glow-in-the-dark ball and tied it onto the pull switch. No trouble finding it now.

QUICK CORD AND PLUG I.D.

When I work on projects around the house, I often have to use a couple of different power tools and switch from one to the other on the same extension cord. With non-grounded plugs, figuring out which way the plug should be connected was slowing me down. So I started color-coding the wide neutral slot on extension ends and wide neutral prongs on my cords. No more fumbling around.

COMPRESSED AIR

AIR-BLOWN FISH TAPE

A buddy was helping me run electrical wiring through conduit mounted underneath my dock to my patio light out by the pool. But after hours of trying to snake the fish tape through the conduit's twists and turns, we were getting nowhere. Then he came up with a brilliant solution: Use an air compressor to blow twine through the conduit. It worked like a dream! Within seconds, the twine was at its destination. We tied off the wiring and pulled it back through. We were able to finish the project with enough time left for a swim.

EXTENSION CORD SMARTS

To prevent tangled extension cords, use hook-and-loop tape to keep long cords organized. Wind the cord in 10-ft. loops and wrap each coil with hook-and-loop tape. That way you can easily unwrap only what you need for a given job. It keeps the work site safer and you don't have to unwind and rewind 50 ft. of cord when you only need 11.

GreatGoofs®

A shocking e-mail

I'll tell you right off that I hate working with electricity because it scares the heck out of me. But I had to replace an outlet, so I shut off the proper circuit breaker and checked the outlet with a voltage tester. The power was off. OK, no big deal. I started unscrewing the wire from the outlet, and just as the screwdriver touched the head of the terminal screw, someone sent me an e-mail, which caused the BlackBerry phone hanging at my hip to vibrate. Thinking I was being electrocuted, I threw the screwdriver across the room, where it crashed right through the window. This is one time that hiring an electrician might have been cheaper.

PRO | WIRING TIPS
SECTION
Wire faster, better, neater

by **Jeff Gorton**

Even if you have years of wiring experience under your belt, there are always a few tricks you may not know. And a good way to discover them is to watch another veteran at work. That's what we did. And it didn't take long to discover some real gems.

For this article we gleaned tips, tricks and techniques from two master electricians with decades of experience between them. From straightening cable to labeling wires, here are tips to help you wire better and faster.

Pack boxes neatly

If you've done much wiring, I'm sure you've had times when you could barely push the switch or outlet into the box because there were so many wires. The solution is to arrange the wires neatly and then fold them carefully into the box. Here's how to keep wires neat and compact: First, gather all the bare ground wires along with a long pigtail and connect them. Fold them into the back of the box, leaving the pigtail extended. Next, do the same for the neutral wires. If you're connecting switches as we show here, you don't need a neutral pigtail. Leave the hot wire extra long and fold it back and forth across the bottom of the box. (See "Multiple Switches, One Hot Wire" on p. 88 for how to connect switches to this wire.) Put a wire connector cap on the hot wire to identify it. The neatly packed box makes it easy to identify the wires and leaves you plenty of room for the switches.

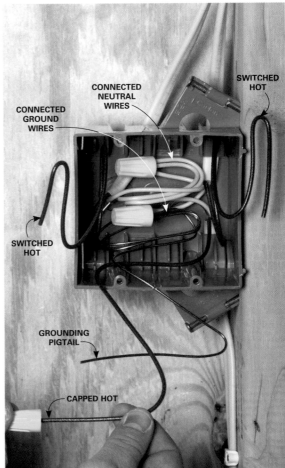

CONNECTED
NEUTRAL
WIRES

CONNECTED
GROUND
WIRES

SWITCHED
HOT

SWITCHED
HOT

GROUNDING
PIGTAIL

CAPPED HOT

Uncoil without kinks

Pulling plastic-sheathed cable through holes in the framing is a lot easier if you straighten it out first. If you simply pull the cable from the center of the coil, it'll kink as you pull it through the studs. The trick is to lift a handful of coils from the center of the roll (Photo 1) and toss them across the floor as if you're throwing a coiled rope. Next, walk along the length of cable, straightening it as you go (Photo 2). The electricians we talked to prefer this method because they can keep the cable contained in the plastic wrapper for easier handling and neater storage.

1 Avoid kinks. Don't just pull cable from the roll. Instead, lift a few loops from the center of the roll. Four loops will reach about 12 ft.

2 Straighten before pulling. Toss the coil across the floor. Then straighten it by hand before pulling it through the framing.

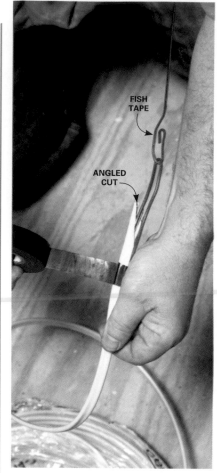

FISH TAPE

ANGLED CUT

Peel UF like a banana

Underground feeder (UF) cable has a tough plastic sheathing that allows you to bury it directly in the ground without running it through a conduit (of course, it has to be buried deep enough to satisfy the electrical code). But that tough sheathing is also difficult to remove—unless you know this trick. Start by separating the black and white wires from the bare copper by grabbing each with pliers and twisting (Photo 1). They're easy to tear apart once you get them started. Pull them apart until you have about a foot of separated wires. Next, remove the sheathing from the insulated wires by grabbing the end of the wire with one pliers and the sheathing with another pliers and working them apart. After you get the sheathing separated from the insulated wire at the top, just peel it off (Photo 2). Repeat the process to remove the sheathing from the black wire. Finally, cut off the loose sheathing with scissors or a knife.

No-snag fish tape connections

After going to all the trouble of working your fish tape to its destination, the last thing you want is to lose the cable or get your tape stuck on something inside the wall as you pull it back. Here's how to avoid both problems (photo left). Start by stripping an 8-in. length of cable. Using a side cutters, cut off all but one wire. Cut at a steep angle to avoid a "shoulder" that could catch on something. Then bend the single wire around the loop on the end of the fish tape and wrap the whole works with electrical tape to form a smooth bundle. Now you can pull the wire without worrying that it might fall off, and the smooth lump won't get snagged by or stuck on obstructions.

Connect it securely. Bend one wire back to form a big loop and wrap the whole works with electrical tape.

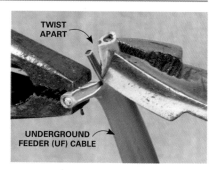

TWIST APART

UNDERGROUND FEEDER (UF) CABLE

1 Separate the end. Twist the end of the UF with two pairs of pliers to separate the wires.

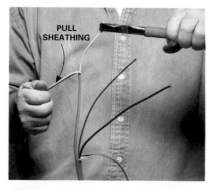

PULL SHEATHING

2 Strip off the sheathing. Peel the sheathing from the wires and cut it off.

Identify roughed-in wires

Save yourself a lot of headaches by identifying the wires as you install them. It's a lot harder to figure out which wires go where when they're covered with drywall. The electricians we talked to use a "code" for marking wires, and so can you. **Photo 1** shows one example. Another method is to use a label (**Photo 2**). But by the time you get back to connect switches and outlets, you might find that drywallers, tapers and painters have covered the label or knocked it off. That's why it's best to use non-label coding whenever possible. Develop a system and write it down. You'll never have to guess which are the "line" and "load" and which wires are the travelers for your three-way switch.

Two ways to I.D. wires

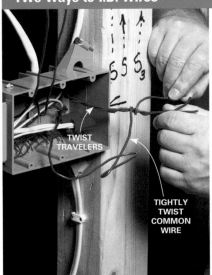
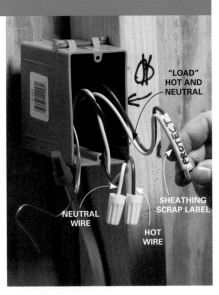

1 Code your wires. Here's one example. Wrap three-way switch "travelers" loosely and wrap the common wire tightly around them for easy identification later.

2 Label wires. You can also use scraps of plastic sheathing to label the wires. Here we labeled the wires that will be GFCI protected.

Test before touching

When you've done a lot of wiring, it's easy to get complacent about whether the power is off. But don't. Use a noncontact voltage detector to check every wire in the box or area you're working. Always check the tester on a wire or cord you know is live to make sure it's working before you rely on it. Noncontact voltage detectors are available at home centers, hardware stores and online and range in price from $5 to $25. The Klein NCVT-1 tool shown here ($16 at amazon.com) has a green light that indicates it's turned on and working—a nice feature that's well worth the extra money.

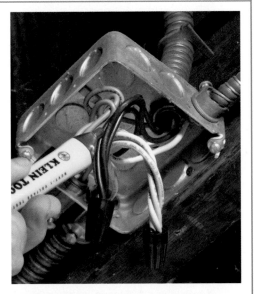

Avoid surprises. Test all the wires in a box with a noncontact voltage detector before you touch anything.

Troubleshooting GFCIs

We asked our electrical pros what problems they run into with GFCIs and how to solve them. For starters, we found that most complaints occur when several outlets are protected by one GFCI. There are several possible causes, ranging from a light or appliance with a ground fault that's plugged into a downstream outlet, to a defective GFCI or even a circuit with too much cable. To determine whether the problem is with the GFCI itself, or downstream, turn off the power to the GFCI and disconnect the wires from the "load" terminals. Push the reset button (if it doesn't click, you'll have to reset it after the power is back on) and plug a GFCI tester into the GFCI outlet before you turn the power back on. If the GFCI trips after you turn the power on, replace it. If it holds, then the problem is with one of the downstream outlets. To avoid the time-consuming process of troubleshooting the "load" outlets, the easiest and best solution is to replace each of them with a new, tamper-resistant GFCI.

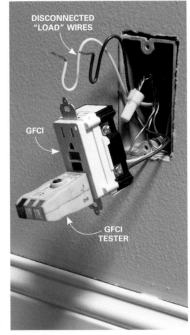

Multiple switches, one hot wire

A box with three switches is crowded enough without adding extra wire connectors and pigtails. Here's a wiring method that eliminates extra connections and creates a neater installation. Instead of running a separate pigtail from the hot wire to each switch, just leave the hot wire extra long. To connect the switches, simply score the wire with your wire stripper and push the insulation to expose about 3/4 in. of bare wire (**Photo 1**). Wrap this bare section at least three-quarters of the way around the screw terminal of the first switch. Repeat the process for the remaining intermediate switches (**Photo 2**). Connect the last switch in the usual manner, looping the wire around the screw in a clockwise direction.

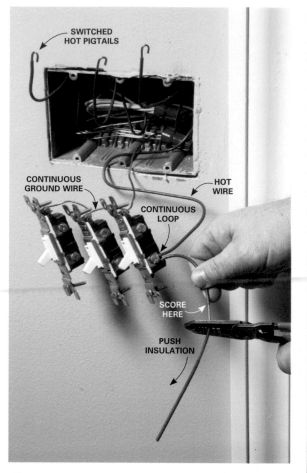

SWITCHED HOT PIGTAILS

CONTINUOUS GROUND WIRE

HOT WIRE

CONTINUOUS LOOP

SCORE HERE

PUSH INSULATION

1 **Save box space.** Run a continuous hot wire from switch to switch. Score the insulation and slide it to expose bare wire.

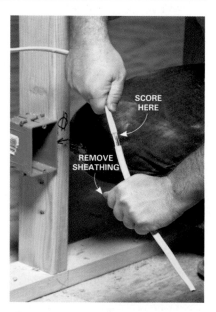

2 **Go from switch to switch.** Wrap the exposed section of wire around the screw and run it to the next switch.

LOOP AROUND SCREW

Strip sheathing first

It's tempting to push your roughed-in cable through the knockouts in the box and worry about how to strip the sheathing later. But that's the hard way. It's much easier to remove the sheathing before you push the wires into the box. The only trick is to make sure you have the cable in about the right spot before marking it (**Photo 1**) and removing the sheathing (**Photo 2**). As long as you don't have the cable stretched tight, there will be enough "play" to make final adjustments after you've inserted the conductors into the box. Remember, the electrical code requires that at least 1/4 in. of sheathing be visible inside the box. ⌂

MARK WITH THUMB

1 **Mark the spot.** Hold the cable near the box and mark it with your thumb where it extends slightly past the box.

SCORE HERE

REMOVE SHEATHING

2 **Strip the sheathing.** Score the sheathing at the "thumb mark" and slide it off. Then feed the wires into the box.

3 Plumbing, Heating & Appliances

IN THIS CHAPTER

FOUR TRICKS FOR GETTING OUT OF PLUMBING JAMS

Most faucet repairs are pretty easy—if everything goes well. But when faucet repairs go bad, they can quickly turn into a nightmare. Most of the headaches happen during disassembly. We asked plumbers to tell us how to handle the biggest headaches they face. But know when to say when. There may come a point when you have to say, "Forget it, I'm buying a new faucet!"

#1 Cut and replace

If a cap doesn't twist free, and the cap is metal, not plastic, heat the cap with a heat gun and grip it with the bare teeth of slip-joint pliers.

If heating doesn't work, or your faucet is plastic, cut the cap with a rotary tool and a cutting wheel (**photo below**). Then jam in a flat-blade screwdriver and widen the opening until the cap unscrews. Buy a replacement cap at the home center for about $10. Coat the new cap threads with plumber's grease to prevent it from sticking again.

#2 Get aggressive with setscrews

If the hex wrench that comes with your repair kit won't loosen the setscrew on the faucet, don't force it—you'll just ruin the head. Spend a few bucks for a 3/8-in.-drive hex socket kit. Buy a tube of valve grinding compound (like Permatex No. 80037; $7 at an auto parts store) and apply a dollop to the hex tip to reduce the likelihood of stripping the setscrew. Then use a ratchet to break the screw free (**bottom photo**). If it still won't budge (and the handle is metal and not plastic), try heating it with a heat gun. As a last resort, drill out the center of the setscrew and use a screw extractor to remove the rest of it. Buy a new setscrew and coat it with anti-seize compound before reinserting it.

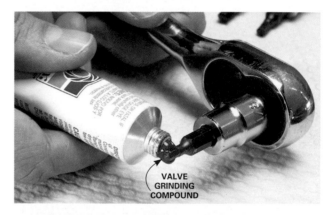

VALVE GRINDING COMPOUND

HEX SOCKET

CUT AND WEDGE
Slice down the side of the cap with a rotary tool and a cutting wheel. Don't worry about cutting the plastic seal (you'll be replacing that). But avoid cutting into the brass threads.

GET A GRIP AND LOOSEN WITH LEVERAGE
Squeeze the hex socket deep into the setscrew with one hand and pull the ratchet handle with the other. Then loosen the setscrew with a quick yanking motion.

#3 Special tools are worth it

Replacement cartridges usually come with a plastic loosening tool. If the cartridge is really stuck, the loosening tool can actually break off the cartridge ears and turn the job into a real nightmare. Even if you get the cartridge to rotate, you may still have to yank hard to get it out. Save yourself a lot of time (and sweat) by forking over a measly $18 for a Danco No. 86712 cartridge puller from amazon.com or a home center. Install it and pull the cartridge in minutes (**photo below**).

TWIST, PULL, DONE
Line up the prongs on the tool with the ears on the cartridge and tighten the screw at the top of the T-bar. Then turn the large nut with an adjustable wrench and twist the T-handle as you turn. The cartridge will pull right out.

#4 Know when to throw in the towel

It makes sense that a pivoting kitchen spout will leak if the O-rings are worn. But brass wears too. So if you've replaced the spout O-rings and the leak reappears in a few months (or weeks), check the inside of the spout.

DON'T FIGHT IT; REPLACE IT
If you feel a groove where the O-rings mate to the spout, the faucet is toast. Don't waste any more time and energy on O-ring repairs—you'll never get a long-lasting seal. Replace the faucet.

DISHWASHER RACK REPAIR

Dishwasher rack tines break off or lose the protective coating at the tips and then you get rust spots on your dishes. New racks cost about $80 (and up). But you can fix yours in less than an hour and for about $13. Buy a bottle of vinyl repair paint and a package of replacement tips to match your rack color (from any appliance parts store or find-a-fix.com). Cut off the rusted tips with a rotary tool and cutoff wheel. Then retip the tines (Photo 2).

To patch a rusted area around a broken tine, first clean off the rust (Photo 1).

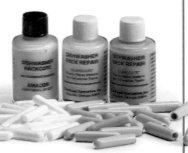

1 Clean the rack. Load a wire brush into a rotary tool and zip off the old rust and vinyl. Keep brushing until you get to fresh metal. Then paint on a new coating.

2 Apply paint and new tips. Coat the freshly cut tip with vinyl paint. Then slip a new vinyl tip over the tine. Let it dry and you're good to go.

HomeCare&Repair

REPLACE A WATER SOFTENER RESIN BED

If your water softener doesn't put out any soft water or it regenerates and runs out of soft water quickly (in just a day or so), you probably have a damaged "resin bed." A resin bed normally lasts 10 to 15 years. But iron in well water and excessive amounts of chlorine in city water can "kill" a resin bed. How do you know if your resin bed has "checked out"? Simple. Check to see if your water softener is using up salt at its regular rate. If it is, and you have no soft water, the resin bed has probably become saturated with iron deposits or been damaged by chlorine and can no longer be regenerated by the brine. If it isn't using much or any salt, the problem is most likely a bad valve head, meaning the resin bed isn't getting recharged with brine water at all. We won't cover that fix here.

First try using iron removal chemicals to clean the resin bed. (Go to familyhandyman.com and enter "water softener" for more informa-tion.) That won't help a damaged resin bed. So if cleaning doesn't work, you'll have to replace the resin. You can do that yourself. It will cost you about $100 and save $150 in ser-vice fees. Figure about four hours to complete the job.

Start by measuring the resin tank to determine how much new resin you'll need (see "How Much Resin to Use," p. 93). Then contact a local water treatment company or shop online for the right high-quality resin (avoid the really cheap stuff) for your particular application. Also purchase a resin funnel, a new riser tube and gravel (if recommended for your sys-tem).

Next, rotate the softener valve to the bypass position (or turn off the main water valve). Turn the dial on the valve head to start a manual regeneration (that'll bleed off internal water pressure). Then disconnect the softener from the plumbing and elec-trical (**Photo 1**). Unscrew the valve

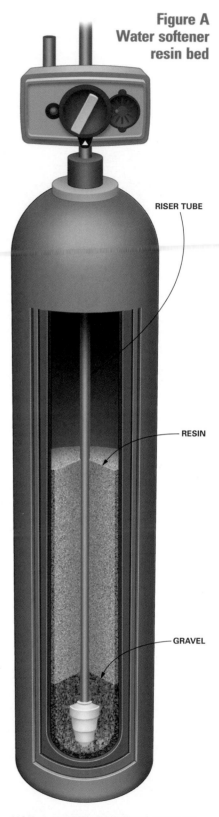

**Figure A
Water softener
resin bed**

RISER TUBE

RESIN

GRAVEL

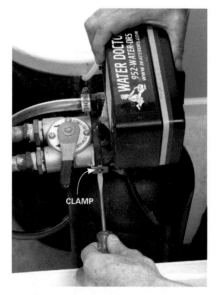

CLAMP

1 Unhook the unit. Remove the fasteners that hold the valve head to the bypass valve and pull the unit away from the plumbing. Watch for O-rings or seals so you can reinstall them in the right place.

IRON-FOULED RESIN

2 Dump and rinse. Pour the water, resin and gravel into a self-drain-ing bucket or tub. Remove the old riser tube and rinse out all remaining resin.

HOW A WATER SOFTENER WORKS
Hard water enters from the valve head and flows down through the resin, exchanging hardness ions for sodium ions. The soft water flows up the riser tube to your plumbing fixtures.

head and set it aside (you may need a helper to hold the resin tank while you twist). Dump out all the resin and gravel (Photo 2).

Before you install the new resin, cut the new riser tube to the same height as the old one and insert it into the resin tank. Refill the softener (Photo 3). Then reinstall the valve head and reattach the unit to the bypass valve. Turn the valve back to the "in-service" position and check for leaks. Enjoy the soft water.

NEW RESIN

TAPED RISER TUBE

3 Add new resin. Tape off the riser tube and position the funnel. Pour in the gravel and shake the tank to help it settle. Then have a friend help you pour the new resin into the funnel. It makes a huge mess if it spills.

HOW MUCH RESIN TO USE
Measure the diameter (the circumference divided by 3.14 equals the diameter) and the height of your resin tank. Then refer to this chart to find how much resin you'll need. Never fill a resin tank to the top—it'll restrict the flow of water.

Tank size	Amount of resin
8" x 35"	0.64 cu. ft.
8" x 44"	0.75 cu. ft.
9" x 35"	0.75 cu. ft.
9" x 48"	1.00 cu. ft.
10" x 35"	1.00 cu. ft.
10" x 40"	1.00 cu. ft.
10" x 44"	1.25 cu. ft.
10" x 52"	1.50 cu. ft.
13" x 54"	2.00 cu. ft.

TOUCH UP A STAINLESS STEEL APPLIANCE

Stainless steel is a great look until you scratch it. Then it looks awful. But you can "sand" out the scratches with sandpaper (400 to 600 grit) and a sanding block, an abrasive pad, or with rubbing compound. Or buy a stainless steel repair kit and get everything you need. (The Scratch-B-Gone kit comes with three pads, a sanding block, lubricant and a video. It's available at home centers and appliance parts stores and at amazon.com for $30.)

The sanding technique only works on plain (uncoated) stainless steel panels. Never try this procedure on simulated stainless steel or stainless panels with a fingerprint-resistant clear coat. Hint: If your appliance fingerprints easily, chances are it's plain stainless steel.

The key to removing the scratch is to start with the finest grit paper or pad and zigzag a stream of sanding fluid on it. Then sand the scratched area (photo right). If the scratch won't come out after sanding for a few minutes, move up to the next coarsest grit. When the scratch disappears, sand the rest of the panel until it blends in.

You'll have to develop a feel for the technique, so start on an inconspicuous area of the appliance panel. Finish by applying a stainless steel cleaner/polish (Sprayway is one brand; $5 at home centers and appliance parts stores).

INSTRUCTIONAL DVD

POLISHING CLOTH

PAD HOLDER

ULTRA SHINE

SANDING FLUID

ABRASIVE PADS

GRAIN

START WITH THE SCRATCH AND THEN BLEND IN
Determine the direction of the "grain" and start sanding in one direction only, following the brushed pattern. Don't sand back and forth and never sand against the "grain."

HomeCare&Repair

OUTDOOR FAUCET

My outdoor faucet squeals every time I turn it. Can you tell me how to silence it?

Outdoor frost-proof faucets eventually develop a squeal when you turn the handle. The brass stem threads are rubbing against the brass threads in the housing. If there's a shutoff valve for the faucet, close it. Otherwise, shut off the main valve. To get rid of the squeal, apply a dollop of plumber's grease.

1 Pull the stem. Remove the handle. Then loosen the packing nut. Reinsert the plastic handle and unscrew out the entire stem.

2 Grease like there's no tomorrow. Apply a generous amount of plumber's grease to the threads. Then insert the stem and try it out. If it still squeals, add more grease. Then reassemble the packing nut and install the handle.

REFRIGERATOR DIAGNOSTICS

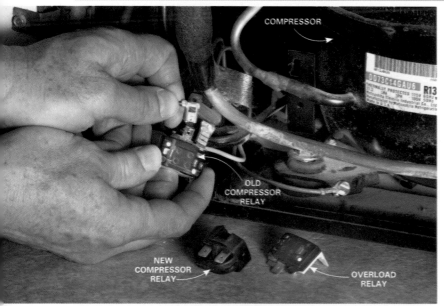

COMPRESSOR

OLD COMPRESSOR RELAY

NEW COMPRESSOR RELAY

OVERLOAD RELAY

TRY A NEW OVERLOAD OR COMPRESSOR RELAY
Pull the fridge away from the wall, unplug it and remove the service panel. Swap in the new compressor and overload relays. Then plug it back in to see if the problem is gone.

A refrigerator that makes a buzzing or humming sound and doesn't keep the food cold may have a blown compressor (big bucks) or just a bad overload or compressor relay (about $20).

I had this exact problem with a refrigerator and called Costas Stavrou, our appliance consultant. To avoid a $100 service call, Costas suggested I first try unplugging the refrigerator for about 20 minutes to allow enough time for the compressor to cool and any on-board computers to reset. When I plugged it back in, the problem returned. So he suggested I buy both an overload and a compressor relay (or a universal relay kit) from the appliance parts store and install it (**photo left**). If the problem went away, it would be a $20 fix. Unfortunately, my compressor noise returned (meaning it was toast). I had to buy a new refrigerator, but at least I didn't have to waste $100 on a service call. Instead I applied that money toward a new fridge.

KEEP YOUR A/C COOL AND SAVE A BUNDLE

Most people assume warm air from their A/C unit means it's low on refrigerant. That's not always the cause. Many times, window and through-the-wall A/C units can't blow cold air because the evaporator and condenser coils or cooling fins are clogged. Professional cleaning costs about $125. But you can do the entire job yourself in about an hour. The supplies cost less than $15. If cleaning doesn't do the trick, you can always call in a pro (or buy a newer, more efficient unit). Here's how to clean your A/C unit.

First remove the plastic filter holder/trim panel. It usually snaps off. Then remove it from the window or slide it out of the wall (get help—it's heavy).

If you're working on a window unit, remove the mounting frame and the case. The case screws are usually located along the bottom edge. Note the location of any odd-length screws since they have to go back in the same spots upon reassembly.

Then straighten the bent cooling fins with a fin comb (Photo 1). The Frigidaire fin comb kit shown here is cheap and fits most brands of air conditioners (No. 5304464988; $7 from apwagner.com).

FIN COMB

Buy two cans of A/C coil cleaner (one brand is AC-Safe No. AC-920; $6 from homedepot. com). Vacuum all visible buildup from both coils (Photo 2). Then spray both coils with the cleaner (Photo 3). While the foam works, clean the fan blades with household cleaner and a rag. If the fan motor has plastic- or rubber-capped oiling ports, pop them and squeeze in a few drops of electric motor oil (pros use the Zoomspout oiler; $5 from zoomspoutoiler.com).

Wash (or replace) the air filter and reinstall the unit. It just might blow a lot cooler. If not, you have other problems!

PLUMBING, HEATING & APPLIANCES

1 Comb out the mats. Match the correct end of the fin comb to the fin spacing on your coils. Then insert the comb and pull up to straighten the fins. Wear leather gloves to prevent nasty cuts.

2 Clean out the crud. Suck up all the spider webs, leaves, dust and dirt before you spray the coils.

3 Apply a foam cleaner. Shoot the spray over the entire surface of both coils and let the foam do the work for you. If the buildup is heavy, brush in the direction of the fins with a nylon-bristle brush.

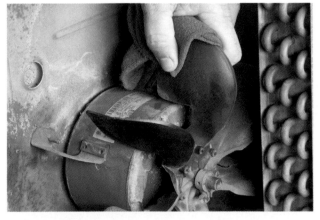

4 Service the fan motor. Pop off the plastic or rubber caps on the motor's oiling ports. Then squeeze a few drops into each port and recap.

HomeCare & Repair

FRONT-LOADING WASHER WON'T DRAIN?

If your front-loading washing machine doesn't drain, there could be an easy fix, especially if you own a newer Maytag washer. Even though some instruction manuals don't mention it, there's a filter near the water pump that catches stuff before it gets into the pump and causes damage. If the filter gets clogged, it can prevent your machine from draining. In some cases, a code number will show up on the digital display. If you look up the code in the instruction manual, it will indicate a problem with suds or tell you to check the filter. On Maytag front loaders, it's easy to avoid these problems by cleaning the filter every six months. On newer Maytag machines, you can access the filter easily by removing the front panel (**Photo 1**). On Frigidaire and some other brands, the filter is part of the pump and you'll have to remove a hose or the entire pump to clean it.

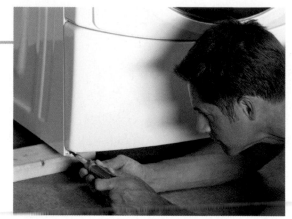

1 Remove the front panel. Tilt the washer back and slide blocks under the front legs for easier access to the screws. Remove the screws and lift off the front panel.

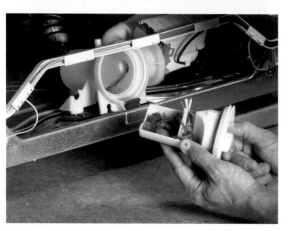

2 Twist off the filter. If your washer has a filter that's separate from the drain pump, you'll see it alongside the pump. Unscrew the filter by turning it counterclockwise. Clean it out and reinstall it.

FIX FOR A CLANGING VENT HOOD DAMPER

Every time the wind kicks up, it opens the damper on my kitchen vent hood. When the wind dies down, the damper slams shut, making a metallic "clang." The noise drives me crazy. What's the fix?

New spring-loaded backdraft dampers ($9 to $30, depending on the size) should solve the problem. Measure the diameter of the vent pipe and order the dampers from a duct supply company (hvacquick.com is one source). Start by replacing the backdraft damper directly above the vent hood. If that doesn't solve the problem, install a second damper near the wall or roof discharge cap. The second damper will greatly reduce the clanging problem.

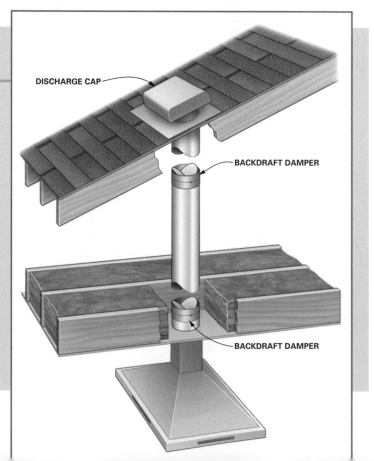

DISCHARGE CAP

BACKDRAFT DAMPER

BACKDRAFT DAMPER

GARBAGE DISPOSER SPLASH GUARD

Got a garbage disposer that spits, um, garbage at you? Forget about replacing the entire unit. You can install a new splash guard (about $10 at a home center) in about 20 minutes. You don't need any special tools.

If your garbage disposer is hard-wired, start by flipping off the circuit breaker. If it plugs in, unplug it. Stack up books or lumber to support the disposer. Then remove the drainpipe and disconnect the quick-connect fitting (**Photo 1**). Replace the old splash guard with a new one (**Photo 2**).

The hardest part of reinstallation is hoisting the disposer up and into place with one hand while you try to engage the locking ring with the other. Forget about that. Use our tip in **Photo 3**.

1 **Disconnect the disposer.** Jam a screwdriver into the locking ring and rotate it away from you. The disposer will drop onto the books. Support it with one hand so it doesn't tip over.

2 **Replace the splash guard.** Grab the lower edge of the old rubber guard and peel it up and off. Then slip the new one on and push it down until it seats.

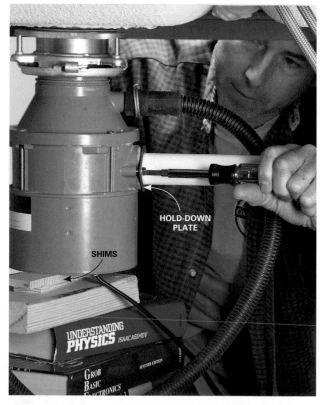

3 **Reconnect the disposer.** Shove several shims between the books and the bottom of the disposer until the locking ring just touches the sink flange. Then just rotate the ring to lock it in place. Reinstall the drain line, do a leak test and grind away.

HomeCare&Repair

REBUILD YOUR WATER SOFTENER

A bum water softener control valve can cause the unit to leak or stop producing soft water. A leak automatically means a rebuild, but if you've run out of soft water, first check the power at the receptacle. If the receptacle works and your softener is more than five years old, chances are good that you're due for a control valve rebuild. Water softener repair pros charge about $200 to do that. But you can do it yourself in about an hour and for less than $60. I'll show you how to rebuild one of the most common valves (the Fleck 5600 series) and direct you to a Web site for rebuild instructions for other brands.

It'll take some detective work to find the make and model of your control valve because they don't have identifying labels. So take a photo of your valve and go to softenerparts.com. Click on "I.D. Your Control Valve" and match your photo to the valves there. If you have a Fleck control valve, buy a complete rebuild kit and follow the instructions here. If you have a different brand, locate the parts and rebuild instructions on the site's menu.

Start the rebuild by relieving the internal water pressure. Turn the bypass valve to the "bypass" position and rotate the dial to the "backwash" position. Unplug the power cord. Then remove the back cover, the housing screws and the screw in the center of the main piston. Tilt the housing and lift it off. Remove the hold-down plate screws and the plate. Then grab the piston and pull it straight up (**Photo 1**). Next, remove the spacers and seals (**Photo 2**). Remove the old brine valve and install the new one (**Photo 3**). Then install the new seals and spacers (**Photo 4**). Insert the new piston and install the hold-down plate. Reinstall the housing, turn on the water and check for leaks. Then turn the dial to put the unit into a manual regeneration and check again for leaks.

1 **Remove the main piston.** Grab the piston by the metal tang and yank it straight up (the uppermost seal may come out with the piston). Toss the piston.

2 **Remove the valve innards.** Stick your finger down into the control valve and pull out the four spacers and five seals. Toss them.

3 **Replace the brine valve.** Pop out the old brine valve and check to make sure the bottom O-ring comes with it. Then push the new valve into the bore.

4 **Load in the new valve parts.** Drop a rubber seal down into the valve body. Then alternate spacers and seals, finishing with a seal at the top.

FLATTEN AIR DUCTS TO GAIN BASEMENT HEADROOM

Don't let low-hanging ductwork scuttle your plans for a basement remodel. If the ductwork is in the way, you have three options. You can reroute it or split it into more but smaller ducts. But the least disruptive and easiest way is to replace the low ducts with new ducts that are flatter but wider. In most cases, you can gain several inches of headroom.

Measure the existing ducts that are too low. Sketch out the current duct layout and note the location of each joint. Take the sketch to a professional heating contractor and get a quote for building new, flatter ducts. If the new ducts provide enough headroom, just deliver the old ducts to the contractor to use as a template for the new ones.

To disassemble a duct joint, remove the drive "couplers" (Photo 1). Then install the new duct (Photo 2). Seal all the joints with aluminum duct tape or duct-sealing caulk.

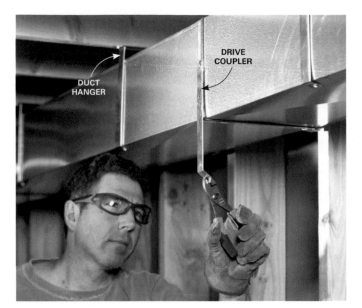

1 Disassemble a duct joint. Unbend the folded portion of each joint's "drive coupler." Pull each one off with pliers. Support the duct with two spring clamps and chain and then remove the duct hangers.

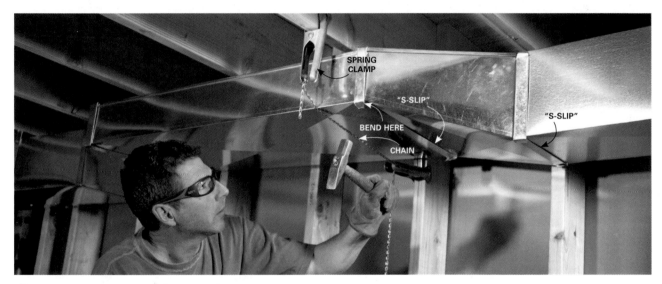

2 Install the new duct. Hoist the new duct into place and hold it with the spring clamps and chain. Line up the joints and insert the top and bottom edges into the S-slips. Install the drive couplers and bend the ends with a hammer. Then install the duct hangers.

RUST STAIN REMOVAL

Throw away the scouring powder and pick up a bottle of resin bed cleaner used for water softeners (about $11 at home centers). Just douse the rust with a foam brush. It's amazing. Usually the rust will disappear in a few minutes. But long-term stubborn rust buildup may take a few treatments. We've even used it successfully on acrylic spas. You really don't want to scour those! Just try it first on a small area to make sure it doesn't damage the surface.

HIGH-TECH
WATER HEATERS

New technology can save energy and money

by **Rick Muscoplat**

Water heater technology is changing—fast! And even though all the new models are more energy efficient, that doesn't mean you'll find them the most cost effective for your family. So before you plunk down big bucks for a high-tech heater, take a minute to understand how each style works, its pros and cons, and its projected payback. Your goal is to find the right balance between performance and efficiency for your particular home. However, if you're really into numbers crunching, use the worksheets at energysavers.gov. Search "13010."

First, check the ratings

There are two ratings to check before you buy any heater: the energy factor (EF), which tells you how efficient it is, and the first-hour recovery (for storage tank heaters) or flow rate (for tankless).

The EF is easy to understand—the higher the number, the more efficient the unit. Interpreting the recovery rate is similar—the higher the number, the more hot water you'll get in the first hour after opening the spigot. But when it comes to ratings for tankless water heaters, keep in mind that lower groundwater temperatures can sometimes cut the heater's flow rate by half. So shop for one that'll provide the flow rate you want, on the basis of incoming winter water temperatures.

ANNUAL SAVINGS BY TYPE

Tankless
(Gas)
$86–
$160[*]

Tankless point-of-use
(Electric)
$79^{**}

Heat Pump
(Electric)
$246[*]
& up

Condensing
(Gas)
$93[*]

A.O. SMITH

* When compared with a conventional storage-tank water heater.
** Annual water savings when installed on faucets farthest from the water heater

TANKLESS

Instead of keeping 40 or 50 gallons of hot water on call 24 hours a day—which wastes energy—a tankless unit heats water only when you need it. A flow sensor detects when you open the faucet. Then the gas valve opens and the burners fire up. The heater measures the incoming water temperature and calculates how quickly the water should flow past the burners. So, if the incoming water is 65 degrees F (typical summer temperature), the heater will provide its maximum flow rate. But if the water is only 35 degrees, the heater will throttle back the flow rate by almost 50 percent. Check with your local utility to find out the water temperature. The average home center price for a tankless heater is $1,000, plus about $200 for a stainless vent.

DOUBLE-WALL VENT CARRIES COMBUSTION AIR IN AND EXHAUST OUT

CONDENSATE TUBE; REQUIRES FLOOR DRAIN

REQUIRES A 110V RECEPTACLE

HOT WATER OUT

REMOTE CONTROL WIRING

COLD WATER IN

REQUIRES 3/4" OR 1" GAS LINE

Pros:

- Nothing beats a tankless heater for putting out lots of hot water—it never runs out.
- A tankless heater saves about 30 to 50 percent in energy costs over a conventional gas heater (minimum EF of .82 vs. .54 for conventional).
- A tankless heater is small and hangs on the wall, freeing up floor space.

Cons:

- With tankless heaters, there's a lag time of three to eight seconds to fire up the burners and heat the water to the set temperature.
- Installation can be a major project.
- Tankless heaters must be flushed annually with special chemicals to remove scale and maintain energy efficiency. You can do this yourself or hire a plumber (about $125).

What to look for:

Shop for one with the highest EF and the best flow rate.

Is it DIY?

You can install it yourself—if you can run a new gas line, follow the venting installation instructions to the letter (and to your local code), install an electrical outlet, and reconfigure the water pipes. It's a big job.

Is it for you?

If you want an endless supply of hot water for long showers or to fill a gazillion-gallon spa, this heater's for you. Just be aware that you may not be able to run several showers at the same time in winter.

The payback on a professionally installed tankless heater is 16 to 22 years, or six years if you install it yourself.

FOR MORE INFORMATION
- boschhotwater.com
- eternalwaterheater.com/products.html
- hotwater.com/lit/spec/r-gas.html#tankless
- navienamerica.com
- rheem.com/products/tankless_water_heaters
- rinnai.us
- statewaterheaters.com

PLUMBING, HEATING & APPLIANCES

ELECTRIC HYBRID HEAT PUMP

Hybrid heat-pump water heaters work by pulling heat out of the surrounding air and pumping it into the storage tank. So if you live in a warm climate and install it in your hot attic or garage, the heat pump alone can save you money. The conventional heating coils come on only when the heat pump can no longer satisfy the demand.

If you install the water heater in a heated room, it will suck some of the heat. However, if you heat the house with gas, you'll probably still come out ahead.

Hybrid heat pump water heaters cost about $1,500 at home centers.

Pros:

An electric hybrid heat pump has the lowest operating cost of any electric water heater on the market, especially when installed in warm climates.

Cons:

- Hybrids cost about $1,000 more than a conventional electric heater.
- The heat pump is taller (and wider in some cases) than your existing electric heater. Make sure the unit will fit.
- Some heaters are "side-piped" to eliminate the possibility of heat pump damage caused by leaking pipes. On those models, you'll have to reconfigure the water pipes.
- You'll have to clean the air filter regularly to maintain operating efficiency.
- The heater needs at least 1,000 cu. ft. of air surrounding it, so it can't be installed in a closet.

What to look for:

EF rating of 2.0 and the highest "first-hour rating."

Is it DIY?

If you can reconfigure the water pipes and connect the wiring, you can install this yourself. But heed this warning: These suckers are big and heavy (about 200 lbs. empty). Get some help!

Is it for you?

If you live in a warmer climate and heat water with electricity, an electric hybrid heat pump will save you the most money over a conventional heater. In colder climates, it'll still save money during the summer when you're not paying to heat the surrounding air. The higher your electric rates and the warmer the year-round climate, the faster the payback. In many cases, the payback can be as little as four years.

FOR MORE INFORMATION
- americanwaterheaternews.com/new_products/hybrid_elec.htm
- geappliances.com/heat-pump-hot-water-heater/
- hotwater.com/products/residential/voltex_hybrid.html
- rheem.com/products/tank_water_heaters/hybrid_electric

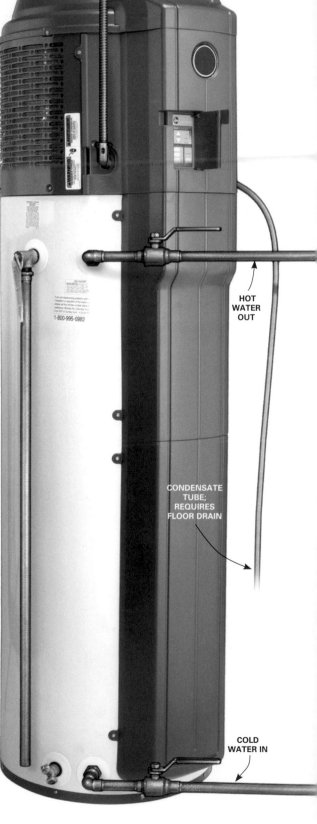

DEDICATED 240V CIRCUIT

HOT WATER OUT

CONDENSATE TUBE; REQUIRES FLOOR DRAIN

COLD WATER IN

CONDENSING GAS HEATERS

Like conventional heaters, condensing gas heaters have a tank. But that's where the similarity ends. Instead of sending hot exhaust gases out the flue, which wastes energy, this heater blows them through a coil at the bottom of the tank. Incoming cold water flows around the coil and collects most of the heat. That's why condensing gas water heaters are so efficient (up to 96 percent thermal efficiency).

Even though it's a storage tank design with "standby loss," the increased efficiency more than offsets that loss.

Condensing gas water heaters cost about $2,000 (from online sources like pexsupply.com—home centers don't sell this style right now). But manufacturers will begin introducing lower-priced models (about $1,200) at home centers.

Pros:

- A condensing gas heater is the most energy-efficient, gas-fired tank-style water heater on the market.
- "First-hour" recovery rate is incredible—you'll never run out of hot water.

Cons:

- A condensing heater costs $2,000. New models coming out will still cost two to three times more than conventional.
- It requires gas line and venting reconfiguration.
- There's no "real-world" experience on tank life or repair costs.

What to look for:

Shop for a heater with a thermal efficiency of at least 90 percent.

Is it DIY?

If you know how to reconfigure gas pipe, install new venting and add a 110-volt receptacle, you can install this heater.

Is it for you?

If you're replacing an existing gas water heater and need lots of hot water for long or multiple showers and tub fills, and want a high flow rate in summer and winter, this may be the way to go. It requires the least amount of repiping and has a faster payback. Figure a 12-year payback at current prices, or an eight-year payback when the lower-priced models arrive.

FOR MORE INFORMATION
- hotwater.com/products/residential/rg-vertex100.html

COMBUSTION AIR IN

1/2" GAS LINE

HOT WATER OUT

COLD WATER IN

EXHAUST TO OUTSIDE

REQUIRES 110V RECEPTACLE

CONDENSATE TUBE; REQUIRES FLOOR DRAIN

A.O. SMITH

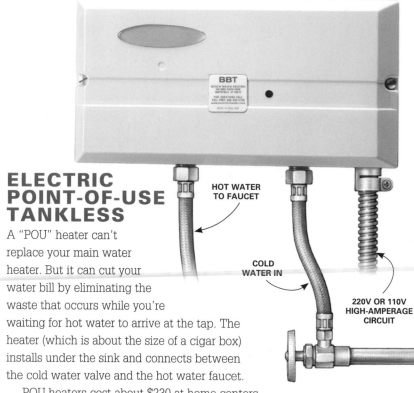

ELECTRIC POINT-OF-USE TANKLESS

A "POU" heater can't replace your main water heater. But it can cut your water bill by eliminating the waste that occurs while you're waiting for hot water to arrive at the tap. The heater (which is about the size of a cigar box) installs under the sink and connects between the cold water valve and the hot water faucet.

POU heaters cost about $230 at home centers and online.

HOT WATER TO FAUCET

COLD WATER IN

220V OR 110V HIGH-AMPERAGE CIRCUIT

Pros:

- A point-of-use heater reduces water waste and dramatically shortens the wait for hot water.
- It boosts the efficiency of your main water heater, eliminating frequent cycling from faucets.

Cons:

- A point-of-use heater adds cost to your water heater project.
- It requires a new 220-volt or 110-volt high-amperage circuit.

What to look for:

The highest EF and best flow rate based on winter water temperatures.

Is it DIY?

If you know how to run a 110-volt or 220-volt circuit, you can install this water heater. The plumbing is a no-brainer.

Is it for you?

If you have long runs from the water heater to kitchen and bath faucets, a POU heater is the best solution. A point-of-use heater offers about a three-year payback based on water savings alone.

FOR MORE INFORMATION
- boschhotwater.com
- hotwater.com/water-heaters/residential/tankless/
- rheem.com/products/tankless_water_heaters/tankless_electric
- stiebel-eltron-usa.com/mini.html

CONVENTIONAL GAS

Conventional water heaters have improved in recent years. They now have thicker insulation, motorized dampers to reduce heat loss, and an EF of at least .67.

Pros:

- Lowest upfront cost.
- Easiest to install.
- No fans or pumps to burn out. Proven reliable over decades of use.

Cons:

- Less efficient; more expensive to run.

Is it for you?

If you need an immediate replacement, you don't plan to stay in your home for years or you just don't use a lot of hot water, a conventional unit may be your most cost-effective option. 🏠

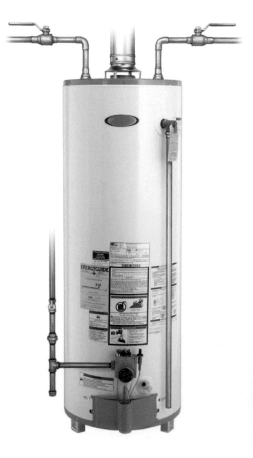

Q&A **ABOUT PEX**

Got questions about PEX? We'll answer them here.

by **Jeff Gorton**

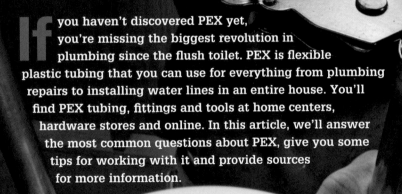

If you haven't discovered PEX yet, you're missing the biggest revolution in plumbing since the flush toilet. PEX is flexible plastic tubing that you can use for everything from plumbing repairs to installing water lines in an entire house. You'll find PEX tubing, fittings and tools at home centers, hardware stores and online. In this article, we'll answer the most common questions about PEX, give you some tips for working with it and provide sources for more information.

What about PEX vs. CPVC?

PEX and CPVC cost about the same. But there are a few reasons why PEX may be a better choice. First, PEX doesn't require glue, which means you don't have to work in well-ventilated spaces or wear a respirator. PEX is less likely than CPVC to burst if it freezes. Also, since PEX is more flexible and is available in long lengths, it can work better for "fishing" through walls in remodeling situations.

CINCH CLAMP   "PRO" CRIMP RING

COPPER CRIMP RING

What special tools do I need?

You can get by without buying a tool to install connectors if you use stab-in or compression fittings to make the connections. But they're too expensive to be practical on large projects (anywhere from $4 to $15 each). For most jobs, you'll want to invest in a special tool to make connections. There are several PEX connection methods, but only two that are affordable enough to be practical for DIYers: crimp rings and cinch clamps, as shown above.

Crimp rings are a band of metal, usually copper, that you slip over the fitting and compress with a crimp ring tool. The main drawback to the crimp ring

CINCH CLAMP

CINCH CLAMP TOOL

method is that you'll need either separate crimping tools for 1/2-in. and 3/4-in. fittings, or a universal tool with a swappable insert (not shown). This adds a little up-front cost to this method. A combo kit with interchangeable crimp jaws starts at about $100.

Cinch clamps work more like traditional band clamps. You slip the cinch clamp tool (shown) over the protruding tab and squeeze to tighten the cinch clamp. The same tool works for all sizes of cinch clamps. Cinch clamp tools start at about $40. The one-handed version shown above lets you hold the ring in place with one hand while tightening it with the other.

The only other special tool you need is a scissors-like cutter for the tubing ($10 and up; **bottom photo**).

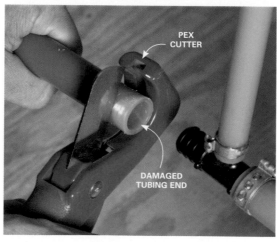

PEX CUTTER

DAMAGED TUBING END

Which is better— PEX or copper?

PEX (cross-linked polyethylene) has several advantages over copper:

- **PEX is cheaper than copper.** Half-inch PEX tubing costs about 30¢ per foot compared with about $1 per foot for copper. Some of the savings will be offset by the need for a special tool to install the fittings, but if you're doing a medium to large plumbing job, you'll usually save by using PEX instead of copper.
- **PEX is faster to install than copper.** If you use a manifold and "home-run" system (shown in the **top photo** on p. 107), it's like running a garden hose to each fixture—super fast and easy. But even if you install PEX in a conventional main line and branch system, the connections are quicker to make than soldering copper.
- **PEX won't corrode like copper.** If you live in an area with acidic water, copper can corrode over time. PEX is unaffected by acidic water and is therefore a better choice in these areas.

How do I splice PEX into my existing pipe?

There are several methods. The easiest is to cut out a section of pipe and slip in a stab-in tee (**top photo, below**). SharkBite is one common brand of stab-in fitting. This method doesn't require soldering, which can be a big time-saver. But check with your plumbing inspector if you're planning to bury this connection in a wall or ceiling. Some locales don't allow stab-in fittings to be concealed. Another method is to solder in a tee and a PEX adapter. Then slip the PEX tubing over the adapter and attach it with your chosen connection method (**bottom photo**). You can also use a stab-in tee to connect PEX to CPVC. Read the label to find the compatible fitting.

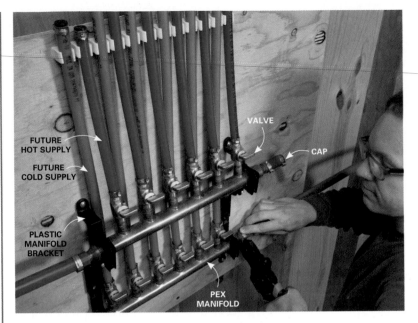

FUTURE HOT SUPPLY

FUTURE COLD SUPPLY

PLASTIC MANIFOLD BRACKET

VALVE

CAP

PEX MANIFOLD

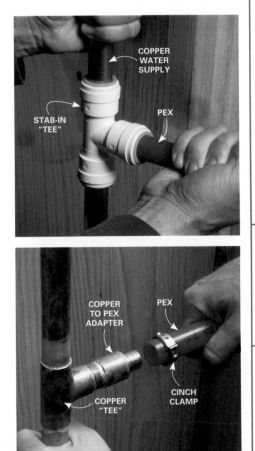

COPPER WATER SUPPLY

STAB-IN "TEE"

PEX

COPPER TO PEX ADAPTER

PEX

COPPER "TEE"

CINCH CLAMP

Does it meet code?

There is no unified national plumbing code. Before starting your plumbing job, check with your local inspector for specific local requirements.

Do I have to use manifolds with PEX?

No. You can install PEX just like you would other pipe, with main lines and branches to each fixture. But you lose a lot of the benefits of PEX with this system since it requires so many fittings. With the "home-run" system shown above, you install a manifold in the utility room or some area that's close to the main water line and water heater, and run a separate PEX tube to each fixture as shown above. This system uses more tubing but is fast and only requires two connections: one at the manifold and another at the fixture end. You can also use a hybrid system where you run 3/4-in. hot and cold lines to a set of fixtures—for example, a bathroom—and install a smaller manifold behind an access panel. Then make short runs of 1/2-in. PEX tubing to each fixture.

Do I have to use red for hot and blue for cold?

No. The colors are just to help you keep track of the hot and cold lines. You can use white PEX for everything if you prefer.

Is PEX reliable?

PEX has been used for decades in other countries, where there are thousands of homes with 30-year-old, leak-free PEX. Most of the problems with PEX systems (in the United States and elsewhere) have been caused by sloppy installation or faulty fittings rather than the tubing itself.

Can I connect PEX to my water heater?

No. First extend a copper pipe 18 in. from your water heater and connect the PEX to the pipe.

Which tubing should I use for interior water lines?

For water lines, there are three grades: PEX-A, PEX-B and PEX-C. They're manufactured differently, PEX-A being slightly more flexible. If you're ordering online, go ahead and spend a few cents extra for PEX-A. But don't go running around town looking for it; the difference isn't that big. The plumbers we talked to would be willing to use any of the three types in their own homes. A good online source for PEX tubing, fittings, tools and information is pexsupply.com. PEX is also popular for in-floor radiant heating systems, for which you need PEX tubing with an oxygen barrier.

How do I connect PEX to my plumbing fixtures?

There are several methods. If the connection will be visible, like under a wall-hung sink, and you would prefer the look of a copper tube coming out of the wall, use a copper stub-out (**top photo, below**). You can connect a compression-type shutoff valve to the 1/2-in. copper stub-out and then connect your fixture. In areas that are concealed, like under a kitchen sink or vanity cabinet, you can eliminate a joint by running PEX directly to the shutoff valve. Use a drop-ear bend support to hold the tubing in a tight bend (**bottom photo**). There are several types of shutoff valves that connect directly to PEX.

If you're using a manifold system with valves, you may not need to install a shutoff valve at the fixture. Ask your plumbing inspector. We recommend adding one, though. It doesn't raise the cost much and is more convenient than running downstairs to shut off the water when a repair is needed.

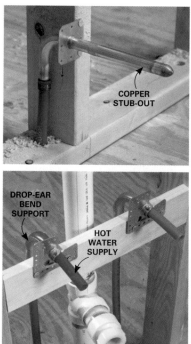

COPPER STUB-OUT

DROP-EAR BEND SUPPORT

HOT WATER SUPPLY

COLD WATER SUPPLY

What about expansion?

PEX expands and contracts more than copper, so don't stretch it tight. Let it droop a little between fasteners. On long runs, it's a good idea to install a loop as shown to allow for contraction. Another advantage of the loop is that if you mess up and need a little extra tubing, you can steal it from the loop. Also, since PEX moves as it expands and contracts, make sure to drill oversize holes through studs or joists so it can slide easily, and don't use metal straps to attach it. Use plastic straps instead.

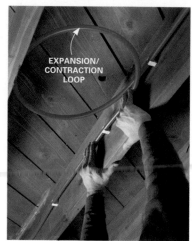

EXPANSION/ CONTRACTION LOOP

Will PEX break or split if it freezes?

Probably not. Manufacturers are reluctant to say so, but reports from the field suggest PEX can withstand freezing. You should still protect the tubing from freezing, but since it can expand and contract, it's less likely to break than rigid piping.

What if I goof? Can I take it apart?

Sure—there's a special tool for cutting off crimp rings, and you can use side cutters to remove cinch clamps. But a rotary tool (Dremel is one brand) fitted with a cutoff blade works great for cutting either type of connector (**see photo**). After you remove the crimp ring or cinch clamp and pull the PEX from the fitting, cut off the end of the tubing to get a fresh section for the new connection. If you damage the fitting with the rotary tool, replace the fitting rather than risk a leak. ⌂

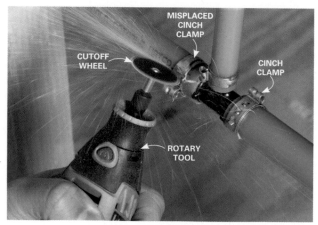

MISPLACED CINCH CLAMP

CUTOFF WHEEL

CINCH CLAMP

ROTARY TOOL

SHOULD YOU GO SOLAR?

5 questions to help you decide

by **Elisa Bernick**

There's no doubt that a solar electric system will cut your monthly utility bill. But will it save you money in the long run? That's a tricky question. The up-front costs average about $15,000 to $25,000 (after financial credits and rebates). For a lot of folks, the discussion ends right there. But for people who live in areas with lots of sun, high electricity rates and significant financial incentives, the payback period for a solar electric system can be less than five years. This article will pose five key questions to help you decide whether solar makes sense for you.

1 Are you a good candidate for solar?

Consider a solar installation if:

■ You live in the Sun Belt. Especially good areas are California, Texas, Florida, the Southeast, the desert Southwest and the Rocky Mountain states. The worst areas are the Great Lakes and Alaska. Foggy or rainy climates will require a lot more solar modules, and the system won't be cost effective.

■ Your electric bill averages more than $125 per month and your rate per kilowatt-hour (kWh) is on the high side (14¢ or more). The more money you spend each month on electricity, the more money your photovoltaic (PV) system will save you. (If you're paying only 8¢ or 10¢ per kWh, the payback period for solar panels would be unattractively long. Investing in new energy-efficient windows might provide a quicker return.)

■ You live in an area with incentive programs. Call your electric utility and visit dsireusa.org to find out which federal, state and local tax credits and rebates are available in your location. In addition to the 30 percent federal solar tax credit (in effect through 2016), states such as California, Pennsylvania, New Jersey, Massachusetts, Colorado and Arizona offer financial incentives that can cut the net cost of solar by 30 to 70 percent.

■ Your utility provides "net metering." For grid-tied systems without batteries, this allows you to sell excess electricity back to your power company to further reduce your electric bills.

How do photovoltaic (PV) solar panels work?

A grid-tied system includes solar panels and an inverter (or micro-inverters) that convert the direct current (DC) produced by the panels into alternating current (AC) that can be used in the house. Excess power flows back into the utility grid. If the solar system can't keep up with demand, power from the grid flows into the home.

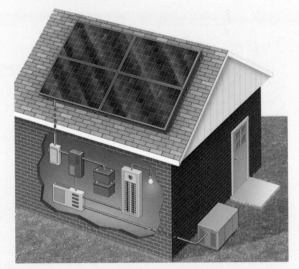

An independent system ("off the grid") provides most or all of the electricity you need and is more common in rural areas where utility connections are expensive. These always include batteries for nighttime use and cloudy weather. Many people with off-the-grid systems also have a backup generator for emergencies. See p. 110 for examples of PV systems.

2 Do you have the right kind of roof?

The optimal roof for a solar installation is south-facing (west is next best) with minimal shading from trees or other buildings. It should also be relatively new. Solar panels last for 30 years, so you want to install them on a roof that won't have to be replaced soon. You will need about 100 sq. ft. of roof area for every kilowatt of system size. Ground-mounted systems are also a possibility (but are more expensive than roof-mounted; see below).

3 Will you install the system yourself?

Doing the installation yourself can save you a third or more of the cost. But you'll need to take a training course and devote a lot of time to researching a potentially confusing host of options. Most areas require a licensed electrician to hook up the inverters and do the wiring. And in many states, a solar electric system must be installed by a certified professional in order to be eligible for solar tax incentives. Research local code requirements before moving forward on this project. Great Web sites for solar DIYers include builditsolar.com, trainingsolar.com and DIYsolarpower.org.

Do you live in the right spot for solar?

To see how much useful sunlight your area averages, go to nrel.gov/gis/solar.html and click on the photovoltaic solar resource map. Find your location and compare the color to the scale. A lower number means the financial incentives will have to be high to make your system cost-effective.

Types of PV

 SOLARCITY

 SEIA / ALAN BLAKE

 INTEGRATED SOLAR DESIGN

 SUNSLATE/ATLANTIS ENERGY SYSTEMS

Roof-mounted panels: Most common installation in urban and suburban areas. For every 1 kW of power generated, you'll need 100 sq. ft. of roof.

Ground-mounted: Used when roof-mounted panels aren't feasible. Additional racking, trenching and mounting equipment add to the cost, and neighbors may object to the appearance of the system.

Integrated into a shade structure such as an awning. This gives you active solar electricity and passive solar shading. May not generate as much electricity, and is more expensive than roof-mounted panels.

Building-integrated PV array: The panels are incorporated into the roofing materials, which then look like standing seam metal roofs, slate tiles and three-tab shingle strips. The most expensive but least visually intrusive installation. .

4 What size PV system will you need?

Sizing a PV system is complex, and you should consult a certified solar electrical contractor for help in determining an appropriate system type and size as well as to get a cost estimate. Visit eere.energy.gov for more sizing information and find-solar.org to find a contractor near you.

Here are some factors to consider before doing the calculations:

Your goals. Do you want to reduce the amount of electricity you buy from your utility or completely replace the power you get from the grid?

Your electricity needs. Check your electric bills and figure out your average annual electricity usage. The more energy efficient your home and the more you can reduce household power consumption, the smaller and less expensive your solar system will be.

Great resource to see if solar makes sense for you

Go to findsolar.com and use the site's solar calculators. You plug in your address and it will tell you which local, state and federal rebates and tax credits are available. You'll learn how big a system you need, the roof size necessary, the estimated cost of the system, your monthly and 25-year savings, your 25-year ROI and the number of years it will take to break even.

5 How much will your PV system cost?

Costs vary widely depending on location and the specific installation. An average cost for a typical 5-kW system, at $7 per watt, would be about $35,000. Solar rebates could reduce this cost significantly. Prices are slowly coming down, especially in California, where state incentives have driven the cost of PV-generated electricity to below 11¢ per kWh. But in other places around the country, it's still likely to be a fairly long payback.

Run the numbers:

- How much can you afford to spend up front? (And how much will you have to finance?)
- What financial incentives are available?
- How big a system will you need?
- What's the best system for your situation?
- How long will you live in the house?
- What will your payback be (the time it takes for the savings to equal the cost)?

How to calculate your payback

(a thumbnail method):

Add up the materials and labor costs and subtract any rebates. Add in any annual costs such as maintenance (minimal), additional insurance and interest payments. Then subtract any tax breaks. Now multiply the actual annual electricity generated in kWh by the cost you would normally have to pay your utility for those kWh of electricity (and the cost will undoubtedly rise each year). Subtract the savings. Continue to do this for subsequent years until the number becomes negative. This is the payback period. If you have a payback of eight years, great. The PV system should last for 30, so you will have 22 years of saving money on your electricity bill. ⌂

5 THINGS YOU NEED TO KNOW ABOUT GEOTHERMAL HEAT

by Elisa Bernick

A geothermal heat pump can save you so much money in energy costs (while helping the environment) that you will be tempted to install one immediately.

However, a geothermal system costs so much to install that you will be tempted to forget the whole thing. Read on to find out whether a heat pump makes sense for you.

1. IT WORKS LIKE YOUR FRIDGE

Your fridge removes heat from its interior and transfers it to your kitchen. A geothermal heat pump uses the same principle, but it transfers heat from the ground to your house (or vice versa). It does this through long loops of underground pipes filled with liquid (water or an antifreeze solution). The loops are hooked up to a geothermal heat pump in your home, which acts as both a furnace and an air conditioner.

During the heating season, the liquid pulls heat from the ground and delivers it to the geothermal unit and then to refrigerant coils, where the heat is distributed through a forced-air or hydronic system. During the cooling season, the process runs in reverse. The pump removes heat from your house and transfers it

to the earth. Many units can provide residential hot water as well.

A geothermal heat pump is vastly more efficient than conventional heating systems because it doesn't *burn* fuel to create warmth; it simply *moves existing* heat from one place to another. And because temperatures underground remain a relatively constant 50 degrees F year round, the system requires a lot less energy to cool your home than conventional AC systems or air-source heat pumps, which use outside air as a transfer medium.

Figure A Geothermal heat pump

BLOWER

HEAT EXCHANGERS

COMPRESSOR

GROUND LOOPS

2. THE UP-FRONT COSTS ARE SCARY

Let's not sugarcoat it—installing a geothermal system is expensive. It costs $10,000 to $30,000 depending on your soil conditions, plot size, system configuration, site accessibility and the amount of digging and drilling required. For a typical 2,000-sq.-ft. home, a geothermal retrofit ranges from $10,000 to $20,000. The system may require ductwork modifications along with extensive excavation. In a new home, installation costs would be on the lower

end. Even so, a geothermal system will cost about 40 percent more than a traditional HVAC system.

Recouping these costs through energy savings could take as little as four years or as long as 15 years depending on utility rates and the cost of installation. It takes some homework and professional estimates to figure out whether a geothermal system makes financial sense in your situation.

3. IT HAS REAL **BENEFITS**

- **Much lower operating costs than other systems.** A geothermal heat pump will immediately save you 30 to 60 percent on your heating and 20 to 50 percent on your cooling costs over conventional heating and cooling systems.
- **Uses clean, renewable energy (the sun).** With a geothermal heat pump, there's no on-site combustion and therefore no emissions of carbon dioxide, carbon monoxide or other greenhouse gases. Nor are there any combustion-related safety or air quality issues inside the house. (However, the pump unit uses electricity, which may be generated using fossil fuels.)

- **Can be installed in both new construction and retrofit situations.** However, it's a lot more expensive in retrofits requiring ductwork modifications.
- **Much quieter than other cooling systems.** There's no noisy outdoor compressor or fan. The indoor unit is generally as loud as a refrigerator.
- **Low maintenance and long-lived.** The indoor components typically last about 25 years (compared with 15 years or less for a furnace or conventional AC unit) and more than 50 years for the ground loop. The system has fewer moving parts and is protected from outdoor elements, so it requires minimal maintenance.

PLUMBING, HEATING & APPLIANCES

4. THERE ARE **DOWNSIDES**

(besides the cost)

- **Not a DIY project.** Sizing, design and installation require pro expertise for the most efficient system.
- **Still relatively new,** so there are fewer installers and less competition (which is why prices remain high).

- **Installation is highly disruptive to the landscape** and may not be possible on some lots. Heavy drilling or digging equipment will definitely crush your prize petunias.

5. TYPE OF LOOP AFFECTS THE **COST**

The three closed-loop systems shown here are the most common. There is also a less common open-loop system that circulates surface water or water from a well through the system and returns it to the ground through a discharge pipe.

The best system, loop length and design for a particular home depend on a variety of factors such as climate, soil conditions, available land, required heating and cooling load, and local installation costs at the site.

Figure B
Horizontal

Layered coils or straight runs (see p. 112) of polyethylene pipe are placed in 6-ft.-deep trenches. This is the cheapest underground option, but it requires a lot of open space. A 2,000-sq.-ft. house requires 400 ft. of 2-ft.-wide trenches.

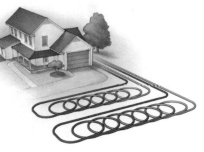

Figure C
Vertical

A vertical system is used when space is limited. Four-in.-diameter holes are drilled about 15 ft. apart and 100 to 400 ft. deep. Two pipes are inserted and connect at the bottom.

Figure D
Pond/lake

This system draws heat from water rather than from the soil. If there's a body of water nearby, this is the lowest cost option. A blanket of water covers coils anchored on racks about 10 ft. deep. ⌂

ADD A **FAUCET** ANYWHERE IN YOUR YARD

And stop lugging that hose around

by **Rick Muscoplat**

SHUTOFF VALVE

3/4" PLUG

3/4" FEMALE ADAPTER

3/4" x 1/4" REDUCER

AIR HOSE ADAPTER

3/4" COPPER TO 3/4" PEX TRANSITION FITTING

CRIMP RING

If dragging hoses around is a constant activity in your yard, install a remote faucet and eliminate that hassle forever. The job will take you a day or two (depending on how much trenching is required) and cost less than $100. Everything you'll need is available at home centers.

The inside connection

To get the best flow rate at the garden, tap into an interior 3/4-in. cold water line. If you can't find one that's convenient, tap into a 1/2-in. line instead (you'll just get a slightly lower flow rate). If you have a water softener, tap into a water line *before* the softener.

The trench

Call 811 a few days before you dig so the utility companies can locate buried pipes and cables in your yard. You only have to bury the water line about 6 in. deep. If you're trenching in hard clay or rocky soil, that's about as deep as you'll want to go. If you're working in soft soil, it's smart to go at least 12 in. deep to reduce the risk of future damage. At any depth, you can easily protect the water line from shovel attacks: Cover the tubing with a couple of inches of soil, then pour in about 2 in. of dry concrete mix before backfilling the trench. Soil moisture will harden the concrete.

The pipeline

Copper pipe is best for the exposed plumbing at the house, but PEX tubing is best for underground. It's a lot cheaper than copper and it's easier to install than CPVC plastic. With PEX, you can make a continuous run from your house and make turns without installing a single fitting. Plus, PEX tolerates mild freezing better than either CPVC or copper (in case you're late blowing out the line). However, you'll have to invest about $50 in a 3/4-in. PEX crimping tool. If you don't want to shell out the cash, use CPVC.

The blow-out system

If you live in a freeze zone, you'll have to blow out the system before the first hard freeze. It's easy to do with a home air compressor, but you'll have to install the components at the time of installation (instead of during a snowstorm).

At the house, splice in a tee and a threaded female 3/4-in. adapter, and cap it with a plug. That's where you'll connect your compressed-air line.

At the garden, install a blow-out valve (a ball valve is best) below grade in a gravel pit. Use a sprinkler system valve box (about $15) to cover it. Before the first freeze, close the shutoff valve and unscrew the plug. Next, screw in a standard air hose fitting and a reducer and connect your air hose. Out at the faucet, open both the faucet and the blow-out valve and let the water drain. Then, close just the faucet and blow out any remaining water with your compressor. Finally, close the blow-out valve and replug the blow-out fitting back at the house.

The post and faucet

We cut a length of hollow PVC fence post to mount the faucet, but you can build your own post out of any material. Make sure the PEX runs inside it to protect it from sunlight—UV rays reduce its life. Set the post at least 18 in. deep. Screw the sill cock flange to the post and install a screw-on backflow preventer. Note: Check with your local plumbing inspector for backflow prevention requirements in your area. ⌂

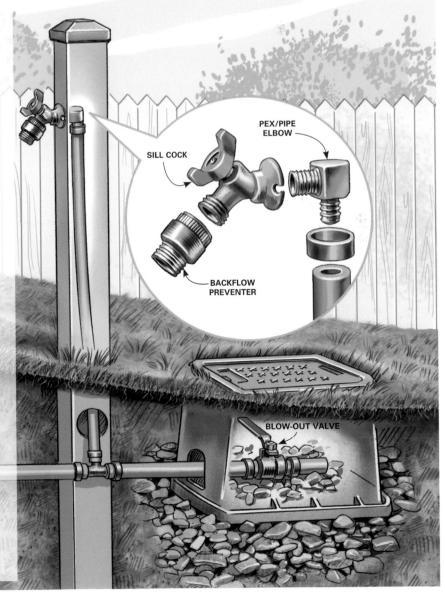

PEX/PIPE ELBOW

SILL COCK

BACKFLOW PREVENTER

BLOW-OUT VALVE

PLUMBING, HEATING & APPLIANCES

GreatGoofs®

CAN YOU HEAR ME NOW?

I was going to install a faucet in our upstairs bathroom and had brought home some slick new quarter-turn ball valves to replace the old shutoffs under the sink. My wife's task was to choose and bring home the new faucet while I got started on the valves. When it was time to turn the main water line back on, I had my 15-year-old son stand in the bathroom with his cell phone to watch for leaks. Out at the street I called him on my cell phone and said, "OK, here we go" as I turned on the water. Then my phone went dead. What a time for a dropped call! I quickly redialed but the call rolled to my son's voice mail. I hung up and my phone rang immediately. "Dad, shut the water off!!!" I did and raced inside and up the stairs to find the entire bathroom and hallway carpet completely soaked. Turns out I'd left my slick new ball valves in the open position when I installed them.

FOURTH TIME'S THE CHARM

Our washing machine was on the fritz. It's a heavy stacked unit (dryer on top) that's tucked into a tight wall recess, so it's tough to maneuver. After 45 minutes of pulling and straining, I got it out from the wall and spotted the problem right away—a broken clutch. But because it was too late in the day to get the part and the unit was blocking the hallway to the kitchen, I had to push the whole thing back against the wall.

The next day I did the backbreaking 45-minute thing over again and replaced the clutch. Then I reattached the supply hoses, pushed the unit back into place and started it. Oh, man—water began coming out from underneath the washer! I'd forgotten to reattach the drain hose! Once again, I pulled the whole thing out from the wall. Then I reattached the drain hose, pushed the unit back yet again, started it and hallelujah, it seemed to work fine—no leaks.

The next day my wife discovered hot water coming out during the cold cycle. I'd switched the hot and cold hoses when I reattached them! Which meant I had to....

THE EVER-FLOWING WATER HEATER

When the plumber replaced one of the heating elements in my electric water heater, I watched carefully, knowing that the other element would eventually need replacing too. Sure enough, a year later the other element went. I checked it with an ohmmeter, confirmed my diagnosis and headed to the plumbing supply store. When I returned home, I killed the power supply at the box and at the wall switch. Feeling proud and confident, I dragged the garden hose into the house, connected it to the heater and ran it into the floor drain to empty the heater—just like the plumber had done. Then I sat and waited for the water to stop flowing. After about an hour of a good, steady flow, it occurred to me to SHUT OFF THE WATER SUPPLY! Fifteen minutes later and hundreds of gallons of water poorer, I replaced the element.

LOW FLOW OR NO FLOW?

Several months ago, my best friend installed a low-flow faucet in her master bathroom all by herself. Her husband had offered to do it, but she decided to tackle it alone and was very proud of her handy work. Her husband immediately complained about the weak trickle of water, and after a few months even she couldn't stand it. She decided her attempts to be "green" weren't worth it, and she went out and bought a different faucet. When she started to uninstall the low-flow faucet, she immediately discovered the problem. She'd never opened the valves under the sink all the way! She was telling me this, but she was definitely NOT telling her husband!

A DATE TO REMEMBER

After our second date, Joe offered to fix my microwave oven, which was installed above my stove. He climbed up a ladder to take a look and asked me for a flashlight. I gave him the only flashlight with working batteries, a gigantic industrial metal one, and then I left him alone. I figured everything was going fine until I heard a crash and the words, "Oh, shoot!" (Not quite.) The flashlight had rolled out of the cupboard above the microwave and smashed onto my glass-top stove, shattering it to smithereens. Long story short, I married him anyway and got a great husband (New England's Best DIY Handyman) and a shiny new stove.

DO AS I SAY...

I'd been riding my kids about emptying their pockets before tossing their clothes into the laundry. So when the washer stopped working in the middle of a load of baseball gear, I was livid. I stared at the gallons of dirty, soapy water in the drum, then I stomped upstairs and read everybody the riot act before I got busy fixing the machine. After messing around with it for an hour, getting angrier and angrier at those kids and the junk they leave in their pockets, I finally found the problem. A drill bit that I'd left in *my* pocket had gotten jammed in the mechanism and was keeping the pump impeller from rotating. I quietly removed the bit, put the machine back together and ate a large piece of humble pie.

Top 10 DIY products

SCREW TOPS FOR 5-GALLON BUCKETS

Hands down, this lid is one of the top 10 products we've published in this magazine. It turns any 5-gallon bucket into a hermetically sealed container. Snap on the outer ring and spin the top shut. It opens and closes in two seconds. Store drywall mud, chemical fertilizer, seed, grain, pet food or anything else that is best sealed in an airtight, pest-proof container. Pay $6 per lid at gammaseals.com.

SHOWER FLOOR FOR DUMMIES

Tiled bathrooms look best with a tiled shower. But a tile shower floor requires some very tricky work: two layers of mortar, both sloped, sandwiching a PVC liner. Plus, you have to fashion a mortar curb that also contains the liner. It's not easy to do. And if it leaks, as such floors often do, you're ripping out a very expensive installation.

Go check out the "goof proof" shower floors at markeindustries.com. Mark E. Industries (866-771-9470) offers a well-designed kit that will help a first-timer install a perfect tile shower floor base. The kit consists of a series of tapered plastic screed strips that you fasten to the floor. You screed the mortar between the strips to create a perfectly pitched floor. Another part of the kit is a plastic curb that you pack full of mortar. Don't get it? I don't blame you. Go to markeindustries.com to see videos, and it'll make perfect sense. If you like it, click on "Dealers" to find a supplier and to figure out how much your kit will run—most likely, it'll be less than $100.

GOTTA DRILL HOLES IN TILE?

If you have to drill holes for pipes in ceramic, granite or marble tile, go to Home Depot and buy a Brutus 1-3/8-in. tile hole saw (model No. 10569; $21). Put a self-stick gasket on the bottom (it comes with six), stick the guide to the tile, splash in a little water and drill away. In about 30 seconds, you'll have a perfect hole. The water keeps the diamond-embedded drill bit cool and eliminates any dust so you can drill the hole right in the bathroom where you're working. I've drilled six holes with this thing—it's fabulous.

MARKE INDUSTRIES (2)

DON'T MEASURE; JUST SLICE

You drywall-hanging veterans might scoff at the possibility of a replacement for the 4-ft. T-square, but the Wallboarder's Buddy was developed by one of your own. Gary McCallum has hung drywall for 30-plus years, and he developed a new way to score rock. It's basically a T-square equipped with a pivoting knife on the tongue.

The Wallboarder's Buddy ($60) does take some getting used to: You don't drag the blade, you push it—and then pull it to finish the last few inches of scoring. And since it's only 2 ft. long, you have to do all your rips from the top. Length cuts are made from the ends. That also takes some getting used to because there are several different scales depending on the length of the rock you're installing. And last but not least, because nearly every single measurement you need is imprinted on the square, you rarely need a measuring tape. You can watch a video demonstration and order the tool at wallboardersbuddy.com.

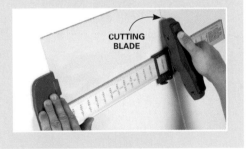

CUTTING BLADE

PARACHUTE BAGS— NOT JUST FOR SKYDIVING ANYMORE!

I bought some "parachute" bags more than 20 years ago and I love them. They contain nearly every type, size and style of fastener I'll ever need, all stacked up inside a 5-gallon pail. Whenever I travel (even up on the roof) to do any building, repairing or remodeling, that bucket, or the bag with the appropriate fasteners in it, goes along. Parachute bags don't tip over and take up very little room, and a drawstring cinches off the top so nothing falls out—ever. They're an exceptional way to store and carry plumbing or electrical fittings or any other small parts that need to be kept separate. There are many varieties available now. (My old one is shown above.) The latest version of the style I have, the 25002 Parachute Parts Bag, costs about $11 at amazon.com. Or just search for "parachute bag fastener" to see the varieties available.

WET-CAST CONCRETE LOOKS LIKE STONE

Silver Creek makes molds from actual stones to produce paving products that are almost indistinguishable from the real thing. Using this "wet-cast" method, Silver Creek makes slate, limestone and travertine landscape tiles in several colors and three sizes. These stone look-alikes are less expensive than the real thing, and since they're all a uniform thickness, are also easier to install. Expect to pay about $6 to $7 per sq. ft. For inspirational photos and product and dealer information, go to silvercreeksw.com.

DECKRITE (X6)

DECK REDUX

The Deckrite deck covering system is for those of you who have: (A) a very ugly deck that's still structurally sound and/or (B) an area beneath it that you would like to remain completely dry. Here's how it works. You screw down 1/2-in.-thick treated plywood to the existing deck and then glue down a polyester fabric (several colors available). Metal edging holds it down around the perimeter. You use various flashing systems from the company, or the material itself, to make waterproof tie-ins to walls, shingles or whatever else the deck meets. It looks a lot like vinyl flooring, but it's designed to stand up to the elements and has a nonskid surface. The guys at Deckrite will help you figure out exactly what you need and ship the materials right to your house. For help finding a dealer, go to deckrite.com or call (888) 450-3325. At deckrite.com, you can also see the material choices and flashing options and watch an installation video.

Top 10 DIY Products

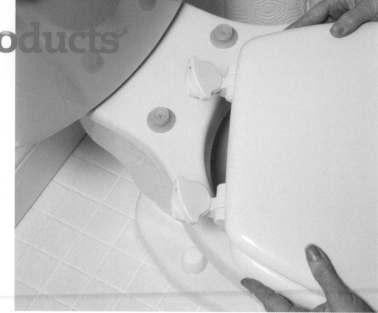

CARGO RACK POPS UP WHEN YOU NEED IT

Want a cargo rack but hate having it in the way when it's not needed? The Invis-A-Rack ($700 from invisarack.com) mounts on your truck-bed side rails with clamps (**photo below**). To set it up, just pull up both sets of front and rear vertical bars and lock them in place. The whole operation takes about 60 seconds. Then load it up with ladders, lumber, a canoe or a small boat. The rack holds up to 500 lbs.—enough to handle just about any project.

AND SNAP!

LIFT

POP, SNAP AND LOAD
Lift up the front and rear vertical supports. Then fold out the horizontal bars and lock them together—instant cargo rack.

A GROSS CHORE MADE EASIER

Toilet seats may not be the sexiest topic, but cleaning toilet seats is even less sexy. Why, in my otherwise enlightened household, does this odious (and odiferous) task always fall to me? Has my husband ever cleaned the toilet? Don't get me started. But I recently switched out our toilet seat for a Bemis toilet seat with an Easy-Clean and Change Hinge, and my cleaning chores are now a tiny bit more pleasant. Flip the levers on the special hinges, and the entire seat, including the brackets, pulls off, leaving the rim clear for cleaning. I know that every member of your household will appreciate this toilet seat because everyone takes turns cleaning the toilet at your house...right? The most basic seat costs $15, or $35 with the Whisper-Close option at Home Depot.

FINGER-SAVING SPRAY PAINT TOOL

I love spray paint because it's so easy to use and there's zero cleanup. But I hate the sore, paint-covered fingertips and hand cramps you get from holding down the little button, especially on multi-can jobs. That's where the Rust-Oleum Comfort Grip spray handle ($5) comes in. You slide it on, press the trigger and paint away distress-free can after can. But believe me: Keep it away from precocious preteens. It's way too easy to use. Available at home centers in the spray paint aisle.

4 Woodworking & Workshop Projects & Tips

IN THIS CHAPTER

ShopRat

STEEL WOOL— FINISHING A FINISH

One of Stephen Evans' special talents is achieving high-quality finishes on all his pieces. No matter what type of finish he applies, he rubs down the final coat with No. 0000 steel wool to eliminate dust motes and other fine flaws. Just unroll the steel wool, form a pad and rub with the direction of the grain. Start out with light pressure and push harder if necessary to achieve a uniform texture and sheen. The harder you rub, the lower the sheen. Apply paste wax, buff and you're done.

NO. 0000
STEEL WOOL

HANG IT HIGH FOR FINISHING

Dave Munkittrick is a furniture builder who's my go-to guy whenever I need finishing advice. When he finishes flat workpieces like frames, plywood panels or doors, he hangs them from pieces of light chain hooked to screws stuck in a board along the ceiling. He drives screw hooks into the project where the holes won't be noticed. That way he can finish both sides at the same time, and no dust settles on the vertical surfaces during drying.

BENCH HOOK

When you have to hold something in place while you chisel, plane, belt-sand or do anything else that requires a lot of pushing or pulling motion, build yourself a bench hook. Build it to suit the job at hand, any size, in only moments. Make the stop a tad thinner than the workpiece, especially if you're belt-sanding.

STOP

CLEAT

SQUIGGLE OUT YOUR BAD LINES!

We all do it. Draw a line or two in the wrong place for cutting a piece of wood. Then it happens. We proceed to follow one of those lines when we're cutting and wreck the wood. So scribble out your mistakes right away. Then you can't go wrong.

MELAMINE WORKBENCH TOPPER

Dave Munkittrick, the designer and builder of the bookcase on p. 127, is justly proud of his 4 x 8-ft. assembly table. At one point, he was ready to resurface its scarred 20-year-old top, but instead he had the brilliant idea of throwing a sheet of 3/4-in. melamine on top and screwing it down.

"I can write on it—it erases easily—and when I clamp glue-ups, the dried glue drips pop right off with a chisel," Dave says. "Varnish drips and spills don't stick either. Heavy projects slide around on the slick surface for easy positioning."

Dave used two-sided melamine so he'll be able to unscrew the top when it's finally worn out, and flip it over to expose a brand new surface.

A 4 x 8-ft. sheet of melamine (plastic-coated particleboard) costs about $35 at home centers.

MELAMINE SURFACE

RAG DAMPENED WITH DENATURED ALCOHOL

NO MORE PENCIL MARKS, NO MORE BOOKS...

Most woodworkers write notes all over their projects, but at some point, those pencil notes and marks have gotta go. Stephen Evans doesn't use erasers, though; he uses denatured alcohol. He just dampens a rag and wipes away the graphite. The wood is easier to clean up before finishing, and pencil erasers will last longer.

BBQ SKEWER

A FIX FOR MISPLACED HOLES

My buddy Dave Munkittrick discovered a new helper for his shop while grilling shish kebabs. He realized that the wooden skewers would be the perfect size for filling misplaced screw holes or worn-out ones that are too big for a toothpick to plug. The skewers, available at most grocery stores, are essentially long, fat toothpicks—perfect for No. 6 and even No. 8 screw holes.

When Dave drives a screw in the wrong place, he puts a little glue in the hole and then taps in a skewer with a hammer as far as it will go. Then he snaps the skewer off flush and tries again.

ShopRat

PENCILS, PENCILS, EVERYWHERE!

If you spend one-third of your time woodworking, one-third looking for tape measures and the other third searching for a pencil, here's what to do about the pencil part. Cut 3-in. lengths of 1-1/2-in. PVC pipe and hot-glue them near every tool and work surface in your shop. Choose a spot where they're out of the way. Stock them all with pencils and you'll have a third more woodworking time. We'll get to work on the tape measure part next.

SPLITTING WEDGE

STAY-PUT EDGE BANDING

When you're edge-banding, Ken Geisen (who happens to operate a cabinet shop), suggests this trick. Make a quick, light pass with the iron just to tack the banding in place. Then run over it again more slowly, following right behind the iron with a thick piece of metal (a splitting wedge works nicely). The metal sucks the heat out of the veneer to make the adhesive set up immediately. That means your edge banding won't pop free right after the iron passes.

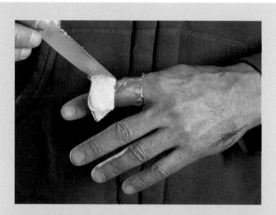

WORKINGMAN'S BANDAGE

Over the years, as a shop rat and a carpenter, I've managed to cut myself probably about 5,000 times. An ordinary bandage will stay on for about 2.5 minutes if you're working. So for years I've made my own bandages that'll stand up to a day's worth of shoveling, hammering or any other hands-on activity. I wrap a small gauze patch around the cut and fortify it with a strip of duct tape. It's pretty much bulletproof for the entire day. When it's time to peel off the tape, just remember: Big boys don't cry.

ALL-TIME BEST FIX FOR GLUE SQUEEZE-OUT

When you finally reach the stage of staining or finishing your project, the last thing you want to see is blotches caused by glue squeeze-out along the joints. It can be tricky to prevent, too: If you use water to clean up the excess glue when it's wet, you'll only spread it around or even weaken the joint. If you try to sand the glue off when it's dry, it will turn to gum and clog the sandpaper. And if you try to scrape if off when it's hard, you'll gouge your workpiece.

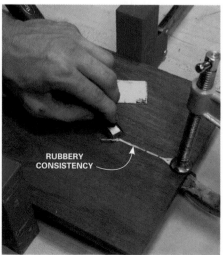

RUBBERY CONSISTENCY

So what's a woodworker to do? Let the glue dry about 20 minutes (until rubbery), then scrape it off with a sharp chisel. Use a *slightly* damp rag to get rid of glue residue. When the piece is dry, lightly sand, then apply a stain and finish.

STACKABLE SAW PONIES

For years, Ken Collier, my boss here at *The Family Handyman*, and I have been debating the merits of collapsible metal sawhorses vs. clunky, heavy, hard-to-store homemade wooden ones. (Guess which side I'm on?) He finally came up with a design that actually makes some sense to me. They're short, compact, stackable mini horses that you can throw together from scraps in about 30 minutes. Short is the key. Ken uses his to work on projects that are too tall for the workbench but too short for the floor, such as cabinets that need finishing. They can also be used as mini scaffolding for working overhead. OK for now, Ken, but if mini collapsibles hit the market, all bets are off. Your horses will be belly up.

TOP
2x6 OR DECK BOARD

32"

30"

SPLINE
2x4

15° BEVEL

GUSSET
1/4" PLYWOOD
(SCRIBE TO FIT)

LEGS
1x4

16"

15° BEVEL

Cloning saw ponies

To build your own ponies, you'll need an 8-ft. length of 1x4, 3 ft. of 2x4, a 3-ft.-long chunk of either 1-in.-thick decking or 2x6, and a few scraps of just about any plywood. Shown is 1/4-in. plywood, but you can use 1/2-in. or any other thickness you have lying around. Then:

1 Cut all the boards to length, including parallel 15-degree bevels on the ends of the legs.

2 Rip the 2x4 edges on the spine to 15 degrees on the table saw. Screw the top to the spine with equal overhangs at all four sides, then screw the legs to the top.

3 Scribe the ends of the plywood gussets and staple, nail or screw and glue them to the legs.

4 Saddle up and ride into the sunset.

LONG-LASTING OUTDOOR FURNITURE

Any wood resting on the ground will rot, especially if it's end grain. That's because water wicks up into the same channels the tree used to transport water. So whenever I build outdoor furniture, I do two things: First I seal the end grain with Titebond III (or any other waterproof woodworking glue). And if the legs are resting on masonry, I pound in plastic furniture buttons ($3 per set at home centers). That keeps the wood slightly elevated so it won't be sitting in puddles.

FURNITURE
BUTTON

EXTERIOR
WOOD GLUE

ShopRat

KNOW WHERE TO STOP

This used to puzzle me. When you're making a blind rip or dado that has to stop in the middle of a board, how do you know when to stop sawing? I figured it out a couple of months ago and it's easy. Push the fence aside so the wood just fits between the fence and the blade. Place the wood so the end of the cut exactly matches the point where the blade emerges from the throat plate. Then clamp a stop block to the fence at the end of the board. Slide the fence over to the proper rip width and make the cut. The stop will automatically end the cut at precisely the right place. If you have a rip that's longer than the fence, just clamp a temporary extender to the fence.

This tip isn't just for ripping thick stock. It also works when you're ripping plywood or any other thin material and you need to stop the cut on the underside where the blade isn't visible. I've also used this tip to cut rabbets in the edges of boards in cases where the rabbet doesn't continue all the way from end to end.

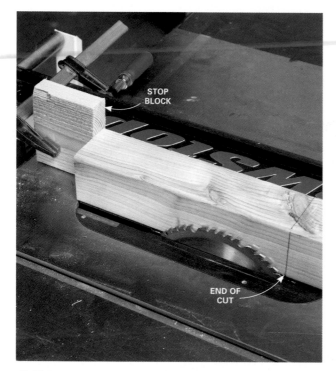

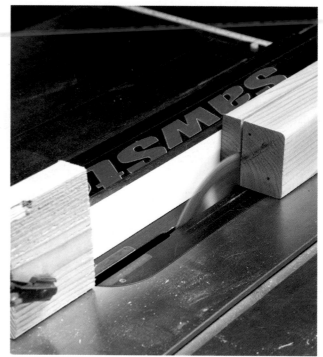

1 Slide the fence over so you can place your board next to the blade, and place the board where the blade meets the end of the cut. Clamp a stop on the fence at the end of the board.

2 Readjust the fence to rip exactly where you want it on the board and make your first cut. Turn off the saw, flip the board over and readjust the fence to complete the cut.

DON'T SKIP THE SEALER!

Finishing bare wood with a clear coat can be daunting. There's a lot that can go wrong, but laying down a sealer first will give you better results. Stephen Evans' favorite sealer is clear shellac because it can be used under just about any clear finish. Penetrating deep into the wood fibers, it improves topcoat adhesion, flattens out the surface and improves the "depth" of the final finish. Brush or spray it on, allow it to dry and then lightly sand with 320-grit sandpaper before applying topcoats. A single coat is enough. This coat isn't meant to be heavy, so don't be tempted to build another layer. Too much sealer can cause problems.

FLAT SCREEN TV BOOKCASE

Traditional style designed for high-tech entertainment

by **Dave Munkittrick**

FOOTBALL IMAGE: ©WISCONSINART1DREAMSTIME.COM

Although bookcases and entertainment centers have been my bread and butter for the past 30 years, this is my first bookcase and entertainment center in one. Until recently, it was hard to pack a high-quality sound system into a traditional bookcase. Today's smaller systems finally let me combine big sight and sound with classic design.

You don't need a huge shop or industrial equipment to build this bookcase. I'll show you how to cut and machine plywood perfectly without a pro-grade table saw. If your shop has enough open space to lay a sheet of plywood on sawhorses, then it's big enough for this project. Plus, you won't have to wrestle full sheets of plywood across the table saw. If you've been thinking about buying a new router, now is the time—this project will give it a good workout.

This bookcase will accommodate most 42-in. flat screen TVs, but not all. So make sure to measure your TV before you build. The total materials bill for my entertainment center—built from cherry—was about $1,250. Using less costly wood, such as oak, would cut the cost by about $400. My building method requires four different router bits. If you don't already own them, expect to spend $170.

WOODWORKING & WORKSHOP PROJECTS & TIPS

Meet a pro
DAVID MUNKITTRICK
Dave is an airline pilot turned professional woodworker. His workplace is a pig barn he turned into a woodshop.

1 Rough-cut the plywood. Keep the saw blade at least 1/8 in. from the cutting line so you can trim the plywood to final size later. Don't cut the cabinet sides apart until you've cut the dadoes (Photo 3).

Slice up the plywood

I like to rough-cut plywood with a circular saw and then clean up the cuts with a router. That gives me perfectly smooth, straight, splinter-free cuts and lets me skip the struggle of steering full sheets across the table saw.

Mark out your cuts following the cutting diagram on p. 132, then rough-cut (**Photo 1**). Keep the rough cuts at least 1/8 in. from the cutting line. Don't worry about getting a perfectly

Tip Trim 1/2 in. off the plywood's factory edges to remove nicks and dents from handling.

square cut at this point—close counts. Be sure to keep the pairs of parts A, D, B and E together so you can dado them in one pass (**Photo 3**) and later cut them apart. Don't forget to leave a little extra width on these grouped sections to accommodate saw cuts.

Finish the rough cuts with a router and a pattern bit (**Photo 2**). Set the straightedge against the line, clamp and rout. For shorter pieces such as shelves, I rough-cut with

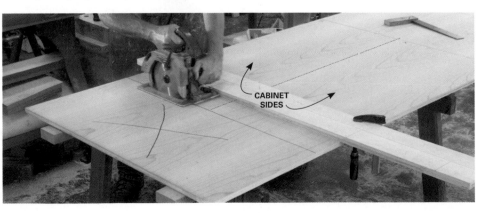

CABINET SIDES

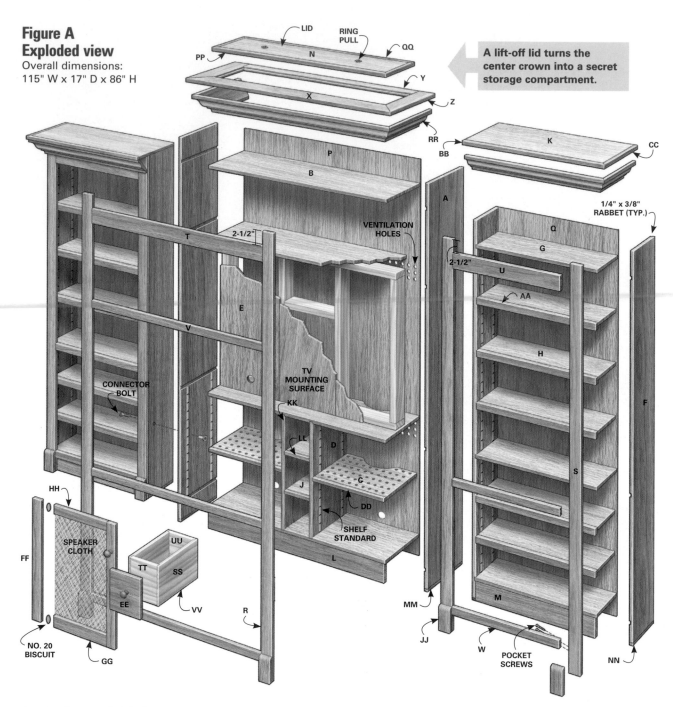

Figure A
Exploded view
Overall dimensions:
115" W x 17" D x 86" H

LID

RING PULL

PP

N

QQ

A lift-off lid turns the center crown into a secret storage compartment.

Y

X

Z

RR

BB

K

CC

P

B

A

1/4" x 3/8" RABBET (TYP.)

VENTILATION HOLES

2-1/2"

Q

G

2-1/2"

U

AA

E

V

H

TV MOUNTING SURFACE

CONNECTOR BOLT

KK

LL

D

J

C

S

DD

SHELF STANDARD

HH

F

SPEAKER CLOTH

UU

FF

TT

SS

M

EE

VV

R

L

MM

W

NN

NO. 20 BISCUIT

GG

JJ

POCKET SCREWS

the circular saw, finish the cut on one end with the router, then cut to final length on the table saw.

Cut the dadoes

Plywood has a good side and a not-so-good side. Keep this in mind when you lay out your dadoes. You want the best face turned toward the outside of the cabinets.

Lay out the dadoes using a square and a straightedge. Be sure to mark an "X" or two alongside the line where the dado goes. If you forget to do this, I guarantee you'll eventually run a dado on the wrong side of the line. Believe me, I've been there.

You can cut the dadoes with a standard 3/4-in. bit,

but I like to use a special 23/32-in. "plywood" bit, which matches the actual thickness of so-called 3/4-in. plywood. You'll need to add a bearing and stop collar to a plywood bit. Unfortunately, a 3/4-in. bearing is as close as you can get to the 23/32-in. plywood bit. This creates a tiny, 1/64-in. offset, an amount so slight I ignore it. My measurements for shelf placement are not that critical.

Cut dadoes in the bookcase sides and the two dividers (**Photo 3**). Then split the paired parts by ripping them on the table saw. Before doing any other machining, dry-fit the lower half of the center bookcase (including the dividers, drawer runners, middle and bottom shelves and sides) to make sure all your pieces fit properly. This is a good

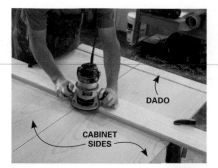

2 Trim rough edges smooth. Clean up the saw cuts with a pattern bit and a straightedge. Take your time to position the straightedge for a perfectly square cut.

PATTERN BIT

3 Dado two sides at once. Cut the shelf dadoes with a plywood bit, which matches the thickness of the plywood. Then cut the cabinet sides apart to get perfectly matched dadoes.

PLYWOOD BIT

4 Rabbet the back edges. Cut the rabbets for the backs with a rabbeting bit. There's no need for a straightedge here; the bearing rides right on the plywood edge.

RABBETING BIT

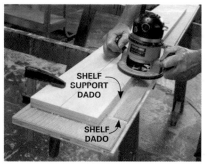

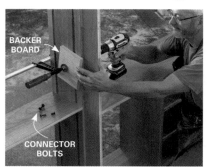

5 Cut grooves for the shelf supports. Rout shallow dadoes with a mortising bit. Center the bit in the shelf dado before you turn on the router. Shelf standards recessed in a dado look neater than surface-mounted standards.

MORTISING BIT

6 Start your finish. Finishing the insides of the cabinets is a lot easier before assembly. Keep the polyurethane off the surfaces that will be glued later. Glue won't stick to poly.

7 Bolt the cabinets together. Clamp the cabinets together and drill holes for the connector bolts. Be sure the backs line up flush and use a backer board to prevent blowout where the bit exits.

CONNECTOR BOLTS

time to cut the edging for the drawer runners and dividers. Glue and clamp these while the lower half is dry-fitted together. After the glue has set, disassemble and sand the hardwood edges flush to the veneer.

Next, cut 1/4-in. x 3/8-in. rabbets in the bookcase sides (**Photo 4**). These grooves create a recess for the 1/4-in. plywood backs. Finally, cut the shelf standard slots with a router and a 5/8-in. top-bearing mortise bit (**Photo 5**). I like to use a router rather than a dado blade in my table saw. It's a lot harder to get a consistent groove depth on a table saw because you're forced to keep a long bookcase side flat on the table while feeding it over the dado blade.

Glue hardwood skids onto the bottom edge of each bookcase side and toe board. The skids protect the delicate veneer from catching and tearing when the cabinets are moved. Sand the edging flush.

Prefinish to save time

Cherry is hard to stain evenly, so I skipped the stain and finished the bookcase with three coats of oil-based poly.

Apply all but the final coat on the interior (**Photo 6**). Prefinishing lets you work on flat horizontal surfaces. It's much easier than brushing into the back of a cabinet with all those corners or working on the underside of a shelf. Best of all, it prevents sags and drips.

Use painter's tape to line the dadoes and tape off the front edge where the face frame attaches. Brush on two coats of poly, sanding between coats. When you sand the second coat, skip the underside of the fixed shelves. These nonwear areas need only two coats.

The dry fit

Now it's time to dry-fit the entire bookcase. The dry fit is a dress rehearsal. It lets you discover problems, work out clamping strategies and avoid disasters. (It's no coincidence that "glue-up" rhymes with "screw-up.") Start from the inside of the big cabinet with the drawer runners and dividers. Add the shelves on the top and bottom of the

8 **Air out your door parts.** A couple of days of air circulation allows fresh-cut wood to stabilize. If any of the parts warp, you can cut new parts and avoid door warp after assembly.

9 **Gang-drill the vent holes.** Stack up the shelves that will hold your electronics and tack them together with a couple of nails. Set a backer board under the stack to reduce blowout. Also cut notches for cords and cables.

CABLE NOTCH

BACKER BOARD

For the face frames, a little warp is OK since the cabinets will hold them flat. The center cap uses wide stock, but in the end, the crown covers most of it and the upper face is above eye level. That means it's OK to use some less desirable wood with knots and other defects. Try to cut the drawer fronts from a single plank of wood so the grain matches.

Put it all together

Disassemble the cabinets and get ready for the big glue-up (**Photo 10**). For big jobs like this, I always use slow-setting glue. The extra 10 minutes of open time takes some of the pressure off complex glue-ups.

Assemble the bookcases and attach the face frames with glue. Rout and sand the face frames flush to the cabinet sides. Sand all unfinished parts to 180-grit.

Now you're ready to fit the cap parts and install the crown. First, you need to bolt the three cabinets together. If you don't have that kind of shop space, do one set at a time.

Align and mount the caps using countersunk screws to fasten them down. The caps have an even 3-in. overhang on the exposed sides of the cabinets. The caps on the side cabinets butt squarely into the side of the center cabinet.

Add lid stops along the bottom of the inside edge of the center cap. The stops will keep the lid from falling into the open-

dividers and work your way out. Use screws wherever an adjoining cabinet will later hide them. Screws are easier and faster than clamps.

Once all three cabinets are dry-fitted, stand them up and clamp them together, making sure the backs line up flush. Bore the holes for the connector bolts (**Photo 7**). I used four bolts along the front edges and two in the back.

The hardwood parts

With the cabinets together, you can cut and fit the other cabinet parts, such as adjustable shelves, drawer and door parts, and the plywood caps. Double-check to make sure the cut parts fit properly on the assembled bookcases.

Before you start cutting up the hardwood, sort through the boards. Set aside straight-grained pieces for door frames and face frames. On narrow parts, straight grain looks the best and is more stable. You may need to harvest the straight-grained edges from several boards to get the wood you want. For the doors, look for boards with straight grain that are free of warp. Also let them stabilize for a couple of days (**Photo 8**).

10 **Put it all together.** Assemble in stages. Start with the plywood cabinet boxes. When the glue has dried, add the face frames. Use 2x4 "cauls" to apply even clamping pressure to the face frames.

CAUL

FACE FRAME

SHIM

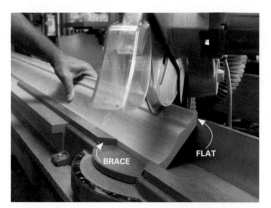

11 **Brace the crown upside down.** Position the crown molding with the bottom edge up. Add bracing to the saw's table to hold the crown at the correct angle. The flats on the back of the crown should sit flat against the fence and table.

12 **Add speaker cloth to the doors.** Pull the cloth tight across the opening and pin it into place with 1/4-in. x 1/4-in. cleats cut to fit the rabbet. Trim away the excess cloth with a utility razor blade.

ing. Cut and fit the plywood lid for the top compartment. Mount the ring pull hardware to the lid.

Cut the crown molding (**Photo 11**). Give yourself extra length for test cuts. Add braces to your saw table to hold the crown in the same position as on the bookcase and to keep the molding from sliding as it's cut. Attach the crown with brad nails and molding glue. The heavy-bodied glue won't run or drip as you hold the crown in place for nailing. Sand the crown smooth.

Cut the door parts to finished dimensions and assemble with biscuits. Rout a rabbet on the back of the opening. Use a wide chisel to square the inside corners. Drill holes for Euro hinges and mount the doors in the openings. Check for fit and even margins. Trim as necessary. Sand the door frames to 180-grit.

Assemble a 2x4 frame inside the TV opening. The setback of the frame depends on the depth of your TV and the mounting hardware you choose. Cover the frame with three panels. Use screws to fasten the middle panel. That makes it a removable access for wiring.

Cut and fit the drawer fronts. I use shims to position the drawer fronts, then pin-nail them to the boxes. Next, I pull the drawer out and clamp the front to the box for added security while I drill pilot holes from inside the box. Fasten the fronts with four No. 8 x 1-in. screws.

Finishing up

Remove the connector bolts and separate the cabinets. Remove the doors as well. Finish the bookcases with three coats of polyurethane. Give the interior its final coat when you brush on the exterior's third coat.

Mount the shelf standards. The standards have a numbering system to help in locating the clips. Be sure you mount the standards so the numbers rise as the standards run up the cabinet. I hold the nails with needle-nose pliers to get them started.

Take the finished doors and cut speaker cloth to fit over the opening with at least an inch of overhang. Press cherry cleats into place, pulling the cloth taut before you brad nail the cleats into place (**Photo 12**).

Mounting your TV

TVs typically can use almost any mount, but be sure your set is not an exception. Check the owner's manual for specific mounting bracket recommendations. Be sure to buy a mounting bracket rated to hold the weight and dimension of your TV. Mount your TV so the screen is slightly behind the face frame. Avoid the tunnel effect caused by setting the TV too far back. 🏠

SHOPPING LIST

ITEM	QTY.
4' x 8' x 3/4" cherry plywood	5
4' x 8' x 1/4" cherry plywood	3
4' x 8' x 1/2" multi-ply birch plywood	1/4
Cherry hardwood (board feet)	35

HARDWARE

Lee Valley Hardware, (800) 267-8735; leevalley.com

Cast steel classic knobs, No. 01W4704	5
3/4" router bearing, 1/2" I.D., No. 16J95.09	1
Bearing lock ring, 1/2" I.D., No. 16J96.08	1

Woodworker's Hardware, (800) 383-0130; wwhardware.com

24" brown KV0255 steel standards	16
48" brown KV0255 steel standards	8
KV0256 WAL brown shelf clips (bags of 20)	3
KV0255 81N BR brown nails (bags of 50)	2
B175H5030.21 mounting plates	4
B071T5650 BLUM cup hinges	4

Rockler Hardware, (800) 279-4441, rockler.com

Speaker cloth (36" x 68")	1
1/4" shank rabbeting bit set (includes bearings for 5/16", 3/8", 7/16" and 1/2" rabbets); No. 91584	1
23/32" mortising (plywood) bit, No. 30963	1
Pattern flush-trim router bit, 3/4" diameter x 1-1/4" height, 1/2" shank, No. 21046	1

Woodworker's Supply, (800) 645-9292, woodworker.com

5/8" x 3/4" top-bearing mortise bit, 1/4" shank, No. 129-140	1

BOOKCASE CUTTING LIST

3/4" CHERRY PLYWOOD (5 SHEETS)

PART	QTY.	DIMENSIONS	NAME
A	2	13-1/4" x 85-1/4"	sides
B	4	13" x 47"	fixed shelves
C	3	12-1/2" x 19-1/8"	component shelves
D	2	12-1/2" x 25"	dividers; add 1/2" edge
E	3	15-1/2" x 33"	TV mount panels
F	4	9-1/4" x 77-3/4"	sides
G	6	9" x 29"	fixed shelves
H	10	7-1/2" x 28-3/8"	adjustable shelves; add 1-1/4" edges front/back
J	2	7" x 12-1/2"	drawer runners; add 1/2" edge
K	2	12-1/4" x 32-1/4"	cap; add 3/4" edges to front side
L	1	4" x 46-1/2"	toe board; add 1/2" on bottom edge
M	2	4" x 28-1/2"	toe board; add 1/2" on bottom edge
N	1	10" x 45"	lid; add 1/2" edging

1/4" CHERRY PLYWOOD (3 SHEETS)

PART	QTY.	DIMENSIONS	NAME
P	1	47-1/4" x 85-3/4"	back
Q	2	29-1/4" x 78-1/4"	backs

3/4" CHERRY HARDWOOD

PART	QTY.	DIMENSIONS	NAME
R	2	2-1/2" x 85-1/4"	stiles; cut to 2-9/16" and trim flush to cabinet
S	4	2-1/2" x 77-3/4"	stiles; cut to 2-9/16" and trim flush to cabinet
T	1	3-1/2" x 43"	top rail
U	2	3-1/2" x 25"	top rails
V	3	1-1/2" x 43"	rails
W	4	1-1/2" x 25"	middle and bottom rails
X	1	4" x 54"	front of cap frame
Y	1	2" x 46"	back of cap frame
Z	2	4" x 17"	sides of cap frame
AA	20	1-1/4" x 28-3/8"	edging for adjustable shelf
BB	2	3/4" x 33"	front trim on cap
CC	2	3/4" x 13"	side trim on cap
DD	3	3/4" x 19-1/8"	component shelf trim
EE	3	7-1/4" x 7-3/4"	drawer fronts
FF	4	2" x 23-3/4"	door stiles
GG	2	2-1/2" x 13-7/8"	bottom door rail
HH	2	2" x 13-7/8"	top door rail

1/2" CHERRY HARDWOOD

PART	QTY.	DIMENSIONS	NAME
JJ	6	2-1/2" x 5"	plinth blocks
KK	2	3/4" x 25"	divider edge
LL	3	3/4" x 6-1/2"	drawer runner edge
MM	2	3/4" x 13-1/4"	skid
NN	4	3/4" x 9-1/4"	skid
PP	2	3/4" x 46"	lid trim
QQ	2	3/4" x 10"	lid trim

CROWN MOLDING

PART	QTY.	DIMENSIONS	NAME
RR	1	4" x 18'	cut to length for front and sides

1/2" BALTIC BIRCH PLYWWOD

PART	QTY.	DIMENSIONS	NAME
SS	6	7-3/8" x 12-1/2"	drawer sides
TT	3	7-3/8" x 6"	drawer fronts
UU	3	6-7/8" x 6"	drawer backs

1/4" BALTIC BIRCH PLYWOOD (COULD USE LEFTOVER CHERRY PLYWOOD)

PART	QTY.	DIMENSIONS	NAME
VV	3	5-15/16" x 12"	drawer bottoms

Figure B
Dado layout

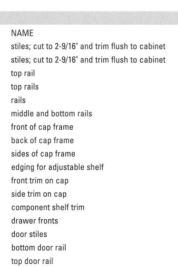

Figure C
Cutting diagrams
(FOR 3/4" PLYWOOD)

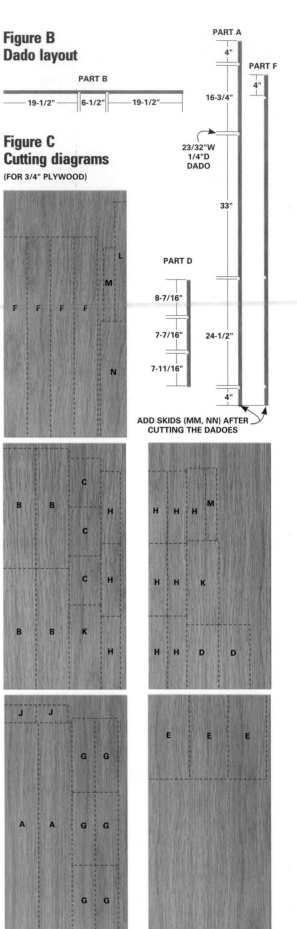

3-TIER
BASKET STAND

An amazingly versatile storage stand, made with an amazingly versatile tool

by Spike Carlsen

You've seen chests of drawers—well, here's a "chest of baskets." It can be used in nearly any room—in the bathroom for storing towels, the entryway for organizing hats and gloves, the bedroom for workout clothes, even in the kitchen for veggies or hand towels.

The total materials bill for our pine stand, including the baskets, was about $50. We bought baskets at a Michaels craft store, but lots of other retailers like Pier 1, West Elm and IKEA also carry them. Make sure to buy your baskets first; you need to construct the stand based on their dimensions.

To keep the frame of the stand both lightweight and strong, we used biscuit joinery. It's a clever way to join wood, and a technique you can use with many other projects. See p. 135 for biscuit joiner tips.

WOODWORKING & WORKSHOP PROJECTS & TIPS

FLAT SCREEN TV BOOKCASE; 3-TIER BASKET STAND   **133**

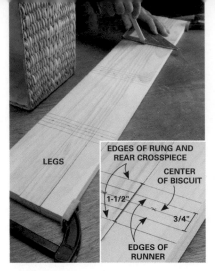

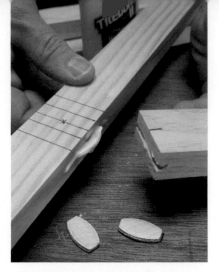

1 **Mark the legs.** Clamp the legs together and mark them all at the same time. That way, all your marks will line up and you'll avoid mismatches.

2 **Cut the biscuit slots.** Cut slots in the ends of the rungs and sides of the legs. Assemble each ladder in a "dry run" to make sure they fit together correctly.

3 **Assemble the "ladders."** Join the rungs to the legs with glue and biscuits, then clamp the ladders together. Work fast! You have to assemble eight joints before the glue begins to set.

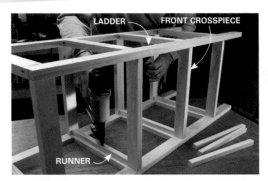

4 **Connect the ladders.** Install the front and back crosspieces with glue and nails. Then add the runners that support the baskets.

5 **Top it off.** Glue and nail the plywood top to the top of the stand, then apply cove molding to neaten up and hide the edges.

HOW TO BUILD IT

Here's the basic process:

You'll start by building the two "ladders" that form the sides of the stand, then glue and nail the crosspieces to join the two ladders.

To get started, cut all the parts to length (see Cutting List, below). Mark the rung and crosspiece locations on the legs. Mark all four legs at the same time to ensure the framework is uniform and square (Photo 1).

As you mark the legs, keep picturing how your baskets will sit on the runners, especially if you're using baskets smaller or larger than ours; it will help you avoid mental errors. Use the biscuit joiner to cut slots in the edges of the legs and ends of the rungs (Photo 2). You'll need to clip the biscuits to suit the 1-1/2-in.-wide legs and rungs (see "Biscuit Tips," p. 135).

Apply glue to the biscuits and slots (Photo 3) and assemble each joint. Clamp the ladders together and set them aside until the glue dries.

Join the two ladders by gluing and nailing the crosspieces between them. Remember that the three front crosspieces that will support the baskets lie flat. Next, install the basket runners (Photo 4) even with the flat crosspieces that run across the front. Glue and nail the 3/4-in. plywood top to the stand, then apply cove molding to cover the edges (Photo 5).

CUTTING LIST

KEY	QTY.	SIZE & DESCRIPTION	KEY	QTY.	SIZE & DESCRIPTION	KEY	QTY.	SIZE & DESCRIPTION
A	4	3/4" x 1-1/2" x 36" legs	E	1	3/4" x 13" x 13-3/4" top	N	2	3/4" x 3-1/2" x 29-1/4" maple (rear top shelf supports)
B	8	3/4" x 1-1/2" x 10" rungs	F	4	3/4" cove molding (cut to fit)	P	1	3/4" x 1-1/2" x 72" maple (top shelf edge)
C	8	3/4" x 1-1/2" x 12-1/4" crosspieces	M	2	3/4" x 3-1/2" x 24" maple (side top shelf supports—not shown)	Q	1	3/4" x 1-1/2" x 15-3/4" maple (top trim)
D	6	3/4" x 3/4" x 10-3/4" runners						

Figure A: Basket stand

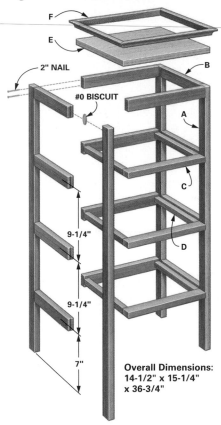

F
E
2" NAIL
#0 BISCUIT
B
A
C
D

9-1/4"

9-1/4"

7"

Overall Dimensions:
14-1/2" x 15-1/4"
x 36-3/4"

Biscuit tips

A biscuit joiner is a superb tool for joining wood where it would be difficult to use nails or screws. The joint is strong, invisible and easy to create. The compressed wood biscuits expand on contact with moisture in the glue. Since the biscuits are placed in slots that are wider than the biscuit, you can adjust the joint a little after butting the two pieces together. Biscuits come in three common sizes: No. 0, No. 10 and No. 20. Whether you're building this basket stand or some other biscuit project, here are some of our favorite biscuit tips:

Clip biscuits for narrow stock
The smallest common biscuits (No. 0) are almost 1-7/8 in. long. That's too long for the 1-1/2-in.-wide parts on this basket stand. But there's an easy solution: Just clip about 1/4 in. off both ends of each biscuit. Your slots will still be too long and visible at inside corners, but a little filler and finish will hide them.

Number the joints
While you're marking the center lines of each biscuit slot, also number each joint. That will eliminate confusion and misalignments during assembly.

Make a glue injector
Spreading a neat, even bead of glue inside a biscuit slot ain't easy. You can buy special injectors online, or make your own using the cap from a marker and a fine-tooth saw.

Always do a dry run
Biscuits grab fast. During glue-up, you don't have time to correct mistakes or dig up a longer set of clamps. So always test the whole assembly—including clamps—before you get out the glue. For complicated assemblies, give yourself more working time by using slow-setting wood glue. Titebond Extend is one brand.

MATERIALS LIST

Here's what we used to make this basket stand: 30 ft. of 1x2, 6 ft. of 3/4-in. x 3/4-in. square dowel, 6 ft. of 3/4-in. cove molding, 3/4-in. plywood, 12 x 12 x 8-in. baskets, No. 0 biscuits, wood glue, 2-in. finish nails, Watco cherry finish.

GreatGoofs®

Screwing up in the driveway

I decided the driveway was a perfect spot to lay out the pieces for the simple collapsible miter saw table I was building. This was such an easy project...my 10-year-old could have done it! All I needed was 2x4s, hinges and two different lengths of screws—1-in. screws to attach the hinges to the single 2x4 and 2-1/2-in. screws to attach two 2x4s. The assembly zipped right along, and after finishing the main section of the table, I stood back to admire my work. It looked perfect. But when I bent down to lift it off the driveway, it wouldn't budge. No matter how hard I pulled, it was stuck fast! Turns out I'd used the longer screws for the hinges, and they had bored straight down through the 2x4 and into the asphalt. I guess I should have let my 10-year-old build the rack after all.

WOODWORKING & WORKSHOP
PROJECTS & TIPS

Handy Hints®

UTILITY KNIFE BLADE I.D.

It's not always easy to tell which side of your utility knife blade has already been used. Skip the guesswork with this simple tip. Before you refill the spare blades in your utility knife, mark the sides of each blade with a "1" and a "2." When it's time to replace the blade, use the No. 1 side first. When the blade becomes dull, flip it to the No. 2 side. When that gets dull, toss out the blade and start over.

HOMEMADE DRYING RACK

I had about 30 fiber cement siding panels to paint, but I didn't have a lot of room in my shop for them to dry. I solved the problem by attaching a piece of wire shelving to some plywood supports. The entire 160 sq. ft. of panels took up only 12 sq. ft. of floor space and dried very nicely. I used the same idea with some deck boards. Since the boards were thicker, I removed every other wire so they'd get enough airflow to dry properly. It worked great!

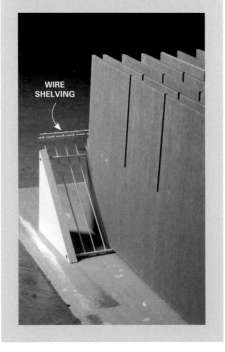

WIRE SHELVING

HOOK-AND-LOOP TAPE

SHOP CUP DISPENSER

Small paper cups are handy in the shop for holding or mixing small amounts of wood glue, two-part epoxy, spray paint and the like. This simple homemade paper cup dispenser works great. Measure the diameter of the cups and attach a short length of the same diameter PVC pipe to your wall with hook-and-loop tape. If the cups sit too loosely in the dispenser, just add a bead of silicone inside the bottom lip to keep them tight.

MARK HARDY

MINI CLIP CLAMPS

When you're gluing thin items together, use binder clips (they're also called "Bulldog" or "Bankers" clips) to keep them in place. The clips come in a variety of sizes at any office supply store and they're inexpensive replacements for C-clamps or bigger spring clamps.

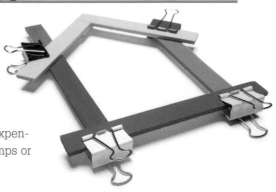

COMFORTABLE SAWHORSE WORKTABLE

After a back injury, I needed a higher worktable so I could sit and work more comfortably. I came up with a solution that's easy on the back and easy to make. Measure how much higher than your sawhorses you want your work surface to be. Cut notches in your four table legs at that height and screw them to the sides of your sawhorses. Set a sheet of plywood on top, and you're all set.

SQUEAKY CHAIR TOURNIQUET

Our dining room chairs creaked and moaned whenever we leaned back in them. I decided to reglue the joints to tighten things up, but I didn't have long enough strap clamps to wrap around the legs while the glue set. Using a tip from my dad, I wrapped thin rope around the chair, tied the end to a stick and twisted the stick until the rope was tight. Then I taped the stick in place and let the glue dry overnight. No more creaks or moans during dinner (from the chairs, anyway).

MARK HARDY

GreatGoofs®

Cutting-edge customer service

A few years ago, my dad decided to replace the vinyl floor tile in the basement. The tiles came up easily, but he couldn't scrape the adhesive residue off the concrete, so he ran to the home center and brought home a slick new razor scraper. But even with the new scraper it was slow going, and I could hear him complaining all morning about how the "@#%$ scraper" didn't work. By lunchtime, he was fed up. He told me to get in the car, and as we drove to the store to return the scraper, he told me to watch carefully and I'd "learn a lesson about how to deal with this kind of situation." My dad stomped over to the service desk, yelled at the poor teenage girl standing there and handed her the piece of junk. She took one look at the blade, clicked the built-in release, turned the blade around to expose the actual razor edge, which had been covered for safety, and cheerfully handed it back. My dad said nothing, but I sure learned a lesson—just not the one he'd intended.

BOMB-PROOF
WOODWORKING
BENCH
World-class workbench in a weekend

by **Dave Munkittrick**

IT DOES IT ALL!

« HOLD LONG STOCK! Clamp one end in the face vise; hold the other end with a pipe clamp under the bench top.

POUND AWAY! » The 2-1/4-in.-thick solid maple top will never flinch.

« SECURE BIG STUFF! An easy-to-build bench jack supports large work.

KEEP IT FLAT! » A dead-flat top keeps your glue-ups flat and true.

« HOLD STOCK! The centuries-old bench dog design secures work for machining.

WOODWORKING & WORKSHOP PROJECTS & TIPS

If you're looking for a "real" woodworking bench but don't want to spend a year and a thousand bucks building one, here's a great design for you. It'll grow with you as your skills improve; it's flat and solid enough to help you do your best work; and it's sturdy enough that you can proudly pass it on to your grandchildren. One weekend and the simplest of tools are all you need to build it.

Time-tested features

This bench includes the signature features of a traditional woodworking bench: a thick, flat top designed to take a pounding; a tail vise and a face vise, mounted one at each end, for securing stock; and an overhanging top that allows you to clamp stock to the edges.

I eliminated the traditional tool tray because it's more of a housekeeping hassle than an effective place to keep tools. Leaving it off gives you a larger work surface. And since most of us are short on workshop space, I added a cabinet base for storage. The sliding doors are a cinch to make and mount, and they keep the contents free of sawdust.

The base is made from inexpensive 2x4s and plywood.

The torsion box legs provide incredibly strong support and a place to mount trays and hooks to hold bench brushes, electrical cords and tools.

What it costs

You can spend as little as $250 if you mount only one vise (you can add the second later) and you make the top yourself (see "3 Top Options" at left). If you go all out like I did with two vises and a massive solid maple top, your cost will be closer to $800. The 2-1/4-in.-thick maple top I used comes prefinished from Grizzly Industrial. It cost $385 plus shipping. All you have to do is drill the dog holes, mount the vises and you're done. Grizzly also sells 1-3/4-in.-thick tops for $250, but if you go this route, you'll need to put spacer blocks under the vises so they fit properly. You can buy unplaned maple for about half the cost of these tops, but you'll face many hours of surfacing, gluing and finishing—and getting the top dead-flat is tough, even for an expert.

3 top options

We used a ready-made, prefinished maple slab from Grizzly Industrial. The 2-1/4-in.-thick top cost $385 plus shipping. It's very flat and stable. You could also use a 1-3/4-in.-thick Grizzly top ($250).

You can make a top from three sheets of 3/4-in. plywood. Cut them oversize, then glue and screw two of them together and then add the third. Use plenty of screws; they can be removed after the glue is dry. This top probably won't be perfectly flat. Cost: $100.

Use a solid-core exterior door. You can find them wherever recycled building materials are available or buy one at a home center. If you add 1/2-in. plywood as a wear surface, you'll have a 2-1/4-in.-thick top. It should be very flat and stable. Cost: $20 to $50.

1 Build the torsion box legs. Assemble a 2x2 frame with screws. Be sure the joints are flush. Run a heavy bead of wood glue, then screw or nail the plywood skin so all edges are flush.

2 Attach the back. Screw the back to the shelves and legs. It's best to paint the plywood surfaces before final assembly.

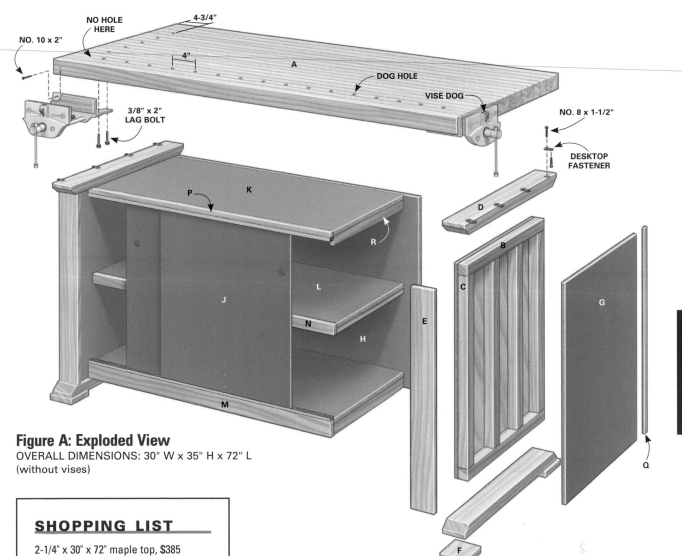

Figure A: Exploded View
OVERALL DIMENSIONS: 30" W x 35" H x 72" L
(without vises)

NO. 10 x 2"

NO HOLE
HERE

4-3/4"

4"

A

DOG HOLE

VISE DOG

NO. 8 x 1-1/2"

3/8" x 2"
LAG BOLT

DESKTOP
FASTENER

P

K

R

D

B

C

E

G

J

L

N

H

Q

M

F

SHOPPING LIST

2-1/4" x 30" x 72" maple top, $385

5 bd. ft. of maple, $20

Sheet of 3/4" plywood, $38

1-1/2 sheets of 1/2" plywood, $45

1/2 sheet of 1/4" plywood, $12

Three 8' 2x4s, $8

Two 9" bench vises, $160 plus shipping

Two packs of desktop fasteners, $8

SOURCES:

Grizzly Industrial, grizzly.com,
(800) 523-4777.

2-1/4" x 30" x 72" maple top, part
No. T21250, $385 plus shipping.

Shop Fox Quick-Release Vise,
9" Jaw, part No. G9851, $80 plus
shipping.

Rockler Hardware, rockler.com,
(800) 279-4441.

Desktop fasteners, part No. 21650,
$4.40 per pack of 8.

WORKBENCH PARTS LIST

PART	QTY.	DIMENSION	MATERIAL	DESCRIPTION
A	1	2-1/4" x 30" x 72"	Maple	Top
B	4	1-1/2" x 1-1/2" x 23-1/2"	2x2	Torsion box rails
C	8	1-1/2" x 1-1/2" x 26"	2x2	Torsion box stiles
D	4	1-1/2" x 3-1/2" x 28"	2x4	Top/bottom support
E	2	3/4" x 3" x 29"	Maple/pine	Front trim
F	4	3/4" x 4" x 4"	Maple/pine	Feet
G	4	1/2" x 23-1/2" x 29"	Plywood	Torsion box sides
H	1	1/2" x 29" x 48"	Plywood	Back
J	2	1/4" x 22" x 25-1/2"	Plywood	Doors
K	2	3/4" x 20-1/4" x 43"	Plywood	Top/bottom shelf
L	1	3/4" x 19-1/4" x 43"	Plywood	Middle shelf
M	1	3/4" x 2-1/4" x 43"	Maple/pine	Bottom shelf trim
N	1	3/4" x 1" x 43"	Maple/pine	Middle shelf trim
P	1	3/4" x 3/4" x 43"	Maple/pine	Top shelf trim
Q	2	1/4" x 3/4" x 29"	Maple/pine	Side trim
R	6	3/4" x 1-1/2" x 19"	1x2	Shelf cleats

To build a bench

Building this bench couldn't be easier. The base is made with 2x4s, fir plywood and a little maple trim. Start with the torsion box legs. Torsion boxes are strong yet don't add a ton of weight, and they're super easy to make (**Photo 1**).

Cut the plywood shelves and back and the shelf cleats (K, L, H, R). Screw the base together to check the fit. Disassemble the bench and paint the pieces. It's a lot easier to paint all the plywood pieces before final assembly. After the paint's dry, attach the shelves to the legs. Cut the 2x4 supports (D). Add the feet to the bottom supports and attach them to the legs with screws. Turn the base upright and attach the back (**Photo 2**). Add the top supports and the maple trim (M, N, P, Q). The trim piece Q is glued and nailed to the exposed edge of the back. Then secure the door tracks in the cabinet opening to complete the base (**Photo 3**). Cut the doors to fit.

Now turn your attention to the top. No matter what top you use (see "3 Top Options," p. 140), the following steps are the same. Set the top on a pair of sawhorses and lay out the bench dog holes. Use a guide to drill the holes so they're square to the top (**Photo 4**). We spaced the holes on 4-in. centers, 4-3/4 in. from the edges. Skip one hole in the front left corner, where it would interfere with the vise.

Flip the top over and mount the vises (**Photo 5**). Line up the metal dog on the vise with the dog holes in the top. To protect wood that will be held in the vise, make wooden faces and attach them to the vise jaws. Use a soft wood such as basswood or pine.

Mount figure-eight or other tabletop fasteners to the top supports. They may need to rest in a shallow hole in the support. These will allow the top to expand and contract without cracking. Get someone to help you set the top onto the base, then secure with screws through the fasteners. That's it. Your bench is ready for your first furniture project! ⌂

DIY ACCESSORIES

Bench jack

The purpose of a bench jack is to support long, wide stock such as a door. To make a jack, screw together a couple of pieces of 3-in. x 36-in. pine or plywood to form a "T." Drill 3/4-in. holes in the face of the jack. Clamp the bench jack in the tail vise, and insert a dowel at the desired height (**see photo**, p. 139).

Bench dogs

Bench dogs work with the vise to hold stock on the bench surface (**see photo**, p. 139). They're easy to make. Drill a 1-in.-deep hole in 1-1/2-in. x 1-1/2-in. blocks of hardwood, then epoxy 3/4-in. dowel stock into the holes. To accommodate different stock thicknesses, cut the block to 1/4-in., 1/2-in., 3/4-in., 1-in. and 1-1/2-in. heights.

3 **Mount the door tracks.** Apply a bead of construction adhesive and clamp the door tracks in place. Cut the bottom track about 1/2 in. shorter than the opening. Center the track to leave gaps at each end so the door motion sweeps out accumulated sawdust.

4 **Drill the bench dog holes.** Fit a corded drill with a 3/4-in. drill bit and drill the dog holes. A drill guide made from a couple of plywood scraps attached at 90 degrees ensures perpendicular holes.

5 **Bolt the vise to the top.** Mount each vise so the metal jaws are slightly below the surface of the wood top. This may require some shimming. I used metal fender washers to fine-tune the vise position.

TRAVIS'S TERRIFIC
TOOL TRAY TOWER

by **Travis Larson**

BUILT-IN PULL

Because most hand tools are relatively flat, piling them in deep drawers wastes a lot of space and makes them hard to find and dig out. This rather fetching cabinet separates and organizes all those tools. Best of all, you can remove the tray containing, say, the open-end wrenches, and take the whole collection to wherever you're wrenching.

I've seen several plain versions of this design: a few drawers made from MDF with utilitarian handles. I decided to bump it up a notch and build a 10-tray unit out of cabinet-grade birch plywood. And rather than use handles, I made the tray bases with built-in "paddle pulls."

Shaping the paddle pulls is the trickiest part of the whole project. You'll get the best results by clamping the tray bottoms together and "gang-cutting" the paddle pulls all at once with a band saw. Sanding them all at once also saves lots of time and ensures that the parts are

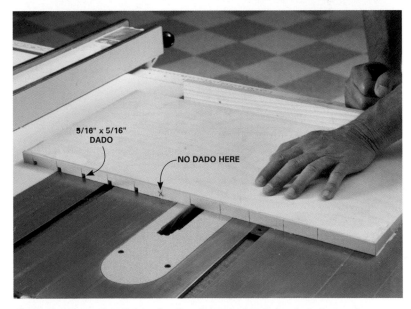

5/16" x 5/16" DADO

NO DADO HERE

1 **Mark and cut the dadoes for the drawers.** Mark the dado bottoms on the edges beginning at 13/16 in. up from the bottom and then every 2 in. Don't cut a dado in the center—that's where the stretcher goes. After cutting all 10 dadoes, cut off the top, 2-3/4 in. above the last dado bottom.

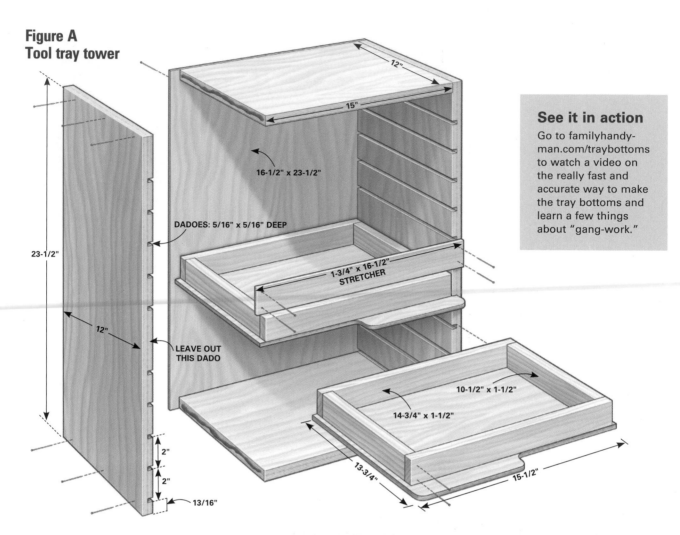

**Figure A
Tool tray tower**

12"

15"

16-1/2" x 23-1/2"

DADOES: 5/16" x 5/16" DEEP

23-1/2"

12"

LEAVE OUT
THIS DADO

1-3/4" x 16-1/2"
STRETCHER

10-1/2" x 1-1/2"

14-3/4" x 1-1/2"

13-3/4"

15-1/2"

2"

2"

13/16"

See it in action
Go to familyhandy-
man.com/traybottoms
to watch a video on
the really fast and
accurate way to make
the tray bottoms and
learn a few things
about "gang-work."

identical (**Photo 5**). (Then get the alternating paddle pulls by flipping over half of
the tray bottoms.)

If you don't have a band saw, a jigsaw will do. If you're jigsawing, mark one
paddle pull on a tray bottom and use it to
scribe and gang-cut five at a time. You can
also just skip the paddle pulls and add the
drawer pulls of your choice. To do that,
cut the tray bottoms to 15-1/2 x 12 in., but
"gang-sand" them all as shown in **Photo 5**.

This project calls for a table saw and a
dado blade. The good news is that absolutely no hardware is needed, including
fussy, expensive drawer slides to mess
around with.

This project is a real plywood eater.
You'll need a full sheet of both 1/4-in. and
3/4-in. plywood to build one. Build it with
more or fewer trays; it's up to you. If you
choose to make a wider or taller cabinet
with more trays, fine. But it'll take more
than two sheets of plywood!

SIDES

BACK

MASK GLUE
JOINTS

BOTTOM

2 Prefinish the interior surfaces. Protect the gluing areas with masking
tape and varnish surfaces on the cabinet interior. It's much easier to do
now than later. For smooth tray operation, be sure to brush out any varnish
pools or drips inside the dadoes.

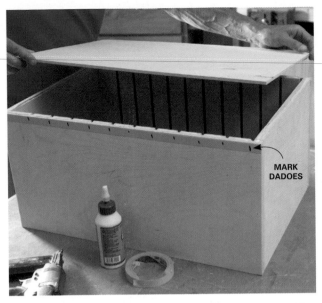

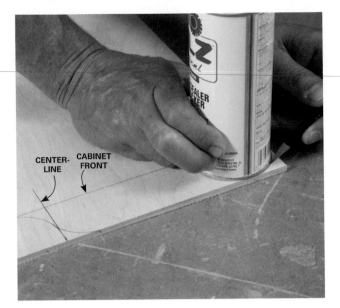

3 **Assemble the box.** Glue and nail the box together with 1-1/2-in. brads. Then mark the dadoes to avoid misses when you nail on the back with 1-in. brads. Glue the perimeter, then nail one edge flush with the box side. Square up the box with the back to nail the second side. Then finish nailing the remaining two sides.

4 Mark the paddle pulls. Cut the tray bottoms into 15-1/2 x 13-3/4-in. rectangles. Draw a line 12 in. from the back edge of the trays and mark a centerline. Use the centerline and one of the corners as a guide while you trace around a spray paint can to mark the curves. Then cut the shapes with a band saw or jigsaw.

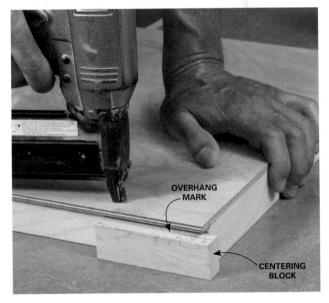

5 **Gang-sand the tray bottoms.** Clamp the tray bottoms together and sand the fronts of them all at once. Get them roughed out and then finish up with a random orbital sander. (If you have a dedicated drum sander or drum sander accessory for your drill press, use that for the inside curves.)

6 **Build the trays.** Glue and nail the tray sides together. Center one of the bottoms with equal overhangs, then mark a centering block to guide you while you glue and nail on the bottoms. You'll need to use the block on just one side for each tray.

Cut the back and sides a little oversize

Cut the 1/4-in. back first. Take a notch out of a corner of the sheet rather than ripping a whole strip or you won't have enough leftover plywood to make the drawer bases. Cut the back 1/8 in. larger than the illustration calls for. After the cabinet is assembled, you can get extremely accurate measurements and either cut the back to fit or use a flush-trim router bit after it's attached. Cut the sides a full 24 in. tall

and cut them to length after the dadoes are cut. (You don't need to cut a dado in the center where the stretcher goes. I forgot and cut one there, but it's hidden anyway.)

Gang-sand the exposed tops of the tray sides before assembly. After you get the cabinet box and trays assembled, finish sanding and apply the clear coat. A nice finishing touch is to line the tray bottoms with squares of indoor/outdoor carpeting. 🏠

Using Tools

IMPACT DRIVER 101

by **Gary Wentz**

A few years ago, cordless impact drivers were a specialty tool, rare on job sites and scarce on store shelves. Today, you'll see several models at any tool retailer and hear their machine-gun chatter wherever there's construction. When a tool gains popularity that fast, you have to wonder what's going on. And, more important, what you're missing.

To sort out the pros and cons of impact drivers, we put them in the hands of our staff editors and field editors, who are pros on the job and DIY guys at home. Here's what we learned:

Prepare for impact

Pick up a set of hex-shaft accessories for about $25 (drill bits, driver bits, socket adapters). You'll want most of that stuff sooner or later, and buying a kit will save you a few bucks. Check the label and get a set that's tough enough for impact-driver duty.

Not just for driving screws

Impact drivers make great drills. With small bits (up to 1/4 in. or so), they act like a drill—but at nearly twice the rpm of most cordless drills. With bigger bits, they kick into high-torque impact mode so you can bore a big hole with a small driver.

Loud. Really loud

An impact driver can bring a heavy-metal drummer to tears. Wear muffs or earplugs—or get fitted for a hearing aid. Your call.

One-handed driving

With a standard driver, you have to get your weight behind the screw and push hard. Otherwise, the bit will "cam out" and chew up the screw head. Not so with an impact driver. The hammer mechanism that produces torque also creates some forward pressure. That means you don't have to push so hard to avoid cam-out. Great for one-handed, stretch-and-drive situations.

It's not a hammer drill

An impact driver works kind of like a hammer drill and sounds a lot like one. But it's no substitute for a hammer drill. An impact driver's innards are engineered to generate torque, not powerful forward blows.

It's all about torque

Impact drivers have one overwhelming advantage over standard drills and drivers: enormous torque. Basically, that means you can drive a big screw (or bore a big hole) with a small driver. In this photo, we sank 3/8 x 10-in. self-drilling lag screws into cedar lumber. No pilot holes, no cheating.

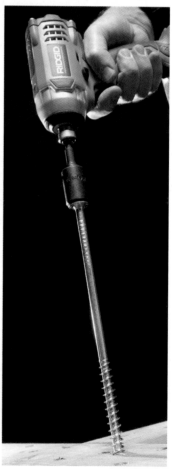

The only driver you'll ever need?

Maybe. An impact driver will handle just about any job, and some of our testers have already retired their old drivers. But when high torque isn't needed, most of us like to avoid the noise and reach for standard cordless drills or drivers instead.

Easy to handle

You might think that extreme torque puts extreme strain on your arm. Nope. For reasons Isaac Newton could explain, an impact driver actually generates less wrist twist than a standard driver. Don't be fooled by the macho-man feeling you get when you effortlessly sink a big screw. A little princess can do the same thing.

Good for gearheads, too

They don't have nearly the torque of big impact wrenches, but cordless impact drivers can be a time-saver when you tinker with engines. They're perfect for small engines, where less torque is usually enough. For automotive work, consider an "angle" version, such as the Craftsman shown on the bottom of p. 149. Hitachi, Makita, Ridgid and others also make angle impact drivers.

Small and smaller

Generally, there's a big torque difference between 12- and 18-volt models. But some of the 18-volt sluggers are amazingly compact—not much bigger than their 12-volt cousins. Big torque in a compact tool—that's why most of our testers favored the 18-volt versions.

HEX SHAFTS ONLY

The chuck on an impact driver makes for quick changes; just slide the collar forward and slip in the bit. But you'll have to buy hex-shaft drill bits. Regular bits won't work.

CONSIDER A COMBO KIT

For a few bucks more than an impact driver alone, you can add a driver, a drill or a hammer drill to your tool collection. This driver/impact driver twosome cost us just $25 more than either tool sold separately. We couldn't resist.

They look alike outside, but . . .

The difference is how they transfer torque from the motor to the chuck. On a standard drill or driver, the motor and chuck are locked together through gears; as the workload increases, the motor strains. An impact driver behaves the same under light loads. But when resistance increases, a clutch-like mechanism disengages the motor from the chuck for a split second. The motor continues to turn and builds momentum. Then the clutch re-engages with a slam, transferring momentum to the chuck. All of this happens about 50 times per second, and the result is three or four times as much torque from a similar-size tool.

Impact driver
Torque: 930 in.-lbs.

Standard driver
Torque: 265 in.-lbs.

Using Tools

IMPACT DRIVER ROUNDUP

It wasn't easy, but after weeks of testing, retesting and arguing, we settled on six favorites. The models shown here are widely available at home centers and hardware stores. If you're willing to do some hunting, you'll find several other models and manufacturers.

Our overall favorite

MILWAUKEE 2650-22
Cost: $320 (Ouch!)
Torque: 1,400 in.-lbs.
Weight: 3.5 lbs.
Battery: 18V lithium (2)

Of our 10 testers, eight gave this one the top rating. In our lag-screw races, it consistently matched or exceeded the others. In addition to raw power, it has all the features we loved: a tool-belt hook, a bright work light and a battery "fuel gauge."

Bummer: No onboard bit storage.

Dissenting opinion: The DeWalt DCF826KL is better. It has almost as much torque, but it's lighter, more compact and comfortable.

The Family Handyman EDITORS' CHOICE

Compact bargain

Hitachi WH10DFL
Cost: $115
Torque: 840 in.-lbs.
Weight: 2.2 lbs.
Battery: 12V lithium (2)

You can find a smaller and lighter driver, or more torque, or a lower price. But for a combination of all three of those traits, you can't beat this light, powerful, affordable little gem.

Cramp warning: If you have big hands or wear gloves on the job, the handle might be too short. Otherwise, it's one of the most comfortable drivers we tested.

The Family Handyman EDITORS' CHOICE

MILWAUKEE 2450-22
Cost: $120
Torque: 850 in.-lbs.
Weight: 2.3 lbs.
Battery: 12V lithium (2)

Well-made and pro grade with a tempting price tag.

PORTER-CABLE PCL120IDC-2
Cost: $140
Torque: 950 in.-lbs.
Weight: 2.6 lbs.
Battery: 12V lithium (2)

Lots of power and one of only two 12-volt drivers with a belt hook (the other is the DeWalt). Battery gauge too.

MAKITA BTD141
Cost: $280
Torque: 1,330 in.-lbs.
Weight: 3.4 lbs.
Battery: 18V lithium (2)

A great tool with ample power and a compact, comfortable design.

ROCKWELL RK2515K2
Cost: $200
Torque: 800 in.-lbs.
Weight: 3 lbs.
Battery: 12V lithium (2)

A lifetime battery warranty and two cool features: a clutch like the one on standard drivers, and adjustable impact mode.

HITACHI WH14DAF2
Cost: $145
Torque: 1060 in.-lbs.
Weight: 3.8 lbs.
Battery: 14.4V NiCad (2)

The work light is in the belt hook and operates by push button. Some testers liked it; most didn't.

RIDGID R86031
Cost: $170
Torque: 1,440 in.-lbs.
Weight: 3.5 lbs.
Battery: 18V lithium (1)

A pro-grade performer, and the lifetime battery warranty is a huge bonus.

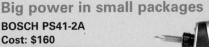

CRAFTSMAN 17428
Cost: $110
Torque: 830 in.-lbs.
Weight: 2.1 lbs.
Battery: 12V lithium (1)

A good performer at a good price. Batteries are interchangeable with other tools in Craftsman's Nextec line.

Watch for falling prices

Don't be surprised if you find lower price tags than listed here. We watched prices during a six-week period and saw prices drop on one out of every four models shown here. The discounts (sometimes sales, sometimes permanent price cuts) were in the 10 to 20 percent range.

ROCKWELL
RK2800K2
Cost: $200
Torque: 1160 in.-lbs.
Weight: 2.9 lbs.
Battery: 18V lithium (2)

Light and affordable, plus a lifetime battery warranty.

Big power in small packages

BOSCH PS41-2A
Cost: $160
Torque: 930 in.-lbs.
Weight: 2 lbs.
Battery: 12V lithium (2)

Among the 12-volt models we tried, this one takes two prizes: lightest and most compact. Plus, it's a runner-up in torque.

BONUS POINTS: Battery fuel gauge!

DEWALT DCF815S2
Cost: $160
Torque: 950 in.-lbs.
Weight: 2.3 lbs.
Battery: 12V lithium (2)

This driver tops our list for 12-volt torque. And although it's taller than most, it's lightweight and comfy.

DISSENTING OPINION: Torque—it's THE reason to have an impact driver. So these 12-volt models just don't make sense. Get an 18-volt.

Terrific torque, low prices

PORTER-CABLE PCL180IDK-2
Cost: $170
Torque: 1,600 in.-lbs.
Weight: 3.6 lbs.
Battery: 18V lithium (2)

You can't beat this combination: Top-tier torque at a price that's about $100 below most of the competition.

SKEPTICISM: Top torque rating by far, but in our tests it performed about the same as other pro-grade 18-volt models.

RYOBI P230
Cost: $100
Torque: 1,200 in.-lbs.
Weight: 4.5 lbs.
Battery: 18V NiCad (2)

Though not as powerful as most of the other 18-volt models, this driver has plenty of torque for all but the toughest jobs—and a crazy-low price tag.

CURMUDGEON'S NOTE: I wouldn't buy anything with a NiCad battery. Lithium is the only way to go.

DRILL MASTER 67028
Cost: $30 (driver, one battery, charger; each sold separately)
Torque: 850 in.-lbs.
Weight: 4.2 lbs.
Battery: 18V NiCad (1)

Unbelievable price: a fraction of the cost of any other model we tried. Available at harborfreight.com.

Makita TD090DW
Cost: $120
Torque: 800 in.-lbs.
Weight: 2 lbs.
Battery: 10.8V lithium (2)

Just 10.8 volts, but as much torque as some 12-volt models. Very light and comfortable, too.

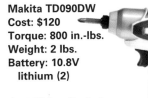

DEWALT DCF826KL
Cost: $260
Torque: 1,330 in.-lbs.
Weight: 3.1 lbs.
Battery: 18V lithium (2)

Most compact and lightweight of the 18-volt models, but it has lots of power.

CRAFTSMAN 17562
Cost: $100
Torque: 700 in.-lbs.
Weight: 3 lbs.
Battery: 12V lithium (1)

This is the only "angle" driver we tested. High torque for tight spots. The Nextec battery works with other tools. Nice price.

Using Tools
BUILD A TABLE SAW SLED

To get dead-on square cuts every time.

by Jeff Gorton

If you own a table saw, you know it works great for ripping long pieces. But did you know that you can crosscut wide pieces with the same ease and accuracy? All it takes is a table saw sled. A table saw sled rides in the miter gauge slots and has a fence that's mounted exactly 90 degrees to the blade, enabling accurate square cuts. We'll show you how to build a sled using a 42-in. square sheet of 1/2-in. plywood.

We used top-quality nine-ply birch, but any flat plywood with smooth faces will work. The tricky parts of the construction are cutting runners that slide smoothly in the tracks, and getting the fence perfectly square to the blade. We'll show you how to accomplish both as you construct the sled.

Start by cutting strips of plywood for the stiffener, front fence and blade cover (**Figure A**). Cut them 1/4 in. wider and 1/2 in. longer than the finished size to allow for trimming. Then spread wood glue on the mating faces and clamp them together. Clamp them onto a perfectly flat surface like the top of your table saw. Try to keep the layers lined up as you clamp them. After about 20 minutes, scrape off the partially hardened glue. Then run the pieces through the table saw, removing about 1/4 in. Using **Figure A** as a guide, mark the shapes onto the pieces and saw them out with a jigsaw. Smooth the curves with a belt sander.

The next step is to cut the runners from strips of hardwood. If you have standard 3/4-in.-wide miter gauge slots, sand or plane a 1x3 hardwood board until it slides easily in the slots (**Photo 1**). (For narrower slots, you'll have to plane or cut the 1x3 to reduce its thickness.) Then rip strips from the 1x3 that are about 1/16 in. thinner than the depth of the slot. **Photos 2 and 3** show how to attach the strips to the sled base. Let the glue set for about 20

CAUTION: You must remove the blade guard on your table saw to use the sled. To prevent accidents:
- Adjust the blade so that no more than 1/4 in. is exposed above the board you're sawing.
- Keep your hands well away from the path of the blade.
- After completing a cut, turn off the saw and let the blade come to a complete stop before moving the sled.

minutes. Then remove the assembly from the table saw and scrape off excess glue from the edges of the runners and bottom of the base. You'll also have to clean out any glue that has gotten into the slots on the table saw. Slide the sled back and forth in the slots. If the sled doesn't slide easily, inspect the runners for darkened areas where the metal has rubbed on the wood. Use spray adhesive to attach a piece of 80-grit sandpaper to a square-edged block of wood and sand the darkened areas to remove a little wood (**Photo 4**). Repeat this process until the sled slides freely.

FENCE BLANK

MITER GAUGE SLOT

1 Slide a hardwood board in the miter gauge slot on your table saw to check the fit. If it's too tight, sand and plane it until it slides easily with no slop. Work on this while you're waiting for the glue to set up on the fence blank (about a half hour).

SHOPPING LIST

ITEM	QTY.
42" x 42" x 1/2" plywood	1
3/4" x 2-1/2" x 3' hardwood board	1
1-1/2" screws	11
3" screws	4
2" carriage bolts and nuts (for stop block)	2
Wood glue	

CUTTING LIST

KEY	PCS.	SIZE & DESCRIPTION
A	1	32" x 24" x 1/2" base
B	2	24" x 4" x 1/2" stiffener
C	3	32" x 4" x 1/2" fence
D	4	4" x 4" x 1/2" blade guard
E	4	1-1/2" x 3-1/2" stop block

Figure A: Sled pieces

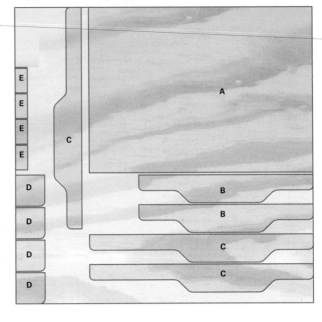

Figure B: Table saw sled

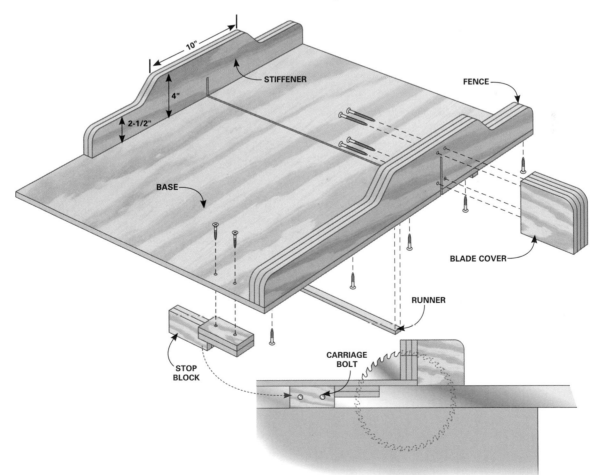

UsingTools

Glue and screw the stiffener to the front edge of the base, being careful to keep screws away from the path of the table saw blade. Then set the table saw blade to about 3/4 in. high and slide the base into the blade. Stop cutting when you get within 3 in. of the back of the base. Turn off the saw and let it come to a stop before removing the sled. Align the fence with the back edge of the base and drive a screw into the right end. **Photo 5** shows how to square the fence to the saw blade and clamp it in place. Screw the blade cover to the back of the fence, being careful to keep the screws well away from the path of the blade.

Test the cut

With the clamp firmly in place, set a 12-in. or wider scrap of plywood on the sled and cut it in two. Test the accuracy of the sled by flipping one side of the cut scrap over and pushing the freshly cut edge against the other half (**Photo 6**). If the two pieces fit perfectly with no gap, the sled is

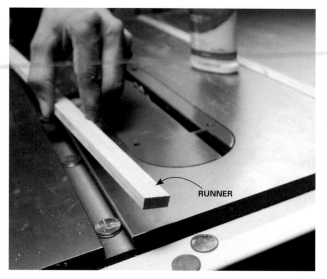

2 Rest the runners on pennies to elevate the top edge above the surface of the saw. Apply a thin bead of wood glue down the center of the top of the runners.

RUNNER

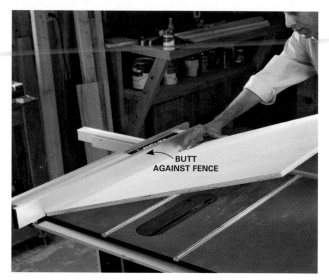

BUTT AGAINST FENCE

3 Glue the base to the runner, using the table saw fence to position it. Make sure the edge farthest from the fence overhangs the table saw at least 2 in. Set weights on the base until the glue dries.

80-GRIT SANDPAPER

OAK RUNNER

4 Sand the edges of the runners where they rub on the sides of the miter gauge slots. Dark spots indicate areas that need sanding.

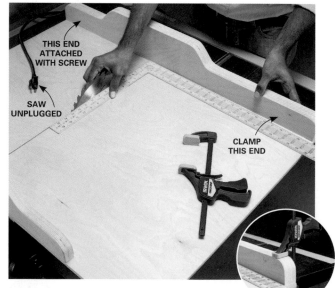

THIS END ATTACHED WITH SCREW

SAW UNPLUGGED

CLAMP THIS END

5 Square the fence with the blade. Raise the blade and press a framing square against it. Swivel the fence on a single screw in one end, and clamp the opposite end when the fence is square to the blade.

cutting squarely and you can drive three additional screws into the fence to hold it in place. Otherwise, tap the clamped end of the fence with a hammer to nudge the fence a bit. Then make another test cut. Repeat this process until the cut is perfect. Then add the screws.

Complete the sled by adding the stop blocks. With the blade half covered by the fence and blade cover, screw a block to the bottom of the sled. Use carriage bolts to attach another stop block to the table saw bed (Photo 7). 🏠

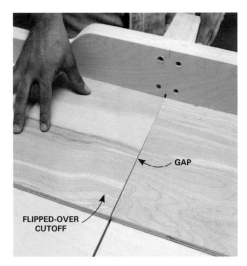

6 Check the position of the fence by cutting a scrap of plywood. Flip one side over and butt the two pieces together. A gap means the fence isn't square.

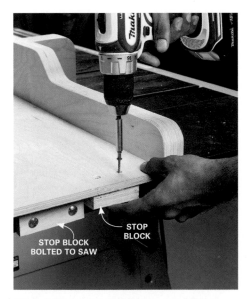

7 Install stops to prevent the blade from cutting through the blade cover.

DRUM SANDER TABLE

If you don't want to pop for a dedicated oscillating drum sander, a sanding drum chucked into a drill press is a quick way to sand contours. But unlike the real deal, there's no dust collection, and since the drum doesn't oscillate up and down, only the lower edge of the sanding surface gets used.

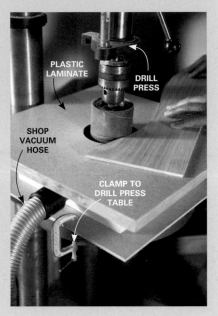

It also means there's always a little gap where the drum is slightly above the drill press table. This simple sander table solves all these problems automatically.

Use 1/4-in. or any other thickness plywood for the base, and size it slightly smaller than the drill press table so you can clamp it down. Build a 1x4 frame, a few inches smaller than the base, so there's room for the clamps, and glue and pin it to the frame. Then glue and nail 3/4-in. material to the frame for the top.

This one is 16 in. square. Build it longer or deeper if you want to sand wider or longer stuff. Cover the top with plastic laminate if you wish. It's worth the trouble because using a drum sander is tricky, and the slippery surface makes it much easier to control sanding.

Finally, drill a hole slightly larger than the drum in the center of the top and a dust-port hole in the frame sized to fit your shop vacuum hose. Move the drill press table up and down to use the entire sanding surface as it wears.

Drum-sanding ABCs

The biggest mistake drum-sander neophytes make is to remove too much material on each pass. Don't be overly aggressive: Use coarse grits only when necessary, and use very light pressure on each pass. Feel for imperfections with your fingertips, and mark the high spots with a pencil.

Figure A: Drum sander table

You can build a drum sander table from just about any scraps you have lying around your shop.

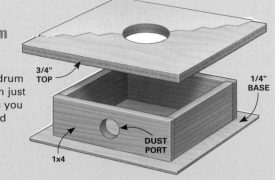

Using Tools

BENCH GRINDER CARE AND FEEDING

Lots of DIYers own a bench grinder. But not everyone knows which wheel to use for which metal or how to care for the wheels. So we consulted the experts and came up with these nuggets to keep you in the grind.

First, use aluminum oxide wheels for ferrous metals and silicon carbide for all the others (brass, copper, aluminum).

Next, dress the wheels regularly to remove clogged grains. Use either a "star wheel" dresser (right; Palmgren No. 82901, $14) or a diamond dresser (like the Commando No. 167-8101; $14). Both are available from amazon.com. The diamond style (not shown) "retrues" the wheel a bit. But don't expect either tool to "resquare" your wheel—that kind of rig costs a bundle.

Theoretically you can keep using your wheels until they wear down to the label. But you should replace them when they're too small to use with the tool rest.

Before you install a new wheel or reinstall a used one, always "ring-test" it to make sure there are no cracks (**Photo 2**). Tighten the wheel only enough to prevent it from slipping. Overtightening can crack the wheel.

WHEEL DRESSER

1 Unclog the pores. Rest the dresser on the tool rest and start the grinder. Then turn it off and press the tool against the grinding wheel as it slows. Repeat several times until the wheel feels rough to the touch (wait until it stops, please!).

2 Ring-test new and used wheels. Slide the wheel over your finger and tap the wheel in four places with a screwdriver handle. All taps should sound the same. If they don't, scrap the wheel. It's cracked.

MARK YOUR BRADS!

When you're in the shop, rip off the tops of all your boxes of brads and mark the sizes on the little tabs (**photo, right**). No more digging around or guessing for the correct length. And when you're working away from the shop and have just a little bit of trim work to pin up that requires more than one size brad, use this tip. Preload the magazine of your gun with an inch or two of the sizes you'll need (**photo, left**). Swap them around as you need them. No more hauling around boxes of brads or dealing with broken, hard-to-pack strips.

MITER SAW NIRVANA

The folks who brought you the Kreg pocket screw jig have something else you should know about—the Kreg Top Trak Fence and Flip Stop. Slide the stop on the track to whatever length you want and you can make cut after identical cut over and over. No tape measure or pencil required. For longer cuts, flip up the stop arm and it's out of the way. You'll of course need an extended miter saw table for mounting it, but you should have that anyway by now! Buy a $140 complete kit (Kreg No. KMS8000 from Amazon) or do what I did; order à la carte from rockler.com and put your own custom one together. Mine is an 8-ft.-long system that handles nearly any length of repeatable cut I ever run across. The flip stop has a little play in it, just enough that I don't trust it for really fine work. But for most cuts, it's fantastic.

Use the flip stop when you need to make multiple cuts that don't have to be super accurate.

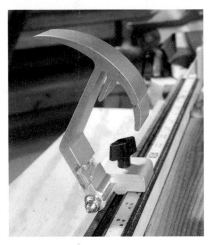

Flip the flip stop up and out of the way for the occasional longer cut.

When your cut requires exact tolerances, slip in the beefier production stop.

BACKWARD JIGSAW

The other day I was cutting an opening for an electrical outlet in the cabinet back directly below a breakfast bar. The cutout was so close to the counter that I couldn't run the saw upside down without the saw body hitting the counter. Ordinarily I'd finish the side cuts by nibbling away with the saw held horizontally. Then I got the brilliant idea of putting the blade in backward and pulling the saw toward the floor. It worked perfectly! Wish I'd thought of it 30 years ago. This is only for small jobs, though. The blade teeth ride against the guide wheel, so they wear down rather quickly.

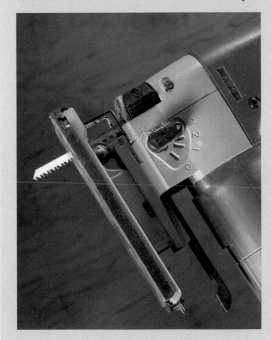

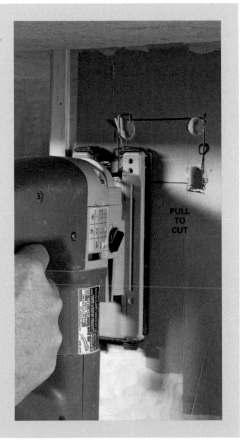

PULL TO CUT

Using Tools
CIRC SAW
SAVVY

Circular saws can do so much more than crosscut and rip wood. Here are a few tricks to put in your carpenter's quiver.

by Travis Larson

Circular saws are the go-to tool for crosscutting and ripping lumber and plywood. And we can teach you a lot of tricks to help you make those cuts more efficiently. But a circular saw's strengths don't stop there. You can cut nearly anything with a circular saw, provided you use the right blade. We'll show you a few of our favorite techniques for cutting practically anything.

But first, a word about safety. Cutting wood is dangerous enough. When we start talking about dicing up metal, shingles and nails, you'd better take the safety glasses and hearing protection very seriously. A face shield is an even better idea than simple safety glasses, and gloves and long sleeves will protect your skin from the shrapnel.

Work off the stack

Don't pick up sheets of plywood and place them on horses every time you have a cut to make. Save your back and your time. Get down on your knees and work off the stack. Slip a couple of 2x4s under the sheet undergoing surgery, make your marks and then your cut. It's that simple. By the way, a drywall square is the perfect tool for marking crosscuts on plywood.

4' DRYWALL SQUARE

Nonbinding compound cuts

Cutting steep angles, especially if they're compound (cuts with a bevel and an angle), requires one special step. That's pulling the guard back from the blade as you begin the cut. Skip this step and your guard will get bound up as you enter the cut and make it impossible to continue.

Cutting through stone and masonry

Forget about those throwaway abrasive masonry blades. Diamond blades have dropped in price in recent years ($25), and they're the key for this task. Find a volunteer to hold a slow-running garden hose right at the cut while you saw your way through. That'll keep the blade cool, speed up the cut and eliminate dust. And don't worry. It's safe as long as you're plugged into a GFCI-protected outlet.

8d NAIL

8d ripping assistant

Whenever you have to rip boards and there's no table saw around, nail the board down to the top of the horses with 8d nails. Just keep the nails away from the cut. It's much safer than holding the board with one hand while you cut with the other. And you'll get a straighter cut. When the cut is complete, pull the board free, tap out the nails to expose the heads and jerk them out.

Perfect, painless, safe siding cuts

Cutting lap siding is tough because it's awkward to "four-wheel" the saw over the laps. Next time you're faced with cutting through siding, make a plywood cutting jig (**Photo 1**). Screw the guide right to the siding with the edge of the plywood directly over the desired cutting line, and set the cutting depth to cut just through the siding, including the thickness of the jig. The saw's base will ride on the flat surface and you'll get a perfect cut every time. With a diamond blade, this trick works great for stucco, too.

LAP SIDING

SCREW THROUGH SIDING

CHALK LINES

1 **Build a jig.** Screw a 1x3 or 1x4 fence to a 12-in. strip of plywood about 6 in. from the edge. Then rip off the excess plywood.

2 **Screw it to the wall.** Snap guidelines on the siding, then align and screw the jig to the siding so the edge follows the cutting lines. Make your cut.

Using Tools

Steep bevel cuts

Most circular saws will make bevel cuts of only 45 degrees. Here's a trick for cutting bevels that exceed 45 degrees. Let's say you need a 55-degree bevel. Subtract 55 (or whatever bevel you're after) from 90 and set your saw at that bevel (in this case, 35 degrees). Next, clamp or screw a block even with the end of the board to support the saw base while you cut. The blade probably won't complete the cut, but it's easy to finish it with a handsaw or reciprocating saw. This trick works for compound cuts as well. Cut the angle first with the saw at 90 degrees, and then use the off-cut to support the saw while you cut.

BLOCK

COMPOUND CUT

55° BEVEL

20° ANGLE

Your foot as a sawhorse

Master this trick and you won't have to lug lumber to the sawhorse for every cut. It's simple and saves countless trips back and forth. It's also perfectly safe as long as you keep your foot at least 12 in. away from the cut. Just prop the board on your foot with the other end resting on the floor or ground. Tilt the board up and make the cut.

COPPER **STEEL** **PVC** **ABS**

Dealing with pipe

A circular saw makes short work of pipe—any kind but cast iron. Use a fine-tooth carbide blade for PVC, ABS or copper. Choose a metal-cutting blade for cutting up steel, such as fence posts, and metal plumbing pipe.

6" LEFT-TILT SAW

7-1/4" STANDARD RIGHT-TILT SAW

Mini circ saws

If you have a yen for an extra circular saw, consider picking a mini saw with a blade in the 5- to 6-in. range. You'll love it. It's much lighter than a standard 7-1/4-in. saw, yet you can still cut 1-1/2-in.-thick material at 90 degrees. But here's the big reason. On most mini saws, the blade is on the left side of the motor (called a "left-tilt saw"). Sometimes, this saw will fit in places where a larger saw won't. Other times you'll need it to cut bevels that are awkward or impossible with conventional right-tilt saws.

Blades that make the cut

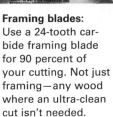

Ferrous cutting blades: Called "ferrous" because they can cut iron-containing metals such as steel, these can cut any metal up to 1/4 in. thick. But *not* cast iron.

Framing blades: Use a 24-tooth carbide framing blade for 90 percent of your cutting. Not just framing—any wood where an ultra-clean cut isn't needed.

Finish blades: Grab a 40-tooth finish blade to make finish cuts such as cutting off door bottoms, veneered plywood or plastics.

Diamond blades: You'll need these for cutting concrete, stone, pavers or any other masonry. Segmented blades will give you the fastest cut.

Recycled blades: Don't toss your old blades. Stick one in your saw for demo work, cutting shingles and nail-embedded lumber, and cutting up exterior doors so they'll fit in the trash can.

Cutting curves

If you grab your jigsaw whenever there's a curve to cut, next time try your circular saw instead. It'll do a sterling job for long, gradual curves in a fraction of the time a jigsaw will. Plus, you'll get a much smoother cut. If you're cutting plywood, set the saw to cut just deep enough to cut through the wood. The deeper the blade, the harder it'll be to make the cut because it'll get bound in the kerf. If you're cutting thicker material, cut halfway through on the first pass and then make a second, deeper final cut following the original cut. This trick isn't for super-tight curves, though. If it's too hard to push the saw through the cut, you'll just have to go with the jigsaw—sorry.

Cutting thin metal

With a metal-cutting blade in your circular saw, metal roofing cuts as easily as aluminum foil. No magic to it—just place the show side down for a nicer finish. If you have metal to get rid of, like old exterior doors or even old metal tanks, you can cut them up into bite-size chunks that'll fit in the trash can or make them easier to haul to the dump.

One-step roof cuts

Sometimes you need to cut a hole in a roof for roof vents, chimneys, skylights, whatever. You don't have to remove shingles before you cut. Just stick an old carbide blade in your saw and plunge-cut right through the shingles and decking.

Using Tools
FLATTENING ROUGH-SAWN WOOD

by **Travis Larson**

If you're an aspiring woodworker who wishes to move on to more advanced projects, there's only one path. That's learning how to flatten rough-sawn wood. Continuing to buy S4S (smooth all four sides) at the home center will limit your project portfolio for two reasons. First, you're stuck with 3/4-in.-thick stock. Advanced woodworking calls for a myriad of thicknesses only available in rough-sawn form. Second, by flattening dry, rough-sawn wood, you'll end up with boards that are perfectly flat, straight and true, which is rare with store-bought boards.

The must-have flattening tools

It takes an investment to flatten wood, though. You can't pull this off without a jointer, surface planer and table saw. You could spend a ton of money on a jointer, but a basic 6-in. jointer will do most everything you'll need; prices start at about $400. If you're only doing small projects, you can get away with a 4-in. jointer for less money, but you won't be able to flatten wider boards. Surface planers start at about $350. But you won't get good results with either tool unless you keep them equipped with sharp knives. As for the table saw, any type will work fine, including portables.

The flattening process

Woodworkers all have their own system for flattening wood, some of which are pretty complex. This is one simple method that'll get you started. As you get comfortable with flattening, you're sure to develop your own.

1 Lay out the parts. Use chalk to lay out the parts you expect to get out of the board. Work around knots, cracks and edges with deep tree bark. If there are several parts coming from the same board, draw yourself a paper sketch to remind you of the layout. Then cut the board to lengths corresponding to the parts. Cut each part at least 2 in. longer than the final length. Do so even if knots, checks or cracks are part of the waste at the ends. That'll allow you to remove any checks on the ends of the boards or snipe (gouges) left over from the planer. Don't work with long boards unless they're called for; it's much easier to flatten short boards.

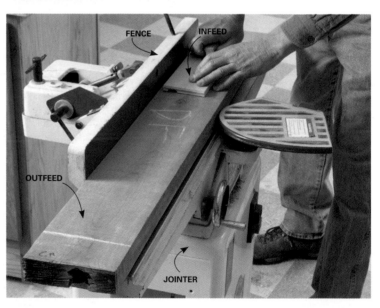

FENCE   INFEED

OUTFEED

JOINTER

2 Flatten one side. First, sight down the board to find out if there's a bow. Set the jointer depth at 1/32 in. or so and push the board through the knives with the bowed side up. You'll hear the knives cutting off the high spots as you push it through. Don't worry about holding it tight against the fence. Keep most of the downward pressure on the board over the infeed bed of the jointer, with little or no pressure on the outfeed side. Keep making passes until the entire board is flat. When you're making the last couple of passes, apply a bit more pressure on the outfeed side.

Jointer smarts

- Be persnickety and square the fence to the bed before any jointing. That's the only way to ensure square sides.
- A rust-free polished bed and fence will give you much better results.
- When you're jointing edges, move the fence every dozen or so passes to spread the wear over the entire edge of each knife.

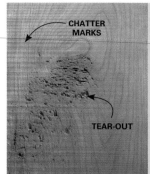

CHATTER MARKS

TEAR-OUT

Dealing with tear-out

If you have tear-out or chatter during jointing, swing the board around and send the other end through first. If the tear-out is still there after the side is flat, let it go and send that side through the planer after the other side has been flattened. The planer gives a smoother cut than the jointer. If that doesn't do it, you'll just have to sand your way out of the jam.

From rough-sawn to flat, straight and true

It's simple, fast and rewarding to turn gnarly, cupped and twisted rough-sawn lumber into beautiful furniture-grade wood. Here are the basic steps.

ROUGH SIDE UP

3 **Flatten the opposite side.** Send the highest point (at either end) of the board through the planer first, with a very small cut. Sneak up on the cutting depth; there are likely to be high spots that might stall the planer as they come through the knives. After the first pass, you can cut a bit deeper, but shallower passes will be less taxing on the tool and less likely to produce tear-out, stalls and burning. As with the jointer, swing the board around and send the other end through if you get any tear-out. Before you get to the final thickness, plane out any tear-out on the first side.

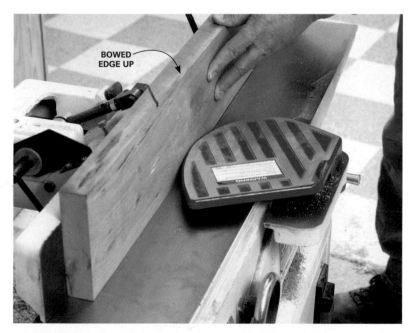

BOWED EDGE UP

4 **Flatten one edge.** Sight the board to find any bows. Hold the board against the fence with the bowed side up and send it through the jointer just as you did for the sides. Stop when the edge is flat.

JOINT ONE SIDE
Send it through the jointer with the bowed side up.

PLANE OPPOSITE SIDE
Send it through the planer with the freshly jointed side down.

JOINT ONE EDGE
Joint with the bowed edge up.

RIP TO ROUGH WIDTH
Rip 1/8 in. wider than finished width.

JOINT TO FINAL WIDTH
Then cut to final length.

Using Tools

Finding rough-sawn lumber

If you have a hardwood retailer near you, that's great. If not, you can shop online. Many rural woodworkers, including pros, buy all their wood online. Search for "hardwood suppliers" to find many sources. We've listed a few here.

Board thicknesses are always listed as "X/4." A 4/4 board is 4 by 1/4 in., or 1 in. Always get 1/4 in. thicker than the finished thickness you're after. For example, if you need a 1-in.-thick final thickness, you should order a 5/4 board. Select widths that are 1/2 in. or so wider than the finished width.

Buying hardwood online

walllumber.com

hearnehardwoods.com

gilmerwood.com

WASTE

JOINTED EDGE

5 **Rip away the waste.** Place the jointed edge against the table saw fence and rip the board to within 1/8 in. of the final width.

6 **Joint either edge to the final width.** If the board is 1-1/2 in. or thicker, you can use the planer for this step. Or if you have several thinner boards of the same thickness, you can "gang-plane" them all at once. Hold the boards together as they enter and exit the planer. Cut the boards to final length and you're ready to start your project! ⌂

ONE PROJECT, ONE TAPE

Tape measures are not all created equal. Different tape measures will give you different results, and even a 1/16-in. variation will cause you major headaches on a close-tolerance project. So if you have more than one tape measure in your workshop, use only one throughout your project. Label it with a strip of tape.

A MACHINIST'S TOOL FOR WOODWORKING

A 1-2-3 block is a machinist's tool. It's a 1-in. x 2-in. x 3-in. block that has perfectly square sides with sharp corners, ideal for simple layout and setup. Use it to check for square, to true up saw blades and to do lots of other tasks. Search online for "1-2-3 blocks." A set of two costs about $34.

REBUILD A FRAMING NAILER

Nothing beats a top-quality nailer for cutting hours out of a framing project. But all that heavy-duty nailing depends on a handful of rubber O-rings. When they fail, your project grinds to a halt. You don't have to wait a week for the shop to rebuild it. You can do the entire job yourself in about two hours and save about $50 in the process. I'll show you how to rebuild a Bostitch framing nailer with a master O-ring kit and a trigger valve assembly. If you have a different brand, don't worry. The rebuild is similar for others.

Framing nailers usually fail in one of these ways: deteriorated O-rings that cause air leaks, a trigger valve that won't fire, or a leaking cylinder seal or a worn driver bumper, which prevents the gun from making a complete stroke. A complete rebuild fixes all those problems. Buy the rebuild kit at a local service center or online. It'll come with all the O-rings and seals. If you've put a lot of nails through your gun, buy new bumpers and a trigger valve at the same time. Then download the gun schematic from the manufacturer (bostitch.com, senco.com or, for Duo-Fast and Paslode brands, itwserviceparts.com).

Start the disassembly at the cylinder cap (Photo 1). Lay out the pieces on a spotlessly clean workbench in the order you removed them. Then remove the old O-rings using a blunt, straight-blade screwdriver (Photo 2). Apply O-ring grease (usually included in the new kit) to the new rings, then replace the rings one at a time, matching each one to its replacement. Install the new bumpers, piston seals and piston stops and reinstall the cap. Then replace the trigger valve (Photo 3).

Prolong the life of your air nailer by using only *nail gun oil* (photo below).

The right oil for your gun

Lube your nail gun regularly with the right oil. NEVER use impact air tool oil, WD-40 or motor oil—they can destroy the O-rings in your gun. Also, use special winter grade oil when operating your gun in cold weather.

1 **Work from the top down.** Remove the four hex screws and then the cap. Then remove the entire cylinder and driver assembly.

BAD TOP SEAL

CYLINDER

O-RING GREASE

2 **Walk the ring off and on.** Pry up the old O-ring. Then slide the round portion of the screwdriver under it. Circle the screwdriver around the O-ring to "walk" it off. Reverse the procedure to install the new, freshly greased ring.

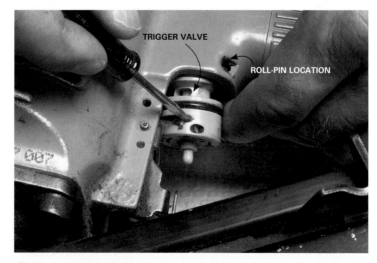

TRIGGER VALVE

ROLL-PIN LOCATION

3 **Swap out the trigger valve.** Locate the roll-pin driver tool and tap it out with a small hammer. Then pull out the valve and install the freshly greased replacement.

Using Tools

POWER COPING

The usual way to get tight inside corners on trim is to "cope" them—to cut a profile on one part that will fit over the adjoining part. That means lots of slow, fussy work with a coping saw. Next time you have some inside corners to cope on standard 3-1/4-in. baseboards, try this method for doing the whole process on your miter saw. It works for ranch and Princeton styles. It takes a bit of practice to master the trick, but once you do, you'll be able to achieve a perfect cope in less than 60 seconds and never grab for the coping saw again.

If you have a low fence on your miter saw, add a 1x4 **(Photo 1)** to fully support the baseboard. Your saw has to be adjusted so it cuts perfectly square in the vertical direction. There will be wood shrapnel and your saw will be running for long periods, so wear vision and hearing protection.

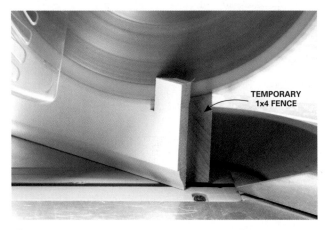

1 **Expose the profile.** Make a reverse 45-degree cut to expose the profile.

TEMPORARY 1x4 FENCE

TEMPORARY FENCE

STOP THE CUT HERE

2 **Cut off the straight part.** Swing the saw around to the other 45-degree setting and cut the vertical part of the cope, stopping just before the profile starts, and snap off the waste.

Install base in the clockwise direction around a room if you're right-handed and counterclockwise if you're a lefty. That'll be playing to your strong hand, and you'll always be coping the same way joint after joint—no confusion.

Rest your elbow on the table or the saw miter adjustment arm for stability. Don't try to get a perfect cope with the saw alone; you'll be able to quickly clean it up with a file. And lastly, don't take your finger off the trigger until you're clear of the cut. The blade will plunge the instant you shut off the power and you'd wreck the cope.

3 **Whittle away the waste.** Nibble away most of the waste above the profile, then fine-tune the profile, stopping about 1/32 in. above the finished cut. Once you get used to the process, you can work even faster by dragging the base sideways while lowering the blade at the same time.

4 **Tune up the cope.** Follow the finished wood surface with a "4-in-hand" file to finish up the cope. With any luck, you'll still have a line of raw wood to follow with the file to get a perfect cope. Be careful even with base that's made from hardwood—the file carves away wood very quickly.

5 **Check your work.** Test the cope with a scrap of base.
■ If the base is going to be painted, don't be a perfectionist— a small gap is easy to fill with caulk.
■ If it will be stained or varnished, take your time to achieve a perfect cope.
■ If you completely blow it, who cares? You can recut another one in seconds.

5 Exterior Maintenance & Repairs

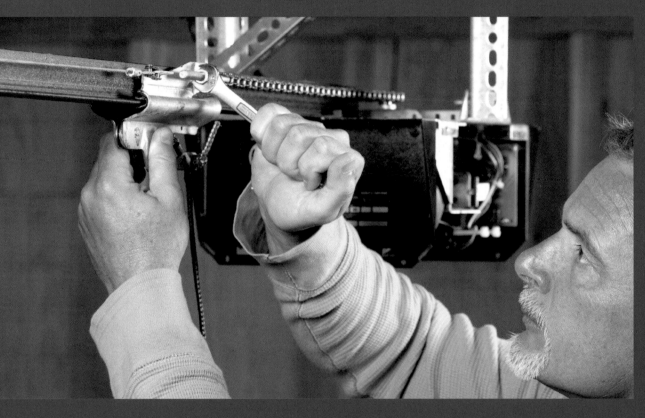

IN THIS CHAPTER

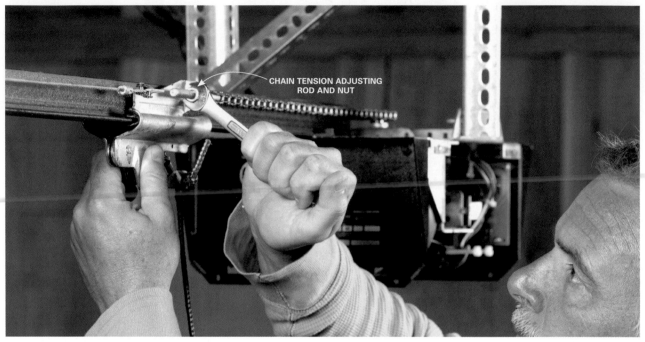

CHAIN TENSION ADJUSTING ROD AND NUT

REBUILD YOUR GARAGE DOOR OPENER

If you press the garage door opener button and hear either a humming or a grinding sound, but the door won't open, you may think you need a new opener. And you might. But before you give up on the old unit, pop off the cover and check for stripped gears. That's a common problem and one that you can fix yourself for less than about $25.

You'll have to get a replacement gear kit (two new gears, grease and washers), which may take some running around. But once you have the kit in hand, you can do the repair in about two hours. You'll need a 2x4, a small drift punch, a standard 1/4-in. drive socket set, hex wrenches, a circular saw, a drill and a hammer. I'll show you how to remove and replace the gears without damaging the shafts.

Start by unplugging the opener. Then remove the retaining screws for the metal cover and put it aside. Shine a flashlight directly at the gear set. If you see chewed-up teeth, you've nailed the problem. If the gears are in good shape, you've got a more serious problem and your best bet may be to just replace the entire unit. To find a replacement gear kit, write down the make, model and serial number of your opener (you'll find it on a label on the back of the opener). Then call a garage door opener repair company. It'll probably charge a bit more than an Internet site, but at least you'll have the parts right away and be up and running the same day.

1 Remove the chain. Unscrew the outer nut on the chain tensioning rod. If necessary, use pliers to prevent the chain from turning. Then slip on a pair of gloves and remove the greasy chain from the sprocket at the top of the opener.

RETAINING SCREWS

MOTOR START CAPACITOR

SHREDDED HELICAL GEAR

2 Remove the helical gear assembly. Unscrew the hex-head screws that hold the helical gear assembly in place. Save the screws for reassembly. Then lift the entire assembly (sprocket, plate, shaft and helical gear) up and out of the top of the unit.

Getting out the gear shafts

Use a combination wrench to loosen and remove the chain (**Photo 1**). Next, use a 1/4-in. drive socket, extension and ratchet to remove the helical gear assembly retaining screws (**Photo 2**). Take a digital photo of the wiring connections from the motor or label them with masking tape. Disconnect the motor wires and remove the entire motor assembly. Move the helical gear assembly and the motor assembly to your workbench.

Remove the helical and worm gears

Cut a shallow groove into a 2x4 with a circular saw. Then slice off about a 3-in. section to make a jig to hold the helical gear assembly circular plate (**Photo 3**). Place the plate in the groove, hold the gear assembly level and mark the end of the shaft on another 2x4. Drill a hole in the wood and insert the end of the shaft. Then remove the roll pin (**Photo 3**). Slide the old gear off the shaft and replace it with the new gear. Reinstall the roll pin using the same jigs.

Next, remove the retaining collar and thrust washers on the end of the motor shaft (**Photo 4**). Pull the motor out of the chassis and slide the worm gear off the shaft (the roll pin stays in place on this shaft). Slide on the new worm gear with the notched end facing the roll pin.

Reassemble the motor assembly and place it back in the opener. Then install the helical gear assembly. Coat the gear teeth with new grease. Reattach the chain and tighten it to the proper tension (see your owner's manual). Test your repair with the garage door disconnected from the opener trolley.

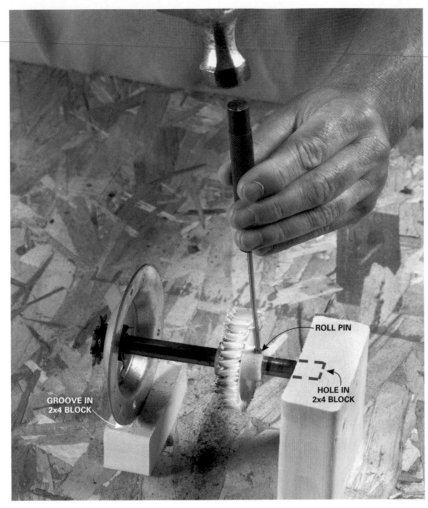

ROLL PIN

HOLE IN 2x4 BLOCK

GROOVE IN 2x4 BLOCK

3 **Remove the helical gear from the shaft.** Support both ends of the helical gear assembly with the two jigs. Hold a small drift punch over the roll pin and tap the pin out of the shaft with a small hammer.

MOTOR RETAINING SCREWS

WORM GEAR

4 **Remove the worm gear.** Loosen the collar setscrews with a hex wrench and slide the worm gear off the shaft. Then remove the motor retaining screws.

HomeCare&Repair

HEARD ON THE FORUM: NOISY GUTTERS

TFH forum member "LuckyToo" asked about noisy gutters. His contractor installed a lead plate in the elbow and then a magnetic cushioned plate. Those fixes usually just change the tone from a metallic drip, drip, drip to a thud, thud, thud sound.

Here's how to solve the problem. Caulk around the gutter drain and install a length of nylon or poly rope (**Figure A**). The water will wick down the rope instead of free-falling and hitting the elbow.

Figure A
Drip-no-more solution
Squirt a bead of gutter seaming caulk around the drain opening, leaving a 1/4-in. gap. Use the same caulk to glue a 3/8-in.-diameter nylon rope next to the gap and drop it down the gutter and out the opening. Then glue it to the bend in the elbow.

SLIP-PROOF WOOD STEPS

Before winter hits, apply a coat of paint and traction grit on slippery wood steps. Sand and aluminum oxide grit are cheap, but both require constant stirring. And they show up as dark specks as soon as the paint starts to wear. Instead, try polymeric plastic grit (such as Seal-Krete Clear Grip, $9 per bag), available at home centers and bigpaintstore.com. Polymeric grit stays suspended in the paint as you apply it, and because it's clear plastic, it won't show up as dark specks as the paint wears.

If you want grit that's easier on bare feet, add rubber grit to the paint (such as Soft Sand Traction Grit; $23 per pint from softsandrubber.com). Use the broadcast method shown to apply it.

Sprinkle the grit on wet paint
Apply a fresh coat of paint to the steps. Then immediately sprinkle a generous coating of rubber grit to the surface. Allow it to dry. Then add a second coat of paint to seal the grit.

Question&Comment

HOW DO I FIX THESE BRICKS?

The bricks on the front of my house are breaking apart. Is there any way to patch them and make it look natural?

No. Any patch material you apply will just pop out again unless you solve the underlying expansion/contraction problem. From the photo, the bricks look like recycled Chicago-commons (a soft brick used at the turn of the last century). If they were set with any of the newer, nonflexing Portland cement mortars, that would explain your broken bricks.

You have two choices. Either reuse the old bricks but with the right mortar (lime mortar or lime putty), or rebuild with new bricks. Pick a brick that's harder and more weather resistant.

WATERTIGHT CABLE

TV and Internet signals are the only things coaxial cables should be bringing into your house, but improperly installed cables can let in water, which can lead to rot and mold. So the next time you're trimming the bushes, take a quick look where the cable enters the house.

Cable should never run downward and directly into your house. Rainwater will adhere to the cable and follow it right into your home. Ideally, the cable should run upward and then in. If your cable was installed incorrectly, contact your service provider and voice your concerns. If the provider refuses to fix the problem, see if you can reroute the cable in order to gain a couple of feet. Try to avoid splices if you can. They can weaken your signal.

If you're installing new cable, loop the cable before it enters the building. The loop will not only help shed the water but also provide extra cable in case a mistake is made inside.

A properly sized feed-through bushing will allow you to drill a slightly larger hole so you can fish the cable in without damaging it. Dab silicone caulk behind the bushing before pushing it into its final resting place.

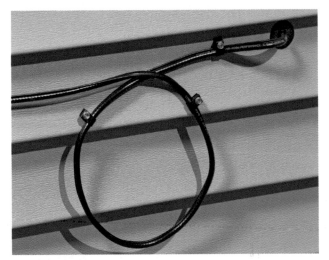

Loop the cable
A loop provides extra length for minor repairs or rerouting later. It also forces water to drip off the cable rather than follow the cable into the wall. A bushing seals around the cable and protects it from the sharp edges of the siding. Fasten the cable with clamps.

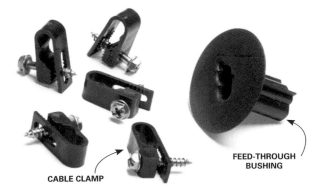

CABLE CLAMP

FEED-THROUGH BUSHING

STOP SOFFIT RATTLE

Aluminum soffits are "maintenance free," they come in a lot of colors and they're relatively inexpensive to install, but they can be noisy!

Most aluminum soffits fit into an aluminum channel mounted to the house. Sometimes, the channel is wider than the soffits and allows them to move. Add a blustery breeze, and the soffits outside your bedroom may have you longing for those restful nights when you had a colicky newborn's cradle parked next to your bed.

The solution may be as simple as a $5 package of screen spline and a $1 putty knife. The first step is to find the offending soffits. Set up a ladder near the area in question and tap on the soffits to see which ones rattle.

Next, take a plastic putty knife and insert a length of screen spline in between the soffit and the aluminum channel. The soffits may have been cut too short, so push the screen mold in far enough so it can't be seen from the ground but not so far that it slides past the end of the soffit. The final step: a good night's sleep.

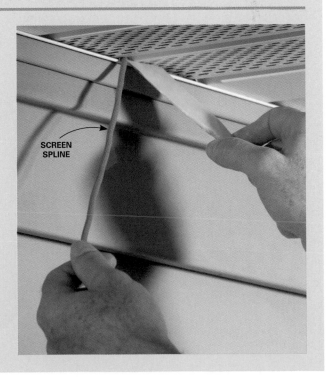

SCREEN SPLINE

HandyHints®

HANDY ROOF TRAY

My husband came up with this handy tool tray for working on the roof. He measured the slope of our roof and built an angled platform for the base. A 1-3/4-in. lip keeps everything in place, and a scrap of carpet on the bottom keeps it from sliding off the roof. Just don't use this tray on really steep roofs or it might slide off and hurt somebody.

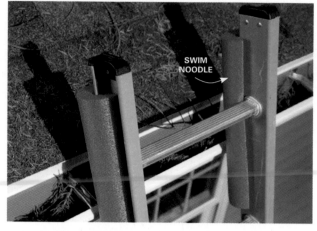

LADDER GUARDS

I recently installed new gutters. When it came time to clean them out, I didn't want my metal ladder to dent or scratch them, so I made ladder protectors out of an old swim noodle (foam pipe insulation would work too). I cut 2-ft. sections of the foam noodle, slit them with a razor knife and stuck them on the sides of the ladder. They were the perfect cushions! If the foam doesn't stay put, tape it on.

Question&Comment

SECRETS OF STEP FLASHING REVEALED!

I see some roofs installed with one long piece of L-shaped flashing under the shingles and behind the siding. The flashing is sealed with roofing cement. Is that a proper way to install flashing?

Well, it's one way to install a roof, but it's not the correct way. It may seem as if a single piece of flashing would offer more protection than many pieces of step flashing. But it doesn't work that way. Once even a small section of roofing cement fails, you'll have a leak. Each additional rain adds more water, and before you know it, you've got rotted wood.

Step flashing offers far better protection from leaks, because even if a single piece of step flashing fails, the water just hits the next lower piece. That flashing directs the water onto the shingle and the water drains down the roof.

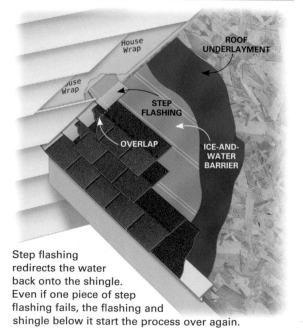

Step flashing redirects the water back onto the shingle. Even if one piece of step flashing fails, the flashing and shingle below it start the process over again.

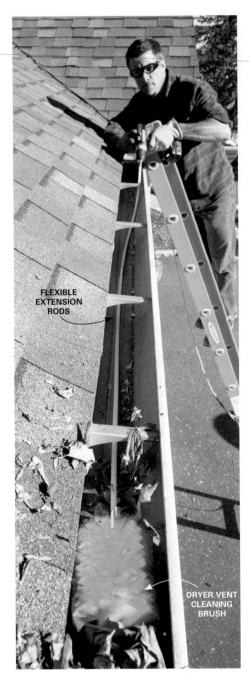

FLEXIBLE
EXTENSION
RODS

DRYER-VENT
CLEANING
BRUSH

EASIER GUTTER CLEANING

To speed up the task of cleaning out your gutters, use a dryer-vent cleaning brush and flexible extension rods. Depending on how many extension rods you use, you can clean 4, 8 or even 12 ft. of gutter from the same spot. Just hook the rod onto your drill, slide the brush under the first bracket and turn it on. As you feed the rod down the gutter, the brush spins and pushes all the debris right over the side.

GreatGoofs®

If the tree falls, will anyone hear you yell?

A storm toppled the oak tree next to my house, but amazingly it ended up leaning against the edge of the roof without causing any damage. I climbed up on the roof to push the tree away, but just as I was going to start pushing, I realized my momentum might carry me right off the roof as the tree gave way! So instead, I got on my back, inched my way to the edge of the roof, put my feet up on the trunk and pushed as hard as I could.

Success! The tree fell harmlessly to the ground. Only then did I realize that my legs were hanging precariously from the roof's edge. With nothing to push off from, I couldn't inch myself away from the edge! I spent two hours stranded in that position until a friend showed up. Two hours is plenty of time to think about thinking things ALL the way through before you do them.

TIDY PAINT SCRAPING

I needed to scrape and repaint my mailbox post, but I didn't want paint chips mixed in with the pebble and wood mulch at the base of the post. I slit a piece of plastic and slid it under and around the pole. That way I could let the paint chips fall onto the plastic and just fold the whole works up and throw it away. This works great for deck posts, bird feeder poles and flower box posts too.

PLASTIC

HandyHints

NOISY-DRIP STOPPER

Do you have a noisy drip coming from your downspout that's driving you nuts? I discovered an easy way to stop the drip—just push a kitchen sponge into the bottom of the downspout. It'll muffle the drip noise without blocking the water flow.

KITCHEN SPONGE

GreatGoofs

Bee careful with that hammer

I was tearing down an old shed that wasn't much more than weathered lumber over a dirt floor. A fair number of bees were flying around, but I kept going until the shed was down and stacked into neat piles. There was one last piece of plywood lying on the ground. With the hammer in my hand, I used the claw to lift up the plywood. Out from the ground came the bees! I dropped the plywood and started running, but one of the bees was gaining on me! My instinct was to start waving my hands to ward off the bee, but I forgot

I was holding my hammer! The emergency room doc was laughing so hard that he had a tough time keeping the stitches straight as he worked on the gash above my eyebrow.

SPRAY PAINT

SINGLE RUNG

IMPROVED LADDER SAFETY

I always feared I would miss a step coming down my extension ladder. The worst moment is when your foot has to transition from a double rung to the single rung (when you move from the extension section to the stationary section). Your foot has to move inward to fit fully on the single rung, and it's a potentially dangerous moment. To make the transition safer, stand on the bottom rung of the extension section and spray-paint a mark on the ladder rails at eye level. When you see the mark as you're descending, you'll know that the next step you take is to the single rung. If people of different heights use the same ladder, use a different color of paint for each person.

6 Outdoor Structures, Landscaping & Gardening

IN THIS CHAPTER

SHARPEN YOUR SHOVEL

Your shovel will slice through dirt and roots easier if it has a sharp edge. If the point of your shovel is ragged with dents or chips, start by smoothing it with a grinder (**Photo 1**). Then switch to a mill bastard file (**Photo 2**) to file a bevel. You don't want a knifelike edge. Instead just bevel the top edge at a 70-degree angle to the back. That's pretty blunt compared with the 25- or 30-degree angle used for knife sharpening.

1 Grind the edge smooth. Use a metal grinding disc in an angle grinder to remove nicks and create a smooth profile. Keep the grinder moving to avoid overheating the metal edge.

2 File a bevel. Hold the file at a 70-degree angle to the back of the shovel. Apply pressure while pushing the file. Lift the file to return for the next stroke. Files cut on the forward stroke only.

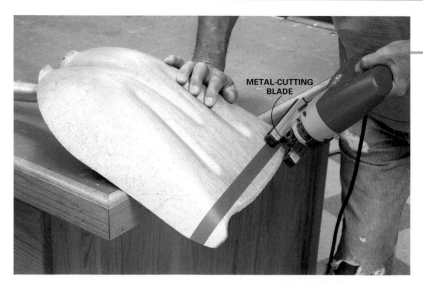

METAL-CUTTING BLADE

RESTORE YOUR GRAIN SHOVEL

Aluminum grain shovels are perfect for snow shoveling, or as a substitute for a big dustpan in your shop. The only drawback is that the soft aluminum edge wears out and gets bent, making shoveling more difficult. Here's an easy fix. Make a straight line across the blade with a piece of masking tape. Then saw along the tape with a jigsaw and a metal-cutting blade to straighten the front edge of the shovel. If you want, you can polish and sharpen the edge slightly with a belt sander.

EASY OIL-CHANGE MODIFICATION FOR YOUR SNOW BLOWER

Most snow blower engines have a drain plug design that's guaranteed to drip smelly oil all over the machine and floor. Instead of cleaning up the mess every time, modify and extend the drain hole with galvanized nipples and a coupler, elbow and cap. Start by tipping the snow blower on its side (remove the gas first with a turkey baster) so you can attach the nipples and fittings without bathing in leaking crankcase oil. Install a nipple to extend the drain out far enough to attach a 90-degree elbow and then take a downward path (**see photo**).

Route the piping so the oil drains right into a shallow pan. Keep it close to the frame of the machine so you won't kick it with your boots as you walk.

WINTERIZING A SPRINKLER SYSTEM

Follow the hookup procedure. Close off both valves on the backflow preventer. Then remove the plug on the blow-out port and screw in a quick-connect hose adapter. Snap on the air hose and connect the other end to the compressor.

Every year I pay the irrigation company $125 to blow out my sprinkler system. I'd like to try it myself, but I don't want to risk leaving water in the system over the winter. Can I do this with my own compressor?

Yes. Just be aware that even the largest home compressor isn't powerful enough to blow out the entire system at once. But you can probably blow it out zone by zone.

If you're into number crunching and you have the original irrigation layout showing the gallons per minute (gpm) of each sprinkler head, just divide the total gpm of each zone by 7.5. That'll give you the cubic feet per minute (cfm) you need to blow it out. Otherwise, just rent a 10-cfm compressor and hose from your local tool rental center (about $35 for four hours).

Set the compressor air pressure regulator to a maximum of 80 psi for rigid PVC pipe systems, or 50 psi for flexible black polyethylene pipe. Then turn off the water supply and set the system timer to open just one zone. Next, open the manual drain valve at the end of that zone (if equipped). Then, connect the air line to the blow-out port as shown (**photo, left**). Connect the other end of the air hose to the compressor and blow out the line. The heads should pop up and spit out water. Disconnect the hose *as soon as they run dry*. Don't overdo the blow-out—without water cooling the plastic gears, they can melt in less than a minute. So move on to the next zone and allow the heads to cool. Then go back and blow out each zone a second time.

OUTDOOR STRUCTURES, LANDSCAPING & GARDENING

PATIO **PERGOLA**

It's perfect for a first big framing project
by **Brett Martin**

Like any other pergola, this one provides partial shade and—if you like—a home for climbing vines. But with its clean, streamlined design, this pergola is easier to build than most. There are no curves or fussy miter joints, no special-order materials or specialty tools required. That simplicity makes this the perfect pergola for DIYers who are ready to tackle their first big framing project—or busy folks who can't spend weeks on a single project.

1x2 BRACES

LAYOUT FRAME

1 Perfect posthole positioning. A 2x4 layout frame makes it easy and foolproof. Drive stakes at the corners to mark the postholes, then set the frame aside while you dig.

WARNING: Before you dig, call 811 to have underground utilities and wires marked.

2 Lock 'em in concrete. No need to mix up all the concrete. Dump in dry mix, leaving the top 6 in. unfilled, and pour in 2 gallons of water. Then mix up concrete to top off each hole. "Crown" the top with wet mix so it slopes away from the post.

3 Build "sandwich" beams. Cut the decorative ends of the 2x10s. Then make a plywood sandwich: Screw pressure-treated plywood to one side of each beam, add the other side and lock the sandwich together with 3-in. screws.

Planting posts in a patio

Any or all of the pergola posts can pass through a concrete patio into the soil below. All it takes is a hole in the concrete that's large enough to let you dig a posthole. That will leave you with an oversize hole in the concrete, of course, but you can patch in around the post with 8-in.-long pavers. After marking the concrete, cut the square with a diamond blade in your circular saw. Also make a couple of diagonal cuts so breaking out the concrete will be easier. Then get to work with a masonry chisel. (If you use a sledgehammer, you'll risk cracking the surrounding concrete.) When the concrete hole is done, set the post as usual.

Mark a posthole on concrete. Set a scrap of 4x4 on the exact post position and wrap it with the pavers you'll use to patch in later. Use a marker to mark the cutout—a pencil line will wash away when you cut.

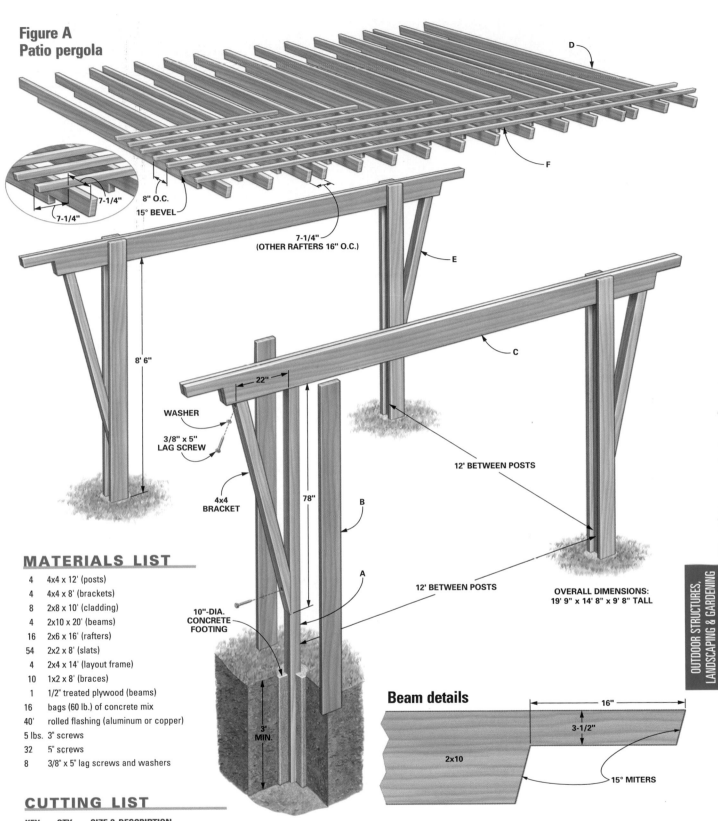

Figure A
Patio pergola

7-1/4"

7-1/4"

8" O.C.
15° BEVEL

D

7-1/4"
(OTHER RAFTERS 16" O.C.)

F

E

8' 6"

22"

C

WASHER

3/8" x 5"
LAG SCREW

78"

12' BETWEEN POSTS

4x4
BRACKET

B

A

10"-DIA.
CONCRETE
FOOTING

12' BETWEEN POSTS

OVERALL DIMENSIONS:
19' 9" x 14' 8" x 9' 8" TALL

3'
MIN.

MATERIALS LIST

4	4x4 x 12' (posts)
4	4x4 x 8' (brackets)
8	2x8 x 10' (cladding)
4	2x10 x 20' (beams)
16	2x6 x 16' (rafters)
54	2x2 x 8' (slats)
4	2x4 x 14' (layout frame)
10	1x2 x 8' (braces)
1	1/2" treated plywood (beams)
16	bags (60 lb.) of concrete mix
40'	rolled flashing (aluminum or copper)
5 lbs.	3" screws
32	5" screws
8	3/8" x 5" lag screws and washers

CUTTING LIST

KEY	QTY.	SIZE & DESCRIPTION
A	4	3-1/2" x 3-1/2" x 12' (posts)
B	8	1-1/2" x 7-1/4" (cladding; cut to fit)
C	4	1-1/2" x 9-1/4" x 237" (beams)
D	16	1-1/2" x 5-1/2" x 176" (rafters)
E	4	3-1/2" x 3-1/2" (brackets; cut to fit)
F	21	1-1/2" x 1-1/2" (slats; cut to fit)

Beam details

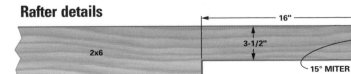

16"

3-1/2"

2x10

15° MITERS

Rafter details

16"

3-1/2"

2x6

15° MITER

COPPER FLASHING

LASER LEVEL

4 Flash the beams. Keep rain from seeping into the beam and causing rot. Center a strip of copper flashing over the beam and fasten it with a few staples. Then bend the edges down with a 2x4 block and staple them.

5 Mark the post height. All the posts must be cut at the same height. A laser level makes marking fast and precise. But there's also a low-tech method: Just measure and mark one post, then transfer that height to the other posts with a string level ($3).

CLADDING

POST

6 Set the beam. Nail one side of the cladding to each post. Then recruit a helper, center the beam and screw it to the cladding.

7 Gang-cut the rafters. After you cut the rafters to length, line them up and clamp them together. Set your saw's depth to 2 in. and make the notch cuts in one pass. Cut individually to complete each rafter end.

Money, materials and tools

Our pergola is built from cedar, and the total materials bill came to about $1,500. Built from pressure-treated lumber, the pergola would have cost about $1,000. Everything you'll need is available at home centers. Aside from a standard set of hand tools, the only tools you need are a cordless drill, a circular saw and a jigsaw. We used exterior screws instead of nails for all the assembly. An experienced builder could complete this project in one weekend. But haste leads to mistakes, so give yourself two or three weekends.

Planning and preparation

■ Depending on local rules, you may need a building permit—check with your inspections department.

■ For stability, the postholes must be at least 3 ft. deep. The frost depth in your region may call for deeper holes.

■ This pergola is sturdy, but shifting soil or extreme winds could move it. Play it safe and keep all parts of the pergola at least 4 in. from any part of your house.

■ The beams require 20-ft.-long lumber, so arrange for delivery of all the materials.

Position the posts

The whole pergola rests on four posts. Planting those posts in perfect position is the most critical and time-consuming part of the project.

The traditional way to position posts is with stakes and strings. But that's slow and fussy; you have to reposition the strings again and again until you get it right. Here's an easier way: Screw together a 2x4 frame with *inside* dimensions of 151 x 151 in. (Cut two of the 2x4s to 151 in.; two to 154 in.) Take diagonal corner-to-corner measurements to make sure the frame is square and then brace it with 8-ft. 1x2s.

Set the frame into place to instantly position the postholes (**Photo 1**). After you've dug the postholes, set the frame back into place. Set each post in its hole and drive temporary screws through the frame and into the post. Then grab your level, plumb each post, and lock it into position with stakes and 1x2 braces. Disassemble the frame and you're ready for concrete (**Photo 2**).

The rest is simple

After the posts are in position, there's still a ton of work to do. But it's not complicated work. If you study **Figure A** and measure and cut carefully, it will all go together smoothly. Here are some building tips:

■ The plywood in the "sandwich" beams isn't structural; it just acts as a spacer. So you can puzzle it in any way you like (**Photo 3**). For better appearance, keep it 1/2 in. away from the bottoms of the beam.

■ The flashing on the tops of the beams is optional (**Photo 4**). We used copper, which looks great and bends easily. Copper is pricey, though: $80 and up for 40 ft. Aluminum flashing is also easy to bend and will cost about $25.

■ To save on ladder work, mark the rafter locations on the beam before you set it on the posts (**Photo 6**). Likewise, mark the slat locations on the rafters before setting them.

■ Coat your pergola with any exterior finish you like. Whatever you choose, finish the rafters and slats *before* you install them. You'd have to be a glutton for punishment to brush on the finish after they're in place. Just saying. 🏠

8 Set the rafters. The notches automatically set the rafters' overhang. Predrill and fasten each rafter end with a single 5-in. screw.

4x4 BRACKET

9 Add the brackets. Hold the 4x4 bracket in place and have a helper mark it along the beam and the post. Cut the bracket, screw it into place and add the second side of cladding.

BACKYARD HEADACHES
AND HOW TO FIX THEM

Real-world situations and expert advice

by **Elisa Bernick**

Headache #1   An eroding slope

"Our beautiful backyard slope was washing down onto our patio with every rain. It was only a matter of time before the whole hill came tumbling down."

Reader Solution: "We built **a dry creek bed** on the slope, and it fills dramatically during a rainstorm. It's a beautiful addition to our landscape, and it seems to be solving our erosion problem."

— Carolyn Rogers

Expert input: "A dry creek bed can work well to control erosion," says landscape architect Susan Jacobson, "if there's a place for the water to go, such as a sandy area somewhere else on your property." In its simplest form, a dry creek bed is simply a gully or trough filled with rocks that directs the flow of water to prevent erosion. To control larger volumes of water, pin landscape fabric in the gully and mortar the rocks into place. Constructing the creek bed with rocks of several different sizes gives it a natural look and maximizes its water-carrying abilities.

But Jacobson says building a dry creek bed won't work in every situation. "You'll create a bigger problem (and a potentially illegal situation) if you direct the water into the street or into your neighbor's yard. And if the slope is too steep, you might just end up with the rocks tumbling down the hill as well."

To control erosion on a steep slope or when there's no reasonable place for the water to flow, consider these suggestions:

■ Terrace the slope with boulders, stone retaining walls or landscape timbers to gradually flatten the incline and slow drainage.

■ Use layered plantings of deep- and shallow-rooted trees, shrubs and ground covers to prevent water runoff.

■ Don't use plastic, straw, mulch, grass or shallow-rooted ground covers alone to control erosion on a slope because they won't be stable over the long term.

Headache #2   Heavy shade kills grass

"My wife wanted grass, so I tried to grow it many times over the years. But thanks to the heavy shade cast by our oak trees, by mid-summer our backyard consisted of small, lonely tufts of grass surrounded by bare earth."

Reader Solution: "My solution was to till most of the backyard (when my wife was gone for the day) and **create a shade garden**. Now that poor, sad grass is just a dim memory, and so far, the garden looks great."

— Bob Rogers

Expert input: A shade garden can be a beautiful way to deal with mature trees. However, planting a garden at the base of a tree can be challenging for both the plants and the tree. Shade isn't the only issue: "The plants will also need to cope with dry soil and root competition," says Doris Taylor, a plant information specialist at the Morton Arboretum near Chicago. "And many trees are sensitive to having their roots disturbed." Taylor offers these suggestions for planting a successful shade garden without harming trees:

■ Consult online resources and the local extension service to choose drought- and shade-tolerant plants for your zone.

■ Newly established plants of any kind (even drought-tolerant plants) need supplemental water the first year. If the tree hates having its feet (roots) consistently wet, spot-water your new plants.

■ Most tree roots are in the top 12 to 18 in. of soil and extend past the canopy. Don't cover existing tree roots with more than 1 in. of soil or they can suffocate. Tilling near a tree can destroy the fine root hairs that take up water. Instead, plant in the pockets of soil between larger roots and add slow-release organic compost to the individual planting holes.

■ Don't plant closer than 12 in. from the trunk, and plant shallow-rooted perennials that don't require frequent division such as hostas, liriope and sedum.

■ Shallow-rooted species like oaks, lindens, magnolias and many maples are sensitive to disturbance and can be easily damaged. Consider adding a bench or planters instead of a shade garden.

Headache #3   "Gumbo" soil won't drain

"Our clay soil is mush when wet and like concrete when dry, and nothing will grow in it."

Reader Solution: "We're in the process of amending our soil with **expanded shale**. It's a gravel-size rock that's pumped full of air. It aerates heavy clay soil, which makes it easier to work and helps it drain better.

 I've already noticed that the part of the garden we've done drained much better than the rest of the garden during the last rain."

— Sue Blackburn

BEFORE

AFTER

Expert input: Sue has definitely done her research. According to Steve George, a horticulturist at the Texas Cooperative Extension service, your clay soil can benefit from expanded shale if it's heavy and sticky when wet "and gets deep cracks when it's dry in the summer." Plants don't grow well in clay soil because they don't get enough oxygen. Expanded shale creates cavities in the soil to hold both air and water. George recommends adding 3 in. of 1/4-in. to 3/8-in. shale, along with 3 in. of compost and tilling them into your soil 6 to 8 in. deep. Then cover your garden bed with a 3-in. layer of mulch.

The good news about expanded shale is that unlike other amendments such as compost or fertilizer, you only need to add the shale to your garden beds once. After that, you'll never need to add compost or commercial fertilizer again. The bad news is that expanded shale costs more than compost (about $10 for a 40-lb. bag; slightly less if you buy it in bulk). But according to George, it's worth it. "Using expanded shale is just so much better. It makes it fun to garden in clay."

Headache #4   Multiplying mushrooms

"We have so many mushrooms in our lawn that they make the weeds seem easy to control. We must have six different kinds, and they're worst after it rains. We've got a dog and grandkids, and those mushrooms are not only disgusting, but I'm worried someone's going to eat one."

 Reader Solution: Elusive. "We've tried using fungicides, but they're expensive, they require twice-weekly applications and you need to treat every single mushroom. If you miss even one application, the mushrooms come back and you need to start over again. We're not sure what to do."

— Eric Lucas

Expert input: We have good news and bad news for you, Eric. The good news, according to University of Minnesota turf expert Bob Mugaas, is that while mushrooms can look unsightly (and they're worse in years with a lot of rain), they're actually beneficial to your lawn. "They're part of the breakdown of organic material in the soil, and they help recycle nutrients."

The bad news, as you've already discovered, is that mushrooms are nearly impossible to get rid of. They're actually the fruit of an extensive underground root system. So even if you remove the visible mushrooms or use fungicides, the source of them is still there (they're like the tip of an iceberg).

According to Mugaas, you have several options. "You can certainly pull them." This won't permanently rid your lawn of mushrooms, but it can give you temporary relief.

You can also make your lawn less hospitable to fungi by correcting drainage problems and eliminating decaying organic matter. Grind down stumps, rake up grass clippings, dig up buried lumber, aerate, dethatch and replace old mulch.

The easiest option (or maybe the hardest for you, Eric) is to make peace with your mushrooms. Their numbers will increase and decrease depending on the season. Teach your grandchildren never to eat mushrooms from the lawn, and during cool, wet periods, keep a close eye on your pets.

OUTDOOR STRUCTURES, LANDSCAPING & GARDENING

Headache #5   Seasonal swamp

"I have a low spot in my yard that fills with runoff from our downspouts during rainstorms. It's not a constant problem, but it's a bear to grow grass there."

Reader Solution:
None yet. Help!
— Alena Gust

ENERGYSCAPES

Expert input: Alena, if you have workable soil (not clay), a rain garden is an easy and effective solution for a short-term, isolated drainage problem. "Building a rain garden means you don't have to fight a losing battle to grow turf," says Douglas Owens-Pike, plant ecologist and owner of EnergyScapes, a Minneapolis landscape design firm. "It's also a great way to treat rainfall as a resource rather than a problem."

All you need is a shallow depression (which it sounds like you already have) that has the soil amended so it drains quickly. Make sure your rain garden is located at least 10 ft. from your foundation so you won't have any seepage problems in your basement. Plant it with shrubs and perennials that tolerate pooling water as well as periods of drought (type "rain garden" into your online browser and you'll find tons of plant lists). The amended soil and water-loving plants capture the excess water, and it slowly percolates into the earth instead of running into the storm sewer or sitting on the surface of your lawn.

And according to Owens-Pike, rain gardens aren't limited to flowers or areas with full sun. "Partially shaded areas planted with lower-growing trees and shrubs can create wonderful wildlife habitat rain gardens that become perfect nesting areas for birds." (For detailed instructions for building a rain garden, search "rain garden" at familyhandyman.com.)

Headache #6   Boggy backyard

"Our house is at the bottom of a slope, and every time we had a hard rain, everything became a muddy mess. We got water in the crawl space and in the basement. We couldn't grow anything since it all just got washed away...our backyard was like a wasteland."

Reader Solution: "We built a **French drain gravel walkway** lined by decorative brick. The digging wasn't easy on my husband and stepsons, but during the first hard rain after we installed it, we all got our slickers on and went outside. There was nothing more beautiful than all that water gushing out the end of the drainpipe, and not a drop of it went into our crawl space or basement. We have a lawn and a garden now—and a beautiful gravel path."
— Nora Spencer

Expert input: "This is a creative solution for controlling a lot of water invisibly," says landscape architect Susan Jacobson. A French drain is similar to a dry creek bed, except the water flows underground through a drainpipe enclosed in a gravel-filled trench. It's effective because water flows through gravel much more quickly than through soil. The water migrates into the trench and flows out of a drain at its end point. The net effect, says Jacobson, is that your lot dries out. "Again, this solution works well if you have a place to dump the water safely such as a sandy area or a side yard that slopes away from your foundation."

If you don't have a place for the water to go, she suggests creating a small holding pond that actually takes advantage of the excess water. "The idea," says Jacobson, "is to work with the natural features of your yard rather than against them." If building a pond isn't an option, an alternative is to build a dry well. This is essentially a holding tank for large water runoff that slowly drains itself into the surrounding soil. (For step-by-step instructions for building a dry well, visit familyhandyman.com and search for "yard drainage.")

START A **GARDEN!**

Create a planting bed (for flowers or veggies) in 8 easy steps

by **Brett Martin**

Ready to start a garden? You could do what a friend of mine did: She threw some topsoil on top of an unused wooden sandbox, let her 6-year-old choose the seeds (strawberries, green beans, watermelon) and watered haphazardly. Net result? They ate a lot of green beans, and most of the rest of the plants were no-shows.

So maybe you'd want to start a garden the right way instead—do the planning, test the soil and cultivate the ideal soil conditions for the plants you choose. Here we'll show you how to start a garden—any size!—from scratch. All it takes is basic garden tools. A sod cutter to remove the grass and a rototiller make the job go faster but aren't necessary.

1 TRACK THE SUNLIGHT

The amount of sunlight your garden gets will determine which plants you should choose. You'll have the widest selection of plants to pick from if you place the garden in full sun to light shade. Vegetables require full sun.

You probably have an idea where you want to plant flowers to enhance the landscape. If so, pick plants suited for those growing conditions (like full sun, partial sun or shade). Take photos of the proposed site throughout the day so that when you shop for flowers, you'll have a reference of how much sun the area gets. If you're flexible on the garden location, choose a spot that suits the sun requirements of the plants you want. Take a trip to a garden center to see what plants are available for your zone and how much sun your favorites will need (visit usna.usda.gov/Hardzone/ushzmap.html for a plant hardiness zone map).

Unless you're planning a rain garden, avoid gardening in low spots in the yard where water collects. In the fall, low areas tend to be frost pockets, which can shorten your growing season. A well-drained area will yield the best plants.

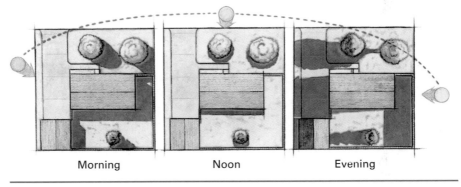

| Morning | Noon | Evening |

Take photos of your garden location in the morning, early afternoon and evening to see how much sun it gets. Vegetables and full-sun plants need six hours of daily sun; partial-sun plants three to six hours; and shade plants two to three hours.

2 OUTLINE THE GARDEN BED

Use a garden hose or landscaping paint to mark the perimeter of the garden bed. Avoid creating tight angles that would make it hard to mow around the garden. Gentle curves look more natural than sharp corners. And make the size manageable—you can always add on later if you decide you want a bigger garden.

Don't dig yet. Wait at least one full day so you can look at the site from various vantage points (like your deck or living room) and at different times of the day. It's a lot easier to change the shape or location now than after you've started digging. Once you decide on the layout, call 811 to have underground utilities marked (for free!). You'll have to identify irrigation lines on your own—they usually run in straight lines between sprinkler heads.

Mark the garden bed and make sure you're happy with the layout before you start digging.

3 TEST THE SOIL

A soil test will tell you whether you need to add amendments such as lime, nitrogen, phosphorus or potassium to the soil.

Test kits are available at home and garden centers, but use a university extension service or a state-certified soil-testing lab instead to get the most accurate results. Enter "university extension service" and your state in any search engine to find the nearest lab. Contact the lab to get the necessary paperwork to submit with your sample. Test fees are usually $15 to $20, and results take one to two weeks. Dig down 6 in. and scoop up a trowel full of soil. Take samples from 5 to 10 areas in the garden and mix them in a clean bucket. Wait for the soil to dry (this can take several days), then mail it to the extension service. Retest the soil every three to five years.

Send the soil sample, paperwork and a check to your local extension service. The service will mail back a report telling you the nutrient content of the soil and the type and amount of fertilizer to add. A lab report tells you what nutrients are needed for your soil.

5 REMOVE THE SOD

The grass has to go—you can't just till it under or it'll grow back and you'll never get rid of it. Digging up turf is hard work, so do yourself a favor and rent a power sod cutter from a rental center ($45 for four hours). Set the blade to cut just below the roots and slice the grass into long strips. Then roll the sod into easy-to-carry bundles. Use the sod to fill bare spots in the yard, or compost it to use later in your garden.

Cut away the sod in the garden with a power sod cutter. Remove the sod and use it in your yard or turn it upside down and start a compost pile.

4 EDGE THE GARDEN

Now that the prep work is done, you can dig and plant your garden

Slice and then dig around the edge of the garden bed to make it easier to follow the shape as you remove or kill the grass.

in a weekend. The first step is edging the garden bed. Use a square shovel or an edger to dig down about 6 in., slicing through the grass roots around the garden bed. After making the slices, dig around the garden edge at a slight angle to remove a 3-in. swath of grass and create a small trench. This keeps the sod cutter or herbicide from going into your yard when you remove or kill grass in the garden.

Ways to get rid of grass

A sod cutter is the fastest way to remove grass, but you can kill it and till it instead. Here are three options:

■ Herbicide. Spray with a non-select herbicide (such as Roundup, $13 for 16 ozs. of concentrate). Spray the herbicide after you've edged the garden so the weed-and-grass killer won't run into the lawn. If anything is still growing after seven days, spray it again and wait another seven days.

■ Plastic. Stake down clear plastic that's at least 2 mil thick ($3 for a 9 x 12-ft. sheet at home centers) over the garden for six to eight weeks to kill the grass.

■ Mulch. Place your mower deck on its lowest setting and cut the grass. Then cover the area with at least 2 in. of newspaper, cardboard, leaves or wood chips and keep them wet. The covering and grass will naturally decompose, giving you rich compost, but this process takes several months.

6 KEEP OUT GRASS

Add a border to keep grass in your lawn from invading your garden; it's hard to get rid of once it does. Home and garden centers sell a variety of border and edging materials.

Strips of steel, aluminum or heavy-duty plastic (starting at $1.60 per ft.) work best on fairly even terrain and are unobtrusive. Pavers (55¢ apiece and up) form a wide border that allows flowers to spill over and provides a flat surface to mow over. A raised stone wall contains the garden and looks attractive, but at $10 per ft. for a two-course wall, it's the most expensive option. Be sure your border extends at least 4 in. into the ground to keep out grass. Interested in building a low-maintenance border? Visit familyhandyman.com and search for "borders."

Borders provide an attractive finish, stop grass from creeping in and make it easier to mow around the garden.

8 ENRICH THE SOIL

Adding organic matter such as compost, manure or peat moss increases drainage in clay soils and water-holding capacity in sandy soils. It also makes the soil more permeable, which encourages root growth and attracts organisms that leave nutrients in the soil. There isn't one best type of organic matter, so buy whatever's the least expensive in your area.

Spread 2 to 4 in. of organic matter over the garden. You can work it into the top 6 to 10 in. of soil with a shovel by digging down, then flipping the load over to mix the organic matter and soil. But a faster, easier way is to use a rototiller ($45 for four hours at rental centers).

Work organic matter into the soil with a rototiller or a shovel. Organic matter improves drainage and adds nutrients.

7 FERTILIZE TO SUIT YOUR SOIL

Your soil test will tell you the type of fertilizer your garden needs. Fertilizer labels list the three main nutrients needed for plant growth. A 10-20-10 formula, for example, contains 10 percent nitrogen (N), 20 percent phosphorus (P) and 10 percent potassium (K).

Buy a slow-release granular fertilizer that contains the appropriate percentage of the nutrients your soil needs. If your soil only needs one nutrient, don't bother adding the others (some fertilizers contain just one nutrient, such as a 20-0-0). Apply the fertilizer just before planting.

Spread a slow-release fertilizer on the garden using a hand-held spreader for even coverage.

Consider a raised bed

If it's almost impossible to grow plants in your soil (heavy clay, poor drainage, rocky), a raised garden bed is the perfect solution. It lets you bring in good soil and create the ideal garden bed. It also lets you garden without bending over as far or working on your hands and knees. Limit the size of the bed so you can reach all the plants from the border, and build it at least 12 in. deep to fill with topsoil.

To begin, cut the grass in the area and cover it with cardboard or layers of newspaper to kill it. The paper will decompose into organic material. Then build the bed and fill it with topsoil, mixing organic matter into the top 6 to 10 in.

STUNNING BRICK FIRE PIT

A masonry masterpiece you can build—with some tips from our veteran bricklayer

by Elisa Bernick

Backyard fire pits are still all the rage, and for good reason. There's nothing like a crackling fire to draw friends and family together. Sure, you could set some stones around a hole or spend a hundred bucks on a steel fire ring. But if you spend twice that, you can build a handsome brick fire pit to create a gathering space in your backyard. We spent $250 on this fire pit. It's maintenance free and easy to clean out, and it will last forever.

If you've ever wanted to learn to lay brick, a backyard fire pit is an excellent project to start with. Even if your brickwork isn't perfect, the fire pit will still look great. We asked Doug Montzka, of Montkza Concrete & Masonry in St. Paul, MN, to show us some tricks and tools of the trade. Set aside several days to complete your fire pit: First you'll pour the footing and let it set up. Then you'll mortar the bricks into place.

Dig the pit

Before digging, call your utility companies (dial 811; for more info, go to call811.com) to check the location of buried utility lines. Also check the fire pit code in your area. Most require a fire pit to be 25 ft. away from any structures and overhanging trees. Think about how the prevailing winds blow through your backyard. Don't locate your pit upwind of your patio or where the smoke will blow into your windows or those of your neighbors.

A 3-ft.-diameter fire pit creates enough room for a good fire, yet keeps everyone close enough to chat (and complies with most codes). To make measuring the pit and pouring the concrete footing easy, we used two cardboard concrete form tubes ($45 for the two from a concrete supply company). You could also make your own forms by screwing together 1/8-in. hardboard. Rip a 4 x 8-ft. sheet ($7) into four 8-in.-wide strips. Carefully bend and screw two strips together to create a 36-in.-diameter circle, and use the other two to make a 48-in.-diameter circle.

Mark the outside edge of the pit (**Photo 1**). Then shovel out the soil to a depth of 8 in. (**Photo 2**). Don't disturb the underlying soil.

Keys to a better fire pit

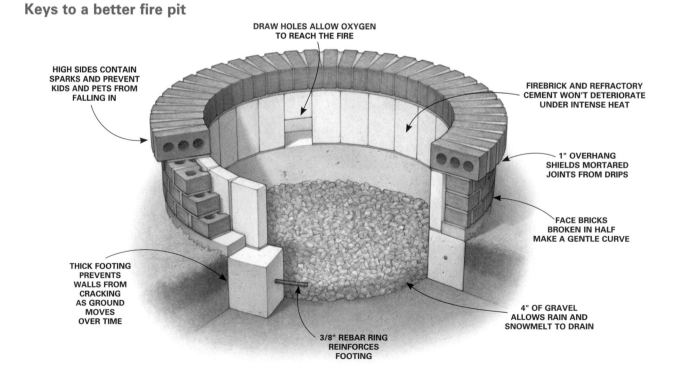

DRAW HOLES ALLOW OXYGEN TO REACH THE FIRE

HIGH SIDES CONTAIN SPARKS AND PREVENT KIDS AND PETS FROM FALLING IN

FIREBRICK AND REFRACTORY CEMENT WON'T DETERIORATE UNDER INTENSE HEAT

1" OVERHANG SHIELDS MORTARED JOINTS FROM DRIPS

FACE BRICKS BROKEN IN HALF MAKE A GENTLE CURVE

THICK FOOTING PREVENTS WALLS FROM CRACKING AS GROUND MOVES OVER TIME

3/8" REBAR RING REINFORCES FOOTING

4" OF GRAVEL ALLOWS RAIN AND SNOWMELT TO DRAIN

1 **Mark out the pit.** Set the larger form in position and spray paint around it. Dig a hole about 8 in. deep and 3 in. larger in diameter than the form.

2 **Level the pit.** Check the bottom of the hole with a level. Remove high spots by scraping off soil rather than digging. That way, you won't loosen the underlying soil. Compact the soil with a hand tamper or a 4x4 post.

3 **Stake the forms.** If the forms aren't quite level, raise one end and drive a screw through the stake. If the forms aren't completely round, reposition the stakes.

4 **Add the rebar.** Bend rebar into half circles and tie them together with wire to make a ring. Fill the forms halfway. Press the ring into the concrete, making sure it doesn't touch the sides of the forms.

Pour a sturdy footing

The concrete footing will create a stable base for the pit walls and keep the sides of your pit from cracking as the ground moves over time. Stake the forms (**Photo 3**) and mix up ten 80-lb. bags of concrete mix ($3.40 per 80-lb. bag at home centers) according to the manufacturer's directions. If you're using hardboard forms, stake them so they're nice and round. Fill the forms halfway and press a rebar ring into the concrete for strength (**Photo 4**). Finish filling the forms to the top and tap the tubes gently with a sledgehammer until the concrete mix is level. Smooth the top of the footing (**Photo 5**). Let the concrete completely set up overnight and then remove the forms.

Dry-set the firebrick liner

Because regular clay brick can crack at high temperatures, we're using firebrick (also called "refractory" brick) to line the inside of the pit walls. Firebrick is a dense brick that's kilned to withstand high temperatures. It's larger, thicker and wider than regular brick, and you can find it at

Meet a Pro

Doug Montzka
Doug Montzka, of Montkza Concrete & Masonry in St. Paul, MN, has been in the concrete and masonry business for 23 years. "I started getting requests for brick fire pits a few years ago. It isn't rocket science, but there are a few tricks to doing the job right."

5 Finish the footing. Shovel in the remaining concrete until the forms are filled. Recheck level, hammering the forms down if necessary, and smooth the top of the footer. Let the concrete set overnight.

CONCRETE FLOAT

6 Dry-set the firebrick. Adjust the spacing between bricks so you won't have to cut the last brick to fit (cutting firebrick ain't easy). Mark the position of every brick on the footing.

FIREBRICK

REFRACTORY CEMENT

1/8" TO 1/4" JOINT

FLUSH WITH INSIDE OF FOOTING

7 Mortar the firebrick. Butter a thin layer of cement on the footer and position your first brick. Butter the second brick and butt it against the first. Continue around the circle checking level side-to-side and back-to-front as you go.

SPLIT FIREBRICK

AIR HOLE

SUPPORT

8 Create air holes. Leave gaps in the firebrick in four spots and then fill them with half bricks. These gaps are "draw holes" that feed air to the fire. Prop up the half bricks until the mortar sets.

most brickyards. Firebrick is more expensive ($2 per brick compared with 75¢ or less), but it will stand up to nightly fires for years to come. You'll need 25 firebricks for a 3-ft. diameter pit.

Because firebrick is so dense, it's tougher to split than regular brick. "Soldiering" the brick (standing it on end) minimizes the amount of splitting and lets you easily accommodate the curve of the pit. You'll only need to split four firebricks (use the technique shown in **Photo 9**), which you'll place across from one another around the pit to create draw holes for oxygen for your fire. After you split your firebricks, dry-set them in place on top of the footing (**Photo 6**).

Mortar the firebrick

Firebrick is mortared with refractory cement, which, unlike regular masonry mortar, can withstand high heat. Refractory cement comes premixed in a bucket ($10 per half gallon at brickyards) and has the consistency of peanut butter.

A margin trowel makes it easier to scoop cement out of the bucket and butter the bricks. A tuck pointer (**Photo 14**) is useful for cleaning up the joints.

Work with four bricks at a time. The secret is to trowel the cement on thin, like you're spreading peanut butter on toast, and use the tightest joints you can (**Photo 7**).

9 **Split 80 bricks in half.** Cup the brick in your hand, keeping your fingers below the top edge of the brick. (Our mason doesn't use gloves, but we suggest you do!) Give the brick a solid tap (a very solid tap for firebrick) on the outside edge near the center hole. Avoid hitting your hand. Repeat 79 times.

BRICK HAMMER

10 **Set the face brick.** Lay a thick bed of mortar and let it harden for 15 minutes. Then lay 3/8 in. of fresh mortar and begin setting brick. Butter one side of each brick before you set it in place.

1/4" GAP

2" MORTAR BED

3/8" FRESH MORTAR

11 **Work in sections.** Working on one-third of the pit at a time, check the level of each course and tap down the bricks as necessary. Stagger the joints between courses for strength.

3/8" STAGGERED JOINTS

12 **Strike the joints.** After you finish each section of face brick, use a jointer to smooth ("strike" or "tool") the joints before the mortar dries too much. The mortar is ready to strike if you press your finger into it and the indentation remains. Striking gives the wall a uniform, polished look.

CONCAVE JOINTER

Continue mortaring the firebrick around the pit, placing the half bricks for the draw holes at four opposite points around the ring (**Photo 8**). Check for level across the pit and the vertical level of the bricks as you go.

Complete the outside walls with face brick

We used SW ("severe weathering") face brick (also called "common" or "building" brick; 25¢ to 75¢ per) to line the outside pit walls. If your climate doesn't include freeze/thaw cycles, you can use MW ("moderate weathering") building brick. Home centers and brickyards carry a large variety of brick. You'll need 80 face bricks for a 3-ft.-

diameter pit. Face brick with holes ("cored") is easy to split with a brick hammer (**Photo 9**). It's easier to form the curve of the pit walls with half bricks. You'll lay three courses of face brick and mortar them together with Type N mortar mix ($5 per 80-lb. bag at home centers, and you'll need about five bags).

Because face brick is smaller than firebrick, you'll need to make up the size difference as you lay your three courses of face brick. The difference between the height of your firebrick and the total height of three stacked face bricks will determine the width of your mortar beds between courses. Dry-set the face brick, marking where each

FLUSH WITH
FIREBRICK

3/8" MORTAR
BED

TUCK POINTER

1" OVERHANG

13 **Mortar the cap bricks.** Lay a 3/8-in. bed of mortar across 10 to 12 bricks at a time. Lay the bricks on edge and butter the face of each brick on the outside edge as you go.

14 **Fill gaps.** Add a small amount of mortar to the joints to fill any gaps. Check level frequently and tap gently with a brick hammer to adjust the spacing. Leave a 1-in. overhang on the outside to allow for rain to drip off. Once all the bricks have been mortared in place, strike the joints for a smooth, finished look.

course of face brick has to hit the firebrick to make the third course of face brick level with the firebrick.

To keep your mortar joints between courses a reasonable width, first lay a 2- to 3-in.-thick bed of mortar right on top of the footing. Let it set up slightly (15 minutes) and smooth out the top. Then, working on one-third of the pit at a time, mortar each course of face brick into place, leaving a 1/4-in. gap between the firebrick and the face brick (**Photo 10**). Level the brick between courses, tapping the bricks down when necessary (**Photo 11**). Remember to leave the draft holes open as you mortar each section of face brick and smooth out the finished joints (**Photo 12**).

Finish off the top lip

Finish the pit with a matching "row-lock" cap using regular face brick set on edge. You'll need about 40 face bricks for this cap, which will help protect the wall joints from rain, keep sparks contained and give you a nice ledge to warm your feet on. We used brick, but you could use natural stone for a different look. Work with 10 to 12 bricks at a time. Lay a 3/8-in. bed of mortar, then butter each brick and press it into place (**Photo 13**). Work your way around the circle, filling any gaps with mortar and checking level and placement frequently (**Photo 14**). Smooth the finished joints with a concave jointer.

Give the cement and mortar a week to cure completely before lighting a fire in your pit. Pour a few inches of gravel on the pit's floor for drainage and you're ready for your first wienie roast. ⌂

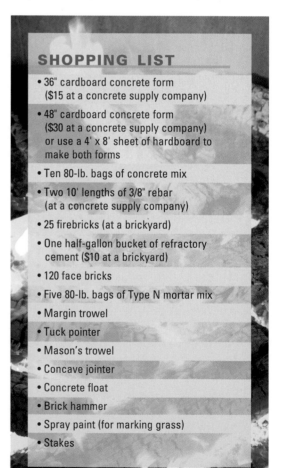

SHOPPING LIST

- 36" cardboard concrete form ($15 at a concrete supply company)
- 48" cardboard concrete form ($30 at a concrete supply company) or use a 4' x 8' sheet of hardboard to make both forms
- Ten 80-lb. bags of concrete mix
- Two 10' lengths of 3/8" rebar (at a concrete supply company)
- 25 firebricks (at a brickyard)
- One half-gallon bucket of refractory cement ($10 at a brickyard)
- 120 face bricks
- Five 80-lb. bags of Type N mortar mix
- Margin trowel
- Tuck pointer
- Mason's trowel
- Concave jointer
- Concrete float
- Brick hammer
- Spray paint (for marking grass)
- Stakes

ONE-DAY RETAINING WALL

The simplest, cheapest, back-friendliest retaining wall in history

by **Travis Larson**

I needed a retaining wall. But I didn't want to abuse my back by schlepping around landscape blocks. Plus, I didn't want to bust the bank buying good-looking blocks. So after accessing my internal carpentry database, I came up with a solution: a wood foundation built as a retaining wall. I've built dozens of wood foundations (yes, made from treated wood for real basements under new homes), so this was a no-brainer—super easy, attractive and cheap.

This 32-in.-high, 32-ft.-long wall was built in one fairly laid-back day by me, Brad and another friend of mine named Bob Cat (meet him in **Photo 7**). The materials cost $500, plus another $500 for Bob and his operator, who supplied gravel and some extra topsoil for fill. Having Bob involved meant there was very little shovel work. And Brad appreciated having Bob there almost as much as I did.

The skeleton of the wall is a treated wood, 2x4 stud wall clad on both sides with 1/2-in. treated plywood. It's held in place with 2x4 "dead men"

Figure A: Wall Anatomy

2x8 TOP CAP

2x4 TIE PLATE

2x4 TOP PLATE

2x4 SLEEPER

ICE-AND-WATER BARRIER

2x4 STRUT

1/2" PLYWOOD

2x4 STUD

2x4 BOTTOM PLATE

DRAIN TILE

1x6 TRIM BOARD

2x6 FOOTING PLATE

assemblies buried in the backfill. The dead men are 2x4 struts bolted to the wall studs and anchored to a perpendicular 2x4 sleeper (see **Figure A**). The weight of the soil on the dead men anchors the wall against the backfill pressure. It's important to locate the bottom of the wall below grade a few inches so the earth in front of the wall will anchor the base in place.

Get the right stuff

Ordinary treated wood will last a good long time depending on soil conditions, although wet sites with clay will shorten the wall's life somewhat. I used ordinary treated wood from the home center, and I figure the wall will last at least 20 years. To build a wall that'll last forever, use foundation-grade treated wood, the material used for basements. It's usually Southern yellow pine, a very strong softwood that accepts treatment better than most, and contains a higher concentration of preservatives. You may find it at lumberyards where contractors shop. Or you

1 **Level the gravel base.** Lay the 2x6 footing plates on edge and use a 4-ft. level to level the gravel. Pack the gravel with the footing plate to drive it down until it's flat and level.

2 **Frame and set the walls.** Frame the walls and stand them on top of the footing plates. Snap a chalk line on the footing plate 1 in. from the edge and then screw the bottom plates to the footing plate even with the line.

can special-order it from any home center or lumberyard, although you'll pay a premium.

Choose nails rated for treated wood: 16d for the framing and 8d for the sheathing. Use 3-in. construction screws for standoffs and dead men connections—again, ones that are rated for treated wood. You'll also need a box each of 2- and 3-in. deck screws for the trim boards. See the Materials List on p. 194.

Prepping the site

I had a gentle slope to retain, not a huge hill. This 32-in.-high wall is designed to hold back a gentle slope and is good for walls up to 40 in. For walls 40 to 48 in, place the studs on 12-in. centers and keep the rest of the wall the same. Don't build the wall more than 48 in. high—a taller wall requires special engineering.

Do the digging with a shovel if you wish. The trick is to dig halfway into the hill and throw the soil on top of the hill. That way you'll have enough fill left for behind the wall. The downside is that if you hand-dig, you'll also need to dig channels for the 2x4 struts and sleepers (see **Photo 5**).

It's much easier to hire a skid steer (Bob) and his

operator to dig into the hill and then cut down a foot or so behind the wall to create a shelf for resting the dead men. Expect to pay a few hundred dollars for skid steer services. The operator can also scoop out the 12-in.-wide by 10-in.-deep trench for the gravel footing, and deliver and dump a 6-in. layer of gravel into the footing. Then you'll only need to do a bit of raking to level off the trench. A yard of gravel will take care of 50 linear feet of wall. If you have extra gravel, use it for backfill against the back of the wall for drainage. Have Bob and his operator return to fill against the back side of the wall and do some final grading.

Get the footings ready

Fill the trench with gravel. Any type will do, but pea gravel is the easiest to work with. Roughly rake it level, then tip one of the footing plates on edge and rest a level on top to grade the footing (**Photo 1**). Use the plate as a screed, as if you're leveling in concrete, and you'll get it really close, really fast. Try to get it within 1/4 in. or so of level. Offset any footing plate joints at least 2 ft. to either side of wall joints. To drive down the plate until it's level, stand on it as you pound it into the gravel with another board, occasionally checking it with a level. If you can't drive the board down to achieve level, scoop out shallow trenches on either side of the footing plate with your hand. Then there will be a place for gravel to flow as you drive down the plate.

Frame and set the walls

Frame the walls in your driveway or on the garage floor. The walls are very light, so you can carry them a long way if you need to. Build them in sections, whatever length you like, and screw the end studs together at the site. Leave off the sheathing for now. Snap a chalk line 1 in. in from the outside of the footing plate to align the walls (**Photo 2**). Place them, screw the joining studs together with four 3-in. construction screws and screw the wall plates to the footing plates in every other stud space with 3-in. construction screws.

Plumb, straighten and brace the walls from the front side and then add the tie plate. Make sure to seam the tie plate joints at least 4 ft. away from the wall joints.

Sheathe and waterproof the walls

Set the plywood panels in place one at a time. Draw and cut 1-5/8-in. x 3-5/8-in. openings spaced 6 in. down from the underside of the top plate and directly next to every other stud. Nail each panel into place with 8d nails spaced every 8 in. before moving on to the next one. Cover the outside with ice-and-water barrier (**Photo 4**). The adhesive won't hold the barrier in place, so staple it as needed. Cut off the excess at the top and cut out the strut openings with a utility knife.

3 **Brace and sheathe the wall.** Plumb and brace the wall, then screw down the tie plate. Dry-fit the plywood to the back of the framing and mark the strut holes and cut out the holes. Then nail the plywood to the studs.

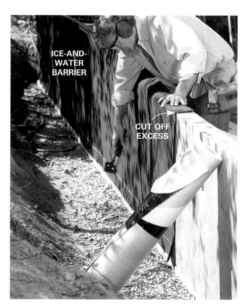

4 **Waterproof the walls.** Clad the back of the wall with ice-and-water barrier and cut out the strut holes with a utility knife.

5 **Assemble the dead men.** Poke the struts through the holes and screw them to each stud. Roughly prop up the struts and secure a continuous 2x4 sleeper to the end of each one with two 3-in. screws.

6 Add the trim. Nail vertically oriented plywood to the top and bottom plates and to the front of the wall. Make sure to seam plywood over studs. Screw a 2x8 top cap to the top plate, hanging it over the front of the wall 1-1/2 in. Fasten vertical 1x6s to the sheathing with 1-1/2-in. spaces between boards.

7 Time to backfill. Plumb and brace the wall from the back. Backfill, starting at the sleeper, to anchor the wall into place as you continue filling the space behind the wall.

Add the struts and sleepers

Slip the struts through each hole. Prop them up so they're close to level, either by piling up dirt or supporting them on chunks of scrap wood. Screw each one to a stud with three 3-in. construction screws. (Predrill the holes to prevent splitting since it's so near the end.) Screw the sleeper to the other end of each strut with two more screws.

Skin and finish the front

Before you can finish the front of the wall and backfill behind it, you'll have to remove the front braces. So prop up the dead men to keep the wall near plumb while you finish the front. Cut the plywood and nail it on, orienting it vertically to the front so the exposed grain will match the 1x6 boards applied over them. Add the 2x8 cap, keeping a 1-1/2-in. overhang at the front. Screw it to the tie plate with 3-in. deck screws. Screw the 1x6 treated boards to the sheathing with 2-in. deck screws. We spaced our boards every 1-1/2 in. using a scrap 2x4 as a spacer. Don't trust the spacer for more than a few boards at a time. Occasionally check a board with a level and make any necessary adjustments.

Backfill and finish

Plumb and brace the wall from the back by nailing braces to the top cap and stake them on the hill. Prop up every other strut and the sleepers with scraps of wood or the fill falling on the struts and sleepers will force the wall out of plumb. Backfill first against the front of the wall over the footing to lock the wall base into place, then fill behind it. Then fill over the sleeper, working your way toward the wall itself. The object is to lock in the sleeper before the fill pushes against the wall. Once the backfill is in place, it's a good idea to run a sprinkler over the fill for several hours to make it settle before you remove the braces.

If you like the look of your wall, you're good to go—no finish required. The treated wood will weather from green to gray in a year or two. We applied two coats of Sikkens Log & Siding in the Butternut color. 🏠

MATERIALS LIST

This 32-ft.-long wall required the materials listed below. If you're building a shorter or longer wall, just figure a percentage of these quantities and you'll get close. For the longer boards, choose them so combinations of whatever lengths will handle the length of your wall.

QTY.	ITEM
1	Roll of ice-and-water barrier
1	50' roll of 4" drain tile
8	Sheets of 1/2" plywood (sheathing)
2	2x6 x 16' (footing plates)
20	2x4 x 8' (studs and struts)
8	2x4 x 16' (sleeper and wall plates)
2	2x8 x 16' (top cap)
20	1x6 x 8' (trim boards)

FAUX STONE PATIO TABLE

The beauty and toughness of stone at a fraction of the cost

by **Gary Wentz**

Like a lot of my other projects, this one was inspired by sticker shock. While I was wandering through a garden center, a stone table caught my eye. It was beautiful and low-maintenance and would last a lifetime. The only trouble was the price: $650 (on sale!). As usual, my solution was to build one myself.

My version isn't real stone, but it fools most people and has all the durability of stone. My total materials cost was just under $150; about $110 for the top and $40 for the pedestal. Everything you'll need is available at most home centers.

A different kind of grout

Construction grout is used mostly for heavy construction projects like anchoring steel columns. But it's also perfect for casting projects because it has a creamy consistency that takes on the shape and texture of the form almost perfectly. Use a smooth form and you're guaranteed a smooth, uniform tabletop. Most home centers carry construction grout in 50-lb. bags, which cost about $13. (Quikrete Precision Grout and Sakrete Construction Grout are two brands.) If yours doesn't, go to quikrete.com or sakrete.com to find a dealer. I darkened the grout by adding cement colorant to the water (see **Photo 2**).

Build the form

Plastic-coated particleboard (called "melamine") is perfect for form work because it's inexpensive and smooth. Cut the form base to 31-1/2 x 31-1/2 in. and then cut 2 x 32-in. strips for the form sides. Attach the sides to the base as shown in **Photo 1**. The overhanging sides make dismantling the form easier; you can just whack them loose with a hammer. Coat the form with spray lubricant (**Photo 1**). Important: Use a lubricant that dries instead of leaving an oily coating. The label will say something like "leaves a dry film." Liquid Wrench Dry Lubricant is one brand.

Next, grab a pencil and sketch a random pattern on the form outlining the areas you'll cover with grout first (**Photo 3**). The pencil lines will determine where the dark veins appear in the finished top. Set the form on a sturdy work surface and level the form with shims. Construction grout is slushy and will overflow if the form tilts. Spilled grout will leave stains, so cover the floor with plastic drop cloths.

The top is made from construction grout tinted with colorant. Tile grout creates the dark veins.

Get ready to mix

Mixing and pouring the construction grout is a three-phase process: You'll use most or all of the first bag to pour a pattern (**Photo 3**), the second to fill in the pattern (**Photo 6**) and the third to completely fill the form.

Forming a crinkled edge

Smooth edges on the tabletop are fine, but a crinkled edge will give it a more natural look. To start, cut four strips of aluminum foil tape about an inch longer than the form sides. Then...

SCRUNCH IT UP.   **STRAIGHTEN IT OUT.**

STICK IT ON THE FORM SIDES.

1 **Build an upside-down form.** Assemble the form, spray on lubricant and wipe off the excess. Cast upside down, the table-top's surface face will turn out as smooth and flat as the melamine form.

2 **Mix one bag at a time.** Add grout to water mixed with colorant. Turn a bucket into a giant measuring cup so you can easily use the correct amount of colored water with each bag.

3 **Pour a pattern.** Sketch a pattern on the form and fill the outlined areas with mounds of construction grout. This pattern will show up on the top of the table.

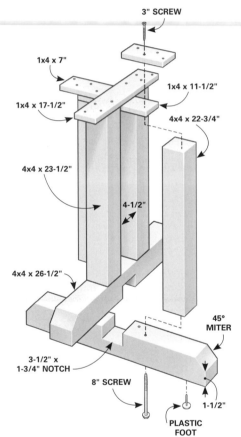

3" SCREW
1x4 x 7"
1x4 x 11-1/2"
1x4 x 17-1/2"
4x4 x 22-3/4"
4x4 x 23-1/2"
4-1/2"
4x4 x 26-1/2"
45° MITER
3-1/2" x 1-3/4" NOTCH
8" SCREW
1-1/2"
PLASTIC FOOT

Figure A: Pedestal
The tabletop height is 30 in. The top itself is 30 x 30 in. and 2 in. thick.

Tabletop materials

150 lbs. of construction grout, 3/4-in. melamine (sold in 4 x 8-ft. sheets), Quikrete Cement Color (10 oz.), spray lubricant, plastic cement tub, 2-1/2-in.-wide foil tape, 2-in. nails or screws, unsanded tile grout (black or charcoal), tile or stone sealer, welded wire mesh.

Turning a bucket into a giant measuring cup (see **Photo 2**) will let you add equal amounts of water and cement colorant to each of the three bags without measuring each time. First, measure the correct amount of water into the bucket (I use 4.5 liters per bag) and mark the water level on the bucket. Measure in more water to locate the other two marks (at 9 and 13.5 liters).

Next, empty the bucket and dump in the cement colorant. Much of it will remain in the bottle. To wash it out, pour in a

little water, shake hard and pour again. Repeat until all the colorant is washed out. Refill the bucket with water and you'll have tinted water, premeasured into three equal amounts. The colorant tends to settle to the bottom, so stir the colored water before each use.

Construction grout hardens fast. In warm weather, it will become stiff and difficult to work with in just 15 minutes. Minutes wasted cutting the wire mesh or searching for a tool can ruin the project. So have *absolutely everything* ready to go before you start mixing. It's best to have a helper, too. To slow down the hardening, use cold water only.

Mix the construction grout in a plastic cement tub ($6). Don't pour the water directly from the bucket into the mixing tub; it's too hard to control the flow. Instead, ladle the water into the tub with a smaller container. Dump in about half the bag and mix it thoroughly. Gradually add the rest of the bag as you mix. If the mixed grout stiffens before you can use it, stir it to restore the slushy consistency. If it becomes too stiff to stir, toss it. The tabletop only requires about 2-1/2 bags, so you can afford to waste some.

■ To cut the half-lap joints, set the cutting depth on your circular saw to 1-3/4 in. Cut a series of kerfs no more than 1/8 in. apart. Break out the slices with a hammer and chisel.
■ Fasten the top to the pedestal with eight concrete screws. Construction grout is easy to drill; you don't need a hammer drill. Wrap tape around the drill bit to mark the depth, and be super-duper careful not to poke through the top.

Pedestal materials

2 4x4 x 8' cedar
1 1x4 x 8' pressure-treated
8" construction or lag screws, 1-3/4" concrete screws, 3" screws, furniture feet, exterior stain.

4 Create the veins. Sprinkle dry tile grout along the edges of the mounds. The colored powder will form dark lines in the finished top.

5 Blow the grout. Turn down the pressure on your compressor and blow the tile grout against the edges of the mounds.

6 Fill in the blank spots. Cover the bare areas of the form. Pour *between* the areas you covered first, not on top of them. Jiggle the form to spread and level the mix.

7 Add the mesh. With the form about half full, lay in the welded wire mesh for reinforcement. Then completely fill the form.

8 Screed it off. Scrape off the excess using a straight board and a sawing motion. Cover the wet grout with plastic. The longer it stays wet, the stronger it will cure.

9 Seal the tabletop. Bring out the color with sealer. Before you apply the sealer, ease the tabletop's sharp edges with 80-grit sandpaper.

FAQs

Can I make it bigger?
Yes, but remember the weight factor. I once made a 3 x 5-ft. tabletop from construction grout. Moving it was like a scene from "The Ten Commandments."

What about other colors?
Home centers typically carry three or four colors of liquid colorant, and you'll find a huge range of powdered colors online (search for "cement colorant"). I've done dozens of color experiments and have learned one big lesson: Coloring cement-based products is tricky. The results I got were sometimes good, sometimes bad, but always a surprise.

Why not use standard concrete mix?
You can. But don't expect to get the same look you'll get from construction grout. With concrete, you're likely to get a rougher surface with more air bubbles and craters. That's not necessarily bad, just different.

Pour, wait patiently and seal

Photos 3 – 9 show how to complete the top. Don't forget to turn down your compressor's pressure to about 5 psi before you blow the tile grout (Photo 5). Cut the 2 x 2-ft. section of mesh (Photo 7) using bolt cutters. Wire cutters won't do the job.

Resist the temptation to tear off the form as soon as the grout is hard. The longer the grout stays wet, the stronger it will get. Give it at least three days. A week is even better. To remove the form, get a helper and flip the form upside down. (Don't let the top tip out of the form!) Then knock the form sides loose with a hammer and lift the form off the top. Don't despair when you unveil the bland, gray top. The sealer will deepen the color and accentuate the black veins (Photo 9). Most sealers can't be applied until the grout has cured for at least 28 days. Before you apply sealer to the top, try it on the underside to make sure you like the look. I used a glossy "stone and tile" sealer to bring out the most color. A sealer with a matte finish will have a subtler look. ⌂

Buy one, get one cheap

You can cast a second tabletop using mostly leftover materials. The only thing you'll need to buy is more construction grout ($40).

CONCRETE PATIO COVER UP

No need to tear out an ugly slab—just hide it!

by **Jeff Timm** and **Gary Wentz**

Before

After

A concrete patio is made for practicality—not beauty. It starts out looking plain and goes downhill from there. As craters, cracks and stains accumulate, it can go from dull to downright ugly in just a few years. But there's a simple solution, whether you want to dress up a bland patio or hide an aging one. Covering concrete with paver bricks is much easier than pouring new concrete or laying pavers the traditional way. It requires less skill and less time, and it's a whole lot easier on your back.

Assess your slab

This project will work with most patios. Surface damage like flaking, chips and craters is no problem. But a few conditions make this method a no-go:

■ **A too-low threshold.** Door thresholds have to be high enough above the existing patio to allow for the thickness of the border pavers, plus an extra 3/4 in. to allow for "frost heave"—rising of the slab when the soil freezes.

■ **Expanding cracks.** This method will work over most cracks—which grow and shrink with seasonal ground movement. But if you have a crack that has noticeably grown in recent years, this method is risky. The crack may eventually "telegraph" through the pavers, creating a hump or gaps.

Money and materials

The materials for this 12 x 14-ft. patio cost about $850, or $5 per sq. ft. Using less expensive pavers, you could cut the cost by almost half. Most landscape suppliers and home centers stock all the materials, but you may have to do a little hunting for the right combination of pavers. The pavers used for the border must be at least 3/4 in.

thicker than the "field" pavers, which cover the area between the borders. That thickness difference will allow for a bed of sand under the field. A difference of more than 3/4 in. is fine; you'll just need a little more sand. If you can't find thick pavers you like, consider retaining wall cap blocks for the border. We used cement pavers for the border and clay pavers for the field.

To estimate how much sand you'll need, grab your calculator. First determine the square footage of the sand bed. Then divide that number by 12 for a 1-in. bed or 18 for a 3/4-in. bed. That will tell you how many cubic feet of sand to get. You can have a load of sand delivered or

Figure A
Pavers over a concrete slab

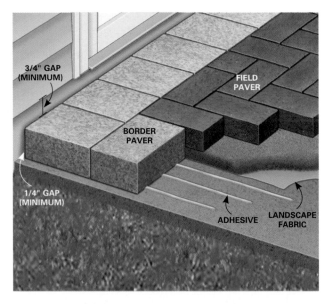

3/4" GAP (MINIMUM)

FIELD PAVER

BORDER PAVER

1/4" GAP (MINIMUM)

ADHESIVE

LANDSCAPE FABRIC

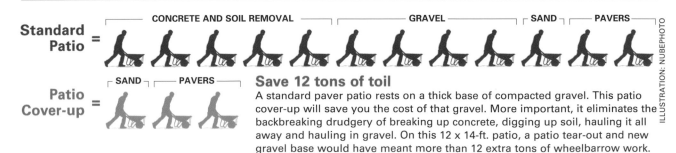

Standard Patio =

CONCRETE AND SOIL REMOVAL — GRAVEL — SAND — PAVERS

Patio Cover-up =

SAND — PAVERS

Save 12 tons of toil
A standard paver patio rests on a thick base of compacted gravel. This patio cover-up will save you the cost of that gravel. More important, it eliminates the backbreaking drudgery of breaking up concrete, digging up soil, hauling it all away and hauling in gravel. On this 12 x 14-ft. patio, a patio tear-out and new gravel base would have meant more than 12 extra tons of wheelbarrow work.

1 Scrub the perimeter. Clean the edges of the patio where you'll later glue down the border pavers. Clean concrete means a stronger glue bond.

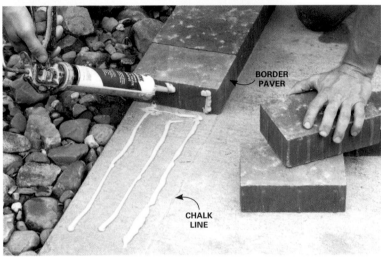

BORDER PAVER

CHALK LINE

2 Glue down the border pavers. After setting each paver, run a bead of construction adhesive up the side of it. That will keep the sand from washing out between pavers.

Figure B
Border layout

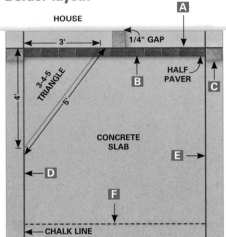

HOUSE

1/4" GAP

3'

A

HALF PAVER

B

C

3-4-5 TRIANGLE

4'

5'

CONCRETE SLAB

E

D

F

◄── CHALK LINE

A Snap a chalk line parallel to the house to mark the location of the border pavers. Remember to leave a gap of at least 1/4 in. between the border pavers and the house.

B Lay out field pavers to locate the side borders. A simple row of pavers will work even if you plan to lay them later in a "herringbone" pattern as we did. The goal is to establish a field width that allows each course to end with a full or half paver, but not smaller pieces. That means less cutting, less waste and a neater look.

C Position the border pavers and mark their locations. It's OK if the border pavers don't quite reach the edge of the patio, but don't let them overhang. Nudge one border outward by 1/4 in. to allow a little extra space for the field pavers.

D Snap a chalk line to mark one side border. To make this line square with the line along the house, use the 3-4-5 method.

E Mark the other side border. Measure from the first side to make sure the two sides are parallel.

F Leave the final border unmarked and install the border after the field is complete. That open end makes screeding off the excess sand easier and lets you position the final border perfectly.

save the delivery fee by picking up a load yourself with a truck or trailer. Most home centers also sell bagged sand. A 50-lb. bag (1/2 cu. ft.) costs about $3.

Lay the border first

To get started, scrub the border area (**Photo 1**) with a concrete cleaner or muriatic acid mixed with water (check the label for mixing and safety instructions). Any stiff brush will do, but a deck stripping brush ($6) on a broom handle makes it easier. Hose down the patio when you're done scrubbing the border.

While the concrete is drying, grab a tape measure and a chalk line and carefully plan the locations of the borders (see **Figure B**). Using the chalk lines

as a guide, glue down the border pavers along the house and two sides of the patio (**Photo 2**). We used polyurethane construction adhesive for a strong, long-lasting bond ($5 per 10-oz. tube). If adhesive squishes up between pavers, don't try to wipe it off. Just let it harden, then trim it off with a utility knife.

A flat bed of sand

If the field area is more than 10 ft. wide, you'll need a screed pipe in the center of the patio (**Photo 3**). A 10-ft. section of black or galvanized steel plumbing pipe ($14) works best. For a 1-in. bed, use 3/4-in. pipe; for a 3/4-in. bed, use 1/2-in. pipe. Keep in mind that each pipe size is listed by its *inner* diameter, but the *outer*

diameter is what matters here: 3/4-in. pipe has an outer diameter of about 1-1/8 in.; 1/2-in. pipe, about 5/8 in. In both cases, you'll get an extra 1/8 in. of sand bed thickness and the field pavers will stand about 1/8 in. above the border pavers. Then, when you "tamp" the

3 **Spread fabric, then sand.** Lay down landscape fabric to keep the sand from washing down into cracks. Then position the screed pipe and spread the sand.

SCREED PIPE

LANDSCAPE FABRIC

SCREED PIPE

NOTCH

4 **Flatten the sand.** Notch one end of a 2x6 to match the depth of the field pavers. The other end rides on the screed pipe. Screed both halves of the field, moving your screed pipe as you go.

5 **Lay the pavers.** Cover the sand with field pavers. When the field is complete, glue down the final border pavers. Then tamp the field with a plate compactor and sweep sand over the pavers to fill in the gaps.

field with a plate compactor, the sand will compact and the field pavers will settle flush with the border.

"Screed" the sand flat with a notched 2x6 (**Photo 4**). The depth of the notch should be 1/8 in. less than the thickness of the field pavers. If the field is less than 10 ft. wide, notch both ends of the screed board and skip the pipe. Screeding is hard work and it's best to have a helper.

Lay the pavers and finish the border

From here on out, this is mostly a standard paver job. Lay the field pavers as you would on any paver patio. Scrape away the excess sand and cut off the excess landscape fabric with a utility knife. Glue down the last border. Let the glue dry for a few hours before you tamp the field pavers and sweep sand across the patio to fill the joints. ⌂

Q&A

Q **Why not skip the sand and glue down all the pavers?**

A You could do that. But gluing down hundreds of pavers will add a few hours to the job and you'll spend at least $100 on adhesive.

Q **I want a bigger patio. Can the pavers extend beyond the current footprint?**

A The pavers could continue onto a standard gravel base. But the gravel base and the existing slab might shift in different ways, creating a gap or hump where they meet. So it's best to keep them separate. If you want to add a grilling area, for example, separate it from the main patio and set a steppingstone or two between the two paved areas.

Q **Can I glue pavers over the steps?**

A Yes. If your patio includes steps, you must cover the treads in order to maintain the height of the steps. Or you can completely cover the steps if you like. Just be sure to leave a gap of at least 1/2 in. between the pavers on the steps and those on the patio to allow for movement.

Q **Do I have to use paver bricks?**

A You can cover the field with any type of paving product: natural or manufactured flagstone, pavers of any size or shape. But paver bricks are best for the border because they provide a flat, even surface for screeding (see **Photo 4**).

Materials

Aside from pavers and sand, you'll need one 10-oz. tube of adhesive for every 8 ft. of border, concrete cleaner or muriatic acid, landscape fabric, a 2x6 and a screed pipe. To tamp the pavers, you'll need to rent a plate compactor ($45 for four hours).

GARDEN SHED

Bright and spacious, easy to access—our best garden shed yet

by **Jeff Gorton**

Framing the roof

If you're a gardener, you'll love this 12 x 16-ft. shed. (And even if you don't garden, I bet you could put all this space to work.) There's plenty of room for all your tools and a planting bench under the windows. You can easily drive your riding mower through the huge sliding doors, or just open them wide for plenty of light and ventilation. Dormer windows provide overhead light, and a bank of end wall windows opens for even more fresh air. To reduce maintenance, we used solid PVC to trim the shed and build the sliding doors, and we covered the walls with fiber cement siding.

You can find most of the materials for this shed at home centers or lumberyards. However, the solid PVC trim boards may have to be special-ordered. We spent about $4,800 on the materials for this shed (not including the concrete slab), and the PVC trim accounts for a big chunk of that cost. If you substitute wood or composite trim, you could save about $1,000.

To build this shed, you'll need standard carpentry tools, including a circular saw and drill. A framing nail gun, miter saw and table saw will save you some time and effort but

aren't necessary. We used a special Ridgid dust-collecting saw to cut the fiber cement siding, but a circular saw will also work.

If you've built a deck or other large construction project, you shouldn't have any trouble with this shed. The framing is straightforward, and with a few helpers you should be able to get the shell up in a weekend. Then expect to spend three or four busy weekends completing the project. Go to familyhandyman.com and search "2011 shed" for a materials list and 13 detailed construction drawings. ⌂

Crabby
Gnomeowner | Happy
Gnomeowner

GIVE HOPELESS GRASS A FRESH START

Kill off the old and seed a healthy new lawn

by **Rick Muscoplat**

L et's get this straight right from the get-go: A healthy lawn doesn't get taken over by weeds. So if it looks like you're raising weeds instead of grass, that's a sign of a more serious problem. And that may mean killing off the grass and starting over. It's a big project that'll take several weekends and may cost you up to 25¢ per sq. ft. for equipment rentals, soil conditioners and seed. If you're willing to spend more, you can lay sod instead of planting seed, but don't skip the soil testing and remediation steps.

Are you ready for a fresh start? Just follow our guide and you'll be the happiest gnomeowner on your block.

Are we talking about *your* grass?

Going "nuclear" shouldn't be your first option. Instead, start with spot applications of weed killer, dethatching and core aeration. But if you still see more than 60 percent weeds at the start of the next growing season, your lawn is too far gone to save. Your best option is to nuke it and replant.

TIMELINE

STEP 1

Get a soil analysis

Don't even think about replanting until you get the results of a soil analysis (cost is usually less than $20). Contact a local extension service or search the Internet for a soil-testing lab near you. Select three different locations around your lawn and collect samples. Mix them together and scoop into a container. Note on the lab form that you'll be planting new grass and whether you bag the clippings when you mow or return them to the lawn. In a couple of weeks, you'll get a report with recommendations about which fertilizers or soil treatments to add.

COLLECT SAMPLES FOR A SOIL TEST
Plunge your spade about 6 in. deep and pull out a plug of soil. Then slice off a section of the plug (top to bottom). Remove the grass and rocks and mix all the samples together.

STEP 2

Kill everything

You can kill the grass with chemicals like Roundup or Killzall. But if you hate the idea of using chemicals and have a large area, rent a sod cutter to remove the lawn surface. Or kill the grass by blocking out its sunlight with black poly film (4-mil or thicker; $100 for a 28-ft. x 100-ft. roll). Remove the poly when the grass is dry and brown (two to three weeks or longer, depending on the weather).

KILL THE GRASS WITH PLASTIC
Lay the poly film over the lawn and secure it with rocks or stakes.

...OR KILL IT WITH HERBICIDE
Cover nearby plants with a tarp. Choose a calm day and hold the spray head close to the grass to prevent overspray.

STEP 3

Remove the dead stuff

Now comes the upper body workout: Rake up the dead grass and weeds before you amend the soil. Yup, it's got to be done.

RAKE OFF THE DEAD GRASS
Rip up all the dead grass and weeds with a rigid tine rake and lots of muscle.

STEP 4

Improve the soil

Don't think you can fix bad soil just by adding a few inches of black soil on top of the old. Instead, rent a tiller (about $45 per day) to till in the soil conditioners recommended by the soil analysis.

"Adding good-quality black topsoil over bad soil is like putting chocolate frosting on a stale cake—it doesn't fix the underlying problem."

Bob Mugaas, Turf Expert

TILL IN THE SOIL CONDITIONERS
Spread the conditioners across the entire lawn. Then till them into the soil to a depth of about 5 in.

Meet our grass guru

BOB MUGAAS is an Extension Educator in Horticulture with the University of Minnesota Extension. Bob has authored or co-authored more than 200 articles on various topics related to turf grass management.

STEP 5

Smooth the soil

Grass seed needs smooth and level ground to get the best germination. And it needs good seed-to-soil contact. So first remove all rocks and debris, then smooth the soil with a rake.

RAKE THE SOIL
Level and smooth the soil with a broom rake. Then drag the rake (tines up) to create "furrows."

STEP 6

Add a starter fertilizer

A starter fertilizer gives grass seed the nutrients it needs to germinate and grow quickly. Consult with a local nursery to find the best starter fertilizer for the seed you select. Follow the instructions on the bag for the proper spread rate for a new lawn and apply the fertilizer.

JUMP-START THE SEED WITH LAWN STARTER FERTILIZER
Spread the fertilizer into the furrows with a spreader. Don't overdo it.

OUTDOOR STRUCTURES, LANDSCAPING & GARDENING

STEP 7

Pick the seed to match your site

Consult with the grass expert at a garden center to select a seed that matches your site conditions, lawn care preferences and budget. Ask about the newer low-maintenance and drought-resistant varieties. Purchase grass seed by the bag or in bulk, by the pound. But buy just what you need. Don't apply the leftover seed—extra seed actually reduces the germination rate.

STEP 8

Prepare the seed

To avoid applying too much seed, mix the seed (4:1 ratio) with a fertilizer/bulking agent (Milorganite is one brand; $15 for a 36-lb. bag).

STEP 9

Spread the seed

Load the seed into a spreader and apply it. Make sure it doesn't fly into nearby gardens. Rake to cover the furrows as shown. Then compact the soil with a sod roller (rent one for about $20 per day) to get good seed-to-soil contact.

MIX THE SEED
Pour the seed and fertilizer into a plastic bucket and mix it thoroughly.

COVER THE SEED
Turn the broom rake upside down and drag it side-to-side over the furrows until only 10 to 15 percent of the seed remains uncovered.

COMPACT THE SOIL
Fill a sod roller halfway with water and roll the seed to pack the soil and seed mixture.

When to plant

There are good and bad times of year for starting a project like this. In cold climates, plant new grass seed in early spring as the lawns are just coming out of winter (early to mid-April) or late summer from about mid-August to mid-September. In warm-weather climates, plant in late spring/early summer. If you're not sure, contact your local extension service to get planting advice from a turf expert.

"Most people overwater new seed. Just keep the soil damp for the best germination."

Bob Mugaas, Turf Expert

STEP 10

Add mulch or grass seed accelerator

Cover the soil with compost mulch to retain water during germination. Or apply a "grass seed accelerator" (one brand is GreenView, greenviewfertilizer.com; about $18 for 30 lbs., which covers 600 sq. ft.). The accelerator absorbs more moisture than either mulch or hay and then slowly releases it. It also degrades naturally, eliminating cleanup.

SPREAD THE SEED ACCELERATOR
Set the spreader to the widest setting and walk quickly to get a light application of the pellets.

SEED ACCELERATOR

STEP 11

Water, but not too much

Water the new lawn generously right after the mulch application, but stop as soon as you see puddles forming. Then keep the soil moist to a depth of 4 to 6 in. for best germination. Keep watering regularly as the seedlings appear and grow. Gradually reduce the watering over a six-week period. Then switch to your normal watering routine.

WATER REGULARLY
Place an impact sprinkler in the corner of the lawn and set it to spray in a quarter arc. Then move it to the other corners.

OUTDOOR STRUCTURES, LANDSCAPING & GARDENING

STEP 12

Cut the grass with TLC

Set the cutting height to 2-1/2 in. Use a new or sharpened blade to make sharp, clean slicing cuts. Avoid using a dull blade—it rips the grass, setting up the conditions for disease. ⌂

MAKE THE FIRST CUT
Mow the new lawn once it reaches a height of 3 in. Use a newly sharpened blade—it's healthiest for the grass. Cut just 1/2 in. per mowing.

BEST IN DIY | CORDLESS STRING TRIMMERS

We compare features and performance of 10 battery-powered trimmers.

by Jeff Gorton

If you're still dragging around the cord for an electric trimmer or dealing with the hassles of a gas engine, it might be time to reconsider cordless models. They've come a long way in the past few years, and they're the best choice for many yards. For this review we rounded up some of the most popular battery-operated trimmers currently on the market. We gave all the trimmers a workout to compare features, ergonomics and run-time. Then we polled our Field Editors and factored in what we learned from online reviews. Read on to see what we discovered.

Convenience vs. power

The advantages of a cordless trimmer are pretty obvious: no gas, no engine maintenance, no starting troubles, less noise. The price you pay for that convenience is a huge power cut. If you have a large lot or need to trim heavy weeds or dense grass, then stick with a gas-powered unit. But for most homeowners, a cordless trimmer is worth considering. If you live on a standard-size city or suburban lot and you choose the right trimmer and you don't expect it to cut thick-stalked weeds, then you'll probably be happy with a cordless trimmer.

Auto feed is a mixed blessing

All these trimmers have an automatic line feed mechanism. Every time the trimmer stops and starts again, the line extends about 1/4 in. The good part: no more bumping against the ground to get more line. The bad: not much control over the line length. Luckily, most of the trimmers also allow you to extend the line by pushing a button near the cutting head while you pull on the line.

This Worx trim head has two nice features: a cap that lifts off easily and a button to release the line.

Safety pains

To prevent accidental starts, all but one of the trimmers employs a lock-off button that you have to depress before you can squeeze the switch trigger. On some, like the Ryobi RY24201 and the Troy-Bilt, the button is on top and easy to release. Side buttons, like those found on the Craftsman and the Ryobi P2002, are harder to engage. We prefer the top-mounted lock-off buttons.

This Greenworks trimmer has a top-mounted lock-off button that's easy to push. The lock-offs on the Craftsman are a little harder to press.

Variable speed – nice but not necessary

The Ryobi RY24201 and the Troy-Bilt have variable-speed switches that allow you more precise control of the cutting line. This is nice when you're near a tree and want to be careful not to damage the bark. But be aware that these require a little more finger pressure to hold in, which can be tiring.

Double up for battery savings

Many of the batteries, like those on the Craftsman, Ryobi, Troy-Bilt and Worx trimmers, can be used in other tools by the same manufacturer, including hedge trimmers, chain saws and leaf blowers. If you have other battery-powered tools or plan to buy some, keep this in mind. Using the same battery and charger for several tools not only is handy but also saves you money.

Run-time ranges

When we gave the trimmers a workout, we found that most of the batteries lasted 15 to 25 minutes, running constantly under load. The Greenworks and Troy-Bilt batteries were the exception. These monsters pack a whopping 6 amp-hour rating, more than twice that of the closest competitors, and run more than 40 minutes under load before they quit. Of course, the bigger the battery, the more expensive it is to replace. Replacing the Troy-Bilt battery will set you back $140—ouch!

In general, we recommend sticking to lithium-ion batteries. They're lighter, charge faster and hold their charge longer on the shelf than nickel cadmium batteries. They also provide more constant power. Don't pay too much attention to the voltage. The amp-hour rating of the battery is a better indicator of how long it will run—larger numbers mean longer run.

They're both 20 volts, but which one do you think will run longer?

Charge ahead with fast chargers

The other big variable is recharge time. One of the Black & Decker trimmers requires nine hours, while the Neuton and one of the Worx models list a 30-minute recharge time. Troy-Bilt offers the best combination, with a long-run battery and a relatively fast two-hour charge. The key is to match the battery and charger to your needs. If you can finish trimming in 15 minutes, you don't need a big battery or a fast charger.

String theory

With the exception of the Troy-Bilt, which uses thicker .080 line, all these trimmers have a single .065 diameter line. You can buy line on prewound spools ($3 to $6 each) or save money by winding your own from bulk line ($10 for 200 ft.). To replace the line, you remove the cutting head cap and lift out the spool. The cap is easiest to remove on the Neuton and Worx trimmers.

It's not the weight that matters

Most of our reviewers didn't object to the weight of the heavier trimmers as long as they were well balanced, while others preferred the lighter units. We've listed the weights for you to compare. The position of the front handle affects the balance. All the trimmers have an adjustable front handle that swivels, slides along the shaft or both. Handles that slide offer the most versatile placement.

Most of the shafts are straight and adjustable for length, but if you're of average height, you'll probably just extend them fully and forget it. Only the Worx models seemed unusually short—if you're over 6 ft. tall, try these for size before committing. The Greenworks trimmer is the only one with a curved shaft. It may not be as good for getting under bushes but otherwise has a nice feel.

Don't run out of power

One of our favorite features is the "fuel gauge" button that displays the percentage of battery charge remaining. No more running out of juice right after you start trimming. You'll find this on the Greenworks, Ryobi RY24201, Troy-Bilt and WeedEater batteries.

Not just for trimming

Dual wheels keep this Worx trimmer steady for precise edging control.

All but the Troy-Bilt employ some method to make edging easier. Some have cutting heads that swivel 180 degrees and some swivel 90 degrees. The 90-degree swivel allows you to walk behind the trimmer, lawn mower style, for a clearer view of the edging path. The Greenworks, Ryobi RY24201 and the Worx trimmers also have wheels for rolling along the walk or driveway as you edge. The Ryobi is the only trimmer with a convenient foot-operated swivel. The rest require you to lean over and mess with the shaft, cutting head or both to convert to the edging mode. The Worx (shown in photo) tools have dual wheels that provide extra stability for edging.

OUR FEATURE-PACKED FAVORITE

Ryobi did its homework on this trimmer. It has almost every feature we like plus the only foot-operated edger conversion. Like the Troy-Bilt, it has a top-mounted lock-off and variable-speed trigger switch. The battery charges in one hour and has a "fuel gauge" button.

RYOBI
RY24201

Cost: $159
(suggested retail)
Battery: 24V lithium, 2.4 Ah
Charge time: 1 hour
Weight: 8.25 lbs.

ECONOMICAL AND POWERFUL

This WeedEater string trimmer includes a better-than-average 2.6-amp-hour battery, an adjustable cutting head angle and a fully adjustable shaft handle. It's the only trimmer without a safety lock-off.

WEEDEATER
LT 20V

Cost: $96
Battery: 20V lithium, 2.6 Ah
Charge time: 1.5 hours
Weight: 6.5 lbs.

GREAT BATTERY

The Greenworks trimmer has the same huge 6-amp-hour battery as the Troy-Bilt. If you're looking for a trimmer with all of the features and long run-time, this is it. Just be sure you're comfortable with the curved shaft.

GREENWORKS

Cost: $160
Battery: 20V lithium, 6 Ah
Charge time: 4.5 hours
Weight: 8.75 lbs.

NO-FRILLS POWERHOUSE

The Troy-Bilt trimmer is a no-frills unit with a fantastic battery and charger. From the solid shaft clamp to the smooth variable-speed trigger and top-mounted lock-off, this tool oozes quality. Our one gripe: It doesn't have an edging feature. Argh.

TROY-BILT
TB57

Cost: $149
Battery: 20V lithium, 6 Ah
Charge time: 2 hours
Weight: 8 lbs.

INTERCHANGEABLE BATTERY

The CR 2000's battery Is compatible with all Craftsman C3 tools. The cutting head pivots for easier trimming on slopes, and it swivels 180 degrees for edging. The side-mounted lock-off button is a little more difficult to engage than the side-mounted buttons on some other trimmers. This is one of two trimmers in our review with a nickel cadmium battery.

CRAFTSMAN
CR 2000

Cost: $110
Battery: 19.2V nickel cadmium
Charge time: 1 hour
Weight: 7.5 lbs.

ECONOMICAL, LIGHTWEIGHT, LOADED WITH FEATURES

The Worx trimmer sports dual wheels for better control while edging. It's also one of the few trimmers with a fast 30-minute charge time and a line cap that's super easy to remove. The battery fits other compatible Worx tools.

WORX
GT WG151.5 (WG165)

Cost: $125
Battery: 18V lithium, 1.5 Ah
Charge time: 30 minutes
Weight: 5.3 lbs.

Same trimmer—different battery

Depending on where you shop, you may also find the Worx 165. It's almost identical and costs just a bit more, but it includes a 24V battery with a three-to five-hour charger. We found that the larger battery ran about five minutes longer.

COMPATIBLE BATTERY

This Ryobi trimmer includes a battery that's compatible with Ryobi's huge line of ONE+ tools. It's missing some features we like, but if you have other ONE+ tools, it's worth considering.

RYOBI
P2002

Cost: $119
Battery: 18V lithium, 2.6 Ah
Charge time: 1 hour
Weight: 6.8 lbs.

POWER BOOST TRANSMISSION

An extra-long shaft makes this trimmer good for tall people. We like the adjustable handle and power boost mode that revs it up to 9,000 rpm for tough jobs. But we're not crazy about the NiCad battery and long charge time.

BLACK & DECKER
NST1024

Cost: $133
Battery: 24V nickel cadmium, 1.7 Ah
Charge time: 9 hours
Weight: 8.8 lbs.

TWO BATTERIES INCLUDED

A second battery means you can finish the job if you run out of juice. Both Black & Deckers have a transmission that the manufacturer claims gives you increased power at the cutting head. We can't verify this. As for the run-time, our test yielded average results—about 20 minutes per battery.

BLACK & DECKER
LST220

Cost: $118
Battery: 20V lithium (2), 1.5 Ah
Charge time: 8 hours
Weight: 5.2 lbs.

SUPER LIGHTWEIGHT

The Neuton trimmer has a handle that swivels and slides on the shaft for maximum adjustability. The line cap is easy to remove and the trigger is comfortable. There's no wheel for trimming, and taller users thought the trimmer felt short.

NEUTON
29317

Cost: $149
Battery: 18V lithium, 2.5 Ah
Charge time: 30 minutes
Weight: 5.3 lbs.

HandyHints®

GARDEN ROCK SIFTER

We replaced our overgrown foundation plantings and wanted to reuse the river rock mulch. But the rocks were mixed with dirt and leaves and looked terrible. We made a garden sifter to separate the rocks from the debris. We built a 2x4 frame and fastened hardware cloth to the bottom with fence staples. Then we elevated the sifter on old bricks and used a power washer to clean each shovelful of rocks. You could use a hose or shake the rocks on the sifter (but that's a lot more work!).

ROLL-ON WEED KILLER

Trying to get rid of pesky weeds growing up through the cracks in a patio or walkway? The overspray from spray-on weed killer can damage healthy grass and plants growing nearby. A better solution is to pour some of your premixed weed killer into a paint tray and use a cheap paint roller to roll it directly on the weeds. This prevents overspray and makes it easy to go around patio corners. Make sure to dispose of the roller properly when you're done.

POSTHOLE PLANTER

I do a lot of gardening and I'm not getting any younger, so watching out for my aching back and knees is a top priority. That's why one of my top planting tools is a posthole digger. It works great to dig holes for all size plants, the depth is consistent, and you get a perfect-shaped hole every time. Best of all, it eliminates a lot of kneeling and bending. Now if I could just get the plants to hop into the holes by themselves, I'd have it made!

POSTHOLE DIGGER

STAY-PUT SOAKER HOSES

Getting new soaker hoses to lie flat and stay put can be tough. They always tend to twist and send water where you don't want it. Try using plastic clothes hangers to make soaker hose anchors. Cut the hanger ends off at an angle and pound them into the ground over the hoses. The anchors are strong, they won't rust or fall apart, and they're easy to pull out if you need to move a hose. You can also use them to root vines and hold plant netting in place. It's a good way to recycle extra hangers.

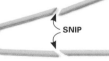

SNIP

SNIP

SIMPLE SPIRAL HOSE STORAGE

Here's a handy tip for storing your spiral hoses next winter so you won't end up with a tangled mess in the spring. Just wrap them around the handle of a rake or shovel you won't be using during the winter. Your long-handled tool will do double duty by keeping your hoses tangle-free.

SIMPLE VEGGIE WASHER

We love growing fresh vegetables in our large garden, but we hate all the dirt that comes inside when we pick them. My husband came up with this great veggie washer. Drill holes in the bottom and sides of a 5-gallon bucket with a 5/8-in. spade bit. Place your fresh-picked veggies in the bucket and hose them off before you bring them inside. The dirt and sand stay out in the garden, and only the veggies end up in your kitchen.

5/8" HOLES

ZIP-TIE VINE TRAINERS

ZIP TIE

It can be challenging to tie your vines to a trellis without damaging the vine. I've had great luck using cable ties (also called zip ties; $5 for 100 at home centers), especially for my tomatoes. They're easier to use than twine, and waterproof, strong and adjustable. You can make the tie loose enough to give the vine room to grow, yet tight enough so it doesn't flop. (Just don't make them too tight or you could damage the stem.)

HANDY BRANCH HAULER

Need a way to haul branches over to your fire pit? Carrying them in your arms is dirty work, and trying to stuff them into a plastic bag is awkward. Try using a sturdy plastic shopping bag with handles. Slit the sides, lay it flat, and fill it with branches and small logs. It loads easily and lets you carry wood without getting your clothes full of sap or mud.

PLASTIC SHOPPING BAG

GreatGoofs®

THE BATHROOM IS OCCUPIED

To save a few bucks, I decided to cut down one of our trees myself. I easily removed all the lower branches with my pole saw and then had the brilliant idea of taking the saw upstairs and hanging out the second-story bathroom window to remove the upper branches. All went well until the last (pretty large) remaining limb. I planned the cut so that the branch would fall into the "safe and open space" in the yard. Unfortunately, the nearly 12-ft. limb had other ideas. I narrowly avoided being skewered as it crashed through the window opening and came to rest a few inches from the doorway. People do a variety of things in their bathrooms—but how many have cut firewood while standing in the bathtub?

RUNAWAY MOWER

My old riding mower works fine, except for a weak battery that needs an occasional jump start. One fine day as I was riding it across the lawn, I had to shut it down to take a phone call. When I tried to start it up again, the engine wouldn't turn over. Luckily, it had died near the street, so I pulled my car up next to the mower, connected the jumper cables and waited a few minutes. Standing next to the mower, I pressed my foot down on the brake, turned the key and sure enough, the engine started right up. I then took my foot off the brake and watched in horror as the mower sped away, ripping the ends of the jumper cables off as it went. I had forgotten to put the transmission in neutral! Thankfully, I was able to hop on and stop it before it got too far, but I got a hearty round of applause from my neighbors, who appreciated the clown show.

DIY Hodgepodge

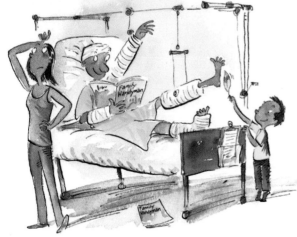

HIDDEN DANGERS of DIY

by Jeff Gorton

If you're grinding without goggles, it shouldn't be a surprise if you get metal in your eye. But there are plenty of ways you can get hurt with DIY that are unexpected. To find out what some of them are, we asked our Field Editors how they've been hurt doing DIY projects. Here's what they told us, along with some of the lessons we can learn from their experiences.

Bump-nailing nails foot

We were using a framing nailer to fasten plywood to joists. The nailer was set to fire in "bump" mode. Instead of pressing down on the nose of the gun and then pulling the trigger, you just hold down the trigger and push the nose against the wood. That's great for speed, but not so great if you bump the gun where you don't want a nail. And that's just what happened. In my rush, I bumped my boot. Luckily, the nail just glanced off my toe. Set your nail gun to the safer sequential-fire mode. It's not worth risking a 16d nail in your foot or forehead just to save a minute or two.

Joe Jenson

Pressure washer peels skin

Charlie Marken says, "I rented a pressure washer to spruce up the concrete patio. After finishing that job, I spotted some dirty patio chair cushions. Holding a cushion with one hand, I used the other hand to operate the trigger on the pressure washer. Not paying much attention, I moved the spray wand right across my hand. Immediately I let go of the cushion and saw the skin on my thumb peeled back and bleeding profusely. I now have a very healthy respect for the power of water when it's pressurized to 2,500 pounds per square inch! I also have a two-inch scar in the shape of a 'Z'—not cut by Zorro, but myself."

Cuts from pressure washers are surprisingly common, and dangerous. Water and bacteria get forced deep under the skin, where they can cause infections. Treat pressure washers as carefully as you'd treat a loaded gun.

Watch out for falling tools

Do you catch yourself leaving stuff on top of ladders or framing? One Field Editor told how his brother had rested a framing nail gun on the top plate of a wall they were building, and while he was working below, the vibrations from his pounding knocked it off onto his head. Tools left on top of ladders, set precariously on framing, or placed unsecured on a roof are an accident waiting to happen.

Zapped by live wires

I plugged a radio into the outlet and switched off breakers until the radio died. I figured it was safe to work in the box and proceeded to disconnect the wires from the outlet. Suddenly, I was knocked back by a jolt of electricity shooting up my arm. It turns out there were two circuits connected to the outlet and only one had been turned off.

It's dangerous to make assumptions about electricity. Always check the wires with a voltage tester and double-check all the wires in the box with a noncontact voltage tester before doing any electrical work.

Elisa Bernick

Wrapped up and reeled in

I was using a large hole saw to drill plywood and leaned in close to apply pressure. The hole saw caught my T-shirt. In my panic, I accidentally pressed the trigger lock (I usually cut the trigger lock button flush to the tool to minimize this problem, but didn't on this drill). The hole saw reeled in my shirt and climbed my chest. Luckily I escaped major injury, but I got some nasty spiraling teeth marks and a shredded shirt before I was able to turn off the drill. I learned two lessons: Avoid loose-fitting clothes around power tools, and be wary of trigger locks.

Jeff Gorton

Blindsided by a beam

Gary Steinmetz was rushing to get done for the day, turned the corner and smashed his forehead into protruding lumber. His baseball cap visor blocked his view and—WHAM! After a trip to the emergency room and a half-dozen stitches, he was more careful about leaving boards sticking out at head level and decided to wear his baseball cap backward.

Jawbreaker bit

My plumber was using his powerful Milwaukee Hole-Hawg drill to bore a big hole through the floor. He was working from underneath, between the floor joists, when the drill hit something and the bit bound up. The drill handle swung around, knocking him in the jaw and off the ladder. He was bruised and couldn't chew for a week, but at least nothing was broken. Even small drills have a lot of torque, so avoid this type of injury by keeping your face away from the drill.

Jeff Gorton

FIELD EDITOR

Karate chop backfires

Here's a cautionary tale from Field Editor William Wilson: "I decided to 'kung fu' a piece of furring strip against the curb so it would fit better in the trash can. The broken piece boomeranged, slapped me in the face at supersonic speed and left a nasty knot over my eye. I played it like it didn't hurt only to go home to my wife and whine when she asked me about it. It's tough being tough."

We received other similar stories of disastrous attempts to break stuff. Take William's advice: A saw is still the best tool for reducing remodeling debris to a manageable size.

Dangerous sawdust

Our crew did a lot of new-home framing, and the last step was the roof sheathing. That involved lots of cutting up there: skylight and vent holes, gable ends, etc. I insisted on having a push broom on the roof and lectured the guys about sweeping the dust away after each cut. The young guns, of course, thought they were bulletproof and wouldn't always do it. Then it happened. Joey's feet went out from under him and he found himself tobogganing down the 5/12 slope and over the edge, then performing a perfect two-point plant on the ground. He was lucky we were building a single story! The broom got used religiously after that.

Travis Larson

Ladder-stretcher disaster

Travis Larson tells this ladder story: "I had a six-foot stepladder and I needed an eight-foot one. What to do? I know—I'll rest it on planks that are resting on sawhorses. Brilliant! Nope, turns out it was really, really stupid. When I climbed nearly to the top, the planks slipped right off the horses like the undersides were greased. Of course, the ladder went down too. The saving grace was that I was near enough to the gutter so I could grab it before I followed the ladder. Fortunately it was strong enough to support my weight. I hung there and bellowed for help until my wife came out to see what the rumble was. She set the ladder back up—on the ground this time—and steadied it so I could 'dismount.'"

Ladders are one dangerous DIY tool. But you can avoid most accidents by following good ladder safety techniques—and using a little common sense. 🏠

ANY DOLT CAN DIG A HOLE, BUT...

IT TAKES A GENIUS TO DO IT RIGHT

by **Travis Larson**

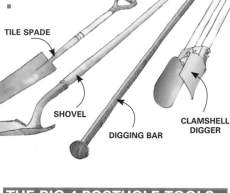

TILE SPADE

SHOVEL

DIGGING BAR

CLAMSHELL DIGGER

SO, you think you know how to dig postholes, eh? Sure you do— anyone can dig a hole. But how hard do you want to work, and how often do the holes end up in the wrong spot and you have to start over? Here are a few tips to get perfectly placed holes—with a little less sweat on your part. Be sure to call 811 before you dig.

THE BIG 4 POSTHOLE TOOLS

If you have more than a couple of postholes to dig, don't stop at a shovel and a clamshell digger. You'll treasure two more tools just as much. Pick up a tile spade. The long, narrow blade will get you places no other shovel can. Also get a tamper-end digging bar.

1 String your line and pound the stakes. String a line marking the outside edges of the posts. Mark the post centers on the line by untwisting the string and pushing a nail through the strands. You can fine-tune the nail position just by sliding it to the exact location. Then pound stakes to mark the center of the holes. If you're using 4x4 posts, that will be just under 2 in. from the string.

2 Carve out a soil divot with a spade. Set the string aside so you don't wreck it while digging. And don't just start digging away; drill yourself a pilot hole first. Carve out a round plug to outline the posthole. That'll get you started in exactly the right spot. Throw the dirt onto a tarp to protect your lawn.

3 Loosen earth with a tile shovel. Unless you have very soft soil, you'll work way too hard digging with just a clamshell digger. Loosen the soil and carve away at the sides with the tile spade. It'll easily slice through small roots.

4 Use your clamshell digger. Plunge the open clamshell digger blades into the loosened soil and grab a load of fill.

5 Use a recip saw on large roots. Don't kill yourself chiseling out roots. Just use a recip saw with a long, coarse blade and poke it right into the soil at the ends of the root and cut it off.

DIG BY HAND UNLESS...

Power augers require a trip to the rental store and a brawny friend. And they're worthless in clay or rocky soil. The truth is, unless you have lots of holes to dig in sand, it's often easier to dig by hand.

USE WATER AND THE BACK OF YOUR SHOVEL

If you're digging in sticky clay soil, dip your clamshell digger in a bucket of water so the soil won't stick. Knock off clumps on the back of the shovel. Spread a tarp to keep dirt off your grass.

SMALL IS BEAUTIFUL

Unless you're a body builder, avoid those giant, heavy-gauge, fiberglass-handled clamshell diggers. You'll just get exhausted; you're better off with a smaller, lightweight digger.

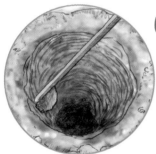

6 Dislodge rocks with a digging bar. Pick out rocks from the hole sides with your digging bar. Let them fall into the hole and pluck them out with your clamshell digger.

9 Cover holes with plywood. If you're walking away from the postholes for a while, cover them with plywood. It just might save a broken leg and/ or keep the sides from caving in during a storm.

7 Tamp soil with the other end. Use the tamper end of the digging bar to compact the soil before setting posts or pouring concrete. That prevents any settling.

8 Mark the post edge locations. Restring the line, pull the nails and mark the exact post edge locations on the line with a permanent marker.

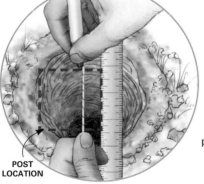

POST LOCATION

STRING

10 Set the posts. Place the posts with one side brushing against the string and the edge even with your mark. Then hold the post plumb while you fill the hole. Pack the soil with the tamper end of the digging bar every foot or so. ⏚

DEFEAT RUST

How to get rid of it. How to keep it from coming back.

by **Rick Muscoplat**

STRIPPING DISC

"ROPE" WIRE WHEEL

FIBER DISC

GRINDING WHEEL

You're surrounded by tools and machines made out of steel. And when the coatings on those products crack, rust starts to bloom and the battle is on. You can attack rust early and nip it in the bud, or you can wait until you have a full-blown war on your hands. The choice is yours. Either way you'll need a battle plan and a complete list of weapons at your disposal. And that's why we're going to show you the five ways to defeat rust—three methods to remove it and two steps to prevent it from coming back.

THE **ELBOW GREASE** METHOD

Grind, sand or scour off the rust

If you're not into chemicals and you want to remove the paint along with the rust, use a power tool like a grinder, sander, oscillating tool or drill. A grinder fitted with a stripping disc, grinding wheel, fiber or flap disc makes quick work of heavy rust on large objects. But keep the tool moving so you don't gouge the metal. For smaller jobs, use a traditional sander. To get into small areas, use a "mouse" sander or an oscillating tool with a carbide rasp or sanding pad attachment.

Whichever tool you choose, always start with the coarsest abrasive to get rid of the rust and pockmarks. Once the rust is gone, switch to a finer grit to smooth out the swirls and grooves caused by the coarse grit. For the smoothest paint job, finish sanding with 400-grit wet/dry paper.

SANDING PAD

CARBIDE RASP

STRIPPING DISC

"CUP" WIRE WHEEL

WIRE WHEEL

80-GRIT CARBIDE PAPER

MATCH THE ABRASIVE TO THE SHAPE
Use flap discs, fiber discs and sanders on large, flat areas. Switch to wire wheels for seams, corners and rounded areas.

THE **CHEMICAL REMOVAL** METHOD

Remove rust with powerful chemicals ...

The old standby rust remover chemicals contain either phosphoric or hydrochloric acid to dissolve the rust. They're harsh chemicals that give off some pretty intense fumes, so suit up with rubber gloves, goggles and a respirator. Find them in the paint department at any home center. You'll also need an old paintbrush, a waste tub, a 3-in. putty knife and rags.

Apply the chemicals with the paintbrush and wait the recommended time for the chemicals to work. Then scrape off the liquefied rust. You won't get it all in a single step—count on multiple applications to completely remove heavy rust buildup. Consider a gel formula when removing rust on vertical surfaces. It'll cling better and result in less runoff.

SELECT FROM THE "OLD STANDBYS"
Brush or spray on any of these acid-based removers. Buy a gel formula for derusting vertical surfaces.

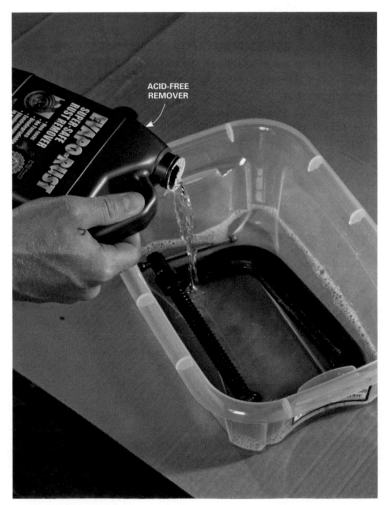

ACID-FREE REMOVER

... or with safer and gentler chemicals

Try one of the newer nontoxic and acid-free soaking solutions shown here. I bought this gallon of Evapo-Rust at an auto parts store for about $25. These chemicals dissolve rust through the process of "selective chelation." I don't know what that is, but I can tell you it works if you're patient.

Start by cleaning off any oil or grease. Then dunk the rusted part in a tub of solution. The product says it'll dissolve rust in either 30 minutes or overnight. Based on my experience, you'd better plan on overnight, because even this minimally rusted C-clamp took that long. Keep in mind that this is a soaking solution— you can't paint it on or spray it on. So, if you've got a large object, you're going to need a lot of solution, and that's going to cost a lot more.

**BUY ENOUGH SOLUTION
TO COMPLETELY COVER THE RUSTED PART**
Clean off any oil or grease before soaking. Pour the solution in a plastic tub. Then drop in the rusted item and walk away.

THE **CONVERSION** METHOD

Convert it—it's the easiest method

If you can live with the look of a rough or pockmarked finish, rust converter can save you a lot of time. It kills the rust, prevents its spread and dries into a ready-to-paint primer. Buy it at any home center or auto parts store. Start by removing any flaking paint and rusty dust with a wire brush. Then either spray on the converter or apply it with a disposable paintbrush (**photo, far right**). Let it dry for the recommended time. Even though the label says you can paint after it dries into a primer coat, I recommend spraying on a real primer. Then paint. Apply a second coat of converter if you're not going to paint. Don't return leftover converter to the bottle—it will contaminate the rest. Toss it in the trash, along with the brush.

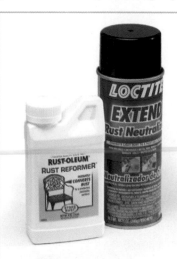

CHOOSE BETWEEN LIQUID AND SPRAY CONVERTER
Rust converter comes in brushable liquid or aerosol spray. Spray provides a smoother finish but doesn't penetrate severe rust as well as brushable liquid.

After

APPLY CONVERTER AFTER WIRE BRUSHING
Pour a small amount of converter into a cup and work it into the rusty patches with a paintbrush. Then smooth out the brushstrokes and let it dry.

THREE WAYS TO REMOVE RUST

	PROS:	CONS:
Grind, sand or scour off the rust	■ No pockmarks and a smooth finish prior to painting. ■ Complete project in a day. No waiting for chemicals to work.	■ Dirty, dusty, hard work. ■ Requires power tools and lots of elbow grease.
Convert the rust	■ Easiest way to stop rust and prime in one operation. ■ Less expensive than chemical or mechanical methods for removing rust.	■ Leaves a rough or pockmarked finish that'll show after you paint. ■ May not inhibit rust as long as traditional removal, priming and painting.
Remove rust with chemicals **TIP** Don't think you can spray rust-inhibiting paint onto a rusty surface and get good results. The rust will bleed right through the paint and ruin your new paint job. You have to deal with the rust with one of the methods we show here. There's just no way around it.	■ Soaking removers can do all the work for you if the item is small enough. ■ Spray removers greatly reduce the grunt work, but they require several applications and some scraping.	■ Long wait times for the liquid removers to do their job. ■ Makes a huge mess. ■ Soaking removers are expensive and can be used only on small items. ■ The surface will still be pockmarked after the rust is gone.

PREVENT RUST: **PRIME FIRST!**

Prime before painting

No matter how you get the rust off, you still have to prime before painting (**photo right**). If the surface is smooth, simply spray on a metal primer (light gray for light-colored paints, black for darker paints). However, if the surface still has pockmarks, swirls or scratches, use a "sandable" or "filler" primer to fill in the depressions.

Surface preparation prior to priming is critical, especially if there's any old paint left on the item. Clean the surface with a wax-removing solvent (buy at any auto parts store) and a tack cloth.

PICK YOUR PRIMER
Choose a regular (nonsandable) primer if the surface is completely smooth. To fill in scratches, choose a sandable primer and lightly sand when dry. Or, use a filler primer to fill in pockmarks.

PREPARE AND PRIME
Clean the metal before priming. Then apply the primer over the old paint and the newly sanded metal.

PREVENT RUST: **PAINT & TOPCOAT**

Pick a high-quality paint

After all the nasty prep work, why risk another bout of rust by using cheap paint? Inexpensive paint contains less pigment, fewer resin binders and no rust inhibitors. Spend a few extra bucks on a premium rust-inhibiting paint. It will contain zinc additives that provide an extra measure of protection against future rust.

Brushing usually provides a better paint bond than spraying, but it leaves brushstrokes in the finish. However, spraying is tricky and if you stay in one spot too long, you can wind up with paint sag marks in the finish.

Whichever painting method you choose, seal the newly painted item with a clear topcoat. That'll add to the gloss and dramatically increase the life of the paint by reducing paint oxidation. ⌂

APPLY A CLEAR TOPCOAT
Allow the color coat to dry completely. Then spray on a clear topcoat to extend the life of the paint.

SHOP FOR RUST-INHIBITING PAINT
Several companies make rust-inhibiting paint. If you don't find the color you like, try the paint department at an auto parts store. Spray on a final topcoat of clear gloss.

GET SMALL ENGINES TO START!

It's all about a clean carb

by Rick Muscoplat

If you can't get a small engine started, or it takes too many pulls to get it going, or it runs poorly, ask yourself this: Did it sit for a long time with gas in it? Like over the summer or winter? If so, your problem is most likely a corroded or gummed-up carburetor. Small-engine repair shops earn about 50 percent of their revenue by cleaning or replacing carburetors that are sidelined by old gas.

Before you rip into the sucker, take a minute to confirm that the carburetor's the problem. I'll show you how to do that, as well as how to rebuild it or replace it. Either way, you'll save about an hour of shop labor (about $70). You can complete the project in a single morning, including the time scouting for parts.

I'll assume the fuel valve is on, there's gas in the tank and you've already checked the condition of the spark plug. Start by shooting

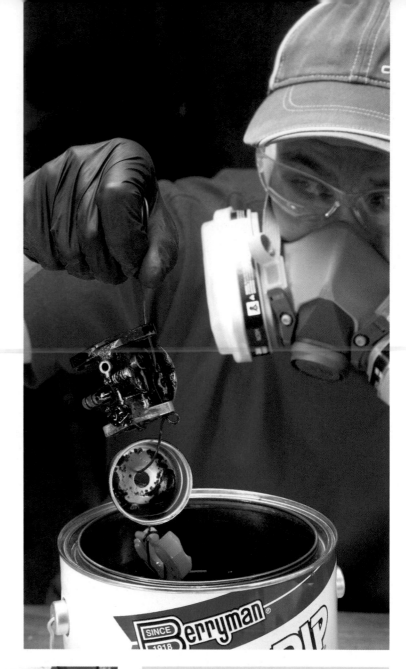

1 Test for gas at the carb. Clamp off the fuel line. Then compress the spring clamp and slide it backward on the fuel line. Pull the tubing off the carburetor nipple and catch the gas in a small bowl.

FUEL LINE

CARB FUEL INLET

How to find carburetor parts and prices

Whether you buy parts from a local small-engine repair shop or online, you may need all this information:

- Machine brand (Toro, Snapper, Honda, etc.), model and serial number.
- Engine brand and serial number (Tecumseh, Briggs & Stratton, Honda, etc.). The engine model and serial number are usually located on a plate above the spark plug.
- You may also need numbers from the old carburetor itself (usually stamped onto the carb body or its mounting flange).

I prefer buying locally, but if you're an Internet shopper, try these sources: smallenginepartswarehouse.com or psep.biz.

a one-second burst of aerosol lubricant or carburetor cleaner down the throat of the carburetor. Then yank the cord. If the engine runs (even just sputters) and dies, you'll know you have a fuel problem. If there's no life after a few tries, it's something more serious and you'll have to haul the engine to your garage for some detective work. If it fired, remove the fuel line at the carb and check for gas (**Photo 1**). It should leak out of both the fuel line and the carburetor. If it doesn't, you've got a plugged fuel line or fuel filter.

Next, remove the carburetor from the engine (**Photo 2**). Place it in a container (to catch the gas) and open the carburetor bowl to check for corrosion (**Photo 3**). If it's corroded, it's toast—buy a new one.

If there's no corrosion, you can choose to rebuild it rather than replace it. But that doesn't automatically mean you should—rebuilding isn't always cheaper, and it might not even do the trick. In fact, sometimes you can buy a new carburetor for less than (or pretty darn close to) the cost of the rebuilding kit plus the cost of the chemicals (see "How to Find Carburetor Parts and Prices," p. 222).

I always just replace bad carburetors, rather than rebuild them. But if you're game, spread out some shop towels and disassemble it (**Photo 4**). Match the new gaskets and O-rings in the kit to the old ones. Then set aside any extra parts (rebuilding kits often include parts for several models, so you might not use all of them). Next, dunk the parts in carburetor cleaner ($20 per gallon at any auto parts store) and let them soak for an hour (**Photo 5**). You can try using spray carb cleaner ($5 per can) instead of the high-priced stuff, but it's a gamble (just be prepared to rebuild it again). Then rinse all the parts with water and blow them dry with compressed air. Install the new carb parts and mount it on the engine. Follow the instructions in the kit for adjusting the idle speed and mixture (or ask the parts supplier for advice). Then fire up your engine and listen to it purr.

2 **The carb comes off easy.** Use a socket or nut driver to remove the two bolts that hold the carburetor to the engine. Then unhook the throttle cable from the carburetor linkage.

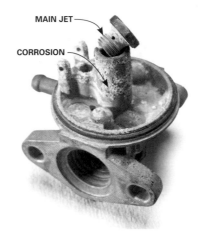

MAIN JET

CORROSION

3 **Corrosion's a deal breaker.** Junk the carburetor if the inside is corroded. Even after cleaning, the corrosion will clog the jets and tiny orifices and restrict the flow of gas.

4 **Dissect the carb on your workbench.** Start the disassembly from the bottom (bowl, float, needle, seat, etc.) and keep all the parts together. Shoot digital photos for help during reassembly.

COAT HANGER

5 **Dunk it and walk away.** Wire all the larger parts together and drop them into a bucket of carburetor cleaner. Wrap the small parts in aluminum screen or use a fine-mesh basket.

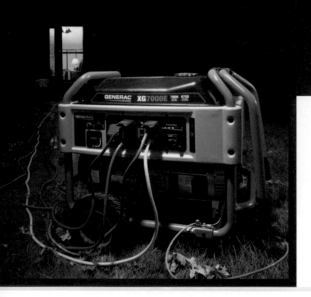

GENERATOR SMARTS

Manufacturers and repair pros share tips to avoid the most common mistakes

by **Rick Muscoplat**

A HEAD LAMP HELPS FOR TANK FILLING After the engine cools, strap on an LED head lamp so you can actually see what you're doing. Pour slowly and avoid filling the tank to the brim.

Don't get burned by wattage ratings

Every generator lists two capacity ratings. The first is "rated" or "continuous" watts. That's the maximum power the generator will put out *on an extended basis.* And it's the only rating you should rely on when buying a generator. The higher "maximum" or "starting" rating refers to how much *extra power* the generator can put out *for a few seconds* when an electric motor—like the one in your fridge or furnace—starts up. If you buy a generator based on the higher rating and think you can run it at that level, think again. It will work for a little while. But by the end of the day, your new generator will be a molten mass of yard art, and you'll be out shopping for a replacement.

8,750 STARTING WATTS

7,000 RUNNING WATTS

WATTS ARE NOT ALL EQUAL
Ignore the higher rating and select a generator based on its "rated," "running" or "continuous" watts.

Chill out before you refill

Generator fuel tanks are always on top of the engine so they can "gravity-feed" gas to the carburetor. But that setup can quickly turn into a disaster if you spill gas when refueling a hot generator. Think about it—spilled gas on a hot engine, and you're standing there holding a gas can. Talk about an inferno! It's no wonder generators (and owners) go up in flames every year from that mistake. You can survive without power for a measly 15 minutes, so let the engine cool before you pour. Spilling is especially likely if you refill at night without a flashlight.

KEEP YOUR GENERATOR HUMMING Pumping out watts is hard on engine oil, and oil-change intervals are short. Store up enough oil and filters to get you through a long power outage.

Stock up on oil and filters

Most new generators need their first oil change after just 25 hours. Beyond that, you'll have to dump the old stuff and refill every 50 or 60 hours. So you need to store up enough oil and factory filters to last a few days (at least!). Running around town searching for the right oil and filter is the last thing you want to be doing right after a big storm.

OUT WITH THE OLD Empty the tank with a hand pump before running the carburetor dry. Reload with fresh gas next time you run the generator.

Old fuel is your worst enemy

Stale fuel is the No. 1 cause of generator starting problems. Manufacturers advise adding fuel stabilizer to the gas to minimize fuel breakdown, varnish and gum buildup. But it's no guarantee against problems. Repair shops recommend emptying the fuel tank and the carburetor once you're past storm season. If your carburetor has a drain, wait for the engine to cool before draining. If not, empty the tank and then run the generator until it's out of gas. Always use fresh, stabilized gas in your generator.

Backfeeding kills

The Internet is full of articles explaining how to "backfeed" power into your home's wiring system with a "dual male-ended" extension cord. Some of our Field Editors have even admitted trying it (we'll reprimand them). But backfeeding is illegal—and for good reason. It can (and does) kill family members, neighbors and power company linemen every year. In other words, it's a terrible idea. If you really want to avoid running extension cords around your house, pony up for a transfer switch ($300). Then pay an electrician about $1,000 to install it. That's the only safe alternative to multiple extension cords. Period.

DON'T!
IT'S JUST PLAIN DANGEROUS
Forget about using a double-ended cord to run power backward into a receptacle. Instead, run separate extension cords or install a transfer switch.

TRIGGER VALVE   FILL PORT

Store gasoline safely

Most local residential fire codes limit how much gasoline you can store in your home or attached garage (usually 10 gallons or less). So you may be tempted to buy one large gas can to cut down on refill runs. Don't. There's no way you can pour 60 lbs. of gas without spilling. Plus, most generator tanks don't hold that much, so you increase your chances of overfilling. Instead, buy two high-quality 5-gallon cans. While you're at it, consider spending more for a high-quality steel gas can with a trigger control valve (Justrite No. 7250130; $65 from amazon.com).

A BETTER GAS CAN MEANS LESS SPILLAGE
The trigger valve on this gas can gives you total control over the fill. There's a separate refill opening so you never have to remove the spout.

Lock it down

The only thing worse than the rumbling sound of an engine outside your bedroom window is the sound of silence after someone steals your expensive generator. Combine security and electrical safety by digging a hole and sinking a grounding rod and an eye bolt in concrete. Encase the whole thing in 4-in. ABS or PVC drainpipe, with a screw-on cleanout fitting. Spray-paint the lid green so it blends in with your lawn. If you don't want to sink a permanent concrete pier, at least screw in ground anchors (four anchors for $20; No. WI652775; from globalindustrial.com) to secure the chain.

GROUND ROD

SCREW LID

STOP CROOKS AND PREVENT SHOCKS
Protect yourself from accidental electrocution by connecting the generator to a grounding rod. Then secure the unit to the eye bolt with a hardened steel chain and heavy-duty padlock.

Use a heavy-duty cord

Generators are loud, so most people park them as far away from the house as possible. (Be considerate of your neighbors, though.) That's OK as long as you use heavy-duty 12-gauge cords and limit the run to 100 ft. Lighter cords or longer runs mean more voltage drop. And decreased voltage can cause premature appliance motor burnout.

100'

LONG CORDS LET YOU GET SOME SLEEP
Invest in some long extension cords to put some distance between you and the noisy generator. But don't exceed 100 ft. between the generator and appliances.

Running out of gas can cost you

Some generators, especially low-cost models, can be damaged by running out of gas. They keep putting out power while coming to a stop, and the electrical load in your house drains the magnetic field from the generator coils. When you restart, the generator will run fine, but it won't generate power. You'll have to haul it into a repair shop, where you'll pay about $40 to reenergize the generator coils. So keep the tank filled and always remove the electrical load before you shut down. ⌂

18 PROBLEM SOLVERS

Tools and materials every DIYer should know about

by Jeff Gorton

Featherweight tile backer

Dean Sorem, our tile guru, had this to say about one lightweight tile backer: "Custom Building Products' EasyBoard is a dream. An average shower requires two to three hundred pounds of cement board, and six to eight trips from the truck to the shower—on the second floor, if you're lucky! My eighty-year-old grandmother could carry 120 square feet of half-inch EasyBoard in one trip, assuming I held the doors for her. Installation is even easier. One steady pass with a sharp utility knife and the board is cut clean through. Fasten it with the same screws used for other backers. Another advantage: no cement dust."

These new super-light backer boards have a hard foam core and water-resistant coating and can be used anywhere you would use other tile backer boards. Custom Building Products' EasyBoard and Schluter's Kerdi-Board are two common brands. EasyBoard costs about $16 for a 3 x 5-ft. piece. You probably won't find foam-core backer board at home centers. Instead, search online for a local source or visit a professional tile shop.

Sticky sand for pavers

Tired of replacing the sand between the pavers on your walk or patio? Sick of pulling weeds from between the stones? Here's a solution. Vacuum or blow out the old sand and replace it with polymeric sand. It's just sand mixed with a glue-like polymer. When wetted, the polymer binds the sand, holding it in place and creating a weed-resistant barrier. It's a little fussy to install because you have to be careful to clean it off the face of the pavers or stones before wetting it, but it's worth the extra effort. Polymeric sand is available at landscape suppliers and some home centers for about $12 for a 50-lb. bag.

Instant electrical connections

Traditional twist-on wire connectors can be a bother to install. The wire ends have to be held in perfect alignment while you twist on the connector. And then you have to fit all those wires and connectors neatly into the box.

Try push-in connectors instead. They're simple to use and almost foolproof. Just strip the wires to the length recommended on the package and press each wire end into a separate hole in the connector. And since they're smaller, they take up less room in the electrical box. They're also the perfect solution for extending wires that are too short.

A few downsides: You'll need to keep a greater variety of connectors on hand, since it wouldn't be economical to use a connector designed for six wires to connect a single pair. Also, push-in connectors cost a little more than the twist-on type. You'll find push-in connectors ($25 for 200) at home centers and online.

Paint-job insurance

Let's face it. Sometimes it's too much work to remove old exterior paint down to bare wood. Zinsser's Peel Stop and XIM's Peel Bond ($22 and $32 a gallon, respectively) are two clear, binding primers that are formulated to seal the edges of paint and prevent peeling. It's a good solution for painting over an area that you've scraped, but that has patches of sound paint you don't want to peel later.

Flat-proof wheelbarrow tire

Is the tire flat every time you go to use your wheelbarrow? Do you use your wheelbarrow on construction sites where nails can be a problem? If so, then you need a "flat-free" wheelbarrow tire. Flat-free tires are filled with foam or made of urethane so they never need air and won't go flat if you run over a nail. And they're not just for wheelbarrows. You can also buy flat-free tires to fit lawn mowers and lawn tractors, handcarts and golf carts. Expect to spend about $30 for a wheelbarrow tire. Find flat-free tires at home centers and online.

Ever-straight wall studs

In most areas of a house, a little wave or bump in the wall caused by a crooked stud won't matter a bit. But in kitchens and bathrooms where you'll be installing cabinetry or tile on the walls, a wavy wall can raise havoc. That's where engineered studs are worth the premium price.

Because they're made of laminated lumber or finger-jointed lumber, they're perfectly straight and more stable than standard studs. Plus, they're available in long lengths for extra-tall walls. They don't come cheap, though. An 8-ft. laminated strand lumber (LSL) stud from LP Building Products costs about $8. Ask for engineered studs at your local lumberyard or home centers. You may have to special-order them.

Waterproof wood glue with no mixing

You old-timers out there may remember having to hunt down and mix resorcinol powder when your project called for waterproof glue. Now you can just reach for the glue bottle ($4 for 8 oz.) to get a waterproof glue-up. It's probably wise to stick with epoxy for boat building, but for everything else these waterproof glues are all you need. Elmer's Wood Glue Max and Titebond's Titebond III Ultimate Wood Glue are two brands.

Faster toggle bolt

Old-fashioned "butterfly"-type toggle bolts are a pain to install. Toggler brand Snaptoggles is a vast improvement. Just drill a hole and slip the metal toggle in. Then slide the retainer along the plastic strips until it's snug to the wall and snap off the strips. With the metal toggle mounted on the wall, it's easy to attach whatever you want by simply screwing in the included bolt. And you can remove the bolt without losing the toggle in the wall. Look for Snaptoggles (about $1 each) near drywall anchors in home centers and hardware stores.

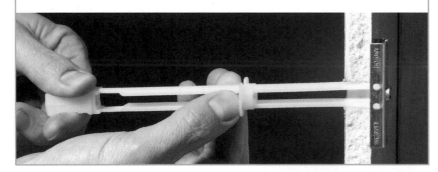

Faster fastening with better screws

Premium construction screws have a few big advantages over the drywall screws we've all been using for years.

For starters, most have improved head designs—hex, Torx or Spider, for example—that eliminate slipping and stripped screws. Premium construction screws are also less brittle than drywall screws, so they won't break off as easily, and they're coated to resist corrosion. Special self-drilling thread designs coupled with a thin shank means you rarely need to drill a pilot hole. Large structural screws can replace lag screws, and the smaller ones are better than drywall screws for woodworking and framing projects.

There are several brands. You'll find GRK screws online and at contractor-oriented lumberyards. Spax and FastenMaster screws are readily available at home centers and hardware stores. Like any premium products, they cost more. Expect to pay about 5¢ each for 1-1/2-in. GRK screws.

Adjustable-depth electrical box

An electrical box that can be adjusted until it's flush with the wall is a perfect solution when you're thinking about adding tile or paneling but aren't sure how thick the finished wall will be. There are a few different versions of adjustable boxes. Turning a screw in the Carlon box shown here moves the box in and out and allows you to fine-tune the box position after you've completed the wall covering. Adjustable-depth boxes cost a little more than regular boxes ($2 to $2.50 each) but are worth every penny in areas where you think you'll add tile, paneling or cabinetry and don't want to guess at the depth.

Waterproof tile is now brush-on simple

A top-notch tiling job in wet areas like showers and around tubs requires a waterproof membrane under the tile. RedGard is a liquid waterproofing that you apply with a brush, trowel or roller. When dry, it forms a flexible membrane that's perfect to tile over.

Here's what our tile consultant, Dean Sorem, has to say: "RedGard saved my sanity! This handy waterproofing has made the installation of a watertight tile job as simple as a brush stroke. Once the tile substrate is securely installed and seams are taped, all you need to do is apply a coat of the pudding-like liquid to the surface, let it dry, and it's waterproofed. This makes waterproofing shower curbs, benches, tub decks and steam showers a breeze."

You'll find RedGard and other brands of brush-on waterproofing at home centers, tile stores and online. A 1-gallon bucket costs about $40.

Arrow-straight drywall joints

This extra-stiff, extra-wide drywall corner system is expensive, but worth every penny in a few situations. First, if you're a novice drywall taper, it absolutely ensures straight inside corners. The stiff material goes on straight, no matter how unskilled you are with a taping knife. For the experienced taper, this stuff makes it easier to handle situations like oddball corner angles or drywall over sloppy framing.

Also, you only need to apply an additional thin coat or two of joint compound over the outermost edge to finish the job. The remainder of the tape is paint-ready and doesn't require more mud. This feature also makes it handy for all inside and outside corners. These products are available at drywall suppliers and online. A 100-ft. roll of No-Coat Ultraflex 450 costs $60. Strait-Flex's Wide-Flex 400 is a similar product ($43).

Moldable wood filler

Nothing beats two-part epoxy wood filler for rebuilding moldings or other architectural elements that have missing or damaged parts. The most common brand is Abatron's WoodEpox. When mixed, WoodEpox has a consistency like Play-Doh that allows you to hand-mold it into the approximate shape of the damaged part. Unlike less expensive fillers, it'll stay put without sagging or running. When the "dough" hardens to about the consistency of soap, you can shave and carve it into the final profile. When it's completely cured, you can sand and plane it like wood. Epoxy wood filler costs about $40 for two pints. Find a local WoodEpox retailer or purchase online from abatron.com.

Ultimate water-base trim paint

A decade ago, if you asked any painters what type of paint they preferred for getting a smooth coat of finish on woodwork, most would have said oil-base paint. But now there are several modern paints that combine the best advantages of water-base and oil paints. These new water cleanup paints have a lower percentage of volatile organic compounds (VOCs) than oil-base paints, so they're better for the environment. And they brush on and flow out like oil, allowing you to get that smooth, brush-mark free finish that is the hallmark of a classic oil paint job. Two popular examples of this new type of paint are Sherwin-Williams ProClassic Interior Waterbased Acrylic-Alkyd and Benjamin Moore's Advance Waterborne Interior Alkyd. Like any superior paint product, these aren't cheap. Expect to pay about $45 a gallon. But if it's a smooth, durable paint job you're after, water-base alkyds are worth every penny.

Cheap, durable, versatile wood filler

Durham's Water Putty is a powder that hardens after you mix it with water. It's a great product to keep on hand for when you need economical, quick-setting wood filler for things like woodpecker holes in your siding or knotholes before painting. You can mix it thin and use it as a floor leveler, or mix it thick for making wood repairs. You'll find Durham's Water Putty at home centers and hardware stores ($10 for a 4-lb. can).

Better foam control

If you've ever used expanding foam with the plastic straw applicator, you know what a mess it can be—sticky foam all over everything and half-used cans that end up in the trash. But it doesn't have to be that way. Applicator guns have an adjustment screw that allows you to fine-tune the flow rate. That, coupled with the long nozzle and trigger valve, gives you much more control over the foam so you don't end up wasting it by overfilling. Plus you can leave the can of foam on the gun for about a month and still use it. You only clean the gun if you remove the can. Then you simply screw a can of foam gun cleaner (about $6) onto the gun and dispense it through the tip.

Foam application guns cost $30 to more than $100. The Great Stuff Pro 14 gun shown here is $50.

Perfect crack filler

If you've ever tried to fill a crack in concrete with regular caulk, you know what a mess it can be. Self-leveling concrete crack filler solves this problem. Just fill the crack and a few minutes later the caulk settles to form a perfectly smooth joint. For wide cracks, insert lengths of foam caulk-backer first to create a better caulk joint and reduce the amount of caulk needed. Self-leveling caulk (about $6 a tube) is available at home centers and hardware stores. Look for the words "self-leveling" on the tube.

Instant, permanent hole fix

Stephen Evans, one of our Field Editors, has a favorite wood filler for special jobs. QuickWood putty stick is a two-part epoxy filler that is the size and consistency of a large Tootsie Roll. Stephen uses it to fill screw holes and make repairs where high strength and a fast set are important.

To use it, just slice a chunk from the tube and knead it until the color is consistent. This activates the epoxy, allowing you about 15 to 25 minutes to fill holes or dings until it starts to harden. A 1-oz. tube costs about $5. Two brands are QuickWood and JB Weld KwikWood. You'll find them online or at woodworking stores and home centers. ⌂

HC&RHodgepodge

SHARPENING SERRATED KNIVES

Serrated knives can be sharpened, but unlike ordinary knives, they need a diamond-coated steel that's properly sized to match the knife.

If you want to master the technique, take your serrated knives to a knife or cookware store and ask to have your knife matched to the correct diameter diamond-coated steel. Its diameter has to match the scallop profiles. If you have more than one serrated knife, choose a tapered steel that'll work for different scallop sizes.

If you examine the blade, you'll see that one side is tapered and the other is flat (this is called a chiseled edge). The tapered side is the only one that gets sharpened. When you're through sharpening, drag the knife through a scrap of corrugated cardboard to knock off any leftover filings.

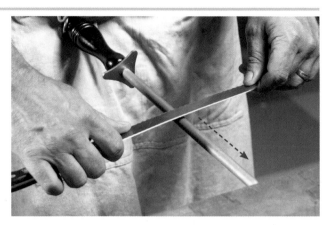

1 Match the bevel to the pushing angle. Sharpen each scallop with the steel. Match the angle of the scallop and push the knife away from you. Do each scallop two or three times, then move on to the next.

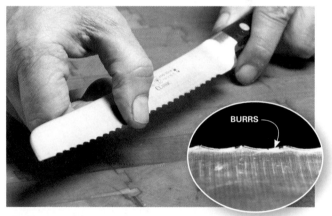

BURRS

2 Create the burrs. Drag your fingertip over the flat side of the knife. If you feel burrs along the whole length, good. If any scallops are missing burrs, flip the knife over and hit those again.

BACK-SAVING TOOL BELT HOLDER

I'm up on a ladder a lot and I'm not as young as I used to be. To save my back and make it easy to move up and down without my tool belt getting in the way, I sling the belt around the top of the ladder. Everything's still close at hand, but I'm lighter on my feet (and a lot less sore at the end of the day).

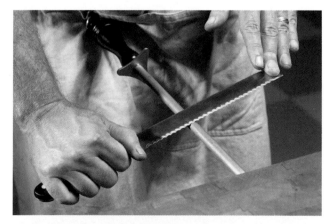

3 Then knock off the burrs. When you're satisfied, pull the flat side of the knife along the rod to knock off all the burrs. Now your knife is sharp.

HandyHints Hodgepodge

DON'T STOCK UP ON SPRAY FOAM

Every spring and fall, home centers offer great prices on insulating spray foam. If you're tempted to stock up, be prepared to use it right away. Most people don't know that the cans have a one-year shelf life—and that's one year from the date of manufacture, not the date of purchase. Some manufacturers print an expiration date on the bottom of the can as shown. But others use a cryptic production code. If you buy that product, make sure you use it as soon as possible.

SPRAY FOAM HAS A ONE-YEAR SHELF LIFE
Flip the can over and check the expiration date before you buy.

NEW LIFE FOR DINGED-UP NIGHTSTANDS

The tops of my nightstands aren't in the best shape, so I covered them with textured wallpaper (that I got at a garage sale!). I cut the wallpaper to the exact size of the table and just set it on top. My lamp and nighttime reading keep the wallpaper in place. When it gets dirty, I cut a new piece from the roll and replace it. You could also cover the wallpaper with a piece of glass. It's an elegant solution for side tables and buffets too.

WALLPAPER

MAGNETIC KNIFE RACK

LADDER TOOL AND SCREW HOLDER

Here's a clever way to keep screws and tools handy when you're up on a ladder. Screw a magnetic tool holder or knife rack (available at home centers for $10) to the top of your ladder. You don't have to worry about losing screws or knocking your screwdriver to the floor. Everything you need stays right where you put it.

LADDER PADDING

I spend a lot of time on my ladder, and leaning against the rungs all day was taking a toll on my shins and thighs. Then I got smart and slit pieces of my kids' swim noodles lengthwise and wrapped them around the front of the rungs. Instant relief! The cushions are easy to move as you work. Just make sure you never stand on them, and always place them higher than you'll step since they can create an uneven step or fall off if you step on them.

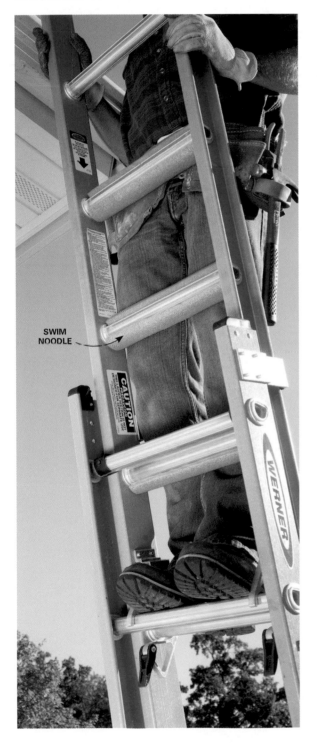

SWIM NOODLE →

NO-SLIDE LAUNDRY LINE

Tired of hanging your clothes on the line and having all the hangers slide to the center? Use plastic chain instead. No more sliding, and the links separate the clothes so they dry quicker. This works great in the laundry room or outside in the yard!

EXTRA CURTAIN ROD

DOUBLE-DUTY SHOWER RODS

It seems like you never have enough wall space to put hooks or towel bars in your bathroom, so why not make your shower walls do double duty? Hang two shower curtain rods instead of one. Hang your shower curtain on the inside rod and use the second rod to hang towels. Plus, you can towel off in the shower—no more dripping your way to the towel bar.

CUSTOMIZED CARTS

To save time, space and my back, I came up with a great way to organize and ferry everything I need for different jobs around the house. I use appliance dollies and bungee cords to create all-in-one carts. I have a compressor cart for nailing jobs, a saw cart with my sawhorses on the back, and a cart of plastic crates loaded with supplies for wiring, painting and other common jobs. The carts make going up and down stairs easier, I don't have to drag along heavy tool cases, and they really cut down the number of trips I make to and from my workshop.

SHOP VACUUM
AIR MATTRESS PUMP

We get lots of guests around the holidays, and blowing up our inflatable air mattresses for guest beds was a hassle until I discovered this trick—use your shop vacuum! It's simple to turn your machine into a temporary compressor. Just hook up the hose to the vacuum's exhaust port and hold the other end to the mattress's release valve. When you're ready to deflate the mattress, connect to the suction port. Now it only takes a minute or two to fill and deflate our mattresses.

EXHAUST PORT

A BETTER STRAW
FOR EXPANDING FOAM

I like expanding foam and its many advantages, but I was ready to give up on it because it's so messy and hard to control. And since you need to hold the can upside down, it's nearly impossible to get it into tight areas like pipe penetrations in rim joists. That all changed when I replaced the short straw with a length of 1/8-in. vinyl tubing. Not only is it way easier to control, but I can hold the can upside down and deliver the foam wherever I need it.

EASY-TO-REMOVE GARBAGE BAGS

Getting a full garbage bag out of the can is always a bear because of the vacuum seal that forms between the bag and the can. I solved the problem by drilling holes in the side of the garbage can near the bottom. The air in the bottom of the can escapes through the holes, and the trash bag slides out with ease.

AIR HOLES

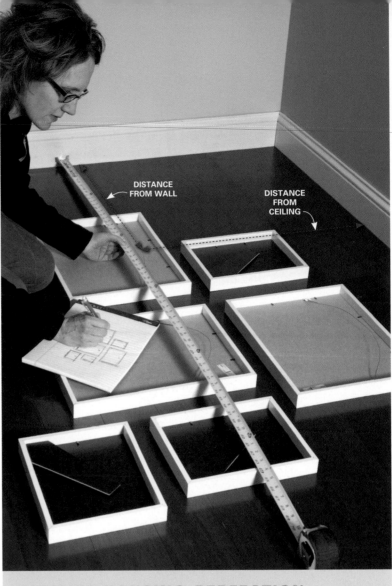

DISTANCE FROM WALL

DISTANCE FROM CEILING

PICTURE-HANGING PERFECTION

When you're hanging a group of pictures, it can be hard to visualize exactly where everything should go. Try this next time: Lay them all out on the floor and get them arranged just how you like them. Then flip them over and make a little diagram of your grouping. Measure the distance of each picture's hanger from the adjacent walls, and jot it down on your diagram. Transfer those hanger locations to the wall and you'll have a perfect grouping every time.

TWO MINI WORK LIGHT IDEAS

Here are two easy ways to make portable work lights that are ideal for cramped dark spots.

1 Cut a small section of foam pipe insulation or a swim noodle and wrap it around a small LED flashlight. Wedge the foam into any crack, crevice or corner.

2 Bolt together a pair of broom clips ($2 at hardware stores) and clamp a mini LED flashlight to one end. Then you can clamp the other end to any fixed object.

GreatGoofs®

MAN-EATING BEANBAG

After remodeling my third-floor home office, I splurged on a new beanbag memory-foam chair that came packaged in a highly compressed cube. No one was around to help, so I decided to carry it to the third floor myself—up two flights of stairs and a narrow spiral staircase. The box wasn't big, but it was heavy—maybe 75 lbs.—and it was hard to get a good grip. After the first flight of stairs, I ditched the box so I could hold on to the shrink-wrapped bundle. Bad idea. After a couple of steps, I snagged the plastic on a piece of rough railing, and I knew I was in trouble when the foam started to expand. By the time I hit the spiral staircase, the beanbag had expanded so much that it sagged into a large, squishy dome around my head and shoulders and I couldn't see where I was going! By the time I found the door to my office, I was completely stuck inside the chair and it took me 15 minutes to push it through the door and extract myself.

FURNITURE FLAMBÉ

I decided to strip my old kitchen chairs using a gel paint stripper. After working on the first chair for hours and making slow progress, I decided that a little heat from my propane torch might loosen the stain in hard-to-reach places. It definitely moved things along—until I suddenly saw that the chair was on fire! I ran with the burning chair out to the backyard and smothered the flames before the fire did any serious damage. I decided to pay a furniture stripper to do the remaining three chairs. I'm still planning to stain and refinish the chairs. But now I'll be using an "ebony" wood stain to hide the burn marks.

FLYING COLORS

My neighbor collects baseball caps, and she decided to run them through the dishwasher to get them clean. To prevent them from shrinking, she stopped the dishwasher before the drying cycle. She was worried that they would shrink in the clothes dryer too, so she came up with the brilliant idea of air-drying the caps by strapping each one to a blade on her ceiling fan. Genius! She turned on the fan, made sure the caps were secure and left to go shopping. When she got back, the caps were definitely dry. But there were crazy stripes of color all over the room. As the caps were spinning around, the dye had bled out and shot color all over her living room walls! ⌂

7 Car & Garage

IN THIS CHAPTER

BUY A WORRY-FREE USED CAR

A four-step plan for buying a used car you can depend on.

by **Rick Muscoplat**

Family and friends used to ask me if a certain vehicle was "a good one" only after they'd bought it. Hello? What am I supposed to say then?

Buying a dependable used car takes a little bit of homework. Here's a four-step plan that you can follow to have the best shot at getting a car that won't turn into a money pit. This step-by-step inspection program works whether you're buying from a car lot or a private party. It's not rocket science, just simple logic.

This story isn't about cosmetic issues like rust, body dents or dirty carpets. Plus, I'm assuming you're buying a vehicle that's out of the factory warranty period.

Step 1: Check out a vehicle's reliability on the Internet

Once you decide on a few vehicle models you're interested in, it's time to begin your research in online forums such as edmunds.com and automotiveforums.com. These are two Web sites where you can read comments and ask questions of a pool of thousands of people who actually own that vehicle. Review the owners' comments and ask about their ownership experience. Find out if there are any recurring problems with that year, make and model and how much the owners have shelled out in repairs. Then ask whether they'd buy the same vehicle again. They'll give you the straight dope. Some forum members respond immediately, but be patient; it might take a few days to get plenty of responses.

Meanwhile, check out rockauto.com's "Repair Index" to compare repair parts costs. You may find, for example, that a certain European sedan's alternator replacement could cost upward of $800, whereas the same item for a similar domestic model is relatively cheap at $150. When you're buying a used vehicle, parts cost is a major concern.

Step 2: The pretest-drive inspection

■ Check the dash lights. Turn the key to the "run" position. The Check Engine (Service Engine Soon), Airbag (SRS), Antilock brakes (ABS), Anti-theft (Security), and traction control lights must come on. After you start the engine, all those lights should go off.

■ Check the tires. If you see cracks in the tread or sidewall areas, or notice any steel wires sticking out, you'll need new tires immediately. So deduct at least $450 from the seller's asking price (more for truck or SUV tires).

Next, use a tread depth gauge (less than $5 at any auto parts store) to check the tread at the edges and center of the tire (photo, below).

Tread wear that's worse on one edge of the tire indicates an alignment problem (minimum $100). Irregular tread depth around the tire (cupping) indicates worn struts or worn suspension components (strut replacement runs about $450 for parts and labor).

■ Check the constant velocity (CV) boots (photo right). If they're cracked, you're looking at big money, at least $400 per side (parts and labor) for rebuilt axle assemblies.

■ Check for engine sludge or severe varnish buildup. Both are signs of neglected maintenance. Remove the oil filler cap and check the engine internals (photo, below right).

■ A cold engine should start right away, without having to "give it some gas." Then it should settle down to a smooth idle. If the idle is rough when the engine is warm, it's a sign of a fuel, ignition or vacuum-related problem. That's going to cost a minimum of $250 to diagnose and fix.

■ Check the fluids. Fresh brake fluid is honey-colored. But dark brown brake fluid may still be good. Your best bet is to buy brake fluid test strips at an auto parts store. Count on $65 for a brake fluid flush.

Engine coolant comes in many different colors, but one color is the kiss of death—rust. If you see that, run, don't walk, away from this vehicle. You'll have nothing but costly repairs (radiator, heater core, water pump, etc.) down the road. Flushing the coolant at this point won't help because the damage has already been done.

Fresh transmission fluid is bright red (bottom photo). If it's light brown, it's due for a change (figure about $175 for a complete change-out with the manufacturer's fluid). If the vehicle doesn't have a dipstick, have your mechanic check it at final inspection.

■ If the owner has maintenance records, great. It probably means that they took good care of their car. Then check the maintenance schedule in the glove box to see if any major repairs are looming. A timing belt change-out can easily cost $500, and a tune-up can cost $250 on some engines. If the owner already did those repairs, great. But if they didn't, you'll get stuck with a large bill right away.

BROKEN CV BOOT

Bring a flashlight and get down. Turn the wheels fully left or right and crawl under the fender. Shine your flashlight on the pleats of the rubber CV boots. Look for tears or grease.

Perform a visual check and then get a finger swipe. Shine your flashlight into the oil filler opening and check the color of the metal engine parts. They should be shiny. Then swipe your finger around the inside of the oil filler opening to check for sludge buildup.

Don't kick the tires— measure them. Measure the remaining tread depth to determine how much tread is left. New tread depth (for cars) is usually 11/32 in., and tires must be replaced when they're at 2/32 in.

If it's got a dipstick, pull it. Yank the transmission dipstick and place a few drops on a white cloth. If it's dark brown and smells burnt, walk away from the car.

WORN-OUT FLUID

GOOD TRANSMISSION FLUID

Step 3: The test drive

This isn't a "once around the block," 10-minute drive. You need to really put the vehicle through its paces on city streets and on the highway. Here's what to look for.

■ As you start the test drive, check for brake pedal pulsation (**photo, below right**). Pulsation is caused by brake rotor runout (warpage), and the fix is usually a brake job ($250 to $500). Pulsation shouldn't kill the deal, but it should reduce your offering price.

■ Check for steering wheel wobble and wander (**photo, top right**). If the wheel vibrates, the cause could be an out-of-balance tire (about $25). But if the vehicle "wanders" and the steering wheel requires constant correction, it's a sign of serious steering or suspension-related problems (minimum $400 for parts and labor).

■ Check transmission shift speeds. Every transmission is different, but as a general rule, the first (1–2) shift should occur at 8 to 12 mph. The next shift (2–3) should happen at about 18 to 25 mph. If the vehicle has overdrive, the last shift should occur at about 40 mph. If you have any doubts about the shifting, ask your mechanic to check it out.

■ Check overall engine performance. Accelerate from a stop without letting up. You shouldn't feel any hesitation, chugging or hiccups. Then put it under a heavy load by driving it up a steep hill or punching it hard on the highway. You shouldn't feel any miss or lag. If you do, it's got "driveability" issues, and that'll cost you a minimum of $100 just to get a scan tool check.

Should be no shakin' goin' on. Accelerate to 50 to 60 mph on a straight, level section of highway and let go of the wheel (keep your hands close). Note any left/right wobble or vibration. The vehicle should drive straight with minimal input from you.

A bouncy pedal is a bad sign. Make several stops to heat up the brakes. Then accelerate to 30 mph and slow to a stop. You shouldn't feel any pulsation. If you do, negotiate a lower price.

Step 4: Negotiate the price first, then take it to a mechanic for a final inspection

Most mechanics charge about $100 for a used-vehicle inspection, and it's the best money you'll ever spend. But before you commit to the inspection, negotiate the best price based on any problems you've already discovered. Then make the final purchase contingent on a clean bill of health from your mechanic. Make sure the final inspection includes a scan tool check for "readiness monitors" and "pending codes." I'm warning you—don't skip the final inspection step just to save $100. ⌂

ASKING PRICE - $4,995

NEEDS: CV BOOTS - 400
BRAKE JOB - 275
TRANNY FLUID - 180

OFFER: $4,140

Handy Hints®

JUMPER CABLES

Editor's Note: While you're storing your cables, it's a good idea to check the tire pressure on your spare tire, too.

TANGLE-FREE JUMPER CABLE STORAGE

Having jumper cables at the ready is serious business in cold climates. For years I never had a good place to store them, and I usually found them stuffed under the seats or tangled up in a heap beneath some other stuff in my trunk. Now I store them coiled around my spare tire under the false floor of my trunk. I always know where they are and they're never tangled.

OIL CHANGE REMINDER

Anytime I change the oil in my car or truck, I reset the trip odometer to zero. This way, I don't have to remember (or forget, usually) when I changed the oil last. When the mileage tells me it's time to change the oil, I do it and repeat the process.

LIFT GATE PROTECTION

When you open the lift gate of your van or SUV, it's easy to hit a cross brace of the garage door and chip the paint on the gate. Protect it by using a swim noodle as a cushion. Just slit the swim noodle with a utility knife and slip it over the brace. You can also use preslit foam pipe insulation. If it slips off, use double-face tape to hold it in place.

SWIM NOODLE

LIGHTED FLOOR JACK

Positioning a jack in the right place under a car usually requires a shop light. I decided to simplify the operation by attaching a battery-powered self-adhesive LED puck light to the base of the jack. Now, I just turn on the light, roll the jack under the car in exactly the right spot and get to work. You can find LED puck lights for less than $10 at hardware stores and home centers.

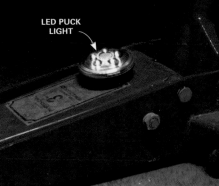

LED PUCK LIGHT

CAR & GARAGE

Car&Garage

DIAGNOSE A HORN PROBLEM

Vehicle horns sit up front where they're exposed to rain and road chemicals. Once that spray gets into the horn's innards, it can short out the coil and kill the horn (and blow the fuse in the process). But an inoperative horn can also be caused by a bad horn switch in your steering wheel, a broken "clock spring" under the steering wheel, a bum horn relay, a broken wire or a corroded ground. Here's how to check the most likely suspects.

Start with the fuse. Refer to the owner's manual for its location. If the fuse is good, jump power directly to the horn with a homemade fused jumper (**top photo**). If the fuse blows, you've got a bum horn. If the horn makes a clicking sound, the problem could be a poor ground connection. Clean the horn's ground connection and try powering the horn again. If the horn still clicks, you'll have to replace it.

If the horn works with jumpered power, the problem lies upstream. Before you waste time searching for a broken wire, try swapping out the horn relay (**bottom photo**). If the relay works, you're looking at a much bigger problem. Take it to a pro.

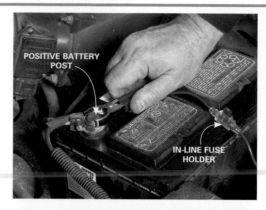

POSITIVE BATTERY POST

IN-LINE FUSE HOLDER

Jump power right to the horn. Make a fused jumper with 16-gauge wire, two clamps and an in-line fuse holder. Connect one clamp to the terminal on the horn and quickly touch the other end to the positive battery terminal.

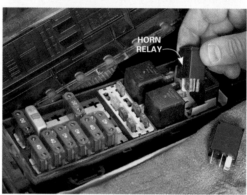

HORN RELAY

Try a different relay. Search the fuse box for the horn relay and then find another one with the same part number to swap with it. If the horn works, buy a new relay.

UNLOCK YOUR RADIO

You replaced the battery in your vehicle and now the radio is locked. Yeah, the radio thinks it's been stolen. Most late-model vehicle radios (2005 and newer) have this anti-theft feature, but check the owner's manual to see if your older vehicle has it. Every vehicle manufacturer has a different procedure for resetting the radio. Some radios (Volkswagen, Jaguar, Land Rover, Mercedes and Saab) can only be reset by the dealer (some charge for this). Other brands can be reset with the radio's serial number and the VIN (see p. 244). That can mean pulling the radio out of the dash. For inexpensive instructions on how to remove a radio, go to carstereohelp.com. To find out how to reset your factory radio, go to forum.ecoustics.com and click on "Car Audio Forum," then "Codes and Everything Else." Post your question there. You'll get a fairly quick (and free) response.

SAVE ENERGY BY <u>NOT</u> FLYING THE FLAG

Think you're sending a green or team message by flying a window flag down the road at high speed? Think again. What you're really announcing is that you like to waste gas. Normal aerodynamic drag accounts for 30 percent of your fuel budget. But add those flags and antenna toppers and you use even more fuel. If you're truly serious about saving fuel, ditch the doodads and drive the vehicle as it came from the factory—naked.

RENEWABLE ENERGY IS AMERICAN SECURITY

UPGRADE THE HANDLEBARS ON YOUR VINTAGE BIKE

If you're still riding around with those "ape hanger" handlebars from the '70s, face it, you're no longer cool. I'll show you how to change out your handlebars yourself and save about $200.

I chose a '70s-vintage Honda because it was one of the more popular bikes back then. On this bike, the wiring harness runs through the middle of the handlebars. The new bar won't have holes for the harness. So you've got two options. You can either drill out the new bar or modify the bracket for the controls and run the harness along the outside of the bar.

Start the project by measuring the diameter of your handlebars (**Photo 1**). Pick the bar style you like, but check with either the bar manufacturer or your dealer to make sure the new bar provides enough turning clearance to avoid hitting the gas tank.

You'll also need shorter brake, clutch and throttle cables and a shorter brake line. Your local dealer can send your old cables out for professional modification (about $30 each), or you can buy new cables ($60 to $80 depending on the brand).

Remove the headlight to access the harness splice area. Then disconnect the wires from the handlebar harness (**Photo 2**). Next, drain the brake fluid reservoir and disconnect and remove the brake line, switches, levers and throttle. Then remove the left hand grip (**Photo 3**). Unbolt the handlebar and move it to the workbench.

Remove the harness from the bar by pulling and feeding at the same time. If the harness binds, squirt in a generous dollop of wire-pulling lube (available in the electrical department at home centers). Once it's out of the old bar, clean off the lubricant and rewrap the harness with new electrical tape.

To run the harness on the outside of the new bar, modify the control brackets (**Photo 4**). Reconnect the wiring harness, controls and levers, and install the shorter cables and brake hose. Secure the wiring harness with zip ties. Then top off the brake fluid reservoir (**Photo 5**). Test all the electrical connections and the brake operation before you take it out for a spin.

1 **Measure before you buy.** Pick any spot along the handlebar to measure its diameter. Then buy the correct bar for your bike.

2 **Disconnect wires, then label.** Find the wires from the handlebar harness and disconnect them one at a time. Apply masking tape to each connector and mark them for reassembly. Don't disconnect any other wires.

3 **Blow and twist off the grip.** Insert a compressed air gun into the grip and squeeze the trigger. That'll inflate the grip enough so you can twist it and break the adhesive.

4 **Make room for the harness.** Grind out a section of the control mounting bracket with a high-speed rotary tool and a cutting or grinding wheel. Then smooth the edges so it won't cut into the harness.

5 **Fill and bleed.** Add fresh brake fluid. Then follow the brake bleeding procedure for your bike.

Car&Garage

TROUBLESHOOT WINDSHIELD WASHERS

If you press the button for windshield juice and nothing comes out, you probably have a clogged nozzle. Start your diagnosis by making sure there's fluid in the reservoir. If so, check for fluid flow at the tee near the cowl (Photo 1). If that checks out, leave the tubing off the tee and clear out the nozzle with a compressed air gun (Photo 2). However, if you couldn't get fluid flow at the tee, you probably need a new pump (search for "windshield washer" at familyhandyman.com).

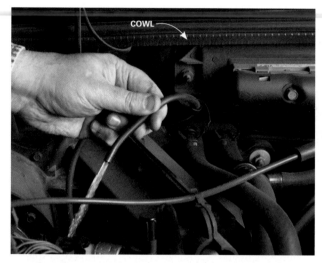

1 **Check pump operation.** Follow the washer tubing from the reservoir to the tee. Disconnect the tubing and have a friend press the washer button. A strong stream of washer fluid indicates a good pump but a clogged nozzle.

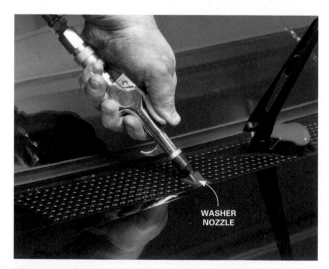

2 **Blow out the nozzle.** Press a rubber-tipped compressed air gun against the nozzle opening and blow air backward through the nozzle (tubing still disconnected at the cowl). Then reconnect the tubing and try the washers again.

Prevent roof-rack liftoff. Secure the leading edge of your roof rack cargo to prevent damage to the roof rack. Tie it down to a location under the front bumper—and reduce your speed.

FACTORY ROOF RACKS CAN BE DICEY!

Roof racks are great for moving lightweight cargo around town. Just secure the stuff to your roof rack and you're good to go. But if you're moving large, flat items like plywood or mattresses, you have to tie the load to the vehicle as well as the rack. A friend tied a mattress to his roof rack and took off for his cabin. As soon as he hit 40 mph, he heard "pop, pop, pop." The "air lift" had ripped the rack mounting bolts right out of the roof (see photo). The body shop repairs cost more than the value of the mattress (and way more than a set of tie-down straps). You've been warned.

FIND YOUR ENGINE CODE

Auto parts stores always ask the year, make and model of your vehicle. But they also need to know which engine you have. Don't know what's under the hood or exactly what year it is? It's all in the vehicle identification number (VIN). Find it in the lower corner of your windshield on the driver's side.

In the series of numbers and letters, the tenth from the left denotes the model year and the eighth is the engine code. Just tell the store clerk those two characters and you're in business.

UPGRADE YOUR CAR'S MUSIC BOX

Your factory tape/CD player may work fine. But why put up with cassette and CD clutter when you can install a brand new MP3 player and listen to all your tunes from a single CD or thumb drive? You can buy a basic MP3 player for about $80 or a full-featured unit for about $200. Save about $40 by installing it yourself. It only takes an hour and it's easy. Just make sure you cough up the $5 or so for radio removal instructions from carstereoremoval.com. Then gather up your tools (screwdrivers, sockets, wire crimpers) and you're ready to rock 'n' roll.

Start the installation by pre-assembling the adapter faceplate (**Photo 1**). Then attach the stabilizing bracket supplied with the player (if equipped). Next, place the new assembly on your workbench and splice the wiring harness adapter onto the player (**Photo 2**). Hold the newly assembled unit near the dash and connect the antenna cable and the wiring harness. Then power up the unit and test the speakers. Switch from left to right and front to back to double-check the wiring connections. Test all the player functions (radio, CD player, iPod connection and USB ports). Once you're sure everything works properly, install it in the dash and refasten the trim panels (**Photo 3**). Then crank up the tunes and rock on.

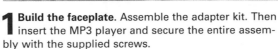
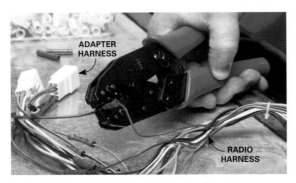

1 Build the faceplate. Assemble the adapter kit. Then insert the MP3 player and secure the entire assembly with the supplied screws.

2 Splice the harness. Locate the speaker and power wires from the new player and match them to the corresponding wires on the adapter harness. Then crimp (or solder) them together.

3 Secure the new unit. Bolt the new unit into place and attach the stabilizing bracket. Then line up the plastic snaps on any trim panels you removed and tap them back into place.

MP3 shopping tip

You can shop for an MP3 player at any car audio or big-box electronics store. But you'll find a much larger brand and model selection online (amazon.com and crutchfield.com are two sources). Find a model that fits your vehicle and your wallet. Then read the reviews for your selection at sites like caraudio.com/forums/head-unit-reviews or reviews.cnet.com/car-audio. Once you decide on a brand and model, order an installation kit and wiring harness adapter for your particular vehicle (some online sources include the kit for free). Buy red "butt-splice" connectors to connect the harness.

Car&Garage

REMOVE A STUCK PHILLIPS SCREW

It's easy to strip out a Phillips screw, especially if you belong to the "more torque is better" club. Rather than mangle the screw head and then have to drill it out, try these tricks.

At the first sign of "slippage," coat your Phillips screwdriver tip with valve grinding compound (about $4 at any auto parts store). Then try removing the screw (**Photo 1**). If that doesn't work, buy a hand-held impact screwdriver (about $10 at an auto parts store). Smack the screwdriver with a hammer (**Photo 2**). The "shock and turn" motion usually frees up the screw.

1 **Coat the tip and turn.** Slip a box-end wrench over the hex-shaped "boss" near the screwdriver handle (if equipped). Then coat the tip with valve grinding compound and jam it into the screw head. Push on the screwdriver while you crank on the wrench.

2 **Hold, smack, turn.** Get a solid grip on the impact tool. Then smack the end with a hammer. The blow automatically forces the Phillips bit into the screw head and twists it at the same time.

THE BASICS OF POURING OIL

Ever notice how oil bottles have an "off-center" spout? It's designed that way to cut down on spills. Most people think the spout should be on the bottom side of the bottle as you pour. That's wrong. Because after just a few seconds in that position, the bottle will start to "burp" and spurt oil. To eliminate the "glug, glug, spurt, spurt," pour with the spout in the "up" position. Yes, that makes it harder to aim, but once you get going, you'll have a smooth stream without any "glugging."

MOUNT A DEVICE HOLDER WITHOUT WRECKING YOUR DASH

Want a great way to mount your electronics without drilling holes? How about a vehicle-specific bracket/adapter mounting system? You can buy a version for just about any car or device from pro-fit-intl.com. The mounting bracket for this 1999 Toyota Camry (Pro.Fit No. 042VSM; $36) fits onto one of the radio fasteners (**Photo 1**). Other versions mount in different places. Then the device-specific adapter mounts to it (**Photo 2**). This adapter (Pro.Fit No. 042TT39; $15 from crutchfield.com) fits the Garmin nüvi GPS.

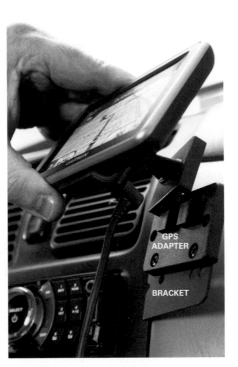

GPS ADAPTER

BRACKET

BRACKET

1 **Attach the bracket to the radio.** Remove the trim bezel and one of the bolts that hold the radio in place. Then attach the bracket and reassemble.

ADAPTER

2 **Install the device-specific adapter.** Connect the adapter to the dash bracket. Then slide your GPS or cell phone into the adapter.

REPLACE WIMPY GAS LIFTS

Worn gas lifts really lose their "oomph" in cold weather. Why risk injury from a falling hatch? You can fix the problem yourself in 20 minutes for less than $50. You only need a small flat-blade screwdriver and a 1/4-in. drive metric socket set.

Buy a pair of gas lifts (always replace them as a pair) at an auto parts store. Have a buddy support the hatch, hood or trunk lid, or buy a lift support clamp (shown is the Lisle 44870; $11 from amazon.com). Don't rely on a 2x4 to hold the hatch open—it's not a safe alternative.

Remove the top portion of the gas lift first. Use a socket and a ratchet to remove the bolted-in-place variety; a screwdriver for the more common C-clamp style (**Photo 2**). Then perform the same procedure on the bottom connection.

1 **Support the hatch.** Lift the hatch slightly higher than its normal open position and have a friend hold the hatch up while you remove the gas lift. Or lock it in place with a lift support clamp.

LIFT SUPPORT CLAMP

2 **Disengage the lift.** Jam a flat-blade screwdriver into the depression in the center of the C-clamp. Then pull the gas lift off the ball stud. Reverse the procedure to connect the new lift.

CAR & GARAGE

Car&Garage

1 **Remove the old thermostat.** Pry off the gooseneck. Then remove the thermostat from the engine or the inside of the gooseneck.

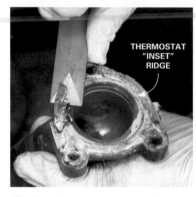

THERMOSTAT "INSET" RIDGE

RTV ON THIS SIDE

SELF-ADHESIVE SIDE DOWN

2 **Clean both mating surfaces.** Use a plastic scraper to remove the old gasket and any sealing compound. Then dry the surfaces with a rag.

3 **Install the new thermostat and gasket.** Place the new thermostat in the recessed groove in either the engine or gooseneck (air bleed toward the top). Hold it in place with a self-adhesive gasket. Then apply a bead of RTV sealant.

REPLACE A THERMOSTAT

In most cases, the cause of an overheating or no-heat condition in your vehicle is a faulty thermostat. And since a new "T-stat" costs only about $8, it makes more sense to replace it than to spend hours diagnosing the problem. If that doesn't fix it, at least you're only out about two hours.

Pick up a new T-stat and gasket, as well as RTV sealant, fresh coolant (to top off the system) and hose clamping pliers at an auto parts store. And while you're there, ask the clerk for the torque specs for the gooseneck bolts. Then gather up your metric sockets, a plastic scraper and a drip pan. Slide the drip pan under the engine to catch the spilled coolant.

The T-stat is usually located near the top of the engine under a "gooseneck" housing attached to the upper radiator hose. If yours isn't there, consult a shop manual to locate it. Remove the two or three bolts that hold the gooseneck in place and remove the T-stat (**Photo 1**). Next, clean both the engine and the gooseneck sealing surfaces (**Photo 2**). If the parts store gave you a plain gasket, coat one side with RTV sealant (self-adhesive gaskets don't need sealant). Then install the T-stat and gasket (**Photo 3**). If the old T-stat used a rubber O-ring instead of a gasket, lubricate the new one with fresh coolant before you insert it. Reinstall the gooseneck and top off the coolant.

1 **Shop smart.** Buy a complete kit. This kit includes tape to mask off the headlight, clear coat remover (activator), sandpaper, polishing compound and cloths, gloves and a bottle of clear coat.

CLEAR UP CLOUDY HEADLIGHTS

Road grit and the sun's UV rays can really do a number on your headlights. The grit literally blasts off the factory-applied protective coating, and the sun takes care of whatever coating is left. Then the lenses cloud over, dramatically reducing the amount of light they project. You've got two choices to see clearly again. You can either restore the old headlights with a restoration kit (**Photo 1**) and a spare hour, or spend $40 to $250 each on new headlights. Tough choice, huh?

We used a $25 kit from Sylvania to show you how it works. But before you buy a kit, make sure the cloudiness is on the outside of the lens (**Photo 2**). If you see moisture droplets on the inside of the lens or hairline cracks, the problem is on the inside and the headlight can't be restored. Buy a replacement at the dealer, auto parts store or an online source such as amazon.com or odonnellsautoparts.com.

All headlight restoration kits include sandpaper and polishing compound, and they all do a decent job. But the better kits also include a bottle of clear coat remover solution and new UV-blocking clear coat (**Photo 1**). That makes the job go faster and the results last longer.

Start by masking off the areas around the headlight to prevent paint damage. Then apply the "activator" solution to soften any remaining clear coat. Wipe the lens clean. Next, wet-sand the lens, starting with the coarsest sandpaper, and work your way to the finest grit (**Photo 3**). Dry the lens and then polish the surface with the "clarifying compound" and the polishing cloth. Finish the job by applying the new clear coat (**Photo 4**).

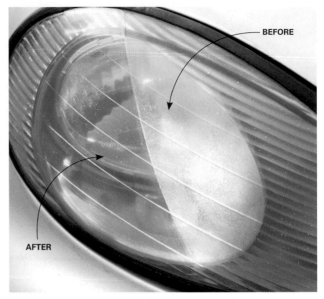

2 **Frosty on the outside.** Check the headlight to see if the wear is on the outside of the lens. If it looks and feels like frosted glass, the restoration will probably work.

3 **Apply some elbow grease.** Wet-sand the lens in a circular pattern with medium pressure. Rewet the lens frequently with clear water.

4 **The final touch—new clear coat.** Clean off all the polishing compound and make sure the lens is dry before you apply the new clear coat. Wipe on the clear coat and let it dry for four to six hours before driving.

Car&Garage

THINGS TO LUBE BEFORE THE SNOW FLIES

Cold weather is tough on your vehicle. Now's the time to lube locks, latches, hinges, window channels and weather stripping. You can lube your entire vehicle in less than 20 minutes. All you need is dry Teflon spray, spray lithium grease, a rag and glass cleaner.

Start with the window channels (**Photo 1**). Proper lube can prevent binding and freezing and save you the cost of a busted regulator ($400, installed). Then shoot the door and trunk/hatch lock cylinders (**Photo 2**). Next coat all the weather stripping (**Photo 3**). Finish the job by lubing the hood, truck or tailgate latches (**Photo 4**).

3 **Coat weather stripping.** Spray all the weather stripping with dry Teflon spray. Then spread it with a cloth.

1 **Lube window channels.** Lower the window glass and shoot dry Teflon spray down the front, rear and top window channels on each door. Soak the channels. Then run the window up and down several times to spread the lube. Finally, raise the window and clean off overspray with glass cleaner.

2 **Lube the locks.** Use the spray straw to force the lock "door" open. Then inject a quick shot of dry Teflon spray into the lock cylinder. Insert your key and rotate the lock to spread the lube.

4 **Grease the latches and hinges.** Spray the hood and tailgate latches with lithium grease. Then spray the door hinges. Operate the latches and doors several times to spread the grease.

FIX A STUCK POWER ANTENNA ON YOUR VEHICLE

If your power radio antenna won't go up and down any-more, the problem is either a burned-out motor or the geared cable inside the mast. Both are easy DIY fixes. You can do the entire repair in about two hours. The parts run about $25 for a new cable/mast, plus the cost of the special wrench. Or, pick up a complete junkyard unit for about $75 (that's half the price of a new antenna).

First, make sure the motor works. Have a friend turn on the radio and listen for motor noise coming from the antenna area. If it makes noise, it's a candidate for repair. If not, you'll have to replace it using the steps we show. Next, order a replacement mast kit from antennamastsrus.com. The kit includes a new geared nylon cable connected to new antenna sections. You'll also need a special wrench to remove the bezel nut (DON'T use pliers; you'll scratch the bezel and the paint). Check an auto parts store for one or order the Steck No. STC21600 for $16 from amazon.com.

Unscrew the bezel (**Photo 1**) and remove the antenna retaining bolts. If your antenna is mounted inside the front fender, remove the wheel-well liner by pulling out the plastic rivets and push-in retainers.

Next disconnect the power and coaxial cable connectors and remove the entire unit from the vehicle (**Photo 2**). If your antenna doesn't have a removable coaxial connector, disconnect the power connectors and perform the mast replacement while the unit is still connected to the coaxial cable.

ANTENNA WRENCH

BEZEL

Remove the cover screws from the antenna. Then lift the cover and note the location of the gears, cable spool, washers and idler roller before you remove them. Next, remove the old mast (**Photo 1**). Thread the nylon cable and mast into the spool and reinsert the gears and rollers (**Photo 3**). Spray all the moving parts with lithium grease. Reinstall the cover, then plug in the antenna and reinstall it in the fender or trunk.

1 **Unbolt the antenna and pull it free.** Tilt the bottom of the antenna away from the fender and pull the unit down and out. That will loosen the rubber gasket and break the unit free.

MOTOR UNIT

OLD CABLE

2 **Out with the old.** Cut the old nylon cable with side cutters. Remove the entire cable, gears and spool and clean all the parts with degreaser.

SPOOL

NEW CABLE

3 **Reinstall the mast and regrease.** Install the mast and nylon cable in the housing and mesh the cable teeth to the drive gear. Install the cover and tighten the screws.

CAR & GARAGE

TURN YOUR TRUCK INTO A GENERATOR

If you need power, here's how to get it.

by **Rick Muscoplat**

No matter how good your battery-powered saw or drill is, sometimes you need a plug-in tool to get the job done. Don't have an AC receptacle nearby? Well, if you have a truck, you already have most of the makings of a rolling AC generator. Just install an AC inverter and you'll have about 1,800 watts at your fingertips. The basic setup runs about $450, and the upscale version (with auxiliary battery and isolator relay) about $700. The installation takes just a few hours and requires only a drill and hand tools.

Component shopping

AC inverters come in two styles: modified and pure sine wave. A modified sine wave inverter (such as the AIMS No. PWRINV1800W; $189 from theinverterstore.com) is less expensive and works great with power tools. For "cleaner" power to run a computer, TV or portable tool battery charger, buy a pure sine wave inverter. Be sure it has built-in overload, over-temperature, over-and-under voltage and fault protection, as well as neutral isolation.

You'll also need one 200-amp fuse block/fuse kit (two if you add a second battery and three if you add a battery isolator). Order separate lengths of 1/0 cable for the positive and negative connections. Adding a 100Ah valve regulated lead acid (VRLA) absorbed glass mat (AGM) battery is optional. It adds about $200 to the cost, but it helps prevent alternator overheating and helps maintain the voltage under heavy loads. Add an isolation relay ($60) at the same time to prevent draining your main battery.

Select a mounting location

Inverters create a lot of heat, so mount yours in a spot with adequate air-flow like your truck bed toolbox or on the floor behind the driver's seat. Open the toolbox lid or the cab door when the inverter's in use.

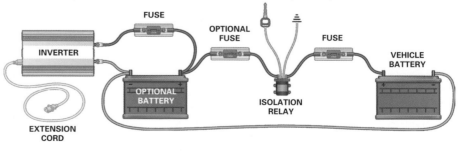

Figure A: The complete system layout
Locate one fuse block between the main battery and the relay. Mount a second one after the relay. Install the third one between the auxiliary battery and the inverter.

INVERTER

EXTENSION CORD

OPTIONAL BATTERY

FUSE

OPTIONAL FUSE

ISOLATION RELAY

FUSE

VEHICLE BATTERY

"SMURF" TUBE
NIPPLE
LOCKNUT
BUSHING
INVERTER

1 **Thread the cables and connect.** Pop 1-in. chase nipples into the holes in the bed and the box and spin on locknuts. Then push the "smurf" tube and cable through the nipples and connect them to the inverter.

FUSE BLOCK

2 **Secure the fuse block.** Clamp the cable ring terminals under the serrated washers and install the fuse. Then tighten the nut and install the protective cover.

Run the cabling

Every vehicle is different, so I can't give you a "one-size-fits-all" wire routing scheme. But the most important rule is to keep both cables away from the engine block, pulleys, steering components, and the exhaust manifold and pipes. And run a separate negative cable from the inverter back to the main battery. To protect the cables under the vehicle, run them (especially the positive cable) inside flexible plastic 3/4-in. conduit. (This Carlon Flex-Plus Blue product, nicknamed "smurf" conduit by electricians, is available in 10-ft. lengths in the electrical department at home centers.) Then drill two 1-in. holes in the truck bed and two in the toolbox and install electrical fittings (**Photo 1**). Next, mount the inverter.

Mount the optional battery isolation relay under the hood and connect the trigger wire to a switch-powered "hot" wire. Install the optional auxiliary battery close to the inverter. See **Figure A** for the complete wiring diagram.

Finish the job at the battery

Connect the positive cable to a fuse block before attaching it to the battery (**Photo 2**). Finish the job by connecting the negative cable to the battery. ⌂

GreatGoofs®

Great Goofs, automotive style

My friend works in a body shop and moonlights by painting cars in his garage. He offered me a paint job for $200, but only if I did the prep work. I washed my car and dried it with a shop rag before taking it over to his place. The car looked fantastic when he was done. But the paint started peeling off in sheets as I drove home. Apparently my rag had car wax on it and I spread it all over the car. That was $200 down the drain.

STORE YOUR CAR
FOR THE SEASON

Time to put your baby away? Here's how to store your car so it's road-ready next spring.

by **Rick Muscoplat**

Step 1: Perform all the maintenance items first

■ Change the oil and filter and run the engine for a few minutes to circulate the clean oil. Fresh oil provides the ultimate in corrosion protection for winter storage.

■ Inject fresh grease into all grease fittings.

■ Prevent corrosion on the hood latch and door hinges by spraying them with white lithium grease.

■ Open the windows, doors and trunk and spray dry Teflon lube or silicone spray on all the weather stripping to keep it from bonding to the doors when the vehicle sits for long periods.

Step 2: Fill with gas and stabilize

Draining all the fuel from your car would prevent gum and varnish buildup. But it's next to impossible to do that, and even trying to do it can ruin a perfectly good fuel pump (a mistake that'll cost you $700 including labor).

Instead, stop at an auto parts store and buy a fresh bottle of fuel stabilizer. Then fill the tank at the gas station and pour in the recommended amount of fuel stabilizer. Drive the car around for about 15 minutes to get the stabilizer mixed into the gas and spread throughout the fuel system.

Step 3: Raise the vehicle on jack stands and lower the air pressure

All tires "flat-spot" during storage (see "Flat Spots Are Real" at right), so jack up your vehicle and set it on jack stands as shown. Then lower the tire pressure to 25 psi or so for the winter.

Forget the blocks—use jack stands. Slip a piece of plywood under the stand to prevent it from sinking into asphalt or leaving rust stains on your garage floor. Then slide the jack stands into place and lower the vehicle.

Flat spots are real

The Internet is loaded with misinformation about which tires "flat-spot" during storage. Most sites say that bias-ply tires flat-spot but radials don't, implying there's no need to jack up your vehicle for storage if your tires are radials. Guess what? They're wrong.

According to Hankook Tire America Corp. engineer Thomas Kenny, all tires can flat-spot after sitting for a while. After short-term storage (about three months), the flat spot usually goes away with a few miles of driving—but not always. Some radial tires (especially high-performance radial tires) can acquire a permanent flat spot when stored longer than six months. So get those tires off the ground during storage.

Step 4: Seal openings to keep out critters

Rodents love the comfy conditions inside your vehicle's heater system, air filter box and exhaust system. To keep them out of the heater, close the fresh air inlet by starting the engine and switching the heater to the "recycle" position. Then shut off the engine and stuff steel wool and a bright reminder flag into the air filter box intake duct (the duct coming into the air filter box, not the one going to the throttle body). Finally, plug the exhaust system as shown.

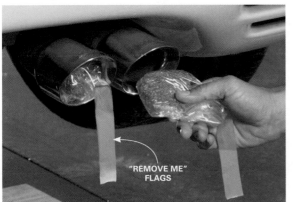

"REMOVE ME" FLAGS

Stuff the tailpipe. Load a steel wool pad into a sandwich bag and jam it into the tailpipe(s). Mark the bags with bright flags to remind you to remove them next spring.

Step 5: Protect your battery

There's no way your battery will stay charged over the winter. And once it loses its charge, it can freeze. Then it's toast. Either remove it and store it indoors, or keep it at full charge by hooking it up to a battery maintainer (shown is the SOLAR No. PL2110 Pro-Logix; $40 from amazon.com).

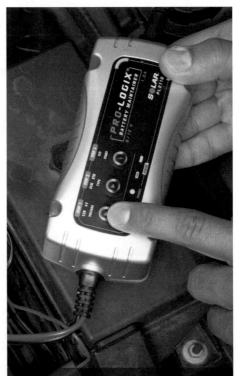

Connect a battery maintainer. Connect the clamps to the vehicle battery (red to red, black to black). Then plug in the battery maintainer and set the voltage and battery type. Press start and close the hood for the winter.

Step 6: Cover with a breathable fabric

If you're storing your car indoors, you can cover it with just a sheet. But if it'll be sitting outdoors, spend the bucks for a breathable water-resistant custom-fitted cover. (A waterproof tarp would trap moisture and create a perfect environment for rust.) Also, make sure you cover the tires to protect the rubber from damaging UV rays. Forget the tire dressing. It doesn't extend the life of the tire at all. 🏠

RESURFACE A PITTED GARAGE FLOOR

A spalled (pitted) garage floor looks horrible. And patches will just pop out eventually. But you can resurface the concrete yourself, usually in less than a day, and for less than $300. You'll need a pressure washer, concrete cleaner (such as Quikrete Concrete & Stucco Wash No. 8601-15; $10 per quart at home centers), a push broom and a floor squeegee. Buy enough concrete resurfacer material (such as Quikrete Concrete Resurfacer; $20 per 40-lb. bag) to coat the entire floor. Refer to the coverage specs on the bag to determine how many bags you need.

The resurfacing material won't bond to loose concrete, paint, grease, algae or mildew. So pressure-wash the entire floor with concrete cleaner and a clean-water rinse. Next, prefill any cracks and pits that are more than 1/4 in. deep (**Photos 1 and 2**).

Saturate the concrete with water and then use a broom to push out any puddles from the pitted areas or low spots. Follow the mixing directions on the resurfacer bag. Then pour out a puddle and spread it (**Photo 3**). If the pits still show, let the material set up and apply a second coat later in the day. But you can stop with one coat if it provides good coverage. To apply a nonslip texture, lightly drag a clean push broom in one direction across the still-wet material (allow no more than five minutes of setting time before applying the broom finish).

Let the new floor dry for at least 24 hours before you drive on it. Follow the manufacturer's directions for additional hot-weather misting procedures or extra drying time for cool weather.

1 **Find the deepest pits.** Make a mark 1/4 in. from the tip of a pencil. Use it as a depth gauge to locate pits that need filling.

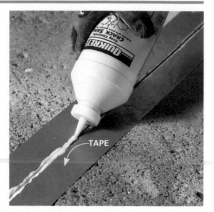

2 **Fill cracks and joints.** Apply tape to each side of the crack or joint and fill with crack sealer. Then level the sealer with a trowel and remove the tape.

POWER MIXER

3 **Apply resurfacer.** Spread from the middle of the puddle and apply moderate squeegee pressure to force the resurfacer into the pores and pits. Then drag the squeegee backward to eliminate the edge ridges. Continue spreading until you get even coverage.

Question&Comment

SHOULD I BUY DEALER PAINT SEALANT?

I bought a new vehicle and the dealer suggested paint sealant. The original quote was $400, but it was lowered to $300. I said no. Is that stuff any good, and does anybody else sell it for less?

Paint sealant really is a good product. But it's nowhere near as perfect as the dealer would like you to believe. If you read the fine print on the "lifetime" guarantee, you'll see that you have to bring the vehicle back for repeat applications on your dime. With routine reapplications, the paint sealant sounds more and more like, uh, car wax.

In fact, paint sealant is nothing more than a polymer-based car "wax" that seals better and lasts longer than traditional carnauba-based waxes. You can apply the same finish yourself (Meguiar's NXT Generation Tech Wax 2.0, $16, or Klasse High Gloss Sealant Glaze, $25, both from amazon.com). Or, you can find an auto detailer shop that'll apply it for about $90.

Apply paint sealant yourself and save bucks. Pour the sealant onto a foam application and spread it around. Wipe off the excess with a microfiber towel.

THE NOT-SO-GREAT ALTERNATOR TEST

My battery goes dead overnight, and I think it's my alternator. I read online that you can just disconnect the negative battery terminal while the engine's running to see if the alternator is putting out enough juice to keep it running. But then I read elsewhere that's not a valid test. Which advice is true?

It was never a good test. But in the pre-computer days, you could pull it off without damaging anything. Today, you risk frying every electrical device in your vehicle. The second you disconnect the battery, the voltage regulator pegs the alternator to put out maximum power. With no battery in the circuit to act as a buffer, the alternator can put out up to 150 volts, depending on engine rpm. When the smoke clears, that "simple test" could end up costing you several thousand dollars for new electronics.

Instead, get a cheap voltmeter (about $15 at any home center or auto parts store). With the engine off, battery voltage should be between 12.5 and 12.8 volts. If it's below that, charge the battery with a battery charger before you conduct the test. Then start the engine and check for increased voltage readings as shown at right. If you see higher readings, chances are the alternator is good (more sophisticated testing equipment is needed to detect an open or shorted alternator diode).

By the way, a dead battery in the morning is usually caused by a computer module that isn't shutting down when you turn off the car. If your alternator tests good, get your vehicle into a shop and pay a pro to find the misbehaving module.

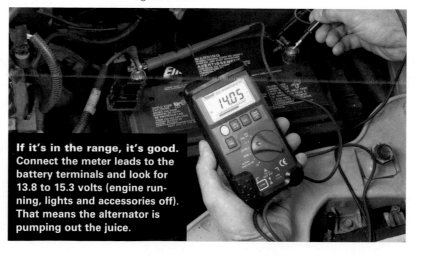

If it's in the range, it's good. Connect the meter leads to the battery terminals and look for 13.8 to 15.3 volts (engine running, lights and accessories off). That means the alternator is pumping out the juice.

Hints & Tips for Storage & Organizing

UTILITY SINK SHELF

To make paint cleanup easier, we cut a section of leftover wire shelving and set it over the front of our utility sink. It's the perfect place to dry sponges, foam brushes and roller covers. We hang the paintbrushes from S-hooks so they can drip right into the sink. When we're done with the shelf, we hang it over the side of the tub so it's right at hand for our next painting project.

WRENCH CADDY

Organize your wrenches in your toolbox by stringing them onto a large, bright colored carabiner (about $6 at camping and discount stores). It will keep your wrenches together and make them portable and easy to spot.

CARABINER

BRILLIANT BUNGEE CORD STORAGE

Bungee cords always seem to end up in a tangled mess. To keep them organized, screw a scrap piece of closet shelving to the wall and hook the cords along its length. It'll be easy to find the one you need.

INSTANT KITCHEN CABINET ORGANIZER

A metal file organizer is perfect for storing baking sheets, cutting boards and pan lids. You can pick one up for a buck at the dollar store. To keep the organizer from sliding around, use rubber shelf liner or attach hook-and-loop tape to the cabinet base and the bottom of the organizer.

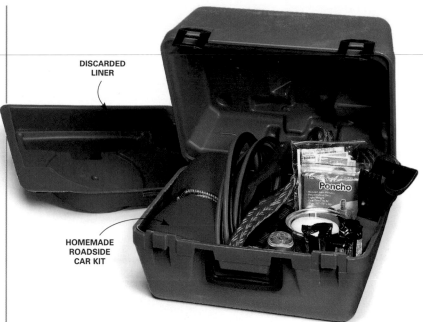

DRILL BOX REUSE

When that power tool finally gives up the ghost, give its carrying case a second life by carefully cutting out the liner with a utility knife. The case can be recycled into a roadside car kit or travel toolbox or holder for just about anything you can cram in there!

STORING PAINT CANS

We've covered paint can storage tips a hundred times before. But this tip comes to us from a house painter with thousands of paint jobs under his belt. Rather than spending time trying to sop all the paint out of the rim, he punches four small holes in the valleys and lets it drain as shown. Then he stores the cans upside down. He swears it works like a charm.

Puncture, drain, store.
Use a small nail to drive four holes in the rim of the paint can. Let the paint drain back into the can and seal the lid with a block of wood and a hammer. Then flip the can upside down for storage.

Hints & Tips for Storage & Organizing

PATIO CUSHIONS AND CAMPING GEAR

Extra-large Ziploc bags (about $2 each at home centers and online) are great for storing camping gear, patio cushions and out-of-season clothes. Here's a slick trick for getting all the air out of the bag before you seal it. Put your items inside and push out all the air you can by hand. Then seal the bag but leave an opening large enough to fit a drinking straw. Use the straw to suck out the remaining air and then finish sealing the bag.

MOUNTAINS OF MAGAZINES

Raise your hand if you have an ever-growing stack of magazines stashed somewhere in your house. Can you actually find anything in that heap? Here's a great way to archive magazines, a method that one of our editors has been using at work for years. All you need is a bunch of hanging folders and a drawer that's set up for hanging them. Cut off the bottom of each folder about an inch below the rod. Drape your magazine over the rod and hang it in the drawer. The spines are easy to read, so you can find what you need quickly.

EXTRA ELECTRICAL CORDS

Ever wish you had one more garage wall to hang stuff on? Well, you do. Your garage door is a perfect place to store lightweight items like extension cords. (Yes, they'll stay put when the door opens and closes.) Install screw eyes diagonally about 8 in. apart and thread bungee cords (with the ends cut off) through them. Now you have a perfect bungee "corral" to hold your extra extension cords.

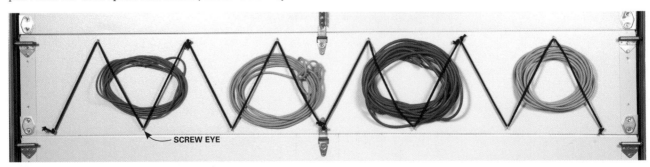

SCREW EYE

MOLDING AND OTHER LONG STUFF

A roll of shrink wrap is essential in any shop. Use it to bundle up pipe, trim, anything that's long and skinny.

REMOTE CONTROLS

Stick them to the underside of your coffee table with hook-and-loop tape.

EXTENSION LADDER

An extension ladder has to be one of the most difficult things to store. When you need to use it, it has to be easy to get to. But there are long stretches when it just gets in the way of everything else in your garage. Here's a good solution: Mount it on your garage ceiling on sturdy racks made of scrap 2x4s that are screwed into the ceiling joists. Use two 3-1/2-in. screws at each joint to make the rack secure. These racks make it easy to slide the ladder out when you need it. Just make sure to position the racks where they won't interfere with your garage door.

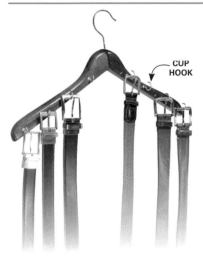

CUP HOOK

BELTS AND OTHER HANG-UPS

Where do you store your belts? At my house, the answer is: (A) on the floor, (B) over a chair, (C) stuffed in a drawer and (D) all of the above. Thanks to one of our readers, I can now choose (E)—on an inexpensive and easy-to-make belt holder. All you need is a wooden hanger and some cup hooks. If some of your belts have unusually thick buckles, just widen the cup hook slightly with a needle-nose pliers. This is a great way to hang small handbags, too.

MUSICAL INSTRUMENTS

UTILITY HOOK

If you occasionally put your hammer down to strum a guitar or banjo, you know how tricky it can be to store them. Floor stands are pricey and they leave your instrument accessible to curious children, rambunctious pets and people who can't carry a tune. It's a better idea to hang your instruments on the wall, but instrument wall hangers cost $20 a pop. Instead of hitting the music store, hit the home center. Plastic-coated utility hooks will hold most instruments at a fraction of the cost ($2 to $4), and they're just as tough. And for those of you DIYers who can't carry a tune...maybe you should leave your instruments on the wall and carry that hammer instead.

Hints & Tips for Storage & Organizing

LISA MCCLINTICK

SCREWS, DOODADS AND MISCELLANEOUS HARDWARE

If you have lots of small hardware on hand, constantly opening drawers or containers to find what you need is a pain. Here's how one of our ultra-organized readers solved the problem. He stores his hardware in small, sturdy zippered craft bags (thicker than sandwich bags and available at hobby stores). He punches a hole in the bag and hangs it on the pegboard in his shop. The clear bags make finding what you need a snap and keep dust and moisture at bay. If you need to find a matching piece of hardware, just hold it up for a side-by-side comparison.

TOO MANY CLOTHES FOR YOUR CLOSET

I don't know anyone who has too much closet space (and if you do, don't brag). Here's an easy way to add space for hanging clothes (or at least clothes that don't require a tall space). Hang a second clothes rod from the upper rod with light-weight chain. Attach the chain to screw eyes directly or use S-hooks or carabiners.

Carabiners make adjusting the height of the extra rod a snap. This system works well in kids' closets since they grow quickly (and their clothes grow along with them). It also works well in an adult closet—you can hang pants on one rod and shirts on the other.

BASKETBALLS (AND OTHER DANGEROUS ITEMS)

If you have kids, you have balls—basketballs, soccer balls, rubber balls and other round objects that roll around underfoot. Here's a perfect way to use that narrow gap between a pair of garage doors (if you're blessed with such an awkward spot). Just install angled "ball ramps" made from scrap wood. The balls fit neatly in the gap, and because the ball ramp is right there at the edge of the garage, kids are more likely to use it on their way back from the hoop.

SHOP AND GARAGE SUPPLIES

Hang inexpensive metal shelves upside down from your ceiling joists. Install the shelves high or low (use lag bolts) and trim the shelf posts with tin snips.

VACUUM GEAR

It seems like the vacuum cleaner always ends up in one closet and the vacuum cleaner bags in another, and the attachments get shoved in a corner or spread all over the floor. Here's a simple tip that will keep everything together and out from underfoot. Screw a hook to the door of your storage closet and hang a mesh or cloth bag on it. You can store all your vacuum cleaner bags and attachments in one place, and the bag lets you carry everything you need from room to room or up and down the stairs in one trip.

YARD TOOLS

Store them in an old golf bag with a cart so you can haul your tools wherever you need them.

GARAGE ODDS AND ENDS

Who couldn't use a few more shelves in the garage? You probably already have shelves in the obvious spots, but what about in the corners? This nifty corner shelf unit takes advantage of existing studs, and it's fast, easy and cheap. Use scrap plywood or oriented strand board to make shelves that fit snugly between the corner studs and support them with 1x1 cleats. These corner shelves are perfect for storing smaller items such as glues, oils, waxes and polishes, which get lost on larger shelves.

WET HATS, GLOVES AND MITTENS

If you don't have radiators, finding a good spot to dry wet hats and mittens can be tough. Tossing them into a plastic bin gets them out of the way, but they never dry and it's no fun putting on damp mittens in the morning. This simple back-of-the-door glove and cap rack allows wet things to dry and keeps easily misplaced items organized. Just string clothespins on aluminum wire (it won't rust) and stretch it between screw eyes on the back of a closet door. This also works great out in the garage for drying garden and work gloves.

BASEMENT JUNK

OK, I don't mean junk. I mean luggage, camping gear, the ugly vase Aunt Martha gave you for your wedding ...stuff you need to keep but don't use all the time. If your house has a set of stairs with a sloped closet underneath, you have a huge amount of space that's mostly wasted. Here's how to get the most out of that black hole. Build a custom rolling cart that fits perfectly in the closet. This one is built like a shelf unit and rides on fixed casters so it slides straight out to keep things organized and accessible. When Aunt Martha comes to visit, just roll it out, grab the vase and you're golden.

TAPE AND RIBBON

A toilet paper holder can hold duct tape, masking tape & more.

Hints&Tips for Storage&Organizing

NO MORE WET BOOTS!

What do you get when you mix boots and winter weather? A dirty, slippery floor (and wet socks). Make life neater and safer for everyone in your house by building this simple boot tray. All you need is a plastic tray or a large metal baking sheet with a lip. Put a layer of medium-size stones in the tray so the boots can drain. To keep the stones in place and give the tray a handsome finished look, build a 1x2 frame around the tray and paint it the same color as the trim in your entryway.

FISHING RODS

This is for all you fishing addicts out there. When the season ends and the gear comes out of the truck, where do you store your rods? You can buy a fancy storage rack or make one of your own. But either way, you're giving up precious wall space until spring. Here's a quick solution: Screw short sections of wire shelving to your ceiling. If the handles don't fit, just clip out some of the wire with bolt cutters. Your rods will be safely out of the way until your next fishing trip.

GLUED
END CAP

1 5/8 Screws

PVC PIPE BLADE AND BIT ORGANIZER

I always seem to have extra bits, jigsaw blades and other small items lying loose in my toolboxes and bags. To keep things organized, I cut different diameters of PVC pipe to the lengths needed for my accessories. I glue one end cap in place, put my items inside and slide on the other end cap. Use a marker to label each container and you'll be able to find all your bits, blades, screws and whatever when you need them.

PVC PLASTIC BAG DISPENSER

After building a PVC fence, I was left with a few extra 2-ft. lengths of fence post. I turned one of them into a home for grocery bags that I reuse. I stuff them into the top and pull them out the bottom. If you don't have any leftover fencing, 3-in.-diameter PVC pipe works well too. Attach it to the door inside a pantry or closet, or to a wall of your workshop or garage.

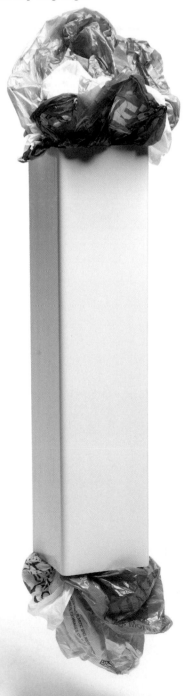

PICTURE-PERFECT TOOL WALL

Having a job that moves me around the country every few years means I have to reassemble my workshop from scratch a lot. I finally decided to photograph my tool wall so that when I land in a new place, I can quickly set up my shop wall placing all my tools in exactly the right spot.

READER PHOTO

CUP HOOK

BBQ TOOL ORGANIZER

We use our grill constantly, and I got tired of all my cooking tools taking up valuable space on my grill's side trays. I came up with the perfect solution: I screwed hooks to the underside of my deck railing. Now I can hang each tool on its own hook. It's a great way to keep the tools out of the way, yet right where I need them.

Hints&Tips for Storage&Organizing

HANDY GARBAGE BAG STORAGE

Here's a good old janitors' tip that a lot of readers write in with. Store your replacement garbage bags right in the bottom of your garbage can. When the old bag is full, the new one is right where you need it. (This tip works best for garbage cans that are unlikely to hold wet, messy stuff.)

ROLL OF GARBAGE BAGS

SPRING CLAMP STORAGE TRAY

Serve up your spring clamps on a tray—a slotted piece of 3/4-in. plywood with 1/4-in. plywood fins glued in the slots. A clamp tray defies the natural tendency of tools to create clutter. Just pull the tray off a peg, take a few clamps off the fins, stick them back on the fins when you're done, and hang up the tray.

SCREWDRIVER ORGANIZER

I found an easy way to store my screwdrivers for quick access and identification. I drilled holes through a length of PVC pipe, screwed it to the wall and organized my screwdrivers by type and size.

MARK HARDY

FISHING ROD STORAGE

Here's a smart way to make your garage doors do double duty—store your fishing rods on them! Make some simple fishing pole racks out of plywood and screw them to the ribs of the door. Then slide your rods onto the racks. The rods stay secure in the holders whether the door is open or shut.

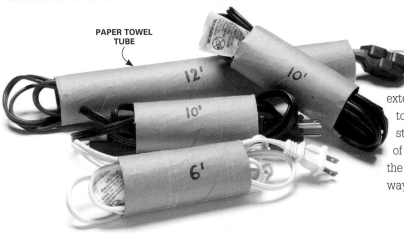

PAPER TOWEL TUBE

EXTENSION CORD STORAGE

I was born in 1929 and this is a hint I've been using for years and years. I keep my extension cords organized by sliding them into toilet paper and paper towel tubes. Before I stick them into the drawer, I write the length of the cord on the tube. That way, I can spot the right cord for the job instantly, and it's a good way to recycle all those paper tubes.

GARDEN AND WORK GLOVE HANG-UP

Our garden and work gloves were in the habit of getting lost in the shed. It was worse than losing socks in the dryer. I'd be lucky to find one glove on the floor and the other one stuck in an empty flowerpot. It was an ongoing battle to find a matched set. Then I came up with the ingenious idea of hanging binder clips on nails to organize our gloves. They're always dry and always together in a matched set. Now I'm trying to figure out a similar system for our socks.

BINDER CLIPS

Hints & Tips for Storage & Organizing

SHEET METAL DRAWER LINERS

If you're one of those guys who uses old kitchen cabinets in your workshop, here's a tip for you. It's a bad idea to throw oily, greasy tools into those drawers, where the wood soaks up everything. Instead, take some careful measurements of the width, depth and height to any HVAC shop. For about $20 per drawer, you can get custom liners for each one. The interiors will look like new, and you'll be able to clean them as needed.

PAINTING GEAR ORGANIZER

I used to have a hard time keeping track of my painting tools, and I could never find what I needed. Then I drilled two holes in the side of a large plastic container and knotted the ends of a bungee cord in the holes. I stand up all my tools in between the cord and the side of the container. Now it's easy to see everything I've got, and I can grab exactly what I need.

BUNGEE CORD

SEE-THROUGH PAINT STORAGE

When I only have a little bit of paint left in the can, I pour it into a clear water bottle. I label each bottle with the name of the paint, the manufacturer and the location it was used. This makes it very easy to find what I need, the paint stays fresher than it would in the can and it sure saves on storage space.

Den
Fire Dance
Benjamin M.

Bath
Gambol Gold
Sherwin W.

Hall
Lagoon
Behr

EASY-ACCESS TARPS

Storing tarps can be a hassle. Big tarps are heavy, and smaller tarps get wedged behind or underneath things. A simple solution is to store them between your garage rafters or basement floor joists. Cut two rebar sections and cover them with plastic conduit cut short enough to roll freely between the joists. Mount the rebar to the framing using plumbing straps. The rolling conduit lets you slide your folded tarps easily up into the joist cavity and down again whenever you need them.

REBAR

PLUMBING STRAPS

SWINGING TRASH

The wastebasket under our bathroom sink was anything but convenient. You had to pull the basket halfway out to throw anything away (which my husband wouldn't do, so his trash ended up on the floor of the cabinet). I solved the problem by screwing wire shelf anchor clips to the inside of the door and hooking the lip of the wastebasket right on the hooks. Now it's easy to use and there's no more trash on the cabinet floor!

WIRE SHELF ANCHOR CLIPS

COPING
TIGHT JOINTS

Make even those complex moldings fit like a glove   by **Jeff Gorton**

Because inside corners are rarely square, simply butting two mitered pieces into the corner almost always looks lousy. The only foolproof method for great-looking inside corners is cutting a coped joint. This age-old carpenter's trick involves cutting the profile on the end of one molding and fitting it against another like pieces of a puzzle. The resulting joint is easy to file and sand for a perfect fit, even on out-of-square corners. It looks difficult, but don't worry—with an $8 coping saw, a few special techniques and a little practice, you'll be cutting perfect copes in no time.

There are few carpentry skills more rewarding than cutting and fitting a cope, but you'll never know until you give it a try. So grab a coping saw and a chunk of molding and follow along as you learn step by step how to cope an inside corner.

A simple hand tool performs magic

Copes are sawed with—you guessed it—a coping saw (**Photo 2**). You don't need to spend a lot of money on one, however. The basic $8 version available at hardware stores, home centers and lumberyards works great. Pick up an assortment of blades. Use fine-tooth blades for thin material and intricate cuts. A blade with 20-teeth per inch works well for most copes. Some carpenters prefer to cut copes with a jigsaw. If you own a jigsaw, install a fine-tooth blade and give it a try.

A coping saw is designed to cut on the pull stroke (with the blade's teeth facing the handle). But many carpenters

COPING SAW

prefer to mount the blade with the teeth facing away from the handle so the saw cuts on the push stroke. Try it both ways and decide for yourself which method you prefer.

Cut a 45-degree bevel to mark the profile

The first step in coping is to establish the cutting line. Cutting a 45-degree bevel (**Photo 1**) is the easiest method if the two moldings you're joining have the same profile. The molding shown has a complex profile, making for a challenging coping job. Most of the moldings you'll encounter will be considerably easier. Crown and cove moldings that rest at an angle against the wall and ceiling require a slightly different beveling technique to reveal the profile for coping. **Photo 7** shows you how to position a crown molding in your miter box to cut this bevel.

The fine blade reaches the tiniest corners

Photo 2 shows you how to start the cope. The technique varies slightly depending on the profile of the molding. Moldings like this, with flat spots on the top, require a square starting cut. If you start angling the cut too soon, you'll see a little triangular gap on the top of the moldings when you join them. Cut a practice cope on a scrap to confirm your starting angle.

Clamp the molding to a saw-horse or hold it in place with your knee while you saw. Don't force the blade. If the blade starts to leave the cutting line, back up a little and restart the cut. On steep curves, the frame of the saw may hit the molding.

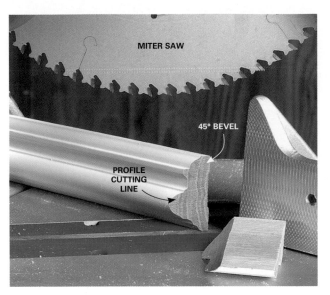

1 Bevel the end of the molding to be coped at a 45-degree angle to reveal the profile.

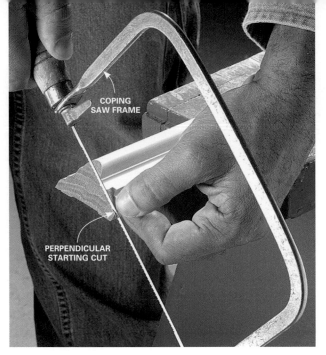

2 Guide the blade with your thumbnail to start the cut accurately. If your molding has a little flat spot on top like the one shown, start the cut with the blade of the coping saw held perpendicular to the molding to make a square starting cut.

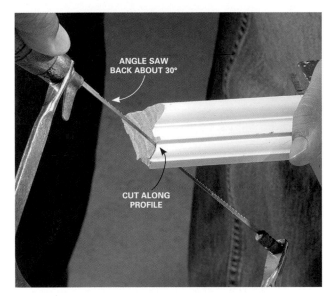

3 Angle the coping saw about 30 degrees to remove more wood from the back of the molding than from the front. Then slowly and carefully saw along the profile. Concentrate on staying just outside the line. You can always sand or file away extra material.

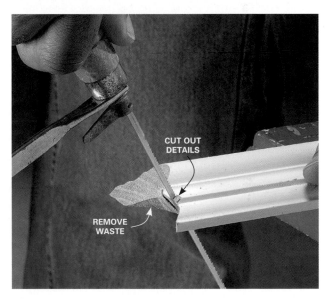

4 Restart the cut to saw around sharp curves or to cut out notches. Complex shapes like this may require three or four approaches at different angles.

If this happens, back the saw out of the cut and saw in from the opposite direction. You may be able to complete some simple copes with one long cut, but in most cases you'll have to approach them from two or three different angles to finish the job (**Photos 3 and 4**).

After a few minutes of sawing, the cut will be complete; now it's time to test-fit the cope on a matching piece of trim. Some copes fit perfectly on the first try. Others require several more minutes of filing and sanding before you get a good fit (**Photo 6**). If the joint is close to fitting, you'll only need to touch up the high spots with 100-grit sandpaper. Use files to remove larger amounts of material.

Crown and cove moldings are a little trickier

Photo 7 shows you how to position the crown molding upside down in your miter box for cutting the bevel. Attach a wood stop to the extension table to hold the molding at the correct angle.

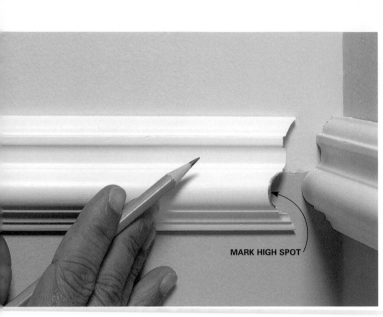

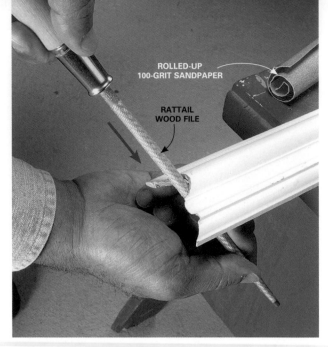

5 Check the fit of the coped joint. Use a sharp pencil to mark spots that have to be sanded or filed.

MARK HIGH SPOT

6 File or sand off high spots. Use rolled-up sandpaper or a rattail file to fine-tune curved sections. Continue checking the fit, then filing or sanding until the joint fits tight.

ROLLED-UP 100-GRIT SANDPAPER

RATTAIL WOOD FILE

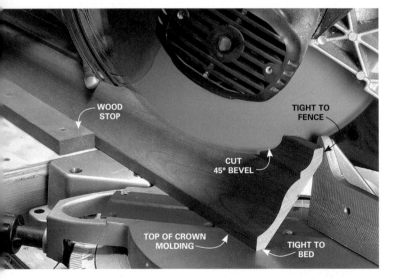

WOOD STOP

TIGHT TO FENCE

CUT 45° BEVEL

TOP OF CROWN MOLDING

TIGHT TO BED

7 Position your crown molding upside down in the miter box at the angle it will rest on the wall (flat spots tight to the bed and fence). Screw or clamp a stop to the extension table to support the crown molding at the correct angle.

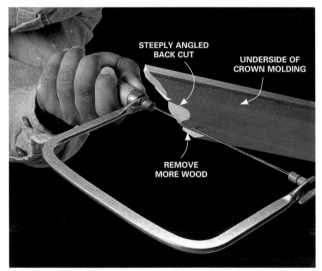

STEEPLY ANGLED BACK CUT

UNDERSIDE OF CROWN MOLDING

REMOVE MORE WOOD

8 Cope crowns at a sharper angle. Recut areas that are hitting in the back. It's common to have to remove large amounts of material in some areas to get a tight fit.

Sawing copes on crowns, especially large ones, requires more effort because the angle of the cut has to be about 50 degrees—much steeper than for a baseboard cope. Even experienced carpenters cut this angle too shallow once in a while. Usually one or two areas will hit in the back and you'll have to remove more material (**Photo 8**).

Switch to a blade with fewer teeth for cutting thick materials like crown moldings. Then expect to spend 10 or 15 minutes on each joint to get a perfect fit.

Before you tackle crown molding copes, practice on smaller moldings like base shoe or simple baseboards to gain confidence. Once you've mastered coping you'll never miter an inside corner again. ⌂

9 Measure and cut the end of the first crown molding square. Butt it into the corner. Don't nail within 16 in. of the corner. Cope the second piece of the crown molding, then file and sand it for a perfect fit.

SCRIBING
FOR A PERFECT FIT

by **Jeff Gorton**

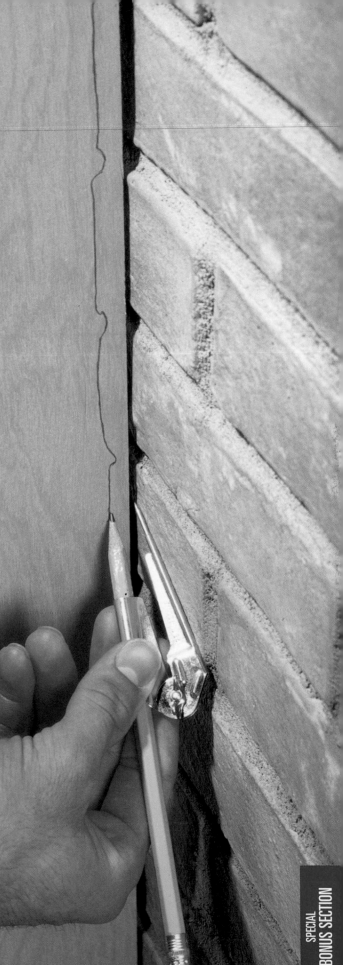

Scribing is a simple technique that lets you fit cabinets, countertops, moldings and almost anything else to crooked walls. Using little more than a $2 compass fitted with a sharp pencil, you can easily transfer odd shapes or the profile of a wavy wall to your workpiece. Once the line is scribed, it's a simple matter of filing, planing or sanding off the excess material to create a nearly seamless fit.

Of course, there are a few techniques you'll need to know for successful scribing. But they're easy to learn, and with a little practice you'll be scribing like a pro. Here you'll learn how to scribe countertops, cabinets, shelves and paneling and even how to fit a panel to a brick chimney. Once you learn how to scribe, a cheap compass will be an indispensable part of your tool collection.

The compass below (available at Home Depot and hardware stores) is my favorite scribing tool, but you don't even need that for many jobs. **Photo 1** shows how to scribe a line with just a carpenter's pencil. **Photo 6** shows how to scribe an even wider gap by adding a scrap of wood.

There are only a few rules to follow for perfect scribing. First, make

COMPASS

CABINETS

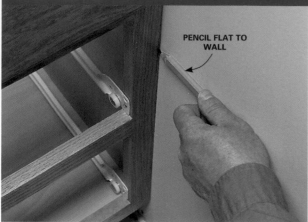

PENCIL FLAT TO WALL

80-GRIT BELT

SAND TO SCRIBED LINE

1 Slide shims under the base of your cabinet until it's level across the top and the side is perfectly plumb. Slide your carpenter's pencil along the wall to scribe a line on the cabinet.

2 Sand to the line with a belt sander. Bevel the wood slightly for a tighter fit by tilting the belt sander as you sand. Remove more wood from the side that's not visible.

COUNTERTOPS

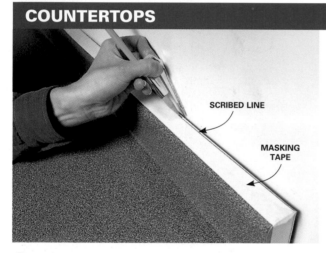

SCRIBED LINE

MASKING TAPE

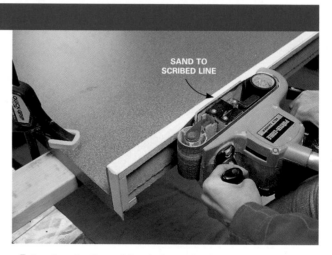

SAND TO SCRIBED LINE

3 Slide the countertop tight to the wall. Measure to make sure the front edge of the countertop is parallel to the front of the cabinets. Adjust the distance between the compass point and pencil tip to equal the widest gap between the wall and the countertop and tighten the thumbscrew. Run the compass point along the wall to transfer the contour to the countertop.

4 Sand to the line with a belt sander fitted with 100-grit sandpaper. Test the countertop's fit and repeat the process shown in Photo 3 to scribe a new line if necessary. Keep scribing and sanding until you get a perfect fit.

sure your workpiece is positioned correctly before you scribe the line on it. Shim a cabinet to make it level and plumb, then place it as close as possible to its final position before drawing the line (**Photo 1**). Don't just shove a countertop against the wall. Make sure it's parallel to the cabinets before scribing the line. To fit boards or moldings to corners that are out of plumb, first hold the workpiece plumb (**Photo 5**), then draw the line.

Next, remember that the distance between the point of your compass and the pencil determines the amount of material you'll remove, which in turn affects the final position of your project. **Photo 7** is a good illustration. The gap between the window stool and the window is 3/4 in., but

you only want a 1/16-in. gap. Set the distance between the compass point and pencil to 11/16 in. and scribe the line. After you cut away the material, the stool will move 11/16 in. closer to the window.

Finally, make sure to hold the compass at a right angle to the surface you're scribing from and maintain this angle while you draw the line. This is especially critical when the compass is spread wider apart or the surface you're scribing is very irregular (**Photo 8**).

Photos 1 – 8 show some of the more common scribing situations and demonstrate the techniques. Once you learn to scribe, you'll never again have to rely on a fat bead of caulk to hide ugly gaps. 🏠

WAINSCOTING

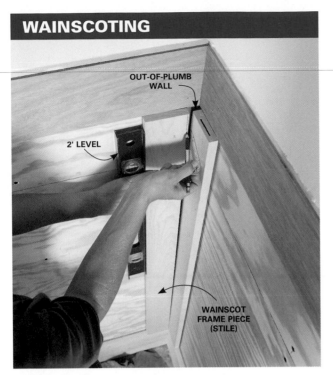

- OUT-OF-PLUMB WALL
- 2' LEVEL
- WAINSCOT FRAME PIECE (STILE)

5 Fit a board to a corner that's not plumb. Use a level to hold the board plumb. Set the compass for the widest gap and scribe the line. Saw or plane away the wood to the outside of the line.

SHELVING

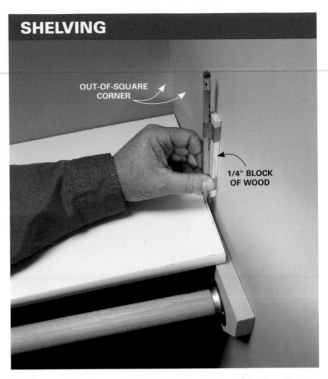

- OUT-OF-SQUARE CORNER
- 1/4" BLOCK OF WOOD

6 Fit a shelf to a corner that's not square. Slide the shelf into the corner, keeping the long back edge tight to the wall. If the shelf fits between two walls, cut it about 1/2 in. too long and set it in at an angle. Run a pencil along the wall to scribe the line. Saw along the line. Repeat the process on the opposite end of the shelf.

WINDOW STOOLS

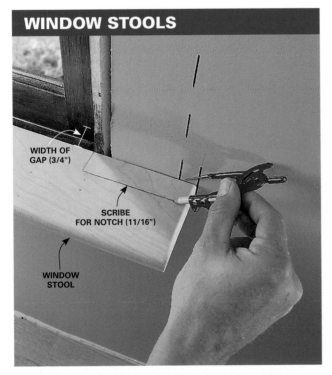

- WIDTH OF GAP (3/4")
- SCRIBE FOR NOTCH (11/16")
- WINDOW STOOL

7 Notch your window stool and set it in place. Measure the gap between the back edge of the stool and the window and set your compass for 1/16 in. less than this measurement. Run your compass along the wall behind each end of the stool. Saw or file away the material to the lines.

IRREGULAR EDGES

- HOLD COMPASS SQUARE

8 Scribing helps you fit a cabinet side, paneling or molding to irregular surfaces like brick. First support the paneling or molding so its edge is plumb. Then set the compass a little wider than the widest gap and scribe the line. Be careful to hold the compass perpendicular to the surface being scribed.

TOENAILING

It's all in the angle.

by **Jeff Gorton**

Toenailing—driving a nail at an angle through the end of a board to anchor it—can be frustrating to learn. But it's an essential carpentry skill, and once you master a few tricks for positioning and driving the nails and get some practice under your belt, it'll be as easy as regular nailing. Toenailing not only makes a strong joint but also is a great way to coax stubborn boards into position.

Photos 1 – 3 walk you through the basic steps of toenailing. The key to success is starting the nail in the right spot and angling it a little steeper than 45 degrees. Visualize the path of the nail by holding it against the boards you're joining (**photo at right**) to determine the right starting spot.

Starting a nail at an angle can be tricky because it'll tend to slide down the board and penetrate too low. It's easier if you begin by tapping the nail point straight in (**Photo 1**). Then tip the nail at the correct angle and pound it in (**Photo 2**). As you pound, you'll discover that toenailing pushes the board off position. Reduce this problem by pressing against the board with your toe to hold it in place while you nail (**Photos 2 and 3**). Also, position the board about 1/4 in. from your mark so the nail will drive it to the right spot.

Driving a toenail requires greater hammer control and precision than regular nailing. Hold the hammer at the

end of the handle with a firm but relaxed grip. Swing from your elbow with a little wrist snap at the end of the stroke for extra oomph. Luckily, you don't have to worry about leaving hammer marks when you're rough-framing walls and floors. As the nail gets close to fully driven, adjust your swing ever so slightly away from you so the face of the hammer will contact the nailhead off center. Catching the head of the nail with the edge of the hammer face allows you to drive the toenail completely.

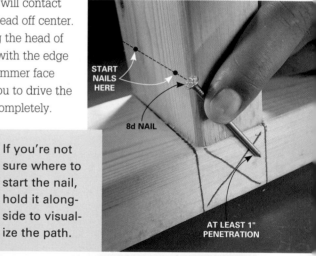

START NAILS HERE

8d NAIL

AT LEAST 1" PENETRATION

Tip If you're not sure where to start the nail, hold it alongside to visualize the path.

TOENAILING BASICS

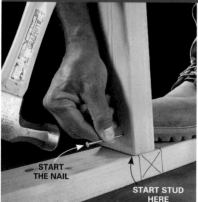

START THE NAIL

START STUD HERE

1 **Start the nail.** Position the board in front of the layout line and place your toe against the back. Start the nail by tapping it about 1/4 in. straight in, not at an angle.

BLOCK WITH TOE

ANGLE NAIL ABOUT 50°

2 **Drive at an angle.** Pull the nail to about a 50-degree angle and set it with a couple of hammer taps. Then let go and drive it in. Brace your toe against the back of the board as you set the nail. It's OK if the board moves slightly past the layout line.

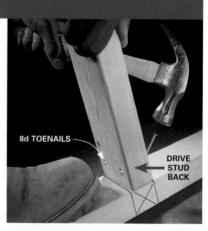

8d TOENAILS

DRIVE STUD BACK

3 **Nail the other side.** Drive toenails into the opposite side to complete the toenailing and at the same time drive the board back to the layout line.

STRAIGHTEN BOWED DECK BOARDS

BOWED DECK BOARD

WIDE GAP

16d TOENAIL

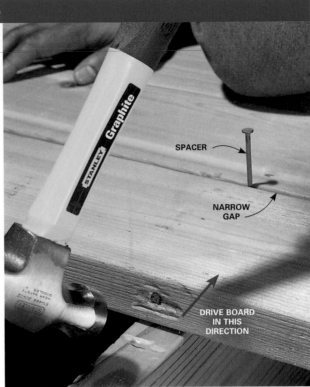

SPACER

NARROW GAP

DRIVE BOARD IN THIS DIRECTION

4 Toenail into the edge of a bowed board to move it closer to the adjoining deck board. Start the nail about one-third down from the top of the board and angle it about 45 degrees to catch the underlying joist.

Here are a few more toenailing tips:

■ Drive the nails until the points barely protrude through the end of the first board before you position it, then position the board and drive the nails home.

■ Drill pilot holes for the nails with a bit about the size of the nail shank. This works great for toenailing in tight spots.

■ Cut a block (14-1/2 in. long for 16-in. on-center studs) to fit between studs when you're toenailing walls. The block acts as a spacer and backer to support the stud while you toenail it.

Put toenailing to work

Toenails have an amazing power to move lumber. This power is especially handy when you're working with framing lumber or decking that's not as straight as you'd like (Photos 4 – 6). Use big nails with big heads like 16d sinkers for these jobs. In fact, if one nail doesn't do the job, drive another alongside to move the board even farther. Some carpenters pound in two 16d nails at once for extra holding power!

So remember, the next time your floor joists or studs stray from the line, coax them into place with toenails. ⌂

5 Pound the nail with heavy hammer blows to straighten the deck board and close the gap between the two boards. Use a shim or nail to maintain a consistent space between boards.

STRAIGHTEN TWISTED JOISTS

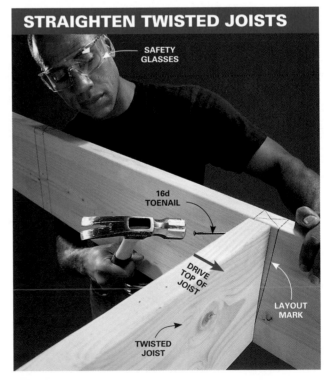

SAFETY GLASSES

16d TOENAIL

DRIVE TOP OF JOIST

LAYOUT MARK

TWISTED JOIST

6 Move twisted framing members into alignment by toenailing in the direction you want the board to go. Continue pounding on the nail until the board is in the desired location. Add a second toenail to move the board farther if necessary.

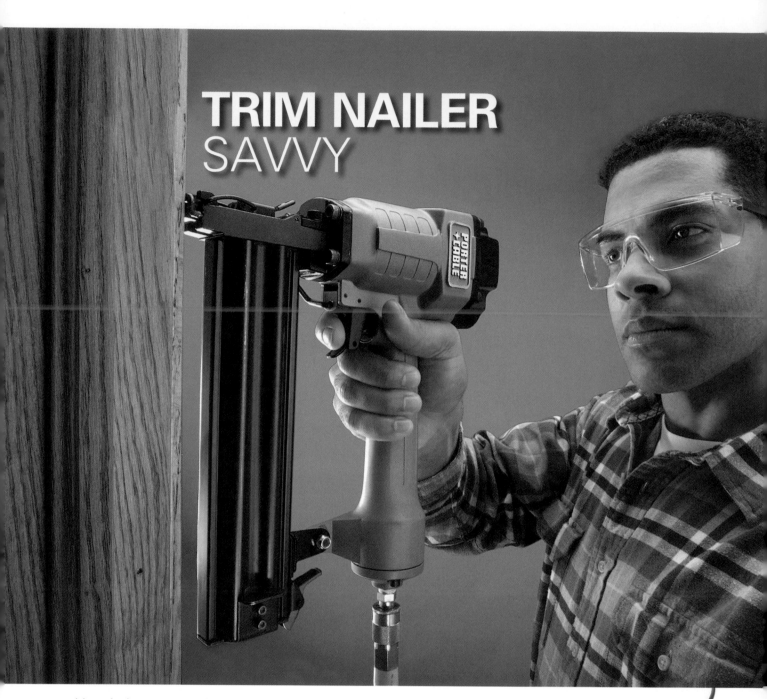

TRIM NAILER
SAVVY

Here's how to avoid common mistakes.

by **Jeff Gorton**

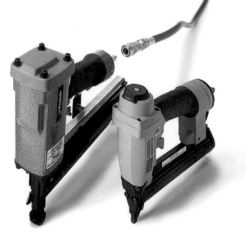

The first time you use a pneumatic trim gun, you'll be hooked. You can install hardwood moldings without predrilling to prevent splitting, and you can leave your nail set mostly in the toolbox. But even better is the fact that nail guns allow you to hold a molding in exactly the right spot with one hand while you instantly nail it in place with the other. And small nail guns called brad nailers allow you to quickly and easily secure thin, fragile moldings without ruining them. That's a job that otherwise requires the dexterity of a surgeon.

But things can go wrong. Here you'll learn the most common problems you'll encounter when nailing trim with a nail gun and the techniques you can use to prevent them.

JAMB   CASING

WRONG ANGLE   BRAD NAILER

1

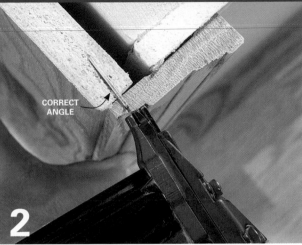

CORRECT ANGLE

2

BLOWOUTS ■ Watch the angle

Once you master this angle technique, you'll have no trouble shooting nails exactly where you want them. Start by positioning the center of the nail gun tip exactly where you want the nail to enter the wood. Then carefully align the nail gun with the path you want the nail to take, just like when you line up a pool cue before striking the ball. **Photo 1** shows what can happen if you get careless and angle the gun wrong. When you're nailing into door jambs

or other areas where only one side shows, point the nail gun slightly to the hidden side where it won't show if the nail pops through (**Photo 2**).

Occasionally nails hit a knot or follow the grain—and pop out despite your best effort. If this happens, break or cut off the protruding nail with a nipper and use your nail set to recess the remainder.

3

CORRECT NAIL PLACEMENT

16-GAUGE NAILER

NAIL TOO CLOSE TO MITER

END SPLITTING
■ Place nails accurately

Driving nails with these tools is so simple that it's easy to get carried away and put nails where they don't belong. (Ask any painter who has to putty all the extra holes!) With practice, you'll get a feel for where the nail comes out of the gun and be able to drive a nail precisely. **Photo 3** shows the result of placing a nail too close to the end of a molding. The same thing will happen if you nail too close to the end of a baseboard, especially on short pieces. Make sure to keep nails a few inches from the end of moldings to avoid splitting the wood. Brad nailers, which drive thinner and shorter nails, are the exception. With these, you can usually nail within 1/2 in. of ends and 1/8 in. of edges without splitting the wood.

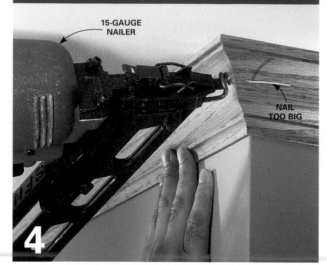

PROBLEM: Exposed nail

15-GAUGE NAILER

NAIL TOO BIG

4

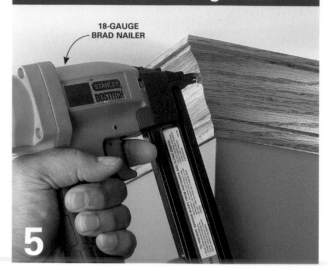

SOLUTION: Use the right size

18-GAUGE BRAD NAILER

STANLEY BOSTITCH

5

WRONG NAIL SIZE ■ Use the right size nail

Changing nail sizes in the middle of a job is bothersome. It's tempting to use the nails that are loaded and hope for the best. But it's a bad idea, as shown in **Photo 4**. A 3/4-in. brad or at most a 1-in. 16-gauge nail should've been used on this miter. A good rule of thumb is to pick a nail long enough to go through the material you're fastening and penetrate the underlying wood about 3/4 in. to 1 in. Allow more penetration for heavy-duty jobs like nailing door jambs, and less for fine work like securing miters.

Some carpenters have a 15-gauge nailer and a brad nailer both connected to separate hoses while they work. (Install a T-fitting at the compressor to connect two hoses at once.) With this setup, it's an easy matter to pick up the brad nailer for intricate jobs like pinning miters (**Photo 5**).

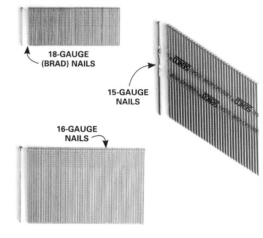

18-GAUGE (BRAD) NAILS

15-GAUGE NAILS

16-GAUGE NAILS

Buying or renting nail guns

If you can afford it, buy both a 15-gauge finish nailer and an 18-gauge brad nailer. The two guns make a winning combination. The 15-gauge nails, ranging in length from about 1-1/4 in. to 2-1/2 in., are strong enough to secure door jambs and other heavy trim materials. Plus, the angled nose on most 15-gauge nailers allows you to nail in corners and drive toenails more easily.

Fifteen-gauge nails are too thick for many fine nailing tasks. And this is where the 18-gauge brad nailer excels. They shoot very skinny 5/8-in. to 1-1/2 in. long, 18-gauge brads. These are perfect for nailing miters (**Photo 2**), nailing the skinny section of door or window casing to the jamb (**Photo 3**) and other nailing jobs

where a larger nail would split the wood or protrude through the other side of the material.

Having both guns connected to your compressor with separate hoses means you can nail the inside and outside edge of casings without having to change nails. And you'll always have just the right size nail for the job at hand.

If you don't do enough trim work to justify the expense of two nailers, a 16-gauge nail gun is a good choice. The 16-gauge nails are a bit skinnier and not quite as strong as 15-gauge nails. But they're less likely to split thin pieces of wood. Most 16-gauge nail guns will shoot nails ranging from 1 in. to 2-1/4 in.

BRAD STICKING OUT

SIDE-CUTTING PLIERS

6

HOSE TO NAIL GUN

PRESSURE-ADJUSTING KNOB

QUICK-CONNECT FITTING

PRESSURE TO NAIL GUN

PRESSURE IN TANK

7

UNDERDRIVEN NAILS ■ Adjust the pressure and nail length

Nails that don't set, or that are left sticking out (**Photo 6**), are usually the result of pressure that's too low, a nail that's too long or an improperly adjusted nail gun. If the nail is sticking way out like the one in **Photo 6**, try increasing the air pressure to the maximum allowable for your nail gun (90 to 100 lbs., or check your instructions). If the nail still won't set, try loading shorter nails or brads.

The nosepiece on some nail guns is adjustable to help control how deep the nail is set. Use this in conjunction with pressure adjustments (**Photo 7**) to fine-tune your nail gun until the head of the nail or brad is slightly recessed. Keep a nail set handy for the occasional protruding nailhead.

Don't bother pounding in nails that protrude more than 1/4 in. They'll just bend over and dent the trim. Instead, grab the shank and bend it back and forth until it snaps, or use side-cutting pliers (**Photo 6**) to cut the nail near the surface. Then recess the rest with a nail set.

Other problems you might encounter

Nail guns can be a little finicky. Here are a few common problems and possible solutions:

■ If the nail gun fires but no nail comes out even though you can see nails in the clip, the nail feed mechanism may be sticking or the nails may be binding in the magazine. Remove the nails and lubricate the magazine and spring feed with spray silicone.

■ If the nail gun doesn't fire even though it's loaded with nails (you won't hear or feel the piston and driver move), it's probably not getting enough air. Make sure the compressor is plugged in and that the fuse or circuit breaker isn't tripped. Then check the gauge to be sure the pressure on both gauges is set high enough.

■ If a nail jams in the nose, disconnect the hose from the gun before you do anything else. Remove the nails from the gun. Then open the nose (check your instruction manual if you're not sure how) and remove the jammed nail.

Nail gun safety

Pneumatic nailers are unbelievably fast and powerful. One careless second is all it takes to lose an eye or put a nail through your finger. Here are safety precautions you should take:

■ Disconnect the air hose from the gun when you're loading nails or clearing a jam, or when you're not using the nail gun.

■ Wear safety glasses and have your helpers and bystanders wear them too.

■ Keep children away from nail guns. Disconnect the gun and put it out of reach when you're not using it.

■ Keep your fingers well away from the nail's path. Use clamps if necessary.

■ Never rest the gun on top of a ladder.

■ Keep your finger off the trigger when you're not firing the gun. 🏠

Electrifying
GreatGoofs®

Electric cake batter

When I was a teenager, I came home from school to find my mother making a cake. She was using her favorite electric mixer. The double-ended electric cord was plugged into the mixer at one end and into the wall outlet at the other. As she happily mixed away, she inadvertently knocked the cord out of the mixer, and it fell into the cake batter. So she fished it out and, not thinking, licked it off. The live cord shocked her tongue, making her jump about 3 ft. in the air. After the initial shock, she was fine, and now we laugh about it.

Real men don't use irons

My friend had installed a kitchen backsplash and asked me to help him change the wall outlets to match the new décor. Since I didn't have my voltage sniffer with me, I needed something to plug into the outlet so I'd know when the power was off. I plugged in a clothes iron, and my friend flipped the circuit breakers until the iron light went off.

I changed the first two outlets and started on the third. Plugged in the iron—yup, the light was off. When I touched the wire, there was a flash of sparks and my entire arm went numb. I was floored—how could I get a shock when the iron showed the power was off? I learned the hard way that the light goes off when the iron reaches the right temperature. I think I'll stick with my voltage sniffer from now on.

Sparks in the dark

Recently I decided to replace a ceiling light fixture with a ceiling fan in my computer room. Instead of turning off the power at the breaker, I just shut off the light switch and got to work. I changed the box and was finishing up the electrical work when a storm passed over outside. The storm darkened the room a bit, but I could still see fine to complete the job. Just then, my wife came into the room to help out. I asked her to hand me some parts and then she said, "Why are you working in the dark?" Taking matters into her own hands, she instinctively turned on the light switch and sparks flew from my screwdriver. Thank goodness my hands weren't touching the wires. Next time I'll turn off the power at the breaker!

Shocking wallpaper

Several years ago, I hung metal foil wallpaper in the bathroom and installed a new light fixture on the wall. The next day, my daughter told me that she got a mild shock when she touched the walls. In disbelief, I went into the bathroom and pushed my palms to the wall and yes, I felt a mild current. I quickly called a friend who's an expert at wiring and he pointed out that I'd wired the fixture incor-

rectly. I'd energized the metal fixture, which in turn energized the foil wallpaper! An occasional ribbing now and then is a good tradeoff for a safe bathroom.

Hot closet!

After framing in a new closet with metal studs, I was ready to take a break. I had been working around an old electrical panel in our old house.

As I sat down on the radiator, I grabbed hold of one of the studs to support myself and was greeted with a powerful shock.

Upon investigating, I found that one of my screws had penetrated a wire inside an existing wall and had energized the new metal wall framing. What a wild ride 120 volts gives you! How lucky I wasn't hurt.

SPECIAL BONUS SECTION

INDEX

Visit **familyhandyman.com** *for hundreds of home improvement articles.*

ACKNOWLEDGMENTS

FOR THE FAMILY HANDYMAN

Editor in Chief	Ken Collier
Senior Editors	Travis Larson
	Gary Wentz
Associate Editors	Elisa Bernick
	Mary Flanagan
	Jeff Gorton
Senior Copy Editor	Donna Bierbach
Art Directors	Vern Johnson
	Becky Pfluger
	Marcia Roepke
Photographer	Tom Fenenga
Production Artist	Mary Schwender
Office Administrative	
Manager	Alice Garrett
Admin. Editorial Assistant	Roxie Filipkowski
Production Manager	Judy Rodriguez

CONTRIBUTING EDITORS

Spike Carlsen	Dave Munkittrick
Tom Dvorak	Rick Muscoplat
Duane Johnson	David Radtke
Brett Martin	Jeff Timm

CONTRIBUTING ART DIRECTORS

Roberta Peters	Bob Ungar
David Simpson	

CONTRIBUTING PHOTOGRAPHERS

Tate Carlson	Ramon Moreno
Mike Krivit,	Shawn Nielsen
Krivit Photography	Bill Zuehlke

ILLUSTRATORS

Steve Björkman	Don Mannes
Gabe De Matteis	Paul Perreault
Mario Ferro	Frank Rohrbach III
John Hartman	

OTHER CONSULTANTS

Charles Avoles, plumbing
Al Hildenbrand, electrical
Joe Jensen, Jon Jensen, carpentry
Dave MacDonald, structural engineer
William Nunn, painting
Dean Sorem, tile
Costas Stavrou, appliance repair
John Williamson, electrical
Les Zell, plumbing

For information about advertising in
The Family Handyman magazine, call (646) 293-6150

To subscribe to *The Family Handyman* magazine:
- By phone: (800) 285-4961
- By Internet: FHMservice@rd.com
- By mail: The Family Handyman
  Subscriber Service Dept.
  P.O. Box 6099
  Harlan, IA 51593-1599

We welcome your ideas and opinions.
Write: The Editor, The Family Handyman
2915 Commers Drive, Suite 700
Eagan, MN 55121
Fax: (651) 994-2250
E-mail: editors@thefamilyhandyman.com

Photocopies of articles are available for $3.00 each. Call (800) 285-4961 from 8 a.m. to 5 p.m. Central, Monday through Friday or send an e-mail to FHMservice@rd.com. Visa, MasterCard and Discover accepted.